Muslim Diaspora

Muslim Diaspora identifies those aspects of migratory experience that shatter or reinforce a group's attachment to its homeland and affect its readiness to adapt to a new country.

The contributors to this collection examine many dimensions of life in the Diaspora and demonstrate that identity is always constructed in relation to others. They show how religious identity in Diaspora is mediated by many other factors such as:

- Gender
- Class
- Ethnic origin
- National status

A central aim is to understand Diaspora as an agent of social and cultural change, particularly in its transformative impact on women. Throughout, the book advances a more nuanced understanding of the notions of ethnicity, difference and rights. It makes an important contribution to understanding the complex processes of formation and adoption of transnational identities and the challenging contradictions of a world that is being rapidly globalized in economic and political terms and yet is increasingly localized and differentiated, ethically and culturally.

Muslim Diaspora includes contributions from outstanding scholars and is an invaluable text for students in sociology, anthropology, geography, cultural studies, Islamic studies, women's studies as well as the general reader.

Haideh Moghissi is a Professor of Sociology at York University, Canada. She was a founder of the Iranian National Union of Women and member of its first executive and editorial boards, before leaving Iran in 1984. Her recent publications include the following books: Three volume reference *Women and Islam: Critical Concepts in Sociology* (ed.), London: Routledge (2005); *Feminism and Islamic Fundamentalism: The Limits of Postmodern Analysis*, London: Zed Press, 1999, Pakistan: Oxford University Press (2000) (winner of Choice Outstanding Academic Book Award), and *Populism and Feminism in Iran: Women's Struggle in a Male-Defined Revolutionary Movement*, London: Macmillan Press; New York: St Martin's Press (1994).

Routledge Islamic Studies

Muslim Diaspora

Gender, culture and identity

Edited by
Haideh Moghissi

Routledge
Taylor & Francis Group

LONDON AND NEW YORK

First published 2006
by Routledge
2 Park Square, Milton Park,
Abingdon, Oxon OX14 4RN

Simultaneously published in the USA and Canada
by Routledge
270 Madison Ave, New York, NY 10016

Routledge is an imprint of the Taylor & Francis Group, an informa business

Transferred to Digital Printing 2009

© 2006 selection and editorial matter, Haideh Moghissi;
individual chapters the contributors

Typeset in Times by Keyword Group Ltd

British Library Cataloguing in Publication Data
A catalogue record for this book is available from the British Library

Library of Congress Cataloging in Publication Data
A catalog record for this book has been requested

ISBN10: 0-415-77081-5 (hbk)
ISBN10: 0-415-77915-4 (pbk)

ISBN13: 978-0-415-77081-1 (hbk)
ISBN13: 978-0-415-77915-9 (pbk)

Contents

Figures and tables

Figures

Tables

Contributors

Haleh Afshar teaches politics and women's studies at the University of York, England. She is Convener of the Development Studies Association Women and Development Study books. Besides numerous articles in refereed journals and edited volumes, her publications include 'Women and wars: some trajectories towards a feminist peace' in *Development In Practice* (May 2003); *Quality in Ageing* (Afshar, Franks, Maynard and Wray, May 2002); 'European ideologies and post-revolutionary feminisms in Iran' in *Islam et l'Espace Euro-Mediterranean* (Lehners and Bento eds, 2001); and *Islam and Feminisms, an Iranian Case Study* (1998).

Aylin Akpınar teaches in the Faculty of Communication at the University of Bahçeşehir in Istanbul. She received her Ph.D. from Uppsala University, Sweden. Some of her recent publications are: 'The honour/shame complex revisited: Violence against women in the migration context' in *Women's Studies International Forum,* Vol. 26, Issue 5, September–October, 2003; 'Waged work and Turkish women in the ethnic/gender-segregated Swedish labour market' in *Migration and Labour in Europe: Views from Turkey and Sweden* (Emrehan Zeybekoğlu and Bo Johansson eds, 2003), MURCIR (Marmara University Center for International Relations) and NIWL (Swedish National Institute for Working Life).

Rob Aitken is a social anthropologist and a Lecturer in the Politics Department at the University of York. His research interests focus on forms of belonging, including locality and ethnicity, and how these interrelate with nationalism, state institutions and changing systems of ethnic and cultural distinction.

Reza Baraheni was born in Tabriz, Iran. He is one of two scholars to join the new Scholars-at-Risk Program at University of Toronto's Massey College and is presently a visiting professor at the university's Centre for Comparative Literature. He was President of PEN Canada. Active for the last 35 years in trying to promote democratic liberties in his country, Baraheni was imprisoned both under the Shah's regime and in the Islamic Republic of Iran. He is the author of 54 books, including *The Crowned Cannibals,* a collection of prose and poetry, and *Les Saisons en Enfer du Jeune Ayyaz,* a novel. His *God's Shadow: Prison Poems* is a collection of poems based on a period of 102 days spent in solitary confinement in Iran, during the time of the Shah.

Fataneh Farahani is a Ph.D. candidate at the Ethnology Institution at Stockholm University, Sweden. Her area of interest is female sexuality, violence against women, postcolonial theories, feminist and ethnicity theories, diaspora and multiculturalism. She is writing her dissertation on Iranian immigrant women's self-presentation and understanding of their bodies and sexual desire, within the context of patriarchal culture and religion (Islam) and diasporic experiences. Her recent publications include 'Veiled Sexuality: A Discursive Analysis on Veiling', in *Body-book Collective* (eds) 2004; Corporealities In(ter)ventions in an omnipresent topic. Ulrike Helmer, Königstein/Tanuns, Germany; 'The absent presence: Reflections on the discursive practice of veiling', 2002, in *The Body and Presentation*. Insa Härtel and Sigrid Schade (eds), Leske + Budrich. Opladen, Germany; and 'Shahrzads's Guile' [http://tys.se/kf/eng/fataneh.hun] 2001. She has also written numerous newspaper articles in Sweden and has participated in television and radio shows regarding Islam, women's sexuality and honour-related violence and gendering multiculturalism.

Myfanwy Franks is currently a senior researcher for the Children's Society, a Children's Charity based in England where her brief is to develop research on refugee children and young people in the UK. She has a background in research into gender, ethnicity and religion, especially in Islamic revivalism and has published on these issues. She is currently also a research associate with the School of Theology and Religious Studies, University of Leeds, UK.

Mark J. Goodman's research includes work on links between theory, politics and culture and on families, gender dynamics, labour discipline and violence. He is a co-investigator in the MCRI Project, 'Diaspora, Islam and Gender' and co-author with Haideh Moghissi of 'Cultures of violence and diaspora: dislocation and gendered conflict in Iranian-Canadian communities', *Humanity and Society,* Vol. 23, Issue 4 (November 1999). Goodman is conducting a study of forced migration and cultural change among African-Americans from slavery onwards and a comparative study of the 'disciplining of ethnicity' among several groups. Formerly Chair of Sociology, he is Coordinator of the Certificate in Anti-Racist Research and Practice (CARRP) in the Atkinson Faculty, York University.

Mary Elaine Hegland teaches Social and Cultural Anthropology at Santa Clara University. She teaches courses on the anthropology of the Middle East, women and gender, aging, family and kinship, and Islam. She has conducted field research in Iran, Pakistan, Turkey, Tajikistan and Afghanistan, and among Iranians and Pakistanis living in the US. Hegland's publications have focused on women and gender in politics, revolution, Islam and ritual, and on Iranian village politics at the local level and in the Iranian Revolution.

Denise Helly specializes in studies on national and ethnic minorities, citizenship, and nationalism, policies of cultural pluralism and immigration, and integration of immigrants. She has published articles and books on the Chinese overseas, national minorities in China, Canadian multiculturalism, Québec policy towards ethnocultural minorities, and Quebec social insertion of immigrants. More recently, she joined two European research teams studying the status of Muslims in Europe.

Afsaneh Hojabri was born in Iran and has lived in Montreal since 1989. She works as a freelance researcher and coordinator in the areas of social policy and minority rights. For the past seven years, she has been collaborating with the Canadian Council for Refugees (CCR) and with the McGill Center for Teaching and Research on Women (MCTRW) and is presently coordinator of the Diaspora Islam and Gender (DIG) project in Montreal. Among her publications are: 'Trafficking in women and girls', *Refugee Update,* Summer 2004; 'Women of Iran: A subject bibliography' (co-author) (A two-volume subject bibliography in English and Persian), Cambridge, MA: Iranian Women's Studies Foundation, 2000; and 'Identity construction and the role of Iranian women', in IWSF Conference Proceedings, 10th annual International Conference. Summer 1999.

Marie Mc Andrew teaches in the Department of Education and Administration of Education Studies at the University of Montreal. She has worked extensively in research and policy development and evaluation in the field of education of minorities and intercultural education. She was the Director of Immigration and the Metropolis, the Inter-university Research Centre of Montreal on Immigration, Integration and Urban Dynamics and from 1989 to 1991, served as an advisor to the deputy-minister's cabinet of the Quebec Ministére des Communautés Culturelles et de l'Immigration. Mc Andrew co-ordinates the Research Group on Ethnicity and Adaptation to Pluralism in Education (Groupe de recherche sur l'ethnicité et l'adaptation au pluralisme en éducation [GREAPE]). She is a member of the Intercultural Council of the City of Montréal and holds the Chair for Ethnic Relations.

Haideh Moghissi is a professor of sociology and women's studies at Atkinson Faculty of Liberal and Professional Studies and the Faculty of Graduate Studies, York University, Toronto. Before leaving Iran in 1984, she was a founder of the Iranian National Union of Women and member of its first executive board and editorial board of *Barabari* (equality) and *Zanan Dar Mobarezeh* (Women in Struggle). Her publications include articles in refereed journals and chapters in edited volumes and the following books: *Women and Islam: Critical Concepts in Sociology* (ed.) London: Routledge (2005); *Feminism and Islamic Fundamentalism: The Limits of Postmodern Analysis*, London: Oxford University Press, 2000 (Zed Press, 1999, winner of Choice Outstanding Academic Book Award) and *Populism and Feminism in Iran: Women's Struggle in a Male-Defined Revolutionary Movement*, London: Macmillan Press; New York: St Martin's Press (1994).

Shahrzad Mojab teaches in the Department of Adult Education, OISE, University of Toronto and is presently Director of the Institute of Women's Studies and Gender Studies. Her specialties include educational policy studies with focus on policies affecting the academic life of marginalized groups in universities, and comparative and international adult education policy. She has conducted research on immigrant women's access to employment and training in Canada and the impact of war and violence on women's learning in the Diaspora. She is editor of

Women of a Non-State Nation: The Kurds (2001, Mazda Publishers) and co-editor, with Himani Bannerji and Judith Whitehead, of *Of Property and Propriety: The Role of Gender and Class in Imperialism and Nationalism* (2001, University of Toronto Press). She was the editor of *Convergence, the Journal of the International Council of Adult Education.*

Ezat Mossallanejad works as a Policy Analyst with the Canadian Centre for Victims of Torture (CCVT). Dr Mossallanejad is a member of the Editorial Board of *Refugee Update.* He has been a Board member of the Inter-Church Committee for Refugees and the Canadian Refugee and Immigrant Counselling Services and Canadian Centre for International Justice (CCIJ). He has escaped persecution three times in his life as a result of his struggle against tyranny and for social justice in Iran. Finding himself in India after his escape from Iran, he began giving a series of lectures about his book, *The Political Economy of Oil in Iran.* This made him the target of local Indian fundamentalists as well as Iranian agents. Eventually, he escaped India for Canada in early 1985. He has published four books and more than 150 articles in Persian as well as a book and 35 articles in English. In his mission to protect refugees and survivors of torture, he has travelled extensively to different countries including the United States, Mexico, Rwanda, Switzerland, Austria and Nigeria.

Saeed Rahnema is a Professor of Political Science at York University. He has worked as a senior officer in the United Nation's Development Program and was a Director of the Middle East Economic Association of the Allied Social Science Association, and has been on the Editorial Board of several journals. He is a frequent commentator of Middle Eastern politics in Canadian and international media, and is the author of several books and numerous articles. His recent books include *Iran After the Revolution; Crisis of An Islamic State* (1995), *Re-Birth of Social Democracy in Iran* (1996), and *Organization Structure: A Systemic Approach; Cases of Canadian Public Sector* (1993).

Hammed Shahidian (1959–2005) was an Associate Professor of Sociology and the Chair of the Sociology/Anthropology Program at the University of Illinois at Springfield, where he was honoured with the University Scholar Award. He was an Honorary Research Fellow at the University of Glasgow in 2001–02. Shahidian's focus was on gender and political activism and Iranians in exile. His research involved gender relations, cultural politics, social movements, and diaspora studies. His articles have appeared in *Qualitative Sociology, Current Sociology, Sexualities, Sociological Inquiry, Feminist Studies,* and elsewhere. His Persian articles on the Iranian women's movement and cultural politics have been published inside and outside Iran. He served on the editorial board of *Sexualities* and *Iran Bulletin.* He is the author of *Women in Iran: Gender Politics in the Islamic Republic* and *Women in Iran: Emerging Voices in the Women's Movement* (2002, Greenwood).

Mary Ann Tétreault is the Una Chapman Cox Distinguished Professor of International Affairs at Trinity University in San Antonio, Texas, where she teaches courses in world politics, the Middle East, and feminist theory. Her recent books include *Stories of Democracy: Politics and Society in Contemporary Kuwait* (2000); *The Kuwait Petroleum Corporation and the Economics of the New World Order* (1995); and edited volumes, among them *Partial Truths and the Politics of Community* (2003); *Conscious Acts and the Politics of Social Change* (2000); *Gender, States, and Nationalism—At Home in the Nation?* (2000). Her current research interests include Kuwaiti politics and society; international energy issues; reconciliation after violent conflict; and constructions of public and private space in the context of globalization.

Introduction

Haideh Moghissi

Muslims and peoples from Islamic cultures form a growing segment of the world's contemporary migrant and refugee population. It is estimated that the number of people of Muslim faith has reached 15 million in Europe, making Islam the continent's second-largest religion after Christianity (Hunter 2002). These populations are remarkably heterogeneous. This is not only due to internal differentiation of each community along class, ethnic, rural, urban and sectarian affiliations, but also because of national-cultural idiosyncrasies and the influences on each of the diasporic communities of differing social, cultural and integration policies in the host societies. Nonetheless, we are beginning to witness efforts towards the formation of a group identity and solidarity among migrant communities and citizens who originate from Muslim societies, despite their diverse national and ethnic origins and their distinct political histories, cultures and languages.

What seems to be happening in Western metropolises today is the construction of geographically and socially distinct localities of 'Muslim' populations and the formation of a sort of collective identity and or group affiliation among this nominally Muslim population. It is perhaps this increasingly observable group identity and identification that has animated the popularity of the term 'Muslim diaspora'. But both the currency of the term 'Muslim diaspora', and the increasing tendency of these communities to episodically or consistently band together, may have at its core more a political than a cultural impulse. That is to say, it is based less on historical commonalities founded in the values, religious affiliations and languages of originating countries and more on the urgent contemporary and common concerns and grievances that these diasporic communities experience in relation to the 'host' countries in which they now live.

It has to be emphasized, in any case, that the identities involved here are constructed. The 'primordialist' idea of identities embedded permanently in specific populations has been pretty much abandoned in most writings on ethnicity, but survives, oddly, in writing on cultural groups linked to Islam. This reflects, perhaps, the influence of a persistent Orientalism, or the result of the politicization of cultures, as Mahmood Mamdani (2004) would have it. As is usually the case, one's sense of identity often reflects a response to a real or imaginary threat to a dignified sense of selfhood. It speaks to an individual's psychological need for a sense of belonging and a constructed connection to people who share one's values, or some parts of them. Therefore, identity is about our relations with the 'others' who share our experiences or values and with those from whom we are differentiated because their experiences and values are different from our own. In this sense, the building of identities is both unifying and separating, sometimes both at the same time. In the case of diasporas of Islamic cultures, I want to suggest that the formation of a collective identity, or diasporic consciousness and solidarity, is more often a response to an inhospitable climate in the host societies than an expression of cultural nostalgia. It is a reaction to the stamp of 'Muslim' with which such individuals are automatically branded regardless of whether or not they are believers or practising Muslims, or see Islam as a defining factor in their lives.

This is not to deny the lasting influence of learned cultural values, traditions and practices, or the predispositions that a diasporic community brings to a new country, which can aid or prevent its integration into the host society. Neither does it overlook the fact that some forms of Muslim cultural expression are extreme, and invite unfriendly and intolerant reactions from the host. Admittedly, all this only provides more fuel for psychological resignation for both the 'Muslim diaspora' and the host society, solidifying a marginal location for the diasporic population and deepening racist policies within the host country. The point, however, is that the dichotomizing classification of diasporic Islamic cultures, which sets people apart from the rest of the population, to a large extent helps determine how they behave and how they respond to the pressures of resettlement in a new society. A feeling of being watched disapprovingly, without having done anything to warrant disapproval, encourages the adoption of forms of 'cultural' expressions that were not needed in the warmth of the known and familiar culture and the normalcy of their way of life. Indeed, this feeling of surveillance and cultural suspicion is a feature experienced by displaced groups from many backgrounds. In the contemporary political setting, however, it is especially felt by those who are identified as coming from 'Muslim' countries.

Vicious circles like these can explain why, with changing circumstances and sometimes despite improved material conditions of life, the subjectivity of Muslims in diaspora is recomposed in a direction that does not always represent a healthy departure from the past. That is to say, migration and relocation can shape a new awareness of self, and this awareness, under favourable conditions, can be riveting and transformative. It can help individuals and even communities find positive and revitalizing sides to the experience of migration and gradually adjust to new conditions and circumstances without having to relinquish their sense of moral agency and way of life. Collective values, practices and internalized beliefs, particularly with regards to gender and age hierarchies, can be reassessed in the interests of a more egalitarian and peaceful co-existence in the diaspora. But much of this depends on the quality of the reception by the host. If the reception is hesitant or hostile, the mere fact of migration will not act as a catalyst for integrative change. In fact, it may prevent new roots from re-establishing and, in time, blossoming. For the migrant, the fear of loss of identity may create a profound sense of insecurity and instability and a sharpening awareness of cultural marginality. Identities may change, but the transformation may involve a renewed emphasis on Islam, either as a culture, a religion or an ideology, even for those who were previously completely secular – hence, the growing tendency to identify with cultural values and practices of the originating country, or with an imagined 'Islamic world', indeed with a 'Islam' that is much more conservative, narrow-minded, unforgiving and intolerant than that which was actually experienced by the individual in the home country. Along with this fictionalizing of memory comes the rise of what has been identified as 'long-distance nationalism' (Anderson, cited in Kennedy and Roudmeetof 2002: 3), a process that leads to the development of radicalized cultural identities. These identities are not rooted in a simple repetition of inherited beliefs and practices, but are politically driven. They reflect a sense of belonging that grows from an urgent need to connect with the people who, despite their internal differences and divisions as individuals or as small communities, share the experience of being attacked and undermined, externally, by the larger community.

One can reasonably assume that this is the impetus behind a turn to religious symbols and practices, even by the second and third generations of Muslim diaspora, which is apparent in Canada, Britain and other European countries. The younger generations, raised and educated in the West, have experienced a process of integration generally much less strenuous and painful than that of their parents and grandparents. But, ironically, a large number of younger people seem to be moving away from their predecessors' attempts at fitting in. They express distinctness and contrast, sometimes by resorting to religious exhibitionism, and even to Islamic radicalism. This shift to heightened Muslim identity, however, does not represent increasing adherence to Islam as a religion, but to Islam as an ideology of resistance and the only force that at present seems to effectively challenge global power structures and domination systems. This is the development of a politicized Muslim identity whose religio-cultural import is only symbolic. In Britain, for example, the 1989 Rushdie affair, the first Gulf War in 1990–1 and the headscarf controversy, argues Parveen Akhtar (2005: 169), 'helped people who prior to these events had not paid any attention to that part of their identity to discover that they were Muslim'. Akhtar's interesting observation is of the negative reaction of the older generation of British Muslims to radical Islam and their fear that it might present a role model to the younger generation. In any case, the Islamic regeneration in the West, she suggests, is the result of the experience of cultural exclusion, which is closely connected to experience in the economic sphere.

The 'political hysteria' over the wearing of the Muslim headscarf in France, and the violent revolts of North African youth in the autumn of 2005 in Paris, must also be seen in this light, that is, a reflection of problems of racial and ethnic exclusion, deepening inequalities, and a continuing, virulent racism. In the words of an Arab youth, burning cars was the only way the disenfranchised youth could make their voices heard, and the only means by which they expressed their frustration, even against their parents, who had suffered in silence for long and had done nothing (*Guardian Weekly*: 12). Hence, 'the retreat into religious identity' may be inflicted rather than desired, as Emanuel Terray (2004: 5) argues. In a hostile setting, that which is stigmatized can be transformed into an emblem of pride, along the lines of 'black is beautiful'.

Within this context, the racialization of Muslims and Muslim cultures creates, or at least accentuates, the need for community connections and support networks. One has to be cautious, though, as not all communities of Islamic culture and certainly not all individuals within each community respond to the social pressures and racism of the dominant culture uniformly. For some communities more than others, the need for group connection and the support of the collective prompt an awareness of their Muslim identity, and this awareness is manipulated in pursuit of specific political goals by radical Islam in the diaspora. Others try to create self-sufficient and self-sustained support services and networks and minimize their encounter with the dominant culture and its institutions, without necessarily feeling the need to accent their Islamic identity. The end result in both cases, however, is the segregation, isolation and exclusion of diasporas, an ensuing resistance to integrating into the predominantly white society, and a closure to ideas and practices that can help break down gender and age hierarchies.

The contributions to this collection represent an attempt at challenging the notion of a single, homogeneous 'Islamic' culture. All of the chapters, except for two, were presented and debated as a series of panel presentations at an international conference in May 2004 at York University in Toronto. We wanted to bring before the participants, and those who would read its proceedings later, the idea that communities from Islamic cultures, while originating in countries dominated by Islamic laws and religious practices, are as varied in their experiences, social relations, values and world views as other sections of the population. Indeed, many of the chapters included in this collection are themselves good examples of the various class, ethnic, gender, age, religious and regional factors that differentiate transnational communities of Muslim cultural background, as well as of the diverse perspectives of the scholars presenting them. The conference was organized with the objective of addressing some of the concerns raised in societies that host substantial numbers of people originating in states with Islamic religious institutions – concerns that are voiced increasingly at the global level. Responding to some of the intellectual and socio-political challenges that have arisen from the growing influence of religion in public life was also a primary objective of the meeting.

The chapters in this volume are multidisciplinary and cover a range of issues that were discussed from various theoretical and political perspectives, with the hope of impelling a more nuanced understanding of the notions of ethnicity, difference and rights. Nonetheless, several important themes kept coming up in these presentations, and may help to unify this collection for the reader. Perhaps the most notable is the idea that 'identity' is always constructed in relation to others. Another recurrent idea is an understanding of diaspora as an agent of social and cultural change, particularly in its transformative impact on women (Afshar *et al.*; Mojab; Farahani; Hojabri). Several contributions deal with diaspora as a political reaction to new realities rather than simply a reflection of an ancestral cultural heritage (Rahnema; Mojab). The readings also help us to understand the many dimensions of life in the diaspora for individuals and communities of Muslim cultural background and help us to unravel some of the realities in countries of origin, such as those discussed by Mossallanejad and Akpınar. How life in the diaspora can shed light on countries of origin and the tensions that develop in them between outsiders and insiders (Tétreault; Shahidian) and how Islam helps to provide a foundation for notions of ethnicity as reflected in the policies of host societies (Mc Andrew; Rahnema) fit nicely with Helly's and Goodman's discussions of culture and 'hybridity' and with Baraheni's provocative suggestion that 'diaspora' as a concept can already be discovered in the discourses of three Abrahamic texts – the *Old Testament*, the *New Testament* and the *Koran* – but only if we are prepared to read them as contemporary literary compositions rather than as purely religious documents.

We hope that this study of the varied experiences of diaspora in Islamic cultures helps identify those aspects of migratory experience that shatter or reinforce a group's attachment to its vision of the homeland and affect its readiness to adapt to a new country. It should also enhance our understanding of the complex processes of formation and adoption of transnational identities, and the challenging contradictions of a world that is rapidly being globalized in economic and political terms and yet is increasingly localized ethnically and culturally. The conference was part of an educational and training programme funded by the Ford Foundation, the support of which is gratefully acknowledged.

Organization of the book

Part I of the collection introduces issues of identity and historical memory in diaspora, and suggests a nuanced reading of the intellectual and practical terrains within which the concept of diaspora and the lived experiences of the dispersed populations can be situated. In the first chapter, 'Diaspora: History of an idea', Denise Helly investigates the origin, meaning and historical transformation of the term 'diaspora', suggesting that diasporic experience is more ambivalent than either negative or positive, given that the experience even of Jews, as a 'classical' diaspora, is not always, or only, one of suffering and loss – this despite the fact that, historically, the term was meant to convey loss and dispersion. Helly notes that the meaning of 'diaspora' as a term changed from antiquity to the modern age. In order to define the concept of diaspora, one must distinguish these historical and sociological ideas from folk memory. Helly defines diaspora according to several characteristics, although the significance of these characteristics and their conditions of deployment vary according to context. These include: the consciousness of a destiny, a fate that is always uncertain or even dangerous and which is related to past traumatic events; a collective memory that is sometimes reinvented by elites; multiple seats of establishment and of cultural expression; and the existence of economic and cultural means that are necessary in order to maintain a multinational network between those seats. She poses questions as to whether globalization and the alleged 'decline' in the role of the state will favour the appearance of new diasporas, and whether a lessening ability of nation-states to assimilate could affect the formation of such identities, including identities connected with Islam.

The three chapters by Saeed Rahnema, Reza Baraheni and Ezat Mossallanejad together explain why some people of Muslim cultural background end up in diaspora, why they are drawn to Islam or reject it as an emblem of their heritage, and the challenges that host societies face in trying to integrate them. In 'Islam in diaspora and challenges to multiculturalism', Rahnema provides a context for understanding the nuances of the policy of multiculturalism in Canada. Muslims in Canada, the author argues, are relatively new in the country and constitute the fastest growing and demographically youngest religious community; compared to their European counterparts they are more integrated in an economic sense and benefit from the country's commitment to multiculturalism and its high level of tolerance. However, Canadian multiculturalism has failed to effectively combat racism and discrimination; for instance, despite their relatively high level of education, Muslims face a high unemployment rate and lower levels of income. Noting the tendency among a growing number of Muslims towards stronger religious affiliation and, in some cases, towards Islamism, Rahnema identifies a vicious circle: faced by racism and marginalization, stronger identification with Islam and its symbols and practices creates a sense of belonging and entry into a shared space based on common values or on a common perception of grievances, but this tendency also invites hostility and strengthens Islamophobia, contributing, in turn, to marginalization. Rahnema argues that using the space provided by Canada's policy of multiculturalism, some religious leaders in the Muslim diaspora are pushing for the application of Shari'a as the basis for arbitration on matters of personal status, to the detriment of women. Rahnema points to an important contradiction in an unfettered multiculturalism developed in opposition to extreme assimilationism, the antagonism between the rights of a minority group and the universal rights of all citizens, and the conflicts between the rights of a group and those of its individual members.

Reza Baraheni, in 'Exilic readings of the *Old Testament*, the *New Testament* and the *Koran*', departs from the language of religion and enters the language of literature, inviting us to go beyond traditional methods of studying the *Old* and *New Testament*s and the *Koran* as sacred books. In his linguistic analysis of these texts, Baraheni suggests that these sacred books should be read from a historical perspective and within an exilic framework on their journey to the twentieth century and the Western world – travel, time and space being the triptych on which exilic discourse finds its locus. Following Jorge Luis Borges, Baraheni suggests that the three sacred texts of the Abrahamic religions should be studied as contemporary literary documents within the discourse of exile, keeping in mind modern notions of representation and anti-representation. All three texts use a singular narrative that becomes progressively more universal in tone; each represents a kind of journey, sometimes fictional and sometimes metaphorical; each makes use of ambiguities involving the real and unreal, for example, regarding the ancestry of Jesus in the *Old Testament* and the *New Testament*. Nonetheless, the *Koran* is different. Time passes chronologically in the biblical texts, but not in the *Koran*.

Anti-representational, it revives, repeats and puts together in a new way the fragments, memories and stories presented in the other two accounts. Baraheni argues that the *Koran* is a particularly exilic text.

In 'Islam and consecrated tortures', Ezat Mossallanejad, through an analysis of Shari'a and consecrated torture, offers a snapshot of the state of human rights in Islamic states as a push factor for the formation of diaspora, and goes on to argue that the rule of Shari'a has caused havoc where it has been imposed, and led to various methods of religiously consecrated torture, which seem to particularly target or victimize women. He traces the justification of torture under Islam to concepts in the *Koran* of hell and punishment after death and to perceptions of an ever-vengeful God in whose name divine torment is applied alike to disobedient believer and non-believer. Mossallanejad focuses on two forms of torture in the Islamic Republic of Iran: 'holy' rape in prisons and the stoning of those accused of adultery. Both of these examples show the gendered character of 'divine' torture. As someone who works directly with victims of torture who have survived various tyrannical regimes, the author is well positioned to argue that 'stoning, rape, amputation of limbs, flogging in public are but some aspects of the sinister manifestations of the imposition of the anachronistic rules of Shari'a that have driven hundreds of thousands of people into voluntary or involuntary exile'. He finds it appalling that rape (today universally considered a horrible act and, in some cases, a war crime) has been routinely used in the name of Allah by hypocritical Islamic fanatics in the jails of Iran and other 'Muslim' societies.

In Mark Goodman's 'Diaspora, ethnicity and problems of identity', the idea of what 'diaspora' is and how diasporic subjectivity is constructed is taken further. Goodman differentiates between the 'self-exile' chosen as a self-description by creative artists, as discussed by Stuart Hall and Paul Gilroy, among others, and the deep separation that marks a permanently imposed condition without the possibility of retrieval or return imposed upon persons subjected to economic or political subordination. He looks at the construction of ideas of hybridity, exile and identity, suggesting that 'hybridity' should not be understood as a chosen state, but as an outcome negotiated between diasporic communities and dominant powers. Goodman uses a 'classical' case of diaspora, that of enslaved Africans, to help underline the importance of this distinction. He argues that diasporic communities can be characterized by the degree of freedom they enjoy in ethnic expression, and that 'victim' diasporas, including communities of the enslaved and populations exposed to colonial occupation, are among those who enjoy the least such freedoms. Goodman discusses two theoretical accounts of slavery in the United States, illustrating how deep subordination can reinforce the sense of being helplessly sealed off. In both accounts, the notion of the overpowering physical and cultural violence available to a hegemonic class is deployed to explain subordination and, at the same time, to reduce the expectation and prospect of resistance.

Turning to Part II of the volume, Chapters 6 and 7 together bring out related problems of representation and misrepresentation, giving special attention to tensions between those who depart and those who stay behind. Mary Ann Tétreault's chapter, 'Divided communities of memory: Diasporas come home', begins with the observation that separation sets in motion a series of powerful processes and that, these, from the outset, divide travellers from those they leave behind. Taking as an example the experiences of Kuwaitis during Iraqi occupation in the first Gulf War, Tétreault points to the tensions that develop within diasporic communities when perceptions are stimulated by dramatic events like wars or revolutions. Both exiles and insiders experience trauma, but often exiles are in a stronger position to tell their stories than those left behind. This generates divided 'communities of memory' among groups who imagine themselves to be a single people. During the war, for example, Kuwaiti exiles conveyed to the world that Iraqi soldiers were raping Kuwaiti women, although insiders knew of hardly any rape victims. Exiles also control superior resources to use in post-conflict competition if the leaders of a regime are among them. In the Kuwaiti case, the words of exiles diminished the credibility of truthful insider accounts about life under occupation.

Hammed Shahidian, in '"Our" reflections in "their" mirror: Cultural politics and the representation of the Iranian diaspora in the Islamic Republic', scrutinizes travelogues, popular literature, newspapers, magazines and films to explore the nuances of representation of the Iranian diaspora inside Iran. He shows that the images presented inside the country try to discredit exiles on social, political and cultural grounds and convince potential migrants and exiles to remain; they also aim to persuade professional and affluent men who have already left to repatriate by casting migration as a danger to family life and the integrity of women and the nation. Shahidian shows that Iranians in diaspora are presented as decadent counter-revolutionaries and monarchists or as a tiny minority, remnants of former organizations, who are alienated, immoral, materialistic and unaware of the situation in Iran. This distorting 'mirror' ignores the vast diversity within the diaspora and denies diaspora members the opportunity to articulate their experiences. Like Tétreault, Shahidian views the diasporic experience as an opportunity for those inside and outside the home country to broaden their cultural and political horizons, seeing for those outside an opportunity to make a critical intervention in the cultural politics of the homeland as well as an opportunity for cultural self-criticism. But this cannot occur, he argues, without the creation of open dialogue between those inside and those outside the country.

Political mobilizations that urge the creation or reshaping of a homeland are a central feature of diasporic experience. Shahrzad Mojab's chapter, 'Gender, nation and diaspora: Kurdish women in feminist transnational struggles', examines this topic by examining the experiences of women and women's activism in the newly formed Kurdish communities in Europe and in their homelands, especially in Iraq. Critical of the 'culturalist' focus of the literature on transnational politics, which overlooks its gendered character, Mojab focuses on women's political mobilization and critically examines the concept of 'multiple modalities' of gender, class, religion, language and generation. She argues that while Kurdish patriarchy and strong ties to feudal ways are maintained and reproduced in diaspora, and that violence against women persists, even in its most obvious form of 'honour killing', the same factors also increase resistance among female Kurds to both a hostile state policy and patriarchal violence. Two points in Mojab's argument are of special importance. The first is her observation that even women-centred initiatives within the Kurdish national struggle are influenced or even controlled by masculinist and patriarchal national projects. The second is the argument that the rights demanded by women in this struggle need to be recognized, enacted and implemented by state authorities, the patriarchal and gendered character of the state and legal institutions in feminist theory notwithstanding.

Aylin Akpinar, in 'Discourses of Islam/secularism and identity-building processes among Turkish university youth', also takes up issues of identity and political mobilization by examining the activities of a specific group, in this case an examination of the religious and secular traditions reflected in the experiences of Turkish university students. Akpınar argues that 'homeland' politics and politics within the Turkish diaspora continuously feed and affect each other. This fact is clearly observable in the question of new Islamic religiosity among the Turkish diaspora in Europe, which is directly related to debates in Turkey over 'Islam as ethics' and 'Islam as observance', and over the kind of Muslim identity that is desirable. The central question for youth, both in the diaspora and in Turkey, is how to have an Islamic lifestyle without thereby threatening the democratic and secular society. Akpınar's piece shows the limits of secularism in the modernizing states of the Middle East, and the complexity and contradictory nature of the Turkish republican state, reflected in the inclusion of religious instruction in nominally secular schools and the forcing of students to memorize prayers and demonstrate proficiency to inspectors who represent the 'secular' Ministry of Education. Interestingly, the increase in religiosity in Turkey is generally seen not as a threat to the secular republican project, but as an endorsement of Ottoman heritage. Akpınar suggests that the older generation of Turks, brought up with the republican ideals of neutral public space, considers religion a phenomenon related to the next life, and not a worldly affair. However, the identity politics embraced by the Islamist movement motivated some young Turks to start a search for conscious Muslim identity. Akpınar remains hopeful that it may be possible to open doors to cross-cultural communication and dialogue that would reduce the polarization between secular and Islamic identities in Turkey.

Part III of the collection focuses on host societies in Europe, the United States and Canada. It brings out the diversity of diasporic experience across categories of gender, class and age, addressing complexities in the consideration of the rights of ethnic minorities and specific cultural practices.

Marie Mc Andrew's chapter, 'The hijab controversies in Western public schools: Contrasting conceptions of ethnicity and of ethnic relations', examines controversies over the wearing of headscarves in public schools and the role of education in producing and reproducing ethnic boundaries. She criticizes two approaches: a class-reductive form of Marxism that understands ethnicity only as an expression of power between dominant and dominated classes, adopting a paradoxical and paternalistic stance and attempting to 'liberate' oppressed members of a group against their own will; and a liberal approach that focuses on ethnicity as the production and prerogative of the individual, encouraging cultural and cognitive relativism and seeing the individual as an autonomous subject. Showing the limits of one-sided conceptions of ethnicity, whether essentialist, conspiratorial or individualist, Mc Andrew asks whether respect for cultural pluralism and the recognition of socio-historical inequalities justify interventions in support of minority rights that would simultaneously deprive schools of their 'public' character. Would respects for rights impinge upon the responsibility to expose students to critical knowledge and to perspectives on religion and values that differ from those of a student's community of origin? She also asks what an accommodation to religious diversity in public schools will mean for the commitment to gender equity.

The complexity of the construct of Muslim identity in diaspora is also discussed in 'Islamophobia and women of Pakistani descent in Bradford: The crisis of ascribed and adopted identities', by Haleh Afshar, Robert Aitken and Myfanwy Franks. In this chapter, the authors argue that Muslim women are caught in a divide created by the call for Muslims in Britain either to discard their nationality in favour of their faith or to abandon their faith to save their nationality. They analyse the difficulties of articulating self and identity for Bradford's Muslim women of Pakistani descent in the wake of rising Islamophobia and the implications for women of the 'call back' to the Islamic *umma*. They also show that it is hard for women to carve out an identity because of the gap between who they feel they are and the ways in which they are addressed by both camps; the host society demands that they abandon their faith by removing hijab, while the 'call to unity' by their Muslim brethren demands that they endorse traditional gender hierarchies. Talking to three generations of women, Afshar, Aitken and Franks seek to understand what women of different age groups see as appropriate notions of who they are and how their identities have changed to conform or conflict with the ascribed identities. Despite a shared experience of Islamophobia, the authors suggest, these women have different understandings of the call of political Islam, as some have more in common with their white British sisters than with their Muslim brethren. This is particularly true for second-generation migrant women, some of whom have not even seen their 'homeland' and are aware of the mythologized notion of the ancestral home. Many also question their parents' interpretations of Islam.

Can we, then, identify diaspora experience as transformative for women? This might be the case, as Fataneh Farahani shows in 'Diasporic narratives on virginity'. Farahani uses recorded interviews with first-generation Iranian immigrant women living in Sweden to examine how the concept of virginity is discursively constituted and normalized within Iranian culture. Informants reveal how parental and socio-cultural insistence on maintaining virginity has led to anxiety, and how this has affected their lives with regards to play as a child, sports and recreational activities, politics and even career choice. Farahani analyses the impact of contemporary Iranian-Islamic cultural and legal practices, as well as the influence of the experience of migration and displacement, in the construction and production of women's sexuality. Using a Foucauldian approach, she suggests that sexuality is gendered, historicized and culturally constructed, explaining how cultural values and practices surrounding sex and sexuality enter women's personal narratives, and how cultural and legal restrictions and representations of sexuality, women and their bodies are reflected in these narratives. Interestingly, it is away from the homeland, in exile, that these women are able to interpret the experiences of their childhood as gendered practices.

In her chapter, 'Iranian-American elderly in California's Santa Clara Valley: Crafting selves and composing lives,' Mary Elaine Hegland chronicles the plight and coping strategies of the elderly in Iranian diasporic communities in the United States. Whether as a result of joining children who had stayed on to work after studying in the US, or because of a desire to leave the Islamic Republic of Iran, a large group of Iranian elderly now live in the US. Like Farahani, Hegland employs a qualitative approach. Using open-ended interviews and participant observation to investigate the challenges and difficulties faced by the Iranian elderly and to determine how older Iranian-Americans have found ways of developing meaningful lives for themselves, she describes their encounters in relating to a society different from their own. The elderly, their caretakers and experts dealing with them talk of isolation, depression, anxiety and loneliness. Usually the elderly cannot speak English; they may not live close to other Iranians and most cannot drive in the US. Yet, developing various strategies, among them cocooning, manipulation and separation from other Iranians, they apply Iranian cultural rituals and practices to deal with their alienation.

In the final chapter in the volume, 'Like Parvin, like Najiba, like Heba, we are all different: Reflections on voices of women in diaspora', Afsaneh Hojabri uses the life histories of women from various communities of Muslim cultural background to show the unity of women's experiences in diaspora without neglecting the diversity and specificity of each individual's story. In common with other contributions to this collection, this paper reflects hope and a belief in the possibility of a harmonious and mutually respectful co-existence between peoples of diverse cultural backgrounds regardless of institutions of inequality and the unique experiences that set individuals apart from others in host societies. In fact, in the face of intensified misperceptions and the continuing hostility towards 'Muslims' in the wake of 11 September 2001, it becomes a particularly relevant and timely task to deconstruct stereotypical notions that depict people from Muslim-majority countries as homogeneous and alien, thereby targeting women and men of diasporic communities in the West. The life histories of ten women from Pakistan, Iran, Afghanistan and Palestine show that women's lives and experiences in the diaspora vary in the degree of religiosity and identification with 'Islam' these individuals maintain, in their level of integration into Canadian society, their degree of social and political activism, and their sense of ethnic identity and how they perceive it in connection with other factors, such as age, gender and social class. These women also differ in their dreams, priorities and attachments to a 'homeland'. That said, they still share the powerful reality of displacement and the experience of being made objects of an ethnic and religious identity imposed from the outside. But Hojabri shows that, far from being powerless victims, '… these women actively adjust to new, often harsh conditions', and creatively challenge unequal power relations at personal and political levels.

The ambition of this collection of papers and of the conference in which they were presented is to deepen understanding of concepts of diaspora and gendered identity, particularly in relation to the experience of migrants from Muslim societies. It is hoped that this book will help the reader confront afresh the myths surrounding 'Muslim diaspora' and the new life its members encounter in the societies that host them.

From its inception, this project has benefited from the support and encouragement of Connie Buchanan, knowledge, Creativity and Freedom Programme, Ford Foundation. I am grateful to her. My thanks also go to James Whiting, Acquisitions Editor, Middle Eastern and Islamic Studies at Routledge and to Carol Pollock for her fine editorial work. I am grateful to both of them. Finally, my thanks goes to all contributors to this volume. Sadly, our friend and contributor Hammed Shahidian passed away before this project was completed. This book is dedicated to him.

References

Guardian Weekly, 18–24 November 2005.

Hunter, S.T. (2002) (ed.) *Islam, Europe's Second Religion: The New Social, Cultural, and Political Landscape*, Westport, Connecticut and London: Praeger Publishers.

Kennedy, P. and Roudmeetof, V. (2002) (eds) *Communities Across Borders: New Immigrants and Transnational Culture*, London and New York: Routledge Publishers.

Mamdani, M. (2004) *Good Muslim, Bad Muslim, America, The Cold War, and the Roots of Terror*, New York: Three Leaves Press Doubleday.

Parveen Akhtar (2005) '(Re)turn to Religion and Radical Islam' in Tahir Abbas (ed.) Muslim Britain Communities under Pressure, Zed Book.

Terray, E. (2004) 'Headscarf Hysteria', *New Left Review*, 26, March–April 2004.

Part I

Diaspora, identity, representation and violence

1 Diaspora: History of an idea

Denise Helly

The term diaspora has been in fashion for the past 20 years, although it is more visible in anglophone than in francophone[1] literature. It means loss and dispersion as the result of a forcible displacement of peoples from countries or regions defined as their cultural and historical centres. The meaning of the word has greatly fluctuated depending on context, and continues to do so. However, if diaspora is a specific sociological reality, we must identify its parameters and processes, and we must review its definitional issues, which are subject to much debate (Tölölyan 1996; Chivallon 2002, 2004; Vertovec and Cohen 1999; Dufoix 2003).

If we focus on the most generally accepted definitions of the term diaspora, we can define four broad periods: antiquity, a time during which it had different meanings; the Middle Ages to the Renaissance; the beginning of the nineteenth century to the 1970s; and the 1980s to the present. During antiquity (800–600 BCE), the term was used to describe the Greek colonization of Asia Minor and the Mediterranean; it referred to trade expansion and had a positive connotation. It was first used by Jewish scholars during the third century BCE in a Greek translation of the Bible[2] and had a negative connotation: it referred to the Jewish experience of displacement to Babylon after the destruction of Jerusalem and its temple (586 BCE). So the terms diaspora and Babylon came to mean being cut off from one's roots and being forced to live in a foreign place (Cohen 1997: 118–19). Diaspora conveyed the notion of loss, of suffering, and of exile from a place of origin, as well as the idea of religious punishment of the Jews.

This definition changed as Jews settled freely outside Palestine and diaspora came to mean the gathering of all Jews by the will of God (Paul 1981; Lenoir-Achdjian 2001). By the third century BCE, the term had shed its negative connotation and designated Jews living in the Greco-Roman world and speaking Greek, as well as the Jews living in Mesopotamia and speaking Aramaic (Sachot 1998). But with the Roman destruction of the second temple in CE 70, it became associated once again with exile (*galût*) from a historical and cultural centre, although this meaning waned during the centuries to follow. Jews suffered intolerance and displacement in Europe with the rise of Christian anti-Semitism in the Middle Ages, all the while being recognized and enjoying their status in Muslim countries. Their lives in Northern Europe improved during the Renaissance (Chaliand and Rageau 1991: 15–35).

Diaspora, nation-state, exile and loss

With the creation and predominance of nation-states during the nineteenth century, a coalescence of the notions of nation, state, culture and territory became the rule, and the term diaspora came again to signify exile, suffering and displacement (Marienstras 1989: 120).

A new way of looking at diasporas, and especially the Jewish one, became common, and gave rise to two debates. One was related to the Nationalities Principle adopted in the 1830s by major powers of the time, which was linked to the debate on the rights of national minorities to a state (Helly 2005). It was then commonly believed that it was normal for a human group, be it linguistic or cultural, to have a state. Zionist thinkers, in fact, compared communities in exile to sick creatures, suggesting that the Jewish diaspora was a pathological mode of existence. Others proposed a particular form of federalism, personal federalism (Karl Renner 1899), or national-cultural autonomy (Otto Bauer 1987). Both approaches were meant to protect cultural and religious minorities who lacked territorial continuity and could not claim national independence (Marienstras 1989: 121–3).

The second debate had to do with the political affiliations of diasporas. Members of a diaspora were suspected of allegiance only to their own community and not to the nation and society within which they had settled. The geographic dispersion of the Jewish diaspora was described as a-national or anti-national.

The ideology of national and cultural homogenization in the nineteenth century could only permit a negative connotation to be ascribed to the term diaspora. The term contradicted the precepts of national and state ideologies, since 'nation' implied the superimposition of an ethnic group, a territory and a political system, as well as the absence of loyalty to any extra-national community, group or institution. The expression 'internal enemy', used to designate diasporas, minorities or political opponents, was adopted in France in the nineteenth century. During the years 1870–80, both French Catholics and Jews were accused of disloyalty to France because they followed the dictates of non-national authorities (papacy, rabbinates and diasporas). Members of diasporas and minority groups (such as Gypsies) were disparaged and discriminated against in a number of Western European countries, expelled by autocratic nationalist regimes (Jews in Russia and Central Europe had to emigrate to North America,[3] Turkey's Armenians dispersed throughout the Middle East,[4] France and the United States), or displaced by international accords (e.g. Greeks forced by the Lausanne Treaty,[5] in 1923, to leave Turkey and settle in the north of Greece). The most extreme cases were the genocide of Pontian Greeks between 1919 and 1923,[6] the Armenian and Assyrian genocide in 1915[7] and the Holocaust.

From the 1950s onward, during the creation of Communist China and the accentuation of the colonial conflicts in Southeast Asia (notably in Indonesia and Malaysia), people started speaking of a Chinese diaspora in the region. The term 'fifth column' was used to refer to persons supposedly without local national allegiances who were linked by powerful economic networks and were developing an allegiance to the new China.[8]

This perception of the people of diaspora as rather untrustworthy elements was reinforced by the role they played in the political and economic life of their regions of origin. For instance, Greek émigrés helped finance the Greek independence movement of the 1830s; the *nan yang*, referred to as *hua qiao*[9] from the 1830s on, actively participated in the establishment of the Chinese Republic of 1911; from the end of the nineteenth century, large numbers of European Jews immigrated to Palestine and supported the creation of Israel in 1948.

The definition of a diaspora as a culturally specific population that places little value on the borders of empires, states, nations and majority cultures and religions was hardly questioned until the 1960s. Until this time, the term implied a clear distinction between diaspora and the migratory flux generated by industrial and capitalist development and by the creation of new states in Central and Southern Europe in the nineteenth century, and in the Third World in the twentieth century. Examples included large numbers of Polish, Russian, Irish, Scandinavian, German, Italian and Portuguese emigrants who were not seen as comprising diasporas, but as economic migrants, dispossessed or oppressed and with no sense of internal unity. However, starting in the 1960s, this distinction between diaspora and economic migration tended to be blurred in the anglophone context, notably in North America.

This evolution was a result of a change in relations between minority and majority cultural groups – between Europeans and non-Europeans (Helly 2000, 2001, 2002). The major facts were a shift in American (1965) and Canadian (1967) immigration policies, whereupon borders were opened to non-Europeans, as well as the adoption of the *Canadian Multiculturalism Act* in 1971 and a similar policy in Australia in 1977, the social uprising in African-American ghettos, the African-American elite's demand for equal rights, the advent of the notion of a black diaspora and the protest movements of Native and African-American minorities. The term diaspora seems to embody the fate of a number of non-European individuals having emigrated or been displaced to the Western world, as it overlooks national borders and evokes an experience of victimization, the will to endure and a strong sense of solidarity. Three definitions were to be put forth.

Diaspora, dispersion and ties to a homeland

Starting in the 1970s and 1980s, the term diaspora came to mean a population living outside its homeland (Tölölyan 1996: 13–15). According to the authors of this semantic change (Scheffer 1993; Esman 1986; Connor 1986), minorities of immigrant ancestry who develop strong ties with their country of origin make up modern-day diasporas. We can then refer to Mexican, Filipino, Serb, Kosovar, Croat, Haitian, Irish, Polish, Japanese, Ukrainian, Sikh, Turkish, Basque, Finnish, Korean and Acadian diasporas. The acceptance of this meaning was popularized during the 1980s through the journal *Diaspora*. Its use became so widespread that one of the directors of the journal, Khachig Tölölyan (1996: 8), warned of the possible dissolution of the notion of diaspora, a word that had become so common that it spoke for itself (Dufoix 2003: 123).

When assigned to a migratory movement with strong ties to its centre of origin, the term is indeed denuded of its original content, and its use becomes purely ideological rather than sociological. The reality of the 1990s brings to light the vacuousness of this definition. In view of the globalization of communications, politics and the economy, the majority of emigrant groups can easily maintain ties with their homeland. Rare are those who lose interest in their countries.

This confounding of diaspora with networking by emigrant peoples who maintain ties with their country of origin is upheld by numerous governments that seek to reinforce allegiances for their own interests. This situation is not new, but it has been reinforced by the increased ease of communications. More and more states call on the patriotism of emigrants with the aim of summoning their votes, their financial resources, their expertise and even their return.

Since the 1990s, immigrants and their descendants have been in frequent contact with their homelands, and their political ties, whether trivial or dramatic, are well known (Demetriou 1999). For example, after the fall of the Soviet Union in 1991, the Armenian diaspora mobilized in favour of the independence of Soviet Armenia (Ritter 2005; Lenoir-Achdjian 2001; Norton 1998), while Ukrainians, Baltic peoples and Poles all fought to rebuild their home states. Besides, many emigrant groups, like most members of diasporas, transfer money to their countries of origin. New theories focusing on how migrant families calculate risks (Stark 1991; Stark *et al.* 1986; Congressional Budget Office 2005) and on immigration networks and channels (Gurak and Caces 1992) explain the growth of these transfers within the context of economic globalization. They have become so important over the past 15 years that they now play a key role in negotiations over the control of migratory movement; they are also an issue in the debate on the brain drain from the south (Stark *et al.* 1997). Estimated at about $150 billion, remittances by emigrants can amount up to 5 per cent of the revenue of some states (CBO 2005; Pérouse de Montclos 2005), and represent high percentages of the GNP in some countries: in 2002, 22.8 per cent in Jordan, 13.8 per cent in Lebanon, 9.7 per cent in Morocco, and 5 per cent in the People's Republic of China.

In these conditions, naming a migratory population that maintains contact with its homeland diasporic does not add anything to the sociology of diasporas. Moreover, it overlooks two facts: the violence causing the dispersion of certain populations, and the network linking different centres of settlement.

Diaspora, hybridity, and challenging modernity

Another definition of the term diaspora gained acceptance during the 1960s and 1970s. Taken from *African Studies*, it emphasized the victimization of Africans deported to the Americas and the recreation and invention of hybrid, mixed and plural identities and cultures. Representing oneself as a member of a diaspora took precedence over forming a diaspora, organizing a dispersed population, and linking disseminated groups and individuals. A diaspora was then considered a type of representation, a discourse, a protest rather than a representation and a form of human action and cultural community. Nevertheless, the importance of this definition resides in its denunciation of one of the sinister faces of modernity.

African-Americans showed an interest in their roots and in Africa as soon as they were emancipated. An African Civilization Society was founded in the United States in 1858; African states for free black Americans (Liberia, Sierra Leone; Schama 2005) were created at the end of the nineteenth century, and the Universal Association for Negro Improvement and African Communities League was founded in 1914. The notion of returning to the land from which they were wrenched by force took on a new form in the 1930s along with the notion of a Black Babylon. The Rastafarian movement[10] was born in Jamaica, its main advocate Marcus Garvey, a Jamaican political activist. Largely derived from the *Old Testament*, it promoted a return to Africa of African-Americans, leaving behind oppression. Ethiopia was likened to the promised land, and Prince (Ras) Tafari to the Messiah after his coronation as Emperor Haile Selassie in November of 1930 (Cohen op. cit.: 126). Melville Herskovits (1938) also contributed to this recognition of Africa and the slave descendants' culture.

The independence of European colonies, the civil rights movement in America, and the Rastafarian movement were all factors in the re-emergence of African-West Indians' and African-Americans' pan-African consciousness in the 1960s and 1970s. Terms such as Black diaspora (Shepperson 1966) and African diaspora were used (Ziegler 1971, in Dufoix 2004: 7–8), and a link was made between the Jewish diaspora and the violent displacement of African slaves to the Americas. The 'return of the South' – that is, of slave descendants and non-European immigrants becoming politically visible in white man's land – transformed the notions of Black Babylon and diaspora, and will ensure the success of post-colonial studies.

Colonization is not only a political and economic domination, it is also psychological and intellectual. It destroys or distorts the past; the colonized then have to recreate their past in order to access their history and gain social recognition. Frantz Fanon mentioned the passionate research of identity by post-colonial subjects who hoped to discover an era of splendour and happiness beyond their memories of daily denigration, self-loathing and poverty, and which could rehabilitate them in their own eyes (Hall 1990: 223).

This research of identity is not made easy. Enslaved Africans and their descendants continue to form a diverse population, dispersed among different societies. Their memories of their regions of origin in Africa, of the slave trade and of their emancipation vary greatly. Furthermore, the absence of written materials renders the task of rediscovering and reinterpreting their past difficult – it has to be recreated from signs and traces. The notion of diaspora becomes the trace of a memory of dispersion, of separation, of enslavement, of contempt, of loss of identity and of transplantation. A diaspora is a collective memory as well as something positive built by victims; it is creativity, cross-breeding and cultural hybridization that is best embodied by the West Indians (Hall 1990; Chivallon 2004). Léopold Senghor and Aimé Césaire spoke of blackness and hybridity between African, American and European worlds. Paul Gilroy (1993) refers to slavery in the New World as an experience of violent dispersion, of cultural creation (Chivallon 2002) and as a diasporic experience: Black Atlantic. Drescher (1999) compared the Atlantic slave trade and the Holocaust and spoke of the Black Holocaust.

This definition of the term diaspora is in line with the political struggle concerning minorities' status and the responsibility of the cultural majority and the state towards them. There were many protest movements from the 1970s to the 1990s as groups claimed to be historical victims of a state or a nation and identified themselves with diasporas to validate their point. Accepted as meaning exclusion and forced exile, the term diaspora was and is still used to make such claims. Even in France, where the myth of republican equality reigns, pressure groups of West Indian, African and Arab origin want the state to recognize its colonial past and its practice of slave-trading. African nationals are also asking for status as victims of the state, questioning in a way the exceptionalism of the victimization of the Jews.[11] For those who have forgotten the return of the South or the post-colonial subjects, like Alain Finkielkraut, the link between the Holocaust and the European slave trade is an attack on the national French identity.

According to this second definition, the first modern diaspora appeared in South America, where the notion of European purity, to the exclusion of other races, was first introduced. The diaspora is then a product of European expansion beginning in the fifteenth century, resulting in the annihilation and displacement of native populations (Anderson 1998), the enslavement of thousands of Africans and Asians, and the expulsion and extermination of minorities due to the rise of nationalism. The term diaspora participates in the self-examination of the discourse on modernity and progress. This statement is legitimate, but sheds little light on the notion of diaspora; it just repeats a well-known fact. The logic of diasporas is contrary to the logic of the nation-state.

Diaspora, mobility and transnational networks

During the 1980s, the term diaspora acquired a new, positive connotation. It was used to designate all forms of migratory movement of different communities, such as the Polish, Japanese, Ukrainian, Sikh and Turkish diasporas. To be certain, as Wang Gungwu put it (1997: 16), the current resurfacing of the idea of diaspora reminds us how shallow the roots of nationalism are in comparison with the long history of diasporas; but this does not mean that all emigrants are diasporic.

This new image of the diaspora emphasizes the ties linking local communities originating from a dispersed population rather than underlining exile from a homeland and links with a country of origin. The association of diaspora and transnationalism is a result of the globalization of trade and the dissolution of national and territorial referents. Over the past 20 years, a double dissociation has definitely become widespread: the one between national culture, collective identity, economic practices and the political system that formerly combined to form a nation, and the other between citizenship and rights (Helly 2005). Since 1945, the rights of cultural and racial minorities have been a focal point for Western powers. During the years 1970–80, throughout the West, the legitimacy and effectiveness of the notions of nation and citizenship were greatly affected by debates over the failure of assimilation policies and by the granting of social and civil rights to non-citizen immigrants. Furthermore, the accelerated globalization of markets and of communications, as well as the expansion of the ideology of human rights to transcend borders, has led to a new valorization of geographical and cultural mobility, as well as of migrant peoples and diasporas.

A number of emigrants and their descendants evolve in a space where national borders seem to have lost their meaning. Instead, they create ties with two societies or with a transnational community. Many different studies document the existence of transnational immigrant networks and transnational identities (Heisler 1986; Glick *et al.* 1992; Basch *et al.* 1994; Blanc *et al.* 1995; Kearney 1995; Jones-Correa 1998; Portes 1996, 1999; Glick 1999; Hannerz 1996; Vertovec 1999; Vertovec and Cohen 1999; Helly and van Schendel 2001; Allievi and Nielsen 2003; Cesari 2004). Authors speak of a transnation, of a displaced nation, of deterritorialization and of multiple identities (Appadurai 1991: 191–6; 1996: 172; Basch *et al.* 1995: 48). They want to see in emigrants, as in diasporas, emblematic figures challenging borders, state authority and single-centred and rigid national identities.

Diaspora, multipolarity and community

These three current interpretations of the term diaspora obliterate its potential epistemological value. We have to examine what specific form of migration and settlement distinguishes diasporas. Robert Fossaert (1989: 164) refers to diaspora as a chain of colonies without a homeland. He distinguishes diasporas born of enclaves of foreign merchants located at the crossroads of commercial routes from diasporas born of European and Asian industrial reserves created by capitalism, which prompted migration to the Americas. From the definition in which diaspora and ties with a homeland are assimilated, Gabriel Scheffer (1993) retains three characteristics: the claim to an ethnic identity; strong ties to a transnational community; and contact with a centre of origin. In a definition closer to the Jewish archetype, William Safran (1990) proposes five characteristics: dispersion from a homeland to various regions; collective memory of the homeland; ties maintained with the country of origin and a will to return; responsibility for its reproduction; and uneasy relations with the society of residence. Robin Cohen (1997: 140–1) adds two other traits: voluntary dispersion and links between dispersed communities. Finally, Kachig Tölölyan (1996: 16–17) proposes the following six characteristics to summarize the definition of historical diasporas: forced dispersion; cultural unity; collective memory (written material, history); strong community boundaries; links between different centres of settlement; and ties with a historical centre.

According to the definition of diaspora as a rupture of modernity, illustrated by the annihilation or displacement of Native Americans and African slaves, the diaspora is a representation of dispersion, and not a type of ethnic community. Being diasporic means being on the margins of cultural groups deemed to be stable, and constantly being in flux, in a process of hybridization caused by the absence of a centre. Modern diasporas are made up of the story of victimized individuals crossing borders, the story of people with no history. This definition overlooks the fact that a diaspora is not just a representation. It is a representation shared by a sufficient number of people to develop a network of institutions linked to one another above and beyond national borders (associations, clubs, religious establishments, etc.). Otherwise, any one person having developed a representation or a memory of victimization could constitute a diaspora.

We have two options in defining a diaspora. We can retain a particular form of group organization and debate the observable criteria. In so doing, the notion of a community and of multipolarity and the absence of a cultural, institutional and territorial centre characterize a diaspora. Chantal Benayoun (1998) speaks of a multiplier (démultiplicateur) of relationships to designate this form of social organization of dispersed populations, whereas Amitav Gosh (1989) speaks of groups who are 'multi-centred and not so much oriented to roots in a specific place and a desire for return as around the ability to recreate a culture in diverse locations'. Nonetheless, the question arises as to how this form came to be. We can explain dispersion by distinguishing diasporas resulting from trauma, expulsion and/or threats of annihilation, diasporas resulting from misery and a desire to flee destitution, and diasporas resulting from commerce. But in this approach we only trace routes of dispersion and pinpoint the groups that will follow it without being able to explain why people organize themselves in such multinational communities. This somewhat determinist method boxes people in at particular locations without specifying their form of social organization.

In a more constructivist approach, we can recognize the structural causes forcing or inducing different forms of population dispersion, and concentrate on the forms the dispersed groups give it and the meaning they attach to it. Not all dispersed populations see themselves as a community, or create institutions to link themselves to one another above and beyond national borders. They have a distinct idea of what a community is. There is an 'adaptive constellation of responses to dwelling-in-displacement' (Clifford 1994: 310), and we need to distinguish migrants from diasporics, empirically speaking.

Diaspora and homeland

Threatened by destitution or political repression, populations migrating in search of better living conditions show a certain propensity for maintaining ties with their country or region of origin. Regardless of the meaning it is given, or its status, this is a real place. However, among peoples dispersed by violent means, this place can be a real and historic land to return to and/or defend, or an imagined place, not rooted in history or geography, which serves as an identity reference. These two representations can be complementary or opposite one another within the same population. Third- or fourth-generation post-Zionist Canadian Jews consider Israel a part of their ancestral heritage, and Canada their state (Olazabal 1999, 2006). Anti-Zionists refuse the creation and defence of the state of Israel, and certain authors, such as Clifford (1994), suggest that the consolidation of a land of origin, for example, the creation of Israel in the case of the Jews, signals the end of a diaspora. After a failed attempt at building a democratic Armenian state in 1991, American and European groups of Armenian origin turned their backs on the newly formed state. Faced by insurmountable political and cultural differences with Armenia's Armenians,[12] they invented an Armenia (Ritter 2005). On the other hand, Gypsies are a dispersed population who have organized a community that reaches across many borders, lacking any type of discourse on an original centre.

The notion of an original centre of culture and history has not been central to the history of the three historical diasporas. It must be remembered that these diasporas have not always developed a myth of an original land embodied by a specific country, nor an image of a return to this country. Clifford (1994: 305; Goitein 1993) reminds us that during the Middle Ages, the Rinascimento Jews in Italy did not think of themselves as exiled from a cultural and historical centre, and did not convey any sense of loss. They thought of themselves as coming from diverse cities and regions (Babylon, Palestine, Egypt, Andalusia). The Greek, Armenian and Jewish diasporas did not form the notion of a single point of origin until the advent of nation-states, after which they developed projects to rebuild countries and transform them into states and territorialized nations.

A place of origin, be it real or imaginary, is not the basis for, or a fundamental feature of, the diasporic form. This form differentiates itself from all other forms of migration by its possible notion of a community created without reference to a centre of origin or territory, which can take on various forms, some opposing and conflictual, but not contradictory. The misalignment or inadequacy in relation to hierarchical or centralized state institutions and the dissociation, contrary to the nation-state ideology, between culture, language, history, territory and state, involves a mistrust of or even a resistance to central or state domination according to Boyarin and Boyarin (1993). On account of its multicentred, hydra-like and a-national nature, a diaspora is characterized by networks, organizations and institutions linking up people and communities settled in different countries, without which it could not exist since it could not fulfil its vocation of warding off the threat of dispersion or annihilation.

Nonetheless, reproducing the modern nationalist logic, authors define a diaspora as a people whose sense of identity cannot forgo a reference to a real territory that has been lost as a result of occupation or a redefining of borders. It is even sometimes said that European or American Jews formed a diaspora only during the periods when they showed an attachment to and an interest in Russia, which was the country of origin of a large number of them after the Bolshevik Revolution. This definition leads them to deny the Gypsies any diasporic character, since they never possessed a territory, and to see as diasporas Tibetans living in India and the

West and Palestinians spread throughout the Western and Arab worlds (Bruneau 1995: 12), even though Gypsies were deported from their settlement in the Valley of the Indus to Lower Mesopotamia, then chased to Anatolia and the Balkans, and some of them deported by colonial powers to their American colonies in the sixteenth century[13] (Thernstrom *et al.* 1980: 441).

Diaspora: Culture or memory?

The remembrance of a collective misfortune, genocide or expulsion is a feature of the modern diaspora. Armenian, Jewish, Greek and nineteenth-century Chinese diasporas were born of events that threatened people's lives. Nevertheless, a diasporic memory is not that of a collective misfortune but rather a shared experience of discontinuity, precarity, even denial of humanity. Intellectual and academic circles praise mobility, hybridization and distance from any majority culture – from a centre or from a state. However, centres, states and cultural majorities are still very real, and marginality or simple cultural or religious differences still represent a threat for populations dispersed and historically ostracized. The diaspora is a form of social organization that ensures a social existence beyond that threat and denial of existence.

Regardless of the positive experiences, this meaning remains because of two conditions. In the first condition, the threat reappears periodically under the form of a physical attack, social exclusion or discrimination, as the memory remains only if it serves a present action. Such modern examples of peoples who having suffered collective ostracism and victimization several times over the past two centuries include Jews, Armenians, Greek Ottomans, Palestinians and African-Americans. The second condition: the dispersed populations, or part of them, must have the will and be able to continue to resist denial. Issues surrounding cultural practices, economic resources and social context are as essential as the meaning given to a collective memory of misfortune. A form of social organization, be it diasporic or not, cannot be reduced to a discourse.

These two conditions, the re-emergence of a threat and the will to face it, are clearly controversial. Debates in Europe concerning a new Arab anti-Semitism, Jews refuting the Jewish diaspora and its woes[14] and the refusal of North American Jews, Armenians, Africans or Chinese to see themselves as members of diasporas are illustrations of the controversies and tensions.

Diasporic moments and segments

The economic role of the African and American Lebanese and of the Chinese in Southeast Asia[15] is proverbial. They are emblematic figures of 'middle men', populations accustomed to trade who followed commercial and capitalist expansion and established themselves in the retail, wholesale and import–export sectors in European colonies.

Populations of Chinese origin residing outside Hong Kong, Taiwan and the People's Republic of China dispose extensive, complex and powerful transnational commercial networks. However, they have not developed the notion of a culture or a community, and do not have institutions that would link them together, spanning Europe, Southeast Asia, Australia and the Americas. They are emigrants who have ties to their homeland, who participate in the debate over its democratization, who heavily invest in it and sometimes go back to settle there.

The Sino-Americans are a prime example. The *hua qiao*, notably those living in North America, founded organizations struggling for the political reform of the empire and the republic from 1880 to the 1950s (McKeown 1999: 322). They formed a Chinese diaspora for a certain period of time at the turn of the 1900s. Then, the destiny of these thousands of Cantonese fleeing foreign invasions and destitution in the nineteenth century was obliterated by stories of affluent merchants and storekeepers,[16] as was the fate of thousands of peasants kidnapped in the Pearl River Delta and enslaved on West Indian plantations (The Cuba Commission 1993; Helly 1979).

According to William Safran (1991: 83), one of the criteria for a population to form a diaspora is the myth of return to a land it considers its only life territory. He uses the terms 'diasporic segments' (Safran 1991: 85) to designate the parts of a dispersed population that hold on to this idea. He gives as an example the case of Poles exiled from 1830, after the insurrection, to 1944, who never gave up fighting to rebuild the Polish state, and who created institutions pursuant to that objective. He distinguishes them from Polish emigrants settling in the USA starting in the 1880s.

Poverty, diaspora and dispersion

The diasporic experience is not the emigration of misery. If we look at the structural factors of dispersion and the meanings given to them by the people involved, we cannot assimilate diasporas and misery-forced migrations, past or present, originating from Ireland,[17] Italy, Haiti, Mexico and elsewhere.

Diasporas are strongly socially differentiated, and are by no means made up of streams of proletariat emigration, for it takes financial, cultural and organizational resources to maintain national and transnational institutions, along with the discourses and institutions related to memory that characterize a diaspora. There are no such things as 'labour diasporas' (Cohen 1997: 129) but, rather, a steady flow of poor immigration that over time and following the social mobility of some of its members can build a diasporic consciousness and organization. Armstrong (1976) speaks of proletariat diasporas in reference to Polish, Irish, Portuguese, Spanish and Italian emigrants who were trying, and still are, to influence political life in their countries of origin. He explains how these migratory streams formed a significant part of the labour force of the New World and how, as a result of their acquired riches, they were able to develop their own religious, cultural and socio-political networks. But he fails to mention that these networks remained purely national and that these émigrés did not develop a notion of the oneness of their traumatic history, or multinational institutions across the borders of their various lands of adoption. In fact, these peoples, including the Irish diaspora that is so often mentioned because of the catastrophic nature of the famine between 1845 and 1848, show an acceptance of the unilinear national logic and attempt out of economic or identity interests to play a role in the life of their country of origin or of establishment.

Furthermore, whatever the period, the Jewish, Armenian and Hellenic historical diasporas that are spread out over Europe and the Middle East have always had an ambivalent status, rather than one of only defeat and social exclusion: on the one hand, their often very lucrative and valued occupational specialization, inclusion in political and cultural elites and frontier-runner status useful for the circulation of products and ideas; and, on the other, the denial or limitation of their rights as a result of their cultural, linguistic and religious attributes, which has marginalized them from neighbouring populations.

The diasporic experience appears to be more complex than simply negative or positive. The experience is not always, or only, one of suffering and loss. Significant cultural developments have been produced by diasporas. For example, the dispersal of the Jews and their integration into Babylonian society provided them with the opportunity to construct new cultural traditions.[18] According to Cohen (1997: 12–121), the return of the Jews to Jerusalem and the restoration of the temple (515 BCE) gave rise to fundamentalism, zealotry and highly prescribed rituals (dietary laws, circumcision); the Jewish communities in Alexandria, Antioch, Damascus and throughout Asia Minor as well as in Babylon became centres of civilization and culture. Cohen concluded (1997: 120–1) that after the destruction of the second temple, it was Babylon that remained the centre of Jewish life and thought, and that the Babylonian period of exile could be seen as a period of new, creative energy in a challenging pluralistic context.

The Armenians, whose kingdom had been of the Christian faith since CE 301, formed a very distinctive community within the Ottoman Empire.[19] A minority comprised bankers, artisans and bureaucrats, along with some counsellors to the sultans; the majority, as they could own land, were peasants. In present times, Palestinians[20] of all persuasions are present in the highest echelons of political life in South America.[21] The Russian Jews are also a striking example of the complexities of the diasporic experience. Until the purges of the Soviet elite in the 1930s, they were over-represented within professional orders (Nathan 2001), and made up 'the backbone of the Soviet bureaucracy' because of their frequent adherence to revolutionary tenets (Slezkine 2004).

Historical records show that the socio-economic integration of the Jews into Western societies, where they participate fully in commercial, economic, political and social life, makes them virtually invisible. The integration of some Americans and Canadians of Jewish origin is such that they do not consider themselves members of the diaspora but rather members of a local Canadian or American ethnic or ethno-religious community whose completion they support. This demonstrates how wrong it is to speak of a diaspora when referring to all peoples of Jewish origin, especially since a number of Israelis scorn at Jewish Americans who, according to them, are not aware of their social reality (Olazabal 1999).

So, a diaspora is characterized by:

- the consciousness of a destiny of social precarity, of a fate always uncertain and sometimes dangerous, which past traumatic events, such as a dispersion, symbolize;
- the legacy of this consciousness through narrations and the construction of a collective memory, sometimes reinvented by elites (schools, newspapers, associations, religious institutions and others);
- multiple seats of establishment and of cultural expression;
- economic and cultural means to maintain a multinational network between those seats.

These characteristics are in no way invalidated if we take into consideration cases of populations dispersed by violence, such as the deportation of Chinese and Indian workers to European colonies and African slaves to European colonies, and the emigration of destitute Irishmen, Italians, Scandinavians, Germans and others. They show the obstacles facing the diasporic construction: memories obliterated by the success of the merchant elite and a lack of resources to develop a network of institutions in the case of displaced Chinese and Indian workers; the organization of European immigrants by American or foreign religious institutions and hierarchies; the indifference of most African-Americans to Africa and their rather nationalistic political or religious mobilization to improve their status within American society. If this definition of diaspora is in any way valid, we have to contemplate the socio-historical reasons behind the violent dispersion of populations.

Conclusion: Rivalries, superpowers and diasporas

The globalization of trade, easier means of communication, the so-called declining roles of states and the multiplication of ethnic wars and the displacement of peoples since the 1980s seem to favour the appearance of new diasporas. Moreover, some people think that current financial, economic and cultural globalization tribalizes democratic societies (Barber 1996), thus encouraging the creation of diasporas. Potential cases are in fact numerous, but since the 1980s a number of migratory movements incited by violence, economic dislocation and political repression (Ogata 2005) have not given rise to diasporas: Volga and Crimea Tartars, Khmer, Hmong and Vietnamese (three million), Afghans (over six million refugees), Bosniac (1,520,000 refugees, 700,000 of which live in Europe), Tutsis from Rwanda (800,000 murdered; one million refugees), Kosovar (400,000 refugees; see Ogata 2005 for all statistics) and Kurds. They all have something in common – the lack of the organizational, financial and cultural means to develop as diasporas – but time will tell. A case in point are the Sikhs fighting for the creation of the state of Khalistan, an example of a migratory movement with binational networks (Punjab and a European or North American country) having taken on a diasporic form that confirms the importance of both human and material resources.

The Sikhs have enough financial and intellectual resources at their disposal to rebuild the collective memory of their expulsion, and to expand and link their networks.

Historical diasporas originated in zones where rivalries between superpowers of the time could be found, such as Asia Minor, the Caucasus and the Middle East (Greeks, Jews, Armenians, Assyrians, Parsis), India, Southeast Asia and Southern China (Chinese, Indians), resulting in the exploitation or the deportation of populations.[22] They were born from the expansion of powerful nations, their eventual confrontations and their decline. Examples include the conquest and the decline of the Assyrian, Persian, Roman, Arab and Muslim (from the Middle East to Spain) empires for Jews, the Russian and Ottoman empires for Armenians and Greeks (modern age), the nineteenth-century Spanish, Dutch, British and French colonial empires for Africans, Indians and Chinese, as well as of the foundation and expansion of new countries such as Australia, Canada and the United States. The history of diasporas is valued by powerful nations in times of peace, but their members fall victim to suspicion and repression during times of confrontation, crisis or decline. In view of the conflictual nature of relations between nations and regions, populations are still exposed to the same uncertain future. It is not by chance that researchers are trying to pinpoint the sociological specificity of the notion of the diaspora while ethnic cleansing, forced displacements, destruction of territories and genocides, rather then being exceptions, are part of today's reality.

Notes

1 *Le Dictionnaire des Sciences Humaines* (Dortier 2004) does not include an entry for 'diaspora'.
2 The Jews dispersed throughout the Mediterranean region could no longer read Hebrew; they were reading and speaking the lingua franca of the times, Greek.
3 Emigration to North America started following the pogroms of the 1880s in southern Russia. Nine million Jews were living in Europe at the beginning of the twentieth century, dispersed over 12 countries; two-thirds of them were Yiddish-speaking.
4 In the nineteenth century, socialist nationalist ideas spread among Turkey's Armenians, and they rebelled against poverty and political oppression. In 1894–6 and 1909, they were deprived of their property and forced into exile or killed by Turkish authorities, who accused them of political treason. Two-thirds of the 1.75 million Armenians living in the northeastern region of today's Turkey were deported to Syria and Palestine. In 1914, there were some four million Armenians living in Turkey and Russia. In 1915, 1.2 million of them were murdered under orders of Ottoman authorities or with their complicit involvement, as were 500,000 Assyrians, Chaldeans and Syriacs. In 1918, the Armenians created a republic that lasted only two years before it was absorbed by the Soviet Union to become the Armenian Soviet Socialist Republic. The term 'Armenian diaspora' appeared during the 1920s after the Armenian Patriarcate of Jerusalem used it to distinguish the scattering of Armenians for economic reasons (so-called 'colonies') from their dispersion after the 1915 genocide by the Turks.
5 The exchanges of Muslims and Christians decided as part of the Lausanne Treaty permitted the Hellenization of the northern half of current-day Greece with the arrival of 1.2 million Christian refugees from Asia Minor. These were Turkish-speaking

Christians from the cities of Pondo, Smyrne, Cappadocce and Constantinople, many of whom were of Greek origin.

6 Greeks residing in the Ottoman provinces around the Black Sea (Pont-Euxin) were displaced several times, for example, during the Russian-Turkish wars in the eighteenth and nineteenth centuries, and then officially expelled from Turkish territory in 1923 in accordance with the Lausanne Treaty. The genocide of over 250,000 Pontian Greeks living in the Black Sea area (1919–23) followed the Armenian genocide.

7 The Turkish government does not recognize the Armenian genocide. Under pressure from many parties, it has given free access to Ottoman archives concerning this matter since April 2005.

8 Compared to the Armenian and Jewish diasporas, the Chinese diaspora is recent. It is also larger in numbers: around 30 million people if we exclude Taiwan (22 million) and Hong Kong (six million), and 55 million if including these countries – in other words, more than the Jewish and Armenian diasporas put together. The Armenian diaspora includes some five million members and, as such, represents more than one half of the world's total Armenian population.

9 *Qiao* (temporary emigrant) designated in the Nankin Treaty (1858) the temporary domicile of Chinese officials residing outside the country (Wang Gungwu 1997: 198). The emigration of Chinese subjects remained forbidden and punishable by death until 1893.

10 The movement now has approximately one million adepts.

11 A committee of Muslim community leaders recently (August 2005) asked Prime Minister Tony Blair to change the name of Britain's Holocaust Day in order to include all populations victimized by a state for religious reasons.

12 There are at present three million people of Armenian origin living in Armenia, and six million living outside the country.

13 Gypsies were sent by Great Britain to Barbados and Jamaica starting in 1544, then to Virginia, Georgia and Australia; by Spain to the West Indies as of 1580; by the Portuguese to Brazil and Angola as of 1591; by France to Louisiana as of 1600; by the Netherlands to New Jersey from 1650 on; and by the Germans to Pennsylvania starting in 1758.

14 The Shoah, or Holocaust, remained a taboo subject in Israel until after the Eichmann trial, when the government designated an official day of commemoration.

15 Ninety per cent of the *hua qiao* come from the three southern provinces (Guangdong, Fujian and Hainan) and are dispersed over the five continents. They remain more prevalent in Asia than elsewhere (about 20 out of 30 million, compared with two million in the Americas and half a million in Europe). The reality of this presence and influence is well known: the Chinese of Indonesia, who represent 3 to 5 per cent of the population, control 70 per cent of the country's economy; the Bank of Bangkok was founded by a Chinese rice merchant (Chin Sophonpanich), and in Southeast Asia, two-thirds of retail trade is in Chinese hands.

16 The idea of a Chinese culture that would tie them together was foreign to them, and the closing off of Maoist China rendered it inoperable. As cultural centres, Taiwan and Hong Kong became more active and innovative than mainland China.

17 Descendants of Irish emigrants have developed the image of a population victimized by the state and banished from its territory (Ireland) by a British policy that caused the famine of 1847. Some of them sought political revenge by supporting anti-British movements (land reform in the 1880s concerning Irish farmers' working and living conditions; the Irish Republican Army). The Irish are at present the second ethnic group, after the Jews, to have experienced considerable upward social mobility in the USA.

18 Discussion groups at the homes of the prophets (Jeremiah, Ezekiel) turned into rudimentary synagogues. Jews came to use the Babylonian calendar and the Aramaic alphabet (Cohen 1997: 119), and Jewish law (Torah) was codified in Babylon.

19 From CE 1000 to 1500, a succession of Central Asian hordes destroyed their kingdom in the northeast of Asia Minor, and many fled to the coast of south-central Turkey (Maras, Adana) and established a new kingdom that lasted three centuries (1080–1375). Others fled to Constantinople, Smyrna (Izmir) or Crimea. The western region was conquered by the Mameluk Egyptians in the fourteenth century, and the eastern part of the kingdom by the Ottomans in the fifteenth century; it was to remain under their rule until World War I. The Armenian Apostolic Church, created in 301, was officially recognized by the Ottoman regime and given the status of *millet*, which meant it had some autonomy. Armenians from the eastern region formed another distinct community under tutelage of the Egypt Mameluks after 1375.

20 Seven hundred thousand Palestinians were deported or fled during the war of 1948.

21 In Salvador in 2003, the two main presidential candidates were of Palestinian origin, descendants of families that had migrated from Bethlehem. Carlos Menem, member of a Shi'a Lebanese family, converted to Catholicism – a prerequisite to becoming president of Argentina. Ecuador had two presidents of Arab origin (Jamil Mauhad, Abdulla Bucaram), and Honduras and Guatemala both had one (Carlos Roberto Flores Facussé and Elias Serrano, respectively), without counting the dozens of ministers, parliamentarians and governors in Brazil and Chile. (At www.suffrage.universel, Diaspora palestinienne, 19 March 2003.)

22 Greeks (30,000) fleeing from the Turco-Tartar tutelage and Christian Armenians who settled in Crimea in the eighteenth century and in Ukraine in the nineteenth century, respectively, encouraged by Catherine II and the Tsar of Russia, and who have an autonomous cultural status as well as their own schools, churches and laws. Greeks were also deported to Kazakhstan by Stalin's regime, without being allowed to return until 1956.

References

Allievi, Stefano and Jorgen S. Nielsen (eds.) (2003) *Muslim Networks and Transnational Communities in and Across Europe*, Leiden: Brill Academic Publishers, 344 pages.

Anderson, Alan B. (1998) 'Diaspora and Exile: A Canadian and Comparative Perspective', *International Journal of Canadian Studies/Revue internationale d'études canadiennes*, 18, Fall/Automne: 13–30.

Appadurai, Arjun (1991) 'Global Ethnoscapes: Notes and Queries for a Transnational Anthropology', in R. Rox (ed.) *Recapturing Anthropology: Working in the Present*, Sante Fe: School of American Research Press, pp. 191–210.

Appadurai, A. (1996) *Modernity at Large: Cultural Dimensions of Globalization*, Minneapolis: University of Minnesota Press. 229 pages.

Armstrong, J. A. (1976) 'Mobilized and Proletarian Diasporas', in *American Political Science Review*, 70(2): 393–408.

Barber, B. (1996) *Djihad versus McWorld*, Paris: Desclée de Brouwer.

Basch, L., Glick Schiller N. and Szanton Blanc, C. (eds) (1994) *Nations Unbound: Transnational Projects, Postcolonial Predicaments and Deterritorialized Nation States*, Langhorne: Gordon and Breach. 344 pages.

—— (1995) 'From Immigrant to Transmigrant: Theorizing Transnational Migration', in *Anthropological Quarterly* 68(1) January: 48–63.

Bauer, O. (1987) *La question des nationalités et la social-démocratie*, translation and introduction by C. Weill, Paris-Montréal: Arcantère-Guérin, two volumes.

Bauer, Otto 1907.- La question des nationalités et la social-démocratie. Introduction by Claudie Weill, translation by Nicole Brune-Perrin and Johannès Brune. Review by Claudie Weill, notes drafted by Alain Le Guyader and Claudie Weill. Montreal; Paris: Guérin: Arcantère, 1987.2 Vols. Originally: *Die Nationalitätenfrage und die Sozialdemokratie*, Vienna, 1907.

Benayoun, Chantal (1998) "Diaspora: un concept pour les sciences sociales", communication, Paris: The Howard Gilman Colloquium on Diasporas and Transnationalism, November 18–20th.

Blanc, C., L. Basch and N. Schiller (1995) "Transnationalism, nation-states, and culture", *Current Anthropology*, 36(4): 683–686.

Boyarin, D. and Boyarin, J. (1993) 'Diaspora: Generational Ground of Jewish Identity', in *Critical Enquiry* 19(4): 693–725.

Bruneau, M. (1995) 'Espaces et territoires de diasporas', in M. Bruneau (ed.) *Diasporas.* Montpellier: Éditions Reclus, pp. 5–23.

Cesari, Jocelyne (dir.) (2004) La Méditerranée des réseaux. *Marchands, entrepreneurs et migrants entre l'Europe et le Maghreb*, Paris: Maisonneuve et Larose, 293 pages.

Chaliand, G. and Rageau, J-P. (1991) *Atlas des Diasporas*, Paris: Odile Jacob.

Chivallon, C. (2002) 'La diaspora noire des Amériques', in *L'Homme* 161 (janvier–mars): 51–74.

—— (2004) *La diaspora noire des Amériques*, Paris: CNRS.

Clifford, J. (1994) 'Diasporas', in *Cultural Anthropology*, 9(3): 302–38.

Cohen, R. (1997) 'Diasporas, the Nation-State and Globalization', in Wang Gungwu (ed.) *Global History and Migration*, Boulder: Westview Press, pp. 117–43.

Congressional Budget Office (2005) *Remittances: International Payments by Migrants*, Washington: Congress of the United States (May).

Connor, Walker (1986) 'The Impact of Homelands upon Diasporas', in G. Sheffer (ed) *Modern Diasporas in International Politics*, New York: St. Martin's, pp.16–56.

Demetriou, Madeleine (1999) "Beyond the Nation-State? Transnational Politics in the Age of Diaspora", *ASEN Bulletin*, 16, Winter: 17–25.

Dortier, Jean-François (dir.) (2004) *Le Dictionnaire des Sciences Humaines*, Paris: Éditions Sciences Humaines, 874 pages.

Drescher, S. (1999) 'The Atlantic Slave Trade and the Holocaust: A Comparative Analysis', in *From Slavery to Freedom: Comparative Studies in the Rise and Fall of Atlantic Slavery*, New York: New York University Press, pp. 312–38.

Dufoix, S. (2003) *Les diasporas*, Paris: PUF, Que sais-je?

Dufoix, Stéphane (2004) 'Généalogie d'un lieu commun "Diaspora" et sciences sociales', *Actes de l'histoire de l'immigration*, on line May 3rd htm://barthes.ens.fr/clio/revues/AHI/articles/preprints/duf.html. (2003 *Les diasporas*, Paris: PUF, Que sais-je? 127 pages.

Esman, M. J. (1986) "Diasporas and International Relations", in G. Sheffer (ed.) *Modern Diasporas in International politics*, London and Sidney: Croom-Helm; New York: St Martin's, pp. 333-349.

Fossaert, Robert (1989) "Devenir et avenir des diasporas", *Hérodote*, 33: 158-168.

Ghosh, A. (1989) 'The Diaspora in Indian Culture', in *Public Culture* 2(1): 73–8.

Gilroy, P. (1993) *The Black Atlantic: Double Consciousness and Modernity*, Cambridge: Harvard University Press.

Glick, Schiller, Nina, Linda Basch and Cristina Blanc Szanton (1992) (eds.) *Towards a Transnational Perspective on Migration: race, class, ethnicity, and nationalism reconsidered*, New York: New York Academy of Sciences, 259 pages.

Glick, Jennifer (1999) 'Economic Support from and to Extended Kin: A Comparison of Mexican Americans and Mexican Immigrant to the US', *International Migration Review*, Fall, XXXIII (3): 745–765.

Goitein, S. (1993, first edition 1967) *A Mediterranean Society: The Jewish Communities of the Arab World as Portrayed in the Documents of the Cairo Geniza*, Berkeley: University of California Press (six volumes).

Gurak, D. and Caces, F. (1992) 'Migration networks and the shaping of migration systems', in M. Kritz, L. L. Lim and H. Zlotnik (eds) *International Migration Systems: A Global Approach*, Oxford: Clarendon Press, pp. 150–76.

Hall, Stuart (1990) 'Cultural identity and Diaspora', in Jonathan Rutherford, *Identity: Community, culture, difference*, London: Lawrence and Wishard, pp. 222–237.

Hannerz, Ulf (1996) *Transnational Connections, Culture, People, Places*, London: Routledge, 201 pages.

Heisler, Barbara Schmitter (1986) "Immigrant Settlement and the Structure of Emergent Immigrant Communities in Western Europe", in Martin O. Heisler and Barbara S. Heisler, *From Foreign Workers to Settlers? Transnational Migration and the Emergence of New Minorities*, Special issue, *The Annals of the American Academy of Political and Social Sciences* 484, London: Sage, pp. 76–87.

Helly, D. (1979) *Idéologie et ethnicité, Chinois Macao à Cuba*, Montréal: Presses de l'Université de Montréal, 342 pages.

—— (2000) 'Pourquoi lier mondialisation, citoyenneté et multiculturalisme', in M. Elbaz and D. Helly (dir.). *Mondialisation, citoyenneté et multiculturalisme*, Québec: IQRC, pp. 223–256.

—— (2001) 'Les limites du multiculturalisme canadien', in Michel Wieviorka and Jocelyne Ohana (dir.) *La différence culturelle. Une reformulation des débats. Colloque de Cerisy*, Paris: Balland, pp. 414–427.

—— (2002) 'Minorités ethniques et nationales: Les débats sur le pluralisme culturel', *L'Année sociologique*, 52(1): 147–181.

Helly, Denise (2005) *Courte histoire de deux idées: citoyenneté et nation*, Montréal: Chaire des études ethniques, Université du Québec à Montréal, 103 pages.

—— and van Schendel, N. (2001) *Appartenir: État, nation et société civile. Enquête à Montréal, 1995* (Belonging to State, Nation and Civil Society, Montreal, 1995–96), Québec, Paris: Presses de l'Université Laval–L'Harmattan.

Helly, Denise and Nicolas van Schendel (2001) *Appartenir : État, nation et société civile. Enquête à Montréal, 1995*, Québec et Paris: Presses de l'Université Laval et L'Harmattan, 242 pages.

Herskovits, Melville (1938) *Dahomey: An Ancient West African Kingdom*, 2 volumes, New York: Augustin.

Jones-Correa, Michael (1998) *Between Two Nations: The Political Predicament of Latinos in New York City*, Ithaca: Cornell University Press, 246 pages.

Kearney, M. (1995) "The Local and the Global: The Anthropology of Globalization and transnationalism", *Annual Review of Anthropology*, 24: 547–565.

Lenoir-Achdjian, A. (2001) *Appréhender la nation, vivre la diaspora: regards arméniens*, Thèse de doctorat, Université de Montréal.

Marienstras, R. (1989) 'On the Notion of Diaspora', in G. Chalian (ed.) *Minority Peoples in the Age of Nation-States*, London: Pluto Press, pp. 119–25.

McKeown, Adam (1999) 'Conceptualizing Chinese Diasporas, 1842 to 1949', *Journal of Asian Studies*, 58(2): 306–337.

Nathan, Benjamin (2001) *Beyond the Pale: The Jewish Encounter with Late Imperial Russia*, Hanover: Brandeis University Press, 601 pages.

Norton, R. B. (1998) 'Domestic Determinants of Foreign Policy: Newly Immigrated Ethnic Communities and the Canadian Foreign Policy-Making Process, 1984–1993', unpublished doctoral dissertation, Johns Hopkins University.

Ogata, S. (2005) *The Turbulent Decade: Confronting the Refugee Crises of the 1990s*, New York: Norton.

Olazabal, Ignace (1999) La transmission d'une mémoire sociale à travers quatre générations. *Le cas des Juifs ashkénazes de Montréal*, Thèse de doctorat, anthropologie, Université de Montréal, 317 p et annexes.

—— (2006 à paraître) Khaverim. Les Juifs ashkénazes de Montréal, entre le shtetl et la condition citoyenne, Québec: Nota-Bene.

Paul, A. (1981) *Le Monde des Juifs à l'heure de Jésus. Histoire politique*, Paris: Desclée de Brower.

Pérouse de Montclos, M-A. (2005) *Diaspora(s), Remittances, and Africa South of the Sahara: A Strategic Assessment*, Johannesburg: Institute of Strategic Studies.

Portes, Alejandro (1996) "Globalization From Below: The Rise of Transnational Communities", in W.P. Smith and R.P. Korzcenwicz (eds.) *Latin America in the World Economy*, Westport, CN.: Greenwood Press, pp. 151–168.

—— (1999) "Conclusion: Towards a New World – The Origins and Effects of Transnational Activities", *Ethnic and Racial Studies*, 22 (2): 463–477.

Ritter, L. (2005) *Les recompositions de l'identité arménienne, diaspora/Arménie, de la victime au Sujet*, doctorat de troisième cycle, Paris: École des Hautes Études en Sciences Sociales.

Sachot, M. (1998) *L'Invention du Christ: genèse d'une religion*, Paris: Odile Jacob.

Safran, William (1990) "Ethnic Diasporas in Industrial Societies", in Ida Simon-Barouh et Pierre-Jean Simon (dir.) *L'Étranger dans la ville. Le regard des sciences sociales*, Paris: L'Harmattan, pp. 163-177. (translated 1991) "Diasporas in Modern Society : Myths of Homeland and Return", *Diaspora*, 1 (1): 83-99.

Schama, S. (2005) *Rough Crossings: Britain, the Slaves and the American Revolution*, London: BBCBooks.

Scheffer, G. (1993) 'Ethnic Diasporas: A Threat to Their Host?' in M. Weiner (ed.) *International Migration and Security*, Boulder: Westview, pp. 263–85.

Shepperson, George (1966) 'The African Abroad or the African Diaspora', *African Forum. A Quaterly Journal of Contemporary Affairs*, 2: 76–93.

Slezkine, Yuri (2004) *The Jewish Century*, Princeton: Princeton University Press, 438 pages.

Stark, O. (1991) *The Migration Labour*, Cambridge: Basil Blackwell.

Stark, Oded, Christian Helmenstein and Alexia Prskawtz (1997) *A Brain Gain With a Brain Drain*, Vienne: IHS.

Stark, O., Taylor, J. E. and Yitzhaki, S. (1986) 'Remittances and inequality', in *The Economic Journal* 96: 722–40.

The Cuba Commission Report. A Hidden History of the Chinese in Cuba, 1876 (1993). Baltimore: Johns Hopkins University, 156 pages.

Thernstrom, S., Orlov, A. and Handlin, O. (eds) (1980) *Harvard Encyclopedia of American Ethnic Groups*, Cambridge, Mass.: Belknap Press of Harvard University Press.

Tölölyan, K. (1996) 'Rethinking Diaspora(s): Stateless Power in the Transnational Moment', in *Diaspora* 5: 3–36.

Vertovec, Steven (1999) 'Conceiving and Researching Transnationalism', *Ethnic and Racial Studies*, 22(2): 447–462.

Vertovec, S. and Cohen, R. (eds) (1999) *Migration, Diasporas and Transnationalism* (The International Library of Studies on Migration), Edward Elgar Publishing, 663 pages.

Wang Gungwu (1997) 'Introduction', in Wang Gungwu (ed.) *Global History and Migrations*, Boulder, Colorado.: Westview Press, 309 pages.

Ziegler, J. (1971) *Le Pouvoir africain, éléments d'une sociologie politique de l'Afrique noire et de sa diaspora aux Amériques*, Paris: Le Seuil, 233 pages.

2 Islam in diaspora and challenges to multiculturalism

Saeed Rahnema

Introduction

Much of the Islamic world is in turmoil. Wars, foreign occupation, authoritarian rule, religious fanaticism and economic problems are the prevalent features of many Islamic countries. Whether living under clerical, tribal, military or civilian governments, the regimes in these societies, to different degrees, lack democracy and tolerance. The failure of modernization programmes carried out under the auspices of multinational capital and authoritarian regimes and the suppression of secular left and liberal forces have turned radical Islamists into a potent political force, promising the establishment of 'truly' Islamic states. The regimes in power resort to more violence against these forces while at the same time giving in to pressures for further Islamification of the societies concerned. In countries where Islamists are in power, the imposition of rigid moral codes of conduct alienates and angers a part of the population, and particularly youth, which constitutes the majority of the population.

These political, economic and cultural factors result in the growing migration of people from these countries, mostly to the West, increasing the populations of Muslim diasporas. As their numbers grow and the host societies fail to integrate them, an increasing number of the migrants and refugees become more and more marginalized and alienated. The events of 11 September 2001 worsened this situation, as it subjected Muslims and peoples from the Middle East and Islamic countries to intensified racism and Islamophobia.

The dominant stereotypes in the West, legacies of Orientalist and colonial perspectives that consider Muslims as essentially different and a homogeneous group, have made all people from Islamic cultures guilty by association and cast them as potential terrorists. Right-wing politicians and the media push for policies to impose more limitations on Muslim communities on one hand, and to limit immigration and multicultural rights on the other. In an atmosphere of fear and uncertainty, many Muslims tend to barricade themselves within their communities. Taking advantage of this situation, conservative Islamic leaders claim the leadership of Muslim communities and push for more faith-based rights. Their claims are easily accepted at face value because of the same dominant stereotypes. The negative impact of the roles played by conservative Islamic leaders are not clearly understood, not only by government and media, but also by the progressive forces and activists who support the democratic rights of minority groups.

This chapter focuses on Muslim diasporas in Canada. It discusses the contradictions of Canadian multiculturalism. The policy provides opportunities for ethnic and cultural groups, including Muslims, to preserve their heritage and cultural practices, and yet it fails to remove discriminatory and racist barriers to assist their integration into Canadian society. It is argued that the celebration of different ethnic cultures, costumes, food and music, without serious efforts to address the marginal status and frustration of the immigrant populations, is a major flaw of the country's multicultural policy. Furthermore, by ignoring the vast diversity within the Muslim population, and giving recognition and concessions to conservative religious leaders, the government is changing the nature of Canadian multiculturalism, turning it into a faith-based multiculturalism with serious consequences for Canadian democracy.

Muslims in Canada

Muslims in Canada are a relatively new community. According to the latest Canadian census (Statistics Canada 2001), the total number of people who identified themselves and their children as Muslims in Canada was 579,600, or about 2 per cent of the total Canadian population. Although a relatively small percentage of the total population, Muslims and peoples from an Islamic cultural background are the fastest-growing religious and ethnic groups in the country. In 1991, there were 253,300 Muslims in Canada. Within only a decade this population had grown by 128.9 per cent. Of the total Muslim population, only 137,800, or about 23 per cent, are Canadian-born, making the vast majority foreign-born.

Before 1961, the Muslim community in Canada constituted a small minority with a very low rate of immigration. It was during the 1980s and 1990s that the country saw the high growth rate for Muslim migrants; of the total 415,800 Muslim immigrants in the country, over 275,000, or over 66 per cent, immigrated to Canada between 1991 and 2001. In terms of generational status, over 91 per cent of Muslims 15 years of age and over are first-generation Canadians; about 7.7 per cent are second-generation and only 0.8 per cent are third-generation. Almost all Muslims live in major urban areas.

Muslims in Canada more or less reflect the global profile of Muslims, and thus form a heterogeneous population highly diversified in terms of ethnic, national and sectarian affiliations, and degrees of religious conviction. As shown in Figure 2.1, over 212,000, or 36 per cent, are from South Asia. Arabs constitute 122,130, or 21 per cent, of the Muslim population, followed by other West Asians, including Iranians with over 81,000. Over 51,000 'black' Muslims are reported in the census. Canadian Muslims also come from other parts of the world, including Southeast Asia, China, Korea and the Philippines, with a small number from the United States. (Statistics Canada uses heterogeneous categories for 'visible minorities', some on the basis of geographic origin, some on nationality, and some on the basis of race, including 'blacks'.)

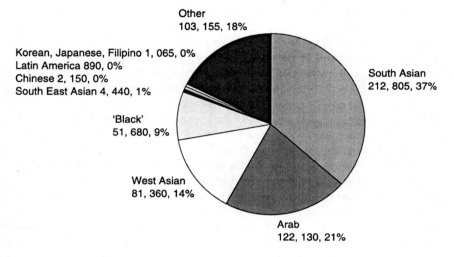

Figure 2.1 Muslims in Canada by ethnic and national origin.
Source: Statistics Canada, Census 2001 Database.

Table 2.1 Muslim population in Canada by gender and age groups

	Total	0–14 years	15–24 years	25–44 years	45–64 years	65–84 years	85 & above
Both sexes	579.654	168.125	94.490	202.525	93.280	20.375	850
Male	303.565	86.775	48.945	104.690	52.660	10.115	380
Female	276.075	81.345	45.545	97.835	40.625	10.255	470
% of Males	100	29	16	34	17	3	0
% of Females	100	29	16	35	15	4	0

Source: Adopted from Statistics Canada, Census 2001 Database.

As shown in Table 2.1, there are more Muslim men (over 52 per cent) than women, and the community is relatively very young. The median age of Muslims is 28, well below the Canadian median of 37. The vast majority, at 59 per cent, are married.

Muslims in Canada are well educated. Being relatively young, 22 per cent of the Muslim population 15 years of age and older attend school on a full-time basis, and 7.4 per cent attend school part time. The distribution of school attendance is more or less similar for both sexes, with women having a slightly higher level of full-time attendance (23 per cent). In terms of level of education, about 25 per cent of Muslims 15 years of age and over have less than high school education. However, over 28 per cent have a university degree. This figure is higher for men, with 33 per cent, compared to women, with about 23 per cent. Over 26,000, or 6.4 per cent, have a Master's degree, and over 6,000 have earned a doctorate.

Muslim women's level of schooling, although lower than Muslim men, is nonetheless quite high. Over 44,000, or about 23 per cent, of Muslim women 15 years of age and above have a university degree. This percentage is much higher than the national level of university-educated women in Canada, which is 14.8 per cent. It is also higher than the related percentages for women of a few other religions, including Roman Catholic (13.4 per cent), United Church (14.2 per cent) and Sikh (16 per cent). However, this percentage is comparable to some, including Hindus (23.8 per cent), and much lower than Jews (36.3 per cent). About 11 per cent of Muslim women have a college certificate or diploma, and about 5.2 per cent have a trade certificate or diploma. Overall, the level of post-secondary education of Canadian Muslims, both male and female, is way above the national level.

Despite a high level of post-secondary education (almost double the national average), Muslims in Canada have a very high level of unemployment, which is almost twice the national average of 7.4 per cent. Of the over 411,000 in the Muslim population 15 years and over, about 252,000, or 61.3 per cent, are in the labour force; over 215,000 of them are employed, and the rest, or over 36,000 (or 14.3 per cent) are unemployed.

The 14.3 per cent Muslim unemployment level is much higher than the percentages of all other major religions, for example: Roman Catholics 7.4 per cent; Baptists 7.1; Buddhists 8.9; Jews 5.3; and Hindus and Sikhs about 9.5 per cent each. The unemployment rate of Muslim women, despite their relatively high level of education, is 16.5 per cent. The workforce participation rate of 61.3 per cent of Muslims is also below the national participation rate of 66.4, in part because of Muslims' higher level of full-time educational enrolment.

Of the total Muslim labour force, 62 per cent are men and 38 per cent women. Based on the North American Industry Classification System (NAICS), about 39,000, or 15 per cent, of Muslims – men and women – work in the manufacturing industry, mostly as wage-workers. Retail trade is responsible for about 35,000, or about 14 per cent of Muslim employment, followed by accommodation and food services. About 20,000, or 8 per cent, work in professional, scientific and technical services, and over 11,000 in educational services. About 7,300 work in public administration for government, which constitutes 2.9 per cent of Muslim employment and is almost half of the national average of 5.6 per cent government employment in public administration.

Muslim men are mostly concentrated in manufacturing, construction, professional, scientific and technical services, and transportation and warehousing, while women are overwhelmingly concentrated in health-care and social-assistance jobs. In several industries, including retail trade, finance and insurance and educational services, Muslim men and women have a more or less comparable presence.

Using a different classification, the National Occupational Classification for Statistics census provides data for the distribution of workforce on the basis of fields and sub-fields of activities. Over 63,000, or 26 per cent, of Muslims work in occupations related to sales and services. The second-largest occupational category is business, finance and administration, followed by management, trades, transport and equipment operation and related occupations.

Women have a stronger presence in health-related occupations and in social sciences, education and government services. In terms of class of workers, of the 235,000 Muslims in the workforce, over 216,000, or about 92 per cent, are paid workers. Over 18,000, or 7.7 per cent, are unincorporated, self-employed business-people. There is also a small percentage of unpaid family workers, notably among women.

Although it is hard to directly correlate the occupations of the Muslim community with levels of education and fields of expertise, both classifications referred to above point to the fact that in the majority of cases, the occupations of Muslims in Canada are not compatible with their levels and fields of education. As an example, despite their relatively high post-secondary education, only 8 per cent work in professional, scientific, and technical services.

A study, of which I am a part, of four Muslim communities in Canada, shows a lack of compatibility of Muslims' occupations with their levels of education and previous occupations. For example, over 32 per cent of Iranians surveyed were in professional and managerial positions before leaving their country of origin, while only 16 per cent were able to occupy positions in the same category in diaspora. On the other hand, a very small number, less than 1 per cent of Iranians, were wage-workers in Iran, while in the diaspora this figure has risen to about 12 per cent. The same trend can be seen for the Pakistanis surveyed, over 29 per cent of whom were professionals and managers in Pakistan; however, only about 22 per cent continued in the same categories in diaspora. The percentage of wage-workers has also risen for Pakistanis, from 2.6 per cent to over 18 per cent. This shows that many of these new, middle-class members of the community have become blue-collar workers in the diaspora. This is a sort of proletarianization of immigrants (Moghissi *et al.* forthcoming).

Despite high levels of education, Canadian Muslims receive very low incomes when compared to the rest of the population. About 54 per cent of them have an income below $20,000. The mean income of the Muslim community, according to the latest census data, is $21,850, compared to $29,769 for the Canadian population in general. The Muslim median income (a better indicator) is $13,963, about 37 per cent lower than the Canadian median income of $22,120 (Janhevich and Ibrahim 2004: 55).

Considering the fact that the vast majority (over 70 per cent) of Muslims live in the large and relatively expensive cities of Toronto, Montreal and Vancouver, it can be assumed that many of them fall below the 'low-income cut-offs'. The 2000 matrix of low-income cut-offs for cities with populations of 500,000 or more put the cut-off figure for a family of two at $22,964 (Statistics Canada 2001: LICO definitions).

The main source of income in the Muslim community, according to the census, is derived from employment, and only a small number rely on government transfers (welfare), or 'other' sources of income. For example, data of the four communities of Afghans, Iranians, Pakistanis and Palestinians in Canada show that, on average, about 80 per cent of their income is derived from employment. This figure is lower for Afghans and higher for Palestinians (Diaspora Project 2005: 20).

Considering the fact that the vast majority of these communities comprise new immigrants to Canada, it is noteworthy that only a small number of them rely on government transfers.

The above data clearly show that Canadian Muslims, with a post-secondary education level twice that of the Canadian average, but an unemployment rate twice the Canadian average, and median income 37 per cent lower than the Canadian median, are in a disadvantageous position. This is partly related to the fact that the majority of new immigrants have completed their studies in their countries of origin and their credentials are subsequently not recognized in Canada; additionally, many do not have 'Canadian experience' in their fields and thus are hired for lower-paying jobs. But major factors that limit the employment of Muslims are biases against them and the implicit and explicit racism in Canadian society.

Racism, Islamophobia and multiculturalism

Canada is a pioneer in multicultural policy. Leaving behind the assimilation-policy legacy of the colonial era, and in an attempt to allow new immigrants and minority groups to maintain their cultural heritage and practices, this policy evolved through time, reflecting demographic changes within the Canadian population.

Prior to the *Canadian Citizenship Act* of 1947, the policy was predominantly Anglocentric. This was despite the fact that centuries earlier, the colonial regime had recognized the special status of Aboriginal peoples in 1763, and later, in the *British North America Act* of 1867, recognized the rights of the French-speaking population. However, '[d]ifferences were tolerated, but deemed to be private and personal and well outside the public realm' (Fleras and Elliot 1992: 71). In 1960, in response to pressures from Québécois and the rise of separatist tendencies, Canadian policy moved towards bilingualism and biculturalism, while at the same time recognizing the contribution of the peoples of other cultures, by then mostly other Europeans (Rex 1996: 128–31).

The early multiculturalism policy focused on cultural preservation, language and culture practices, but in the 1970s, with the changing configuration of immigrants and the arrival of more 'visible minorities' from Third World countries, the policy began to shift. New policies 'intended to balance the cultural program with a program of equality, through the removal of racially discriminatory barriers' (Fleras and Elliot 1992: 75).

In the 1980s, the policy went through more significant changes, and new institutions were created to ensure cultural preservation and the removal of discriminatory barriers. In 1982, multiculturalism was incorporated in Canada's *Charter of Rights and Freedoms* to affirm Canada as a culturally and ethnically 'plural society' and to 'assure the cultural freedom and equality of all Canadians' and provide them 'the protection and equal benefit of law … without discrimination based on race, national or ethnic origin, colour, religion, sex, age and mental or physical disability' (cited in Moghissi 2003: 5). In 1988, the rights and freedom of minority groups was further emphasized in the *Canadian Multicultural Act*, which committed the federal law to recognizing the contribution of culturally diverse communities to the Canadian society. The constitutional character of multicultural policy went beyond a simple recognition of the rights of minorities to practise their language and cultural heritage, and entered the domain of human rights. It emphasized the principle of equality of rights for all citizens, and made the federal government responsible for implementing the principle and the policy of non-discrimination in such important areas as employment, affirmative action, and others (Moghissi 2003: 5).

Despite legal and institutional efforts, and the attention that was given to 'race relations' as a priority, multiculturalism has, in practice, failed to counter racism in Canada. Living in the most multi-ethnic, multicultural society in the world has exposed Canadians to different cultures and modes of behaviour, and has made them tolerant of other cultures; however, being tolerant of ethno-racial minorities and living under a formal policy of multiculturalism has not made the society immune to racism. Though vehemently denied, implicit and systemic racism, and at times even explicit manifestations of it, exist and are practised every day. Walking on Yonge Street in downtown Toronto, touching shoulders with people of all colours and nationalities, one feels as if walking the globe. But if you move up the elevators of the high-rises on Bay Street, the next block over and the centre of Canada's financial world, colour and diversity begin to diminish. In the Canadian social pyramid, the base is the most colourful, and as we move to the apex, colours fade away.

The multiculturalism policy has no doubt positively contributed to the recognition of the plurality of the Canadian society, and has been an integral part of the Canadian democratic system, but it has many contradictory and controversial aspects. If overemphasized, multiculturalism can reduce social cohesiveness and add to a greater fragmentation of Canadian society, and if undermined, the rights of groups and respect for diversity are jeopardized. In every social system, the more cohesive the sub-systems (in this case different ethnic, cultural and religious minorities), the less cohesive the overall system (Canada as a whole), and vice versa. There are advantages and disadvantages either way, and no doubt an optimum mix is required. The opposite extreme of assimilationism, is unfettered multiculturalism, which undermines the universal rights of all citizens. There are contradictions between the rights of a specific group and the universal rights of all citizens, and between the rights of a group and the rights of the individuals within that group.

An uncritical and unconditional push for more autonomy for minority group rights does not take into consideration these contradictions. For one thing, this approach assumes that ethnic and religious groups are homogeneous, and ignores the existence of multiple voices. Moreover, many cultural traditions are authoritarian and patriarchal, and by allowing communities to freely follow and exercise these traditions, the rights of individual members, particularly women, are threatened. Susan Okin (1999), among others, has vividly discussed the contradictions of multiculturalism for women. Even the arguments that differentiate between rights in the private and public domains, and offer that groups should be left alone to exercise their traditions in the private domain, are not without problems, as family is in the private domain, and abuse within family violates the human rights of the individual family member. In recognizing group rights, the most important consideration should be whether such rights contravene universal human rights and the constitutional rights of all citizens.

More recently, Canadian multiculturalism seems to be moving towards a faith-based policy. This is no doubt the biggest threat to multiculturalism and to the rights of the groups that this policy is supposed to protect. The manner in which religious communities in Ontario have taken advantage of the *Ontario Arbitration Act* of 1991 to push for the use of religious laws in arbitrations is a case in point. After the Jewish community began to formally use *halacha* for arbitration, the Islamic Institute of Civil Justice, a small, conservative Muslim organization, initiated the idea of using Shari'a as the basis for arbitration, and other conservative Islamic leaders followed suit.

The Islamic leaders who initiated the idea of Shari'a as a basis of arbitration, and the Ontario government that initially granted them the right, used the excuse that since other religions were allowed to use the Arbitration Act to resolve their conflicts, Muslims should also be allowed to do the same. In a sense, the Ontario government implicitly applied a Most Favoured Nation (MFN) clause without taking into consideration the impact it would have on Muslim citizens, notably women. Religion cannot be treated like international trade, in which any concession given to a second party can be extended to others. In a commentary, I suggested that to protect the pillars of democracy and secularism in Canada, we should have a negative or reverse MFN, whereby any concession denied to a religious community by the government should be extended to others (Rahnema 2004). Under pressure from secular groups and moderate Muslims, the Ontario government eventually reversed the earlier decision and banned all religions in arbitration courts, a sort of reverse MFN. In a real democratic system, all religions should be free but separate from the state, and laws of the land should be equally applied to all citizens. Violations of these principles will only lead to the weakening and erosion of democracy itself. In fact, permitting different religious interpretations and practices to extend their authority to the secular Canadian legal system jeopardizes the human rights of many Canadian citizens, particularly women. This can also reinforce notions of second-class entitlement for some Canadians.

The biggest irony in the attempt to incorporate Shari'a in the legal process was that neither the Islamic leaders who pushed for this controversial decision nor the Ontario government that initially granted this right made it clear which Shari'a they were talking about. Obviously, the prevalent assumption was that there is one, single Muslim community in Canada and that its constituents are all followers of a single, canonic law.

Shari'a, or the Canon Law of Islam, is a broad, abstract, umbrella concept covering several sources of Islamic faith, the *Koran*, Hadith (the Prophet's sayings and traditions), *ijma'* (consensus of the jurists), and for some *qiyas* (analogy), and for others a*ql* (reason). Shari'a is not a single, codified and written text or set of texts that anyone could readily refer to or draw judgement from (Rahnema 2004).

Difficulty of implimenting Shari'a

Rather, it gradually came into existence in diverse parts of the vast Islamic empire over two centuries after the death of the Prophet, and its different versions, occasioned by various emerging sects and schools, came into practice in different parts of the world.

Islam is both a worldly religion and a faith for the other world. It is a religion with strict codes of conducts and very specific do's and don'ts, covering at least five categories of acts, including what is obligatory, what is forbidden, what is recommended to do, or not to do, and what is permissible. There is also a broad and strict system of punishments and rewards for following, or not following, the rules of behaviour. Devout Muslims needed guidance for their day-to-day actions and needed to regulate their moral and religious practices. The scripture, as the most important reference, could not provide unambiguous responses to all of these questions, and gradually the sayings and traditions attributed to the Prophet and his close companions were added to the source. The problem was that there were about a million of these references, making it very difficult to identify which was true and which was fabricated. The jurists of the time attempted to authenticate these references, and although their views were based on supposedly fallible human judgements, they came to be deemed infallible and immutable. This formed yet another source of Shari'a.

It would be wrong to assume, contrary to the simplistic views in the West – shared, ironically, by the Muslim orthodoxy – that Islam is a monolithic religion. Heresiographers have identified over 72 sects, each considering itself the 'saved sect' and the others misguided (Montgomery Watt 1998: 3). Apart from the major division between the majority Sunnis and the minority Shi'as, there are major sub-sects and divisions within each of these sects. An authoritative source on Shi'a sects names over 200 different sub-sects (Mashkoor 1980: 146–51, 168–86). Moreover, like any other religion and ideology, Islam has had a contingent nature, influencing and being influenced by the different cultures and societies that it has come to dominate.

In the Sunni world throughout the eighth and ninth centuries, four major schools – Hanafi, Maleki, Shafei and Hanbali – emerged, and after reaching consensus, the jurists closed the 'doors of *ijtihad*' (forbidding any more jurist's interpretations). By contrast, in the Shi'a world, *ijtihad* was continued by different Shi'a imams who were the direct descendants of the Prophet and who had separated from the Sunnis on the question of succession of the Prophet. Problems of succession also led to different sects among the Shi'as, notably the Twelvers, the Zeidis and the Ismailies. Each of these sects and schools, both among Sunnis and Shi'as, developed their own versions of Shari'a and, more specifically, produced their own *figh* (more specific Islamic jurisprudence).

The complicated system of Islamic laws in different schools and sects covers all aspects of life, body and soul, and while they all agree on the basic principles of religion (and so deny that there are different Shari'as), they are different in other aspects, notably as regards the worldly aspects of Muslim life and family and social relations: issues such as marriage and divorce, child custody, polygamy, temporary marriage, adultery and inheritance. Ironically, these are the aspects that were supposed to be covered by the *Ontario Arbitration Act* for Muslim citizens of Ontario belonging to different sects and schools mentioned above.

Moreover, not everyone in the Islamic world is religious. Islamic countries and communities of Muslim origin, like other communities, comprise practising individuals and non-practising sceptics, along with secular, laic and even atheist members. Among practising Muslims, also, there are radical Islamists (who constitute a very small minority) and a vast majority of peaceful and moderate adherents. This diversity is usually ignored and, in particular, the existence of a large number of secular and laic persons of Islamic background is completely overlooked. In a recent conference, I suggested that there might be a seventy-third sect of Islam that is 'none of the above', that is, a large number of people in the Islamic world who are secular. Unfortunately, these secular muslims (with no capital letter, as they are identified on the basis of cultural origin) are not recognized either by devout Muslims or by average citizens and mainstream media in the West. For devout Muslims, particularly for zealots, the secular muslims are considered *murtadd* (apostate) and, according to Shari'a and *fiqh* (and almost all versions are unanimous on this), they should be put to death. Once a Muslim, you cannot divert, convert or become doubtful.

The faith-based diversity among Muslims should seemingly make it hard for any individual or sub-group to claim representation of the whole group. In fact, the main thrust of the opposition to the Ontario government's decision to allow Shari'a in arbitration courts came from moderate Muslims such as the Canadian Muslim Congress and secular members of the communities of Islamic cultures.

Claim of representation of Muslims in Canada also ignores the existence of other major divisions among Muslims, notably their different ethnic and national identities. In a sense, Muslims in diaspora have at least triple identities, as depicted in Figure 2.2. At one level, they adhere to a single religion and are Muslims. But even at this level they vary, because they belong to different sects and schools, most notably Sunnis and Shi'as and their many sectarian divisions. At another level, Muslims are distinct in terms of ethnic and national groupings, such as Arabs, Pakistanis, Indians, Turks, Kurds, Algerians, Nigerians, Iranians, Somalis, Indonesians, Chinese and many others. Finally, they are, in the majority of cases, citizens of their new home countries, and are therefore French, British, Dutch, German, Canadian, etc., and to different degrees they acquire the dominant culture of these societies. Of course, there are other major differences within these diverse communities in terms of class, gender, age and generational gaps that make them extremely heterogeneous.

These identities are often conflictual and, depending on the condition of diaspora, one identity might dominate the other two. Members of Muslim diasporas may feel they are first an Iranian, an Arab, a Pakistani, an Afghan or a Nigerian, and then a Muslim. This no doubt varies from one national community to the next, as some have a stronger affiliation with their religion than with their nationality. Nonetheless, the strength of ethnic, national and cultural affiliations cannot be denied. A growing number of these communities, and particularly the younger generation within them, also tend to assimilate and absorb the identity of their new home country, considering themselves, first of all, Canadian, British, etc. The

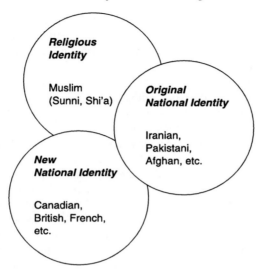

Figure 2.2 The triple identity of the Muslim diasporas.

study of the four communities of Islamic cultures in Canada mentioned earlier shows that while they overwhelmingly identify their original country as 'home', a percentage of diasporic Muslims – about 12 to 15 per cent of the Afghan, Iranian and Pakistani adults surveyed – identify Canada as their 'home country'. The figures for the youth of these communities are much higher; about 31, 26 and 20 per cent, respectively, consider Canada 'home' (Moghissi *et al.* forthcoming).

What has assisted a few Islamic leaders in successfully claiming the representation of all Muslims and peoples originating from Islamic cultures, despite multiple identities and diversity among Muslims in Canada, and what has made Canadian society, government and media accepting of such claims, are the prevalent stereotypes about Muslims in the West. Saleh Bechir and Hazem Saghieh rightly point to the 'essentialist view of the other' in the West, which considers people of diverse cultures and origins as simply 'Muslims' and, in a sense, has 'invented' the 'Muslim community' (Bechir and Saghieh 2005: 2).

Throwing together all these communities, which do not have much in common and are culturally very different, ignoring the existence of a large and growing number of non-religious and secular members within these communities, and giving recognition to several outspoken religious leaders, will change the nature of multiculturalism. A faith-based multiculturalism will only add to the growing problems of racism in Canada and the West in general.

The vicious cycle in Muslim diasporas

With its own unique characteristics, however, the Canadian Muslim diaspora shares some similarities with other Muslim diasporas. That is, Muslim diasporas are diverse, and differ in terms of their country and culture of origin, configuration, diversity and size, and length and extent of their formation, yet they all face more-or-less similar situations in the host country. To different degrees, they are confronted with racism and Islamophobia, and share anger and frustration about the recently intensified Western confrontations with Islamic countries and the Muslim world.

In France, the Muslim diaspora, with a population of over five million – about 8 per cent of the total population – has a long history and strong presence, but is confronted with the equally strong resistance of French society to provide them adequate resources and equal opportunities. As Emmanuel Terray (1994: 2) observes, the Muslim population in France is faced with '… segregated cities, irreducible pockets of misery and unemployment, ghetto schools, educational failure, discrimination in the job and housing markets, workplace racism – and, finally, the retinue of bitterness and violence that these phenomena provoke in their victims, especially the young'. In the United Kingdom, close to two million Muslims (over 3 per cent of the population) with an equally long history and strong presence, face outright racism and discrimination. So, too, is the case in the Netherlands, with about one million Muslims (5.7 per cent of the population). Unlike the situation in Canada, there are open confrontations in these European countries between Muslim religious communities and the authorities, along with growing violence and ethnic and religious hostilities.

The failure of the French society and its governments to integrate and accommodate the large and growing Muslim population has pushed Muslims in that country into further isolation, providing the best breeding ground for conservative religious leaders to push for their conservative agendas. There are 1,685 mosques and other Islamic institutions throughout France, many of them with active memberships of about a thousand each. The French government, fearful of foreign funding and the influence of radical elements, moved to a very controversial decision to fund these mosques and train their imams (*Liberation* 2004: 4). Not until major riots broke out in predominantly Muslim neighbourhoods in France in November of 2005 did the French government and society begin to seriously think about the situation of Muslims in France.

Similarly, in the United Kingdom, apart from earlier conflicts, relations with the Muslim population deteriorated when some Muslim leaders in Britain reiterated Ayatollah Khomeini's fatwa to kill the British author, Salman Rushdie, in 1988. The 2001 riots in Bradford and other confrontations all point to the worsening of relations between Muslims and the British society. Muslim leaders, pointing to the fact that there are more Muslims regularly attending mosques than Anglicans attending churches, have demanded more privileges, including assigned seats in the British House of Lords. Britain's involvement in the second invasion of Iraq angered many Muslims, and led to the disastrous London bombings that further deteriorated relations between Muslim communities and the British public in general. Street attacks, vandalism of Muslim-owned stores and the desecration of mosques, which now number 1,200 throughout Britain, increased, forcing the British government to pass legislation against religious hatred. But this very act has only inflamed Islamophobia further (Gelb 2005: 11).

In the Netherlands, the worsening relations between Muslims and the Dutch society, and the assassination in 2001 of a Dutch right-wing politician who was against Muslim immigration, along with the subsequent assassination of the film-maker, Theo Van Gogh, by a Muslim extremist, have led to one of the ugliest ethnic confrontations in a non-war situation.

In Canada, the Muslim population, compared to its counterparts in European countries, is smaller in size and younger in its history. Moreover, unlike the situation in most European countries, where the majority of Muslims share a single national origin, for example, mostly Pakistani and Bangladeshi in England, Algerian and other North African in France, or Turks in Germany, Muslims in Canada, as discussed earlier, are very diverse in terms of their national and cultural origins. With these features, the Muslim population in Canada is also more fragmented than its European counterparts. At the same time, Canadian Muslims, on average, are younger and more educated, and are not ghettoized, as are their European counterparts. Canadian society is comparatively more tolerant and, as a result, there have not been serious confrontations between the Muslims and the rest of the society and the government.

Nonetheless, the prevailing discriminatory attitudes and practices against Muslims, exemplified, among other ways, in the employment and social exclusions mentioned earlier, continue to be a source of grievance and anger among a section of the Muslim population in Canada. The conservative Muslim leaders taking advantage of this situation have become more and more active and more organized. Since the 1990s, a growing number of new Islamic organizations have sprung up in different provinces and cities, ranging from mosques (*masjids*), prayer halls, Islamic societies (*jama'ats*), schools (*madrasas*), study circles, information centres, and funds and investment firms. There are over 180 such institutions in Canada, 127 of them in Ontario, which has the largest Muslim population. Many of these organizations provide valuable support for their respective communities, which are concerned with and affected by growing Islamophobia, while others implicitly follow Islamist politics.

Although the conservative Muslim leaders in the diaspora are not Islamists in the true meaning of the term, and neither intend to bring about – nor can they envisage – the creation of an Islamic state in the host societies in the West, a good number of them support Islamists in Islamic countries. At the same time, they actively try to expand the Islamification of the Muslim community in diaspora. A growing number of Muslims have willingly assimilated in the host culture, and have distanced themselves from traditional religious practices. Yet, the pressures within these communities, along with lingering racism against Muslims, drive more members to seek shelter within their community and hence increase their religiosity.

The point is that in Canada, as in other parts of the Western world, prevailing racism and discrimination continue to marginalize Muslims; the more marginalized they become, the better the chances are that they will turn to religion and, in some cases, to Islamism, which is fed by radical ideologies produced both in Islamic societies and in the diaspora. Stronger religious and Islamist tendencies, in turn,

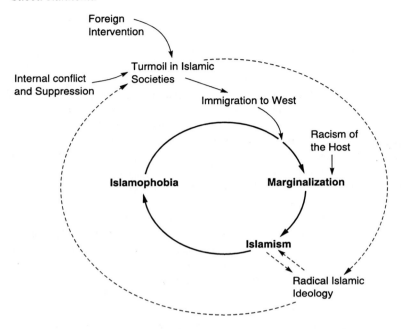

Figure 2.3 The vicious circle of Islamism and Islamophobia in diaspora.

invite more Islamophobia, contributing to further marginalization. Figure 2.3 depicts this vicious circle. In Canada, because of the reasons discussed earlier, this cycle is much weaker. However, if racism and Islamophobia continue to rise, multicultural policy is allowed to become more faith-based, and conservative Islamic leaders are able to take advantage of the situation to pursue their politics, this cycle would be intensified and be more similar to Europe.

Giving prominence to conservative religious leaders and ignoring and, in a sense, silencing diverse voices within communities of Islamic cultures – particularly the voices of the more progressive and forward-looking members, reformers, secular and laic individuals and feminists of these communities – has the most significant impact on intensifying the vicious cycle. For example, after the tragic London bombings, despite the objections of the secular and moderate members of Britain's Muslim communities, Prime Minister Tony Blair met with the conservative imams. So did Prime Minister Paul Martin of Canada. Such actions give credibility to groups that may very well be part of the problem.

When comparing efforts towards social change in societies that host Muslim diasporas (new home countries) with those of Muslims in Islamic countries (originating home) we are faced with a puzzling irony. In the less-developed Islamic countries, the progressive intellectuals act as agents of change, working towards forward-looking transformations in traditional values and practices, whereas in the more developed Western countries that are homes to Muslim diasporas, it is

—not wholly accurate, but interesting

the conservative religious leaders who act as agents of change, working towards regressive transformations, hoping to push back modern values and practices. Moreover, in Islamic countries, the progressive, change-seeking forces are suppressed by authoritarian regimes and conservative elements, while in Western countries, the reactionary, change-seeking forces gain the support of democratic regimes and some democratic elements in the name of multiculturalism. The end results in both home sites are the same: the weakening of secularism, universalism and respect for individual rights.

Conclusion

Muslims in Canada form a relatively new, but the fastest growing and youngest, religious community in the country. Despite their relatively high level of education, they are faced with a high level of unemployment and a lower level of income. Yet, compared to their European counterparts, they are more integrated into the host society. Also, partly as a result of the configuration of the Muslim population, and partly because of the higher level of tolerance in Canada and the country's multicultural policy, generally we see fewer ethnic confrontations in this country. However, Canadian multiculturalism, despite its achievements, has failed to effectively combat racism. With the growth of the Muslim population, lingering racism and increasing grievances, some conservative religious leaders take advantage of the loopholes in Canada's multiculturalism to claim the leadership of the 'Muslim community' and push for faith-based rights. Prevalent stereotypes within Canadian society, the government and the media help the acceptance of this claim. Failing to recognize the extensive diversity of the Muslim population in Canada, a growing number of whom are integrating into the host society, and giving recognition instead to a group of conservative religious leaders would strengthen the shift towards a faith-based multiculturalism. This has serious political and social consequences and, as has happened in many European countries, will intensify the vicious cycle by which the more marginalized Muslims who turn to Islamism are faced with more Islamophobia and, thus, more marginalization.

This trend can be reversed if racism and Islamophobia are seriously addressed and the grievances of the Muslim population redressed. To successfully accommodate religious and national minorities, Canada needs to emphasize and implement a secular and balanced multicultural policy that respects religious minorities' cultures while assisting them to develop a sense of belonging as citizens with equal rights, life conditions and opportunities. The stronger their sense of identity with Canada, the weaker would be their sense of ethnic and religious identity.

References

Bechir, S. and Saghieh, H. (2005) 'The "Muslim Community": a European Invention'. Open Democracy. Online. Available HTTP: http://www.opendemocracy.bet/conflict-terrorism/community_2928.jsp.

Diaspora Project (2005) *Communities of Islamic Cultures in Canada: A Statistical Profile*, York University.

38   *Saeed Rahnema*

Fleras, A. and Elliot, J. L. (1992) *The Challenge of Diversity: Multiculturalism in Canada*, Nelson Canada.

Gelb, N. (2005) 'Britain's Muslim Question', *New Leader*, Vol. 88, Jan/Feb.

Janhevich, J. and Ibrahim, H. (2004) 'Muslims in Canada: An Illustrative and Demographic Profile', in *Our Diverse Cities*, No. 1 Spring 2004, Metropolis Project.

Liberation (2004) 'Islam de France', December.

Mashkoor, M. J. (1980) *Tarikh-e Shi'eh va Fergheh hay-e an Ta Gharn-e Chaharom* (History of Shi'a and its Factions Until the Fourth (Tenth) Century), Tehran: Eshraghi Publishers.

Moghissi, H. (2003) 'Multiculturalism in Canada: Myths and Realities', in Kwansei Gakuin University, *Challenges of Multiculturalism*, Osaka.

Moghissi, H., Rahnema, S. and Goodman, M. (forthcoming) *Muslim Diasporas: A Comparative Study*.

Montgomery Watt, W. (1998) *The Formation Period of Islamic Thought*, Oxford: One World.

Okin, S. M. (1999) *Is Multiculturalism Bad for Women?* New Jersey: Princeton University Press.

Rahnema, S. (2004) 'Which Shari'a?' *Globe and Mail*, October 12, reprinted in Danish in *Information*, 7 November.

Rex, J. (1996) *Ethnic Minorities in the Modern Nation State: Working Papers in the Theory of Multiculturalism and Political Integration*, London: Macmillan Press.

Statistics Canada (2001) 2001 Census, www 12 Statcan.ca.

Terray, E. (2004) 'Headscarf Hysteria', in *New Left Review*, 26, March–April.

3 Exilic readings of the *Old Testament*, the *New Testament* and the *Koran*

Reza Baraheni

Among the various etyma given for the word *exile* by Christine Brooke-Rose in 'Exsul', her article in Susan Rubin Suleiman's *Exile and Creativity* (1998), I find a couple that are specifically relevant to the method I exploit here to discuss my views on the exilic reading of the three sacred books of Abrahamic religions. Discussing some of the more ancient and classic roots of the word, Brooke-Rose states:

> … But then later, in Old French, *exilier* or *essilier* meant 'to ravage', 'to devastate', a shift in meaning still traceable in *exterminate*, literally 'to drive beyond boundaries'. (Brooke-Rose 1998: 10)

My main emphasis is on the concept of 'driving beyond boundaries', not physically and territorially in the form of actual banishment from one's own home and language to foreign lands and languages, but rather, on moving beyond the boundaries of the home of one text to the home of another, while discussing their relationship to each other with a view of the linguistic and narratological transformations the texts have undergone. I also see in 'driving beyond boundaries', in the exilic project, the underpinnings of another 'drive beyond boundaries', namely, the project of the prefix 'post' used in such terms as post-structuralism, post-colonialism and postmodernism, because the prefix connotes the drive to go beyond the boundaries of structuralism, colonialism and modernism. Here we see the march forward of the dynamics of 'post' on the one hand, and, on the other, the inertia to which the three 'isms' have been reduced.

Within this framework, I see the two concepts of the exilic and the postmodern standing conveniently together and conversant with each other, submitting to a happy marriage and offering a new view of the three texts I propose to discuss after my essential remarks by way of introduction to set the stage for what will follow. In this context, the 'driving beyond boundaries' inherent both in concepts of exile and in those of 'post'-based approaches, will be a consideration of the ways in which one text is driven beyond its boundaries towards another, and the second text towards a third. My main contention is that only in this age of ours, with unprecedented upheaval in matters of theory and the practice of theory, could we come up with the notion that there may be – in fact there is – a concealed journey, beyond the boundaries of the three texts of my title, which we have to take into consideration. These texts have travelled beyond the boundaries of their references of time and locus and are now with us, and almost a part of us; and I emphasize *almost*, because in our minds, in spite of their absence from past history and their presence with us today, they are always on the verge of moving away from us towards the unknown future. I am not discussing here faith, revelation, comparative religion, concepts of enlightenment versus faith, the historical development of meaning, the metaphorical and metonymic polarities of literary languages, and the metaphysical world views that ensue from such polarities, in the guise of hermeneutics, in the domains of either religion or philosophy, and their aesthetic and critical bearings on literature. No! I am not dealing with heavy, thickened, coagulated and overtly sophisticated material. I am dealing with 'driving beyond the boundaries' of two elements in the reading of the *Old Testament*, the *New Testament* and the *Koran*, namely: language and narratology. This is simply a matter, within the framework of comparative reading, of assessing the specific space of almost oversimplified similarities and dissimilarities once we move away from the main characteristics of one text towards the second and then the third. The temporal location of this kind of cultural reading belongs not to the past, but to the present; but here, too, a reiteration of locus and focus is required. It is neither the presence nor the absence of religious faith, neither the preference of one belief over the others, nor the combination of aspects of one with those of the others that has relevance here. These texts speak to each other as texts, and as such, all three of them are taken almost self-referentially, erasing whatever trace of history and society they may have behind them and to which they may retreat. I call this the denuding of a text of all its metaphysical attributions.

I have one aim in my mind that arises from the shortcoming of our times, and in order to account for this, I would like to invoke the authority of Jacques Derrida. In his opening remarks to a gathering of philosophers in Capri on 28 February and 1 March 1994, in which Hans-Georg Gadamer, Gianni Vattimo and others participated, Derrida said:

> We represent and speak four different languages, but our common 'culture', let's be frank, is more manifestly Christian, barely even Judaeo-Christian. No Muslim is among us, alas, even for this preliminary discussion, just at the moment when it is towards Islam, perhaps, that we ought to begin by turning our attention to. No representative of other cults either. Not a single woman! We ought to take into account: speaking on behalf of these mute witnesses without speaking for them, in place of them, and drawing from this all sorts of consequences.
>
> (Derrida 1998: 5)

Although hybridity in European languages exists, the Eurocentric nature of the gathering, coupled with discussions based on what Derrida describes as its 'manifestly Christian' nature (Gadamer echoes a similar feeling, particularly with regards to Islam) and the title of the book published on the talks, *Religion*, demonstrates that the concepts of 'alterity', 'difference' and 'différance' have received a great blow at the hands of those who originally formulated them. It makes no difference whether you speak on behalf of, for, or in place of the missing faction, Islam is speaking there as an 'absence', which demonstrates the failures of the organizers in 'presencing' Islam; the so-called ultimate 'difference' is subjected to another 'différance', or postponement, and those who could make contributions to the topic of religion from a different perspective are reduced, with a slight change in Derrida's phrasing, to 'mute[d] witnesses'.

In spite of the stupendous influence of Derrida's thought on the new generation of thinkers in some Islamic countries, the development of the minds of the thinkers, writers, poets and novelists of Derrida's contemporaries in the Islamic world have been shaped differently from the minds of Derrida and his contemporaries in the West. Noteworthy among these differences is the essential recognition of the fact that Judaism and Christianity, both as systems of belief and as frameworks of confabulation, language and poetics, have been major components of the mind-sets of all Middle Eastern peoples, both before and after the advent of Islam. Islam itself, and the *Koran* particularly, are imbued with references to stories of both Testaments. Judaism and Christianity acted first as rivals to the Iranian religions of Zoroastrianism and Manichaeism and, following the rise of Islam and the defeat of the Iranian empire, formed a major component of the influences that led to the supplanting of the two Iranian religions. True, both Judaism and Christianity acted as rivals to Islam, but only as differences in the systematizations of faiths among the various sects of Semitic tribes, which led, with the rise of the caliphate as an empire, to the subjugation of many nations and many religions in the Islamic territories. There were hundreds of lives of Judeo-Christian prophets and saints recorded in classical examples of literature in both Arabic and Persian in the old times, and they are now part and parcel of all Islamic cultures in the world. A great intertextual library, as well as a resourceful storehouse of verbal and folk-loric literature, collected and spread by way of wars, invasions and cultural influences, have educated Muslims from Gibraltar to Indonesia. No such phenomenon existed in Europe before the rise of the new nations on that continent, and since the Renaissance the educational system in the West, compounded first with the colonialist and later with the Orientalist approaches of the last several centuries, have prevented Western thinkers and writers from occupying the same position with regards to Islam as the writers, poets and thinkers of the Islamic world have in connection with Judaism and Christianity.

A new component could be added to this. A new category of thinking and writing was introduced, this time by some of the great names in German poetry and philosophy, from Hölderlin to Nietzsche, Heidegger and Rilke, that made the presocratics from Homer to Euripides the main springboard for the formation of a world view of thinking and writing. Although the main influence on all of this discourse was the figure of Dionysus, and almost everyone on the list spoke of the origin of the god as being Eastern, none of them paid much attention to who he was in the East, and not one even bothered to make a thorough reading of Herodotus and Xenophon to find out about civilizations to the east of Greece. Even in the field of etymology, both Heidegger and Derrida were Greek- and

Latin-oriented, and were not ready to move 'east of Greece' to the actual etyma in Sanskrit and pre-Sanskrit languages of the names Bacchus and Dionysus. This new version of Eurocentrism has risen on the shoulders of the Eastern god *Bagh* (the original name in various forms is *Fagh, Baghe Magh* – the origin of *magus* – and *Fagh* in Chinese and *Beigh* in Turkish), with more than 40 cities erected to the glory of his name in ancient Iran and cities of the surrounding countries, Baghdad being one of them (Dehkhoda 1994), and on the basis of his expropriation, first by the Greeks and Romans themselves, and about 25 centuries later by those who considered themselves the genuine inheritors of the Greeks, not being aware that they were taking the roots of their thinking further back in history, or prehistory, to lands and cultures that had come into earlier conflict with the Greeks or had arisen at the dawn of history. By the same token, in spite of the opposite position taken by Edward Said, there is no doubt that the roots of controversy between East and West were much deeper than he had thought, and it was neither limited to the roots he cited in his book nor to the works of latter-day Orientalists alone. The names of some of the major independent thinkers and poets of the last two centuries who were not emissaries of colonialist regimes or their imperialist descendants, as such, could be included, with a thin partitioning of innocence as a consequence of ignorance among those who had acted as the emissaries of their colonialist and imperialist regimes.

In two different periods of their history, Muslims, and particularly Arabs and Persians, started the translation of foreign works into Arabic and Persian. A great age of hybridity and polyglossia – if I may use Bakhtinian terms to account for what was happening in the first period – started with great philosophy, mysticism and poetry being the linguistic manifestations of indigenous cultures for many centuries. The main sources of inspiration came from India and Greece.

The second period belongs to the beginnings of the last century, when Persians and Arabs, as well as Turks, came into first-hand contact with Western modernity, and a deluge of translations started and continued to flow into all three languages from European philosophy, literature and sociology, as well as translated works from Russia, other parts of the Soviet Union and the United States. The post-colonial literature of revolt against Western domination in the Middle East opened up a new period of translation and transnationalization of art, literature and philosophy, and this has continued to the present day. In the West, this and other periods of Arabic, Persian and Turkish cultures are supposedly represented by Orientalists, gathered together in Middle East or Near East centres in Europe and America. On this world view of Orientalism, we have the testimony of Said himself, in his article 'Orientalism Reconsidered':

> Orientalism of course involves several overlapping aspects: first, the changing historical and cultural relationship between Europe and Asia, a relationship with a 4,000-year-old history, and fantasies about a region of the world called the Orient; second, the scientific discipline in the West according to which, beginning in the early nineteenth century, one specialized in the study of various Oriental cultures and traditions; and third, the ideological suppositions,

images, and fantasies about a region of the world called the Orient. The common denominator among these three aspects of Orientalism is the line separating the Occident from the Orient. And this, I have argued, is less a fact of nature than it is a fact of human production, which I have called imaginative geography.

(Said 2002: 199)

If this is the 'imaginative geography' created by the Orientalist, wherein you have 'on the one hand, the Orientalists, and on the other, the Orientals', the image in the minds of the Orientals themselves and their writers and thinkers is somewhat different. Said does not deal with this. His 'imaginative geography' is quite different. Since the advent of colonialism, the struggle against it in the form of revolutionary upheavals and the production of post-colonial, modern and even, at times, postmodern art, literature and criticism and other forms of thought, the Oriental writer in the Middle East, enchanted by art, literature and philosophy on the one hand, and by democratic institutions and scientific progress of the West on the other – in spite of harassment, repression, imprisonment, invasion and exploitation – has gone through a particular type of education that no single nation, or even groups of writers in the West, could have gone through, except in times of war and invasion. It is not an exaggeration to say that there are thousands of people in the Middle East who know Western cultures to the degree that they can easily carry on a conversation of the first order on Western literature, art, and philosophy with their Western counterparts. Again, it is not an exaggeration to say that it would be impossible to find a sizeable group of people in the Western world of culture who would have an equal knowledge of the literature, art and culture of the Middle East. In the confusion that has arisen due to politics, exploitation and Orientalism, it is also not an exaggeration to say that the Middle Eastern writer is an exilic soul, permanently harassed by his own state when in his own country, in spite of the recognition of his readership, and suffering outside his country because of the absence of both his readers and recognition as a result of the general indifference of both the publishing industry and the public.

It may be surprising to see that the definition of exile by Brooke-Rose as 'driving beyond boundaries' finds its almost exact wording in Said's 'need for greater crossing of boundaries' in *Orientalism Reconsidered*. One can easily understand his definition of crossing boundaries as 'greater interventionism in cross-disciplinary activity, a concentrated awareness of the situation – political, methodological, social, and historical – in which intellectual and cultural work is carried out' (Said 2002: 215). But what about the mind of the person – say, Said, the musician – who pours out his heart to get to the bottom of pieces of music by Bach, Mozart and other great musicians, or the man who stands in front of a miniature from the Babur period, or wracks his brain to find out why some of the chapters of the *Koran* start with simple letters, such as A.L.M., but not words, their combination as phrases and sentences meaning something in spite of the difficulty of the eso-teric diction of the book? What does meaninglessness on the surface mean in a book considered to be God's miracle? And, the main question: is it possible to release a new energy into the veins of the three Abrahamic religions by simply discussing their sacred books within the framework of our contemporary understanding of realism, modernism and postmodernism? Why not take this crossing or 'driving beyond boundaries' to the realm of categories hitherto unthought of and, consequently, left uncrossed? There are no simple answers to these questions. The answer is perhaps in the trying of it; meaning and purpose may follow, or they may not.

One of the main thrusts of my discussion is that there may be a purely stylistic, linguistic and narratological approach to the three major religious texts in the light of the exilic loci of memory, genesis amnesia, remembering, forgetting and dismembering when remembering, in contradistinction to the reading of them, either as purely sacred and religious texts or as purely content-oriented historical and realistic texts. We have to think of the texts of the *Old Testament*, the *New Testament* and the *Koran* from another historical perspective in order to reach this exilic point of view. That historical perspective may be the perspective of what has happened to textual studies in relation to the phenomenon of exile in the contemporary world. Within the exilic framework, and within the concept of 'driving beyond boundaries', all historical views of the past can be nothing but contemporary, because a religious text is supposed to be destined for all times, and as such, the three texts in question have been alienated to their relevant historical pasts to a degree that they are nothing but contemporary. They are exilic texts within the framework of the present world discourse of exile. They have journeyed in time and space (travel, time and space being the triptych on which exilic discourse finds its locus), and in their linguistic and narrative thrust, to the twentieth century and the Western world, finding a new ontology within the framework of modern notions of presentation, representation and anti-representation. What has happened to the three texts in relation to each other in the past may be similar to what has happened to the texts of and on narratology in the last 200 years. The distance between us and the three texts is exilic. Their understanding in these terms was postponed (and is not postponement of this kind an exilic *différance*, to borrow a word from Derrida's lexicon of deconstructionism?) for centuries, until we reach the present age of exile as a postmodern, multi-dimensional phenomenon, characterized by hybridity and fragmentation, in spite of the politically and economically motivated confrontational ideologies and meta-discourses of Samuel Huntington's misnomer 'the clash of civilizations' in his book of the same title. Archaic and ancient structures and perspectives would not have risen to the surface of our present philosophical and psychological perspectives if, by token of the leanings and yearnings of our contemporary predilections, we had not ventured to invoke their presence and participation.

Jorge Luis Borges once said that metaphysics was a part of fantastic literature. But he was not really saying something new, because in Eastern literature, it has always been impossible to draw a line between the two categories. Concepts of linguistic transgression sometimes place literature in the wide-open space of ambivalence. You can move in both directions of the extreme. A religious text is a linguistic operation that can be read both as a religious text and as a literary text; by this token, we can assume that a religious text is a text which has hybridity as its fundamental component. We may immediately add that since hybridity is the dominant element of all exilic literature, all major religious texts are exilic by their very nature. All great prophets of the world were great exilic figures, moving from one territory to another, from one memory of time and space to another, and constantly preoccupied with the process of receiving, retaining, forgetting and reinventing memory.

To my mind, a religious text leaves its own threshold of religiosity, because of the particular type of language that sometimes runs the whole gamut of literary discourse and at other times opens up an angle of relativity with it and attempts to reach out to another threshold. When trying to reach out, the phenomenon of literature as literature in turn moves backwards to meet the first phenomenon halfway, and this space of 'liminality' and 'interstitiality' (which I borrow from Homi Bhabha's *The Location of Culture*, 1994) shares qualities with a similar space in literature; as such, this space could be called religious and literary at the same time. Hence, a kind of journey, sometimes fictional and sometimes metaphorical, is characteristic of the religious discourse. This is another capacity of hybridity, this movement from the territory of prose, or language in the process of saying something beyond language itself, into the land of poetry, or language in the process of saying something about language itself as a performance of language for its own sake.

A kind of departure from the origin is taking place all the time in all great religious texts, followed by a return to the origin of language, the textuality of language as language. Allegorically speaking, the Buddha leaves the castle, and Adam and Eve are expelled from the Garden of Eden. The Buddha is doomed to experience poverty, sickness and death in the space of short journeys. Adam and Eve are expelled from the Garden of Eden, when Eve is tempted by Satan, and have to experience the hardships of life and the closure of death. All utopias turn into dystopias, and in the dystopia, human beings are promised either the return to utopia, or are told they will be taken to another dystopia, the worst of its kind: hell. The return is a return in the memory of the performance of language, because a total and final dissipation of language is impossible.

On the other hand, in both the *Old Testament* and the *New Testament*, there is a kind of realistic presentation. Things move in time; the time of things is known to the person who is narrating and the person who is listening to the narrative or reading it. There is also a semblance of causality, and sometimes a great amount of it, reaching a plenitude characteristic of metaphysical events. This later becomes, in the fantastic novel, a predominant element. Make-believe in this kind of fiction is based on the precise, word-by-word description of the unreal. This is what I call 'linguistic realism', narrating the most unreal situations with such realistic precision (from the story of Ezekiel in the *Old Testament* to the story of the 'Three Beggars' in the early pages of *The Thousand and One Nights* to the surgical detailing of things in *The Blind Owl*, a 1935 postmodern novel by the Iranian author Sadegh Hedayat) that the most fantastic events are written and read as phenomena that are more natural than the everyday events of life. Sometimes this space of the real/unreal is given to us numerically. For example, in the first chapter of 'The Gospel According to St. Matthew', the ancestry of Jesus is given, from Abraham to Jacob and Mary, and then the generations are cited:

> So all the generations from Abraham to David are fourteen generations; and from David until the carrying away into Babylon are fourteen generations; and from the carrying away into Babylon until Christ are fourteen generations.
> *(Holy Bible* 1958: 849)

How can you have this mathematical precision with three blocks of 14 generations? Why not 41, 53, or some other number, instead of a total of 42 generations? In spite of these almost predestined figures of 14 blocks each, in both the *Old Testament* and the *New Testament* an archival reproduction of the genealogy of the prophets, and even non-prophets, becomes an essential requirement of style. One person comes after the other, with a recitation of how his story started, how it developed, and how it ended. This is generally the process of literary archivism as well. For a nation to declare itself as a nation, it is required, almost by an unregistered legislation, that its birth, evolution, shaping up and continuation are reproduced in the first major work of that nation. In spite of a great number of whole passages and chapters dealing with revelations of all categories, revelations by themselves are not the dominant textual phenomenon of the *Old Testament*, because the major characteristic of a revelation is its suddenness in the form of a release from the bondage of time and history. In the *Old Testament*, one thing generally comes after another, and the interpolation of the religio-historical narrative with clusters of epiphanies and revelations is only part and parcel of the narrative technique. The story tries to attest to some kind of reality, as if a kind of history were being written. Here we are dealing with the dominant mechanism of presentation, in spite of the existence of pieces that could be called representational, or even non-representational. In order for this presentation to take place, we have to think – in fact, 'imagine' – that everything is taking place in reality. Some degree of plausibility is required. In order for that plausibility to exist, the existence of yet another element is a requirement. There should be an author for the text of the *Old Testament*. We are never told who is telling the story, and it cannot be God himself, because he is a character, the hero of the text. In order for a story to take place, you need a beginning, an element of time, and a person who tells the story. In order for the story of the beginning of the world to take place, you have to posit someone there before the beginning of the creation, so that he can say that God said: 'Let there be light, and there was light'. So, the time of the narrator comes before the time of the book of 'Genesis', and language opens its mouth before God opens his mouth. In order for God to say what he is saying, there should be someone who knows beforehand that it is his responsibility to make a note of what is going to come: who is going to say what, and what is going to follow after what was said. The trick is that the author seems to have been there before God was there, and language seems to have been there before language was used by God for the creation of the world. The priority of the author and his language is a necessity. Otherwise, the text would not be there. A pre-genesis has taken place, it seems, before genesis takes place, as we know from all scientific discoveries; but now one can argue that somebody was witnessing something and putting it down as a script. He, or she, must have been there prior to the eruption of genesis on the universe.

There is undoubtedly a great difference in the methodology of the *Old Testament* and that of the *New Testament*. In the first book, the narrator is generally narrating and describing everything. The dominant narrator is more or less an omniscient one, certainly with some exceptions. But all the stories are different from each other, because some kind of historical time, or a semblance of it, is being exploited by the author(s), and since history in a book of this kind cannot even be repeated in spirit, reality means the provision of new people, new events, and a timeline that will carry the story forward. In the *New Testament*, the viewpoint has changed, and first-person narrative is being used by different narrators to explain one character standing before them, the major subject, the hero, God or the son of God. It reminds us of modern methods of writing, such as that found in *As I Lay Dying* or *The Sound and the Fury* by William Faulkner (who is said to have read the *Bible* every year), the only difference being the presence of conscious intertextuality in the *New Testament* and subconscious intertextuality in the two works by Faulkner. We can say that the difference between the *New Testament* and the modern works mentioned is only in the degrees of their cubism – the style of their writing – but not in the category of their writing.

The archivism we spoke of in the case of the *Old Testament*, implemented for the building of a collective memory for a nation, can also be found in such non-religious poetic narratives as Homer's two epics and *The Book of Kings* written by Ferdowsi, the Persian poet of more than a thousand years ago. In these epics, things appear one after the other, or in a sequence of time. There are enemies surrounding the nation each of them represents, and all epic poems are full of time sequences taking their course as a result of the journeys of the heroes. However, although they are not devoid of mythical pieces archiving the prehistoric periods of the Greeks and the Persians, the exact structuring and subdivision of all history in the *Old Testament* into three sets of 14 generations of prophets in the beginning of 'The Gospel According to St. Matthew' does not exist in the literary epics. In spite of this major difference, the structural similarity between the *Old Testament* and the books of Homer and Ferdowsi is astonishing. There is the birthplace, the intrusion of the foreign aggressor and the battles, and then either the return home or the failure to return.

One element of national archivism is testimony given to the genealogy of the prophets. All history is documentation, or all history is written history, and it seems that the Semitic peoples were obsessed right from the beginning of their history with documentation. The Greeks and the Iranians also had the same obsession, and there seems to have been a competition amongst them. Did Jehovah appear before Ahuramazda and Zeus? Did Adam appear before the first man in Greece and Kiyoumarth in Iranian mythology? A Judaization of prehistory and an equal Persianization of it was, and still is, on the agenda of both nations. In the Western mind, first came the Greeks, and Hellenization of the world is a major characteristic of Western nations. Each nation presupposes that it came before every other, and the world – the genesis of the world – started only with the first people and the gods of that nation. For a nation to be a nation, there is need for a linguistic, cosmogonic vision of the world: a national cosmogony in words, followed by written history, either in prose, as in the *Old Testament*, or in verse, as in the two Homeric epics and Ferdawsi's *The Book of Kings*. Considering that the dominant element of the narrative in the *Old Testament* is omniscience, and in the *New Testament* cubical, first-person narratives of generally one model figure, Jesus Christ, we can say that the *Old Testament* could be called from the standpoint of style and viewpoint generally realistic and based on presentation. The *New Testament*, with the exception of St. John's 'Revelations' and some other short pieces, could be called representational, and to a certain degree modern, according to our new standards of modernity for texts. Not only the actual narratives, but also all the letters and sermons, are cubically personalized. Many people are talking about the same person, or the same phenomenon. With the coming of Jesus, a new nation is not born; the nation, or tribe, or race, was already there. God in the *New Testament* had no need to create the world all over again. References to the creation are enough. The cosmogony is seen through the other end of the tube; the end, a kind of apocalypse, is in view, and each of the characters is giving his own narration of this approaching apocalypse. Each character in the *New Testament* provides us with his own snapshot, or series of snapshots, of Jesus, on the basis of an autoptic view of the world, and then we, as readers of the text, write or, rather, rewrite the story, in our mind. But we know that each major figure speaks of the entire story of Jesus, and the life of Jesus is the life of a man who is born to a world that has already existed for some time, and if there is a genesis here, it is the genesis, trial and crucifixion of one man only – Jesus.

The major common characteristic of all three texts is that they are made up of words – the words of a language – and they have reached us in their written forms. In short, all three texts are language(s). Textuality is foregrounded when a text's existence is threatened. We have to bring that text to life; we have to present its life in order to show that only when a text is jeopardized as a text do we realize that we are dealing with a significant text. The contents of both the *Old Testament* and the *New Testament* could be produced as narratives in shortened forms, or in forms much longer than the texts of the two books. In other words, there are sustained narratives in both books, and you could reproduce them either exactly, or in shortened and enlarged forms. But you cannot do this with the *Koran*. In order to narrate the story of Jesus according to the *Koran*, you have to go to hagiographies written in Arabic or Persian, or go back to the *New Testament*. In the *Koran*, with one or two exceptions, no story is given in full, even if there may be a semblance of fullness. If the *Koran* had been the only book revealed to the Semitic prophet or written by someone, it would have been almost impossible to understand the narratives. Texts written before the *Koran*, and after it, either in the form of narratives or interpretations and commentaries, are essential for its understanding, because the unique quality of the *Koran* lies in the fact that it is based not exactly on *hekayat*, or narrative, but on *esharat*, allusion.

Language in the *Koran* is the dismembered body of the entire cosmogony of the Semitic peoples in the form of dismembered language, and in spite of the existence of parts of the *Koran* dealing with the exact Islamic laws, and sections giving almost full stories, its overall fragmentariness, its allusive language and its emphasis on the 'language-ality' of language – what I have called in my writings in Persian *zabaniyyat*[1] (Baraheni 1995): the foregrounding of language to a degree that it does not look for a reference outside itself; when referentiality is cancelled altogether or to the utmost degree, and language seems to be sufficient unto itself; and when the *jouissance* of the adventure of language itself, rather than the *jouissance* of meaning or combinations of meanings thrust into language, is brought to the fore – even in those parts dealing with laws and narratives. These characteristics, as well as its total reliance on what has been called by Islamic commentators the miracle of language, make it completely unique, and completely different from both the two earlier texts and all other texts written afterwards as interpretations or even renderings into other languages. In spite of the existence of translations of the *Koran* into almost all languages of the world, it is perhaps, I believe, the least translatable of all literary and religious texts. The original performance of language, the performative capacity of the text, the fragmented nature of the pieces, its total reliance on the sounds and rhythm of the language, and its complete dependence in most cases on rhyme patterns that are totally untranslatable into other languages, its absolute inimitability in both the Arabic of other Arab writers and in other languages, turn the book into a unique phenomenon, and you do not have to be a believer in this book to realize this.

In fact, a good translation of the *Koran* will never exist in other languages. The texts of the translations I have seen in the two major languages of Islam in the Middle East, that is, Persian and Turkish, in spite of the genuine greatness of some of the translators throughout the ages, are in no way comparable with the original text. The translations in English are of the same quality, in spite of the great efforts of the translators. And it is not the fault of the translators in any of these languages. Fragmented works, based on the essence of language, sounds with internal references to each other, and allusions with internal references to allusions both in the memory of culture and language itself, and the participation of the lungs – in fact, the entire chest – in the uttering of the words through the throat, the vocal chords and the mouth, teeth and the lips, in fact the genius of the particular language, which is one language, completely separate from other languages, the absolute and total reliance of the language of the *Koran* on the genius of Arabic as a language, quite different from the genius of other languages, makes translation almost completely impossible. The poetry of the *Koran* and the poetics of its fragmentation make it impossible to imitate. And, as I said, this is not a matter of belief or disbelief.

It is common knowledge in the Islamic world that belief in the *Koran* means belief in the two major works of the Semitic people that preceded the *Koran*. There is a reason for that. The *Koran* itself does not speak of Mohammad's genealogy because the style and method used in the text are so different from the two earlier texts that one can say with assurance that it would have been a literary, rather than a religious, blasphemy to include Mohammad's personal genealogy in his book; its style simply rejects the notion of such an inclusion. But this does not mean that the Arabs did not go for genealogy as did the Jews, the Persians and the Greeks. Rather, the narrative of the *Koran* is different from the narratives of the two previous Semitic texts. The fact is that most of the significant names mentioned in the *Koran* have already been mentioned in the two earlier books; however, the view in the *Koran*, as far as the element of time is concerned, is not chronological. A kind of anachronism, a kind of accidentality, a sort of suddenness, overwhelms the work, and in spite of the hundreds of texts that came after it, some of them fashioning themselves in the style of the *Koran*, particularly among the mystics, the uniqueness of the text is something that can never be matched.

The object of this study is not to claim belief or disbelief in the contents of the three texts. We are dealing with an element that is so positive, and positively so relevant to all three texts, that if we do not deal with it, the text will be left to itself like a closed fist, and the energies of the work will not be released. The positive knowledge of a text is knowledge of the language of that text, the way the text was put together, or the way one sees how its language was put together. The undeniable, irrefutable part of any text is the material, or rather the matter, of which the text is made, and any discussion of this phenomenon means a discussion of the language-ality of the text.

There are two words, perhaps of the same origin, which will clarify the style of the *Koran*: the word *qassah*, and the word *quessah*. Both of them are verbs. The two of them put together would mean 'kill and narrate' or 'dismember and narrate'. Both the *Old Testament* and the *New Testament* are testaments of killing and narrating. Cain kills his brother Abel, and then the incident is narrated; the first story of the *Old Testament* that takes place outside the Garden of Eden is the story of a murder. The narration in the second book is the story of the killing of a Jew by his fellow Jews, with some assistance from the Romans. Two stories of murder are being narrated: someone kills and someone tells the story, perhaps with the killing taking place first and the narrating coming right afterwards, because both of them have the same connotation. 'A crossing of boundaries' has taken place here; murder has turned into a word.

In both Arabic words, you have the connotation of dismemberment. The *Koran*, stylistically speaking, takes the two previous books, and by cutting them to pieces, by means of fragmentation, deletions and additions to the fragments from history, culture, faith, laws and other sources, enters a revolutionary process in language unprecedented until then, and hardly achieved until we enter the battleground of the difference/différance in the controversy between modern and postmodern. Since the world of the Semitic nations has been documented once by the means of presentation, and then by representation, the *Koran*ic text indulges in an anti-representational endeavour by problematizing first the temporal structure of the events of the two previous books, and then by exploiting those elements which are totally fragmentary, which is the closest in spirit to the concept of revelation. This does not mean that the holy book of Muslims lacks linear approach altogether. It means that it is more oracular than narrative; it is more poetic than prosaic;

it is more sonorous than flat; it is more fragmentary than seamless. It is more recitative than bland.

The beginning letters of some of the chapters of the holy book of Muslims are generally sounds or letters, such as A.L.M., T.S.M., A.L.R. or A.L.M.R., generally uttered in the reading of the *Koran* with their original Arabic pronunciation. They appear to be meaningless, but they are extremely important from the standpoint of language-ality. They are broken and fragmented sounds and letters, to which all kinds of interpretations have been attributed, including some very interesting ones by Mansour Al-Hallaj, the dismembered saint of Islamic mysticism of about 11 centuries ago. In my mind, they were perhaps sounds to invite the outburst of the language, and like any linguistic outburst, they were opening the way for language to follow. Then the language flowed, not in the form of a narrative from the beginning to the end, or an exegesis, beginning a discourse and opening it up to further discussions in the continuity of a feeling of time for the duration of the discourse, but more or less in the form of a frequently disrupted narrative, or in the form of independent lines, as if each verse appeared in its final form as a revelation. There certainly were exceptions in the form of narrative lines continued for a longer period of time, such as the chapter entitled 'Qasas', or narrative. The stories of the two earlier books appear as if in the dream of the third book, as if a continent of lost memories had been pushing its way into the mind of someone else or coming generations but, not succeeding in making itself fully available, and always being pushed back by the exigency of the immediacy of what was to be said to the followers, it became piecemeal and fragmented, and consequently it was language or, rather, the language-ality of language, that was foregrounded.

If we move from the language of religion to the language of literature, we might say that what happened in this scripture in connection with the two earlier scriptures is what has happened to Pound's *Cantos* in comparison with the poetry of Homer, Dante and the Chinese, or to the second part of Joyce's *Ulysses* or to *Finnegans Wake* in connection with continental and British literatures. What happens in the mind of the exilic writer is more or less of the same nature. He remembers always in the process of forgetting, and rebuilds memory, weaving and interweaving the past and present into a new texture. And this is always happening in the world of literature, because all writers in the world now, whether at home or abroad, are in exile. With the experience of the last 300 years, with the advent of the processes of presentation, representation and anti-representation, or rather, the process of realism, modernism and postmodernism, we can say that perhaps we have been dealing with a historical déjà vu. What happened to the three ancient religions and their holy books in the ancient world has been happening to many aspects of world literature during the last three centuries. In diasporic thinking, the congruous and the incongruous live unhappily together, and several hands are driven into the same glove, the contemporary glove. The reading of the *Koran* as an exilic text in relation to the two earlier texts – a concentrated reading of it as a text ever reviving, repeating, forgetting and putting together in fragments memories of other tribes and other stories and texts – places the book within the framework of the notion of exile, as the third zone of literature.

The concept of 'Exile, The Third Zone of Literature' (Baraheni, *The Silver Throat of the Moon*, 2005: 264–75), first came to my mind when I read Homi Bhabha's concept of the 'Third Space' in 'Commitment to Theory' in his extraordinary book, *The Location of Culture* (1994). I find it rather strange that those who have been influenced by Martin Heidegger's philosophy, and not his politics – Jacques Derrida, Edward Said, and Homi Bhabha – all deal, from different angles, with the word 'boundary' and the crossing of it. To quote Heidegger: 'A boundary is not that at which something stops but, as the Greeks recognized, the boundary is that from which *something begins its presencing*' (Heidegger 1994: 1). My 'third zone of literature' dealt first with the concept of 'double alienation' of Third World writers, which I first formulated in *Masculine History* (Persian version 1969–70), *Journey to Egypt* (Persian version 1971), and *The Crowned Cannibals* (1977: 92–4). Later, I expanded it further to embrace the concept of exile in 'Exile: the Third Zone of Literature'. The reason I believe Homi Bhabha's formulation of the Third Space is apt here is that he comes to this space through language, which although formulated for a different kind of discourse, could be suitably adapted to the position of the *Koran* in the way it deals with language. A few significant lines will suffice:

> The reason a cultural text or system of meaning cannot be sufficient unto itself is that the act of annunciation – the *place of utterance* – is crossed by the *difference* of writing…. It is this difference in the process of language that is crucial to the production of meaning and ensures, at the same time, that meaning is never simply mimetic and transparent…. The linguistic difference that informs any cultural performance is dramatized in the common semiotic account of the disjuncture between the subject of a proposition (énoncé) and the subject of enunciation…. The production of meaning requires that these two places be mobilized in the passage through a Third Space, which presents both the general conditions of language and the specific implication of the utterance in a performative and institutional strategy of which it cannot 'in itself' be conscious.
>
> (Bhabha 1994: 36)

Following this extremely interesting and sophisticated description of the 'intervention of enunciation', Bhabha speaks of the destruction of the 'mirror of representation' (1994: 37), which in my mind happens in the language of the *Koran*, which rises against all unifying elements of the past, offering fragmentation as a language which will be disruptive in its main thrust, not only of meaning, but even all attempts based on the paraphrasing of meaning. Herein lies, I believe, *zabaniyyat*, the 'language-ality' of language, when language shows its essence, when the poet enters the depths, the entrails, of language, and may not know what he is saying when he comes back, and what he says may have little to do with the obvious structuring of language for the purpose of meaning, communication, or even expression of feelings, when language leaves all elements of representationalism behind, and is born, alone and single, by itself. Then, he will give us the essence of language from its depths.

I believe that, apart from what each verse of the *Koran* says, we are dealing on numerous occasions with language in its role of 'performativity', and like a performativity of the highest order, it does not seem to be conscious of itself, when it is engaged, almost entangled, with driving itself 'beyond boundaries'.

Note

1 The coinage of *zabaniyyat* is mine, a deliberately illegitimate coinage, because the first part, *zaban*, is Persian and *yat* is an Arabic suffix, and generally you are not supposed to combine the two, but here an innovation is shockingly foregrounded to draw attention to the fact that this is different even as an innovation. I have used it generally for a particular type of Persian poetry, but here I am applying the concept to parts of the *Koran*.

References

The Authorized Version of The Holy Bible. Philadelphia: The National Bible Press, 1958.
Baraheni, R. (1977) *The Crowned Cannibals*, New York: Vintage.
—— (1995) *Khatab beh Parvaneh-ha* (Accosting the Butterflies), Tehran: Markaz Publishing House. With a supplement on the theory of *Zabaniyyat* (Lanaguage-ality), pp. 123–98.
—— (2005) In L. Langer (ed.) *The Silver Throat of the Moon: Writing in Exile*, Nottingham, UK: Five Leaves Publications.
Bhabha, Homi, K. (1994) *The Location of Culture*, New York, London: Routledge.
Brooke-Rose, C. (1998) In S. R. Suleiman (ed.) *Exile and Creativity*, Durham & London: Duke University Press.
Dehkhoda Encyclopedic Dictionary, Tehran, Iran: Publications of Moassesseh-ye Loghatnameh-ye Dehkhoda (1994) Vol. III, p. 4235.
Derrida, J. (1998) In J. Derrida and G. Vattimo (eds) *Religion*, Stanford, California: Stanford University Press.
Heidegger, M. (1994) In Bhabha, H., *The Location of Culture*, New York, London: Routledge.
The Qur'an. Bilingual Edition in Arabic and English, translated into English by M. H. Shakir and N. Y. Elmhurst: Tahrike Tarsile Qur'an, Inc., Publishers and Distributors of *Holy Qur'an*.
Said, E. (2002) *Reflections on Exile and Other Essays*, Cambridge, Massachusetts: Harvard University Press.

4 Diaspora, ethnicity and problems of identity

Mark J. Goodman

How are we to understand the concept of diaspora, its relation to ethnicity, and its value for understanding problems of identity? One approach, suggested in Stuart Hall's (1992: 257–8) idea of 'new ethnicities', emphasizes the ways in which diasporic populations can forge a hybrid, emergent or mixed identity. Following a line of reinscribing patterns of inequality based on class and race within a cultural framework, Hall's approach seeks to escape what is seen as an essentialized (and biologically rooted) concept of ethnicity, positing instead the importance of discourse and a variable narrative frame. The move is described as transgressive and potentially libratory, a challenge to ethnic absolutism and, in its progressive appropriation of what W. E. B. DuBois identified for African-Americans as a troubled and troubling 'double consciousness' – facing outward and inward at the same time (Reed 1997) – a way to break free of the polarities imposed by coercive binaries. The aim, conceptually, is to reject absolute racial markers. But we should recognize immediately that what Hall proposes is primarily a movement in thought, a discursive step. Typically, the construction of identities involves both the passive experience of 'being made' by external forces and the active process by which a group 'makes itself'. This involves not only material circumstances but also the intervention of claims imposed by other persons or groups, and typically entails a complex interaction involving cultural assertion and challenge, the reproduction or transformation of cherished ideas of self, and even the repudiation of identities over time (Cornell and Hartmann 1998: 80; quoted in Kibria 1998: 941). Often, the migratory experience initiates this cycle. Groups in diaspora are confronted with new realities and new opportunities – and new challenges. But whether a displaced or dislocated group can seize the possibility of remaking itself is, in the first instance, a question that begs for an appreciation of the materiality of power. As Anthias (2001a: 624; 2001b) suggests in her discussion of hybridity, identities under challenge are not simply merged, but merged under the sway of specific social relations – arrangements for imposing or eliciting difference that are characteristically asymmetric. The exercise of power is fundamental to the equation.

We should also note that, in company with many writings on the diasporic condition and hybridity, Hall's remarks are placed within a privileged imaginative setting. This is what the author understands as 'the new forms of cultural practice' emergent in films like John Akomfrah's 1986 *Handsworth Songs*, a reworking of archival materials and newsreel footage of the 1985 Handsworth and London street disturbances in the UK. Thus, the 'black cultural production' and 'new conception of ethnicity' that Hall recognizes is a single, precarious instance situated in the relatively free space of the artist. Hall explicitly links this idea to Jacques Derrida's notion of *différance*, so his notion of cultural production occupies a space that stretches to include the 'positional, conditional and conjunctural'. It is based, as we see, on a doubly fragmented instance – fragmented in time, and located, for that moment, in a particular place. A similar approach informs Paul Gilroy's (1987) discussion of reggae, soul and other black music in the UK. Labelling this music diasporic and insurgent, Gilroy takes disruptive song texts as markers of an 'anti-capitalist critique' (1987: 199) in which 'work is sharply counterposed, not merely to leisure in general, but to a glorification of autonomous desire' and the 'black body is reclaimed from the world of work and celebrated as an "instrument of pleasure rather than labour"' (1987: 202). Again, we should recognize that what is being described is an interpretive process. Commenting, reinscribing, remaking and transcending, the artist is supposed to take hold of his or her raw materials; yet the process is also charged with its own determinations. To understand the results, one must call into view the practical situation of the artist, filmmaker or musician and his or her intentions. Indeed, if this construction of hybridity, transgressive as it may be, is indebted to and selectively draws upon the experience of colonial and ex-colonial subjects, the selectivity can be pointed in many different directions. If Gilroy, for example, understands the pleasure-seeking he marks in contemporary black lyrics as an instance of the casting-off of Herbert Marcuse's 'surplus repression', could he not just as easily describe it – still staying with Marcuse – as a species of harmless escapism, a performative gesture that keeps order intact? Could not his 'transgressive' example also pay tribute to the repressive tolerance of the liberal state, transforming Public Enemy's insurgent idea in 'Fear of a Black Planet' into a sly, marketable and sustainable commercial property, reinforcing domination rather than escaping from it?

Thus, the 'new ethnicities', in Hall's and Gilroy's arguments, are decisively decoupled from ethnicity as it operates in dominant discourse. In that usual setting, by contrast, ethnicity in the United Kingdom was and could not be free, but was linked to the 'embattled, hegemonic conception of "Englishness"', which, under Margaret Thatcher, so powerfully stabilized a racialized politics, merging it with 'nationalism, imperialism, racism and the state' (Hall 1996). Thus, we must note, there is a difference in the 'difference' that marks racial divisions in a hegemonic state and the 'difference' liable to be entertained, sometimes even playfully, by a filmmaker, musician or poet like the classic Charles Baudelaire, stylized by Walter Benjamin as an exemplar of the rootless *flâneur* and dandy (cf. Shields 1994; Pels 1999: 65). Certainly, there is a difference between the self-exile freely chosen, suffered, and perhaps even enjoyed as an intellectual stance, and the exile confronting those who are permanently ensnared. For the enslaved, the deported, the economically wretched and rejected and those made politically *non grata* without the possibility of return, 'exile' is not a metaphorical but an actual circumstance, not a temporary possibility but a permanent condition. Conceptually, we make a mistake by bringing both conditions under a single term. Thus, according to Hall, in the hands of the insurgent ethnic artist, the gap separating the 'other' does not yield to the 'radical and unbridgeable separation' normally encountered and policed in the street, but provides the basis for an active process of 'unsettling, recombination, hybridization and "cut-and-mix"', a process he calls 'cultural diaspora-ization'. It is precisely this gap, unbridgeable and menacing, that constitutes the being of those who are permanently exiled. And even for those for whom the decision to move is to some extent voluntary, the ways in which values of the homeland are mixed with those of the new country is never a simple choice, but a choice made under constraint and with real practical effects.

To his credit, Hall tries to avoid turning hybridity into a 'notion where everything is wonderful, a place without struggle or pain'. Said (1990: 362–3) and Clifford (1992: 107) also emphasize the sharp differences between the circumstances and considerable freedoms of the self-exiled residing in the West and the realities experienced by the great mass of immigrants or refugees. At the same time, they emphasize the predicament of the self-exiled, the 'contrapuntal' opposition between self-affirmation and feelings of loss, of being 'out of place'. Other writers are not so modest or so concerned about balance. In Braidotti's account (1994: 255–6; also, 1996: 20, cited in Pels 1999: 81n. 18), for example, the space separating the commentator and her object is entirely collapsed, and 'modernity' – linked to a sedentary, masculinist discourse (the 'phallogocentrist' regime) and stable identities, dualities and hierarchies – is contrasted to its disadvantage with a 'female' world and female, nomadic bodily experience. In this nomadic world, the inhabitants are freed by an 'intense desire to go on trespassing [and] transgressing', although the transgressions, so far, seem limited to the development of expertise in the 'treacherous contingencies of language', a determined cheerfulness (these are happy nomads!), and an ability to mix various speaking voices and writing styles.

Although extreme in its expression, Braidotti's self-appreciation illustrates a more general problem in diaspora literature, which as Clifford (1994: 302) remarks, easily slips between 'invocations of diaspora theories, diasporic discourses, and distinct historical experiences', often assuming, as well, the presence of a pluralist and non-oppressive state, and the operation of the 'ideologies (and even the accomplishments) of assimilation'. There are several problems here. Most glaring, perhaps, is the tacit invocation of what Alcoff and Potter (1993: 14) call the 'metonymic fallacy' (assuming that what strikes the observer as valuable or disruptive or liberating is also so valued by those observed). One slips between a meaning contingently imputed to an action by an observer and the activity as understood by the actor herself. Thus, on such an account, migration which is coerced can be reinvented as a libratory 'nomadic' experience, or the literary and musical expressions Gilroy describes can be claimed as 'completing' the project of the African diaspora to 'recover and validate black culture and reincarnate the sense of being and belonging which had been erased from it by slavery' (Gilroy 1987: 219; cf. Gilroy 1993). But we need to ask how did it come to pass that the African diaspora was given such a task? This is teleological thinking.

There is also the logical error of imposing the advertised self-understanding of contemporary hegemonic powers on circumstances and motives in another place and time. One cannot assume a pluralist openness to cultural variation if the object of the analysis is to determine the fluidity of a community, the extent to which it accepts (much less values and cherishes) cultural difference – or whether, instead, it insists on imposing definitions of the culturally required which make the expression of transgressive attitudes a dangerous step. 'Difference' is not always celebrated. It is sometimes made the object of an inquisitor's concern, the basis for suspicion and a police file, or justification for a broad, censorious and harrying intervention in everyday life. We need to pair the concept of a free-ranging and apparently unbounded hybridity and cultural creativity with its polar twin – the disciplining of ethnicities, their policing and narrowing, the substitution of the actively challenging by the opposition that succumbs. But this requires that diaspora is not unhistorically posited but situated instead within a definite historical framework, understood dialectically as an interaction with the dominant – and that the outcome of this interaction is made the subject of empirical study and not imposed as a given. Equally important, at the other extreme, we need to keep open the possibility that attempts to impose a suffocating cultural hegemony can fail – that, despite all efforts at ruling with the iron fist wrapped in a velvet glove, insurgency, recalcitrance and sabotage can break out. Even if we do not impose on this resistance, or stubbornness, the grand name 'project', we can still see it at work, or at least see its gritty possibility as a potential hindrance to the utopian ambitions of rule.

We have argued that the notion of hybridity and self-exile may conceal a romantic self-absorption and the hidden privilege of the few. We have also proposed that there is a certain self-protective and even narcissistic tendency which may falsely link the alienated feelings of the self-exiled to those for whom exile is a hardship imposed from the outside. I believe there is an analytic advantage in keeping the two concepts distinct. I am not arguing for a position of absolute singularity, in which each case must be discussed separately. But we err in stretching ideas until they are emptied of content. For example, 'dislocation' and 'displacement' are terms that can be stretched too far, and for which a metaphorical, privileged usage can slowly bleed away the real violence and pain of the dispersed. In each case, one needs to look at the power relations involved. At one extreme, for example, slavery, like settler colonialism, generally, marks a condition of maximum inequality, disprivilege and asymmetry. It is also a condition that is intended to be permanent and self-renewing. Indeed, enslaved or violently displaced populations confronted by their oppressors find precious little space to remake themselves. They are subject, instead, to great legal and extra-legal stress, not invited to an enriching but to a repressive integration. The truly dispossessed may even be denied their own place of burial. Their graveyards go unmarked; their trees are uprooted; their villages wither.[1] This experience may have a profound effect on the way in which analysts and political actors approach such situations. A certain deep heartlessness becomes the norm.

At the other extreme, certain trajectories of dislocation and displacement can be celebrated as instrumental in establishing the claim to a remarkable privilege.

At the cost of great pressure to themselves and to their children, diasporic populations that achieve material success in the new country can be identified as championing values which make them a 'model minority', embodying through hard work and dedication to education a cultural energy which is taken as a strategic asset in moving ahead. Thus, as Ong (1996, 1997) argues in her analysis of Asian migration to the United States, hierarchical schemes of racial and cultural difference intersect in a complex, contingent way to locate minorities of colour from different class backgrounds. But, breaking away from this complexity, an essentializing discourse can be imposed which 'moves beyond a simple reiteration of "Chinese/Confucian" values to a *homogenizing* description of Asian culture, *legitimating* state policies of capital accumulation, labour, and social control' in the migrants' places of origin, and *orientalizing* Asian traditions as timeless and permanently embodied in a dedication to strong (and patriarchal) families, loyalty to elders, discipline, frugality, and a demanding work ethic (Ong 1997: 353; italics added). This leads to the discursive 'whitening' of migrants whose dedication to Confucian values yields the expected success, and to the ideological 'blackening' of those who fail to demonstrate the demanded cultural competence. In this way, the claim that the USA provides a nondiscriminatory environment can be preserved intact, while differences in achievement are pinned to a group's ability to realize an inherited cultural capital. Thus, in both masking the pain of the forcibly dispossessed and celebrating a singular achievement based on cultural advantages nominally inherited from abroad, the forces that structure the unequal insertion of various 'ethnics' in the racial hierarchy of the USA go undisclosed (Pierre 2004: 143). The focus on cultural narratives and neglect of the practical politics of racial power helps avoid an inquiry into the realities of economic structure in the host country.

But perhaps the greatest difficulty with the concepts of diaspora, hybridity and their many cognates can be located in the singular and monochromatic manner that this approach is intended to replace. I refer, of course, to the assimilation perspective, which underlies so much of social-science thinking about race and culture and is always threatening to make a comeback, notwithstanding the rapid and sometimes bewildering dispersion of diaspora ideas (Brubaker 2001, 2005). Here again, one encounters a deep confusion between accounts that describe assimilative processes of entry and adaptation by migrant populations, invocations of the moral goodness of such a path, and theories explaining why such processes may succeed or fail. In the older literature, for example, the American concern to describe was always connected to an unproblematic, normative Anglo-conformism: the travel towards a 'Protestant "core culture"' (Brubaker 2001: 540). Generations of immigrants were instructed on the need to stop talking with their hands, and to cut down on the consumption of garlic and onions – it did not look good – and these lessons were often laid down with the greatest vigour by one's own kind, in the same way that a cautionary 'minority culture of mobility' can be urged upon aspiring, middle-class African-Americans in negotiating 'interracial encounters in public settings' and problematic 'inter-class relations within the black community'

(Neckerman *et al.* 1999: 947–8). This is assimilation with a vengeance, and it has everything to do with appearances – talking and walking in the accepted fashion – and virtually nothing to do with asserting one's rights.

There is a second meaning to assimilation, however, which attends to the securing of social and economic justice, particularly in respect to equality of opportunity and equality of outcomes in education and jobs. Assimilation of this sort has been under deep threat in the USA since the Supreme Court's controversial split decision in the Bakke case (1978), striking down the admissions programme at the University of California (Davis) Medical School, while upholding, with qualifications, the principle of affirmative action, a legal precedent which has led in recent years to a series of defeats under California Proposition 209, the Washington Initiative 200, the One Florida Initiative and, more recently, the Supreme Court's refusal to overturn *Texas v. Hopwood*, forcing the University of Texas to eliminate Affirmative Action in admissions to its School of Law (Ball 2000). Likewise, in France, Brubaker reminds us (2000: 536), the right to guard against cultural imposition was not urged by diasporic populations intent on preserving a distinct identity but by the old French, the 'real French' clustered around Le Pen. So, rights and cultural absorption are two categories that should not be carelessly intermixed. There is always the issue of power, of whose rights are to be asserted and at what cost. This is why hybridity is at risk if it is understood only as a cultural condition, freely suspended, for example, in an artistic process of choosing and without sufficient attention to the privileged condition of the artist. Attention must also be given to the tense political relationship between the assertion of cultural habits and civil entitlements in the law and before the law. There is a vast difference between a diasporic population that is 'allowed space', but always grudgingly and contingently, at the margins of a dominant regime (but always the subject of suspicion, always liable to dispersal) and one that takes this space as a matter of constitutional right. If economic rights do not guarantee cultural respect in societies in which power is anchored in the possession of property, the absence of such rights certainly makes the assertion of difference a vulnerable undertaking. A more realistic understanding of hybridity forces one to see it as an outcome negotiated between transgressive communities and dominant powers, and therefore an outcome of a political process.

These considerations put into special light the various proposals that have been offered to make sense of the burgeoning literature on diaspora. Several typologies have been offered. Cohen (1997), for example, following Safran's (1991) pioneering efforts, distinguishes between 'victim' and trade, or labour, diaspora. The proposed basis for this division is the element of volition. Although movements across national boundaries are never completely without compulsion, trade or labour diaspora are suggested to include a significant voluntary element. By contrast, the case of the 'victims' is one of pure stick. In the classic instances, these diasporic victims are driven out; their homes are violently stolen from them, and the population, itself – as in the case of chattel slavery or other forms of colonial violence, such as the indentures system – is stolen violently from its home. The new place of toil and settlement is also no home.

This description has been applied to several groups. But the traumatic dispersal of victims is not limited, as Cohen suggests, to being 'taken in shackles' from a single place of origin, or even to a dispersal accomplished merely once. Indeed, the signal characteristic of enslaved diaspora shared with other communities targeted as victims (Margold 1999 points to populations extruded from the rural Philippines) is the peculiar and determining state of being constantly marked at risk for yet another dispersal, displacement, scourging or evacuation, another invasion, another set of rules tightening controls. What emerges is a culture of 'fear and terror', variously overt or quietly, menacingly intrusive, which is normalized as a habit in disciplining a people – often strenuously resisted but deposited, nevertheless, as a layer of identity. In short, diaspora that implicates a continuing struggle, a continuing surveillance – no collective sigh, no point of rest. This, then, is migratory movement at the pole of violent coercion, which Cohen intends to contrast with diaspora impelled by economic motives. But we would do better to see both forms as mixtures of motives and compulsions, a simultaneous pulling and pushing which only at the limit becomes one of pure coercion. Slavery, indentures, and colonial occupation take us to the limiting case.

Here, the accumulative psychological effects are given classic expression in Fanon's *Black Skin, White Masks* (*Peau noire, masques blancs*, trans. 1967: 109). In a difficult and controversial philosophical move (cf. Gordon 1995: 135), Fanon drives past the existential limit, surpassing the Hegelian dialectic of recognition, as refocused by Jean Hyppolite and Alexandre Kojève on the relation between master and slave. Writing of his place as a displaced African, Fanon (1967: 109) declares:

> I came into the world imbued with the will to find a meaning in things, my spirit filled with the desire to attain to the source of the world, and then I found that I was an object in the midst of other objects. Sealed into that crushing objecthood, I turned beseechingly to others. Their attention was a liberation, running over my body suddenly abraded into nonbeing, endowing me once more with an agility that I had thought lost, and by taking me out of the world, restoring me to it. But just as I reached the other side, I stumbled, and the movements, the attitudes, the glances of the other fixed me there, in the sense in which a chemical solution is fixed by a dye. I was indignant; I demanded an explanation. Nothing happened. I burst apart. Now the fragments have been put together by another self.

This famous passage is written in the first person, a ghostly and iconic 'I'. As David Macey (2000: 162) notes in his biography of Fanon, there is no indication here that the author had experienced a relatively privileged, middle-class childhood in Martinique, no reference to the island's politics or political economy, no reflection on the profound alienation of the Old Colony, which had been 'departmentalized' (and stranded) at the height of the Cold War and Korean intervention and of France's hot war in Indochina. Indeed, Fanon's words and referents are elevated to a metaphorical level – he is writing, presumably, of black men and women everywhere, and the fierce tone draws energy from his reworking of a

1952 piece for the French Catholic journal, *Esprit*. There, as a Martinican psychiatrist living and practising in Lyons, Fanon describes the anguish and humiliation of the North African proletariat living in France – to which the editor appends the note that 'if the scandalous way North Africans are treated in France does not provoke a scream of anger, why were we given the ability to scream?' (*Esprit*, February 1952: 219; Macey 2000: 157).

Macey comments that *Peau noire*'s reception was muted, in part because of the confounding variation in the book's narrative register; and indeed, there are also instances of psychoanalytic doctrine deployed in the book that are disturbingly rigid. But there is also much that goes directly to the centre of emotional experience. In 'The Fact of Blackness', for example, novelist Richard Wright is also prominent, and the desperate voice of Bigger Thomas from *Native Son* (1940) – the young black man from Chicago, the child of dispossessed Southern migrants who murders twice out of fear and then is hunted down like a dog – is also to be heard, and very powerfully. As Fanon explained to his editor, 'I am trying to touch my reader affectively or in other words irrationally, almost sensually'. If Fanon wanted to 'sink beneath the stupefying lava of words that have the colour of quivering flesh' (Francis Jeanson, Preface to *Peau noire*: 12; Macey 2000: 159), this device was deployed precisely to break through the neatness and philosophical comfort of formulations that admit oppression but see in the acquiescence of the dominated a stabilizing support. It is this wish to find support in conditions which are, in fact, insupportable, that can lead to an unwitting acceptance of the oppressive circumstance.

On this same point, we can also consider the case of slavery in the American South. In truth, the African-American's condition of being locked up and locked out did not cause terrible concern, even through the 1920s, an era dominated by the Phillips school of historians. Ulrich Phillips was a thoroughgoing racist, pinning much of the blame for antebellum Southern troubles on the laziness of blacks. Writing during World War I from the Army YMCA (Camp Gordon, Georgia) he could still see black soldiers exhibiting, he thought, the same 'easy-going, amiable, serio-comic obedience and the same personal attachments to white men, as well as the same sturdy light-heartedness and the same love of laughter and of rhythm, which distinguished their forbears' on the plantation (Phillips 1918: Preface). But consider, as well, John Spencer Bassett's *The Southern Overseer* (1968 [1925]). As Michael Tadman (1989: 216) reminds us, Bassett's cold appreciation of the African-American family and its fate 'reads like the writings of an antebellum planter restored to the sinister comfort of the Old South'. Indeed, Bassett doubts that tearing slave families apart mattered very much to blacks, for they 'did not esteem marriage as the white people esteemed it'. He explains that 'slavery was a hard school but in it the Africans learned some good lessons'. The overseer, uneducated, confronted a 'child race of black men'. Whipping was needed (Bassett 1925: 5, 18, 22, 16). One does not think in such instances of a diasporic population challenging fixed boundaries, or recasting the host society, but only of ways in which insurgency is suppressed. However, like other terrible wounds, the accumulative violence of enslavement and its racialized inflection cannot simply be taken as fact. Circumstances like these must burn through one's consciousness, and if they are not adequately criticized and resisted, they continue to act. Then they become, as Wright (1935) puts it in his evocation of a ghastly lynching, an 'icy wall' encircling our hearts, indeed a terrible 'night wind' of fear and denial, 'mutter[ing] in the grass and fumbl[ing] the leaves of the trees'. Can one also suggest that such a desperately wished unwillingness to face the historical facts profoundly affects received habits of thought and, perhaps, even prepares for thoughts – and much more than thoughts – that make oppression normal? In such a circumstance, terrible humiliations and tortures can be reinvented, and the appearance of cultural variation and plasticity can be rethought, more conservatively, to mark and even celebrate the loss of challenge, a compulsory harmonization. In a political climate manipulatively saturated with fears of terror and 'terrorism', safety and security become the focus. Indeed, in the post-9/11 period, diasporic hybridity becomes a problem for host countries in North America and Europe. The potential cultural contributions of new peoples are appreciated only with nervousness and anxiety, and there is a selective encouragement to researchers to rethink their work as a means of enabling stability rather than change. If we follow the language used by Thomas S. Kuhn in *The Structure of Scientific Revolutions* (1996 [1962]), we can see here the operation of 'normal science'. Discrepant activities and movements become problems or puzzles that have to be solved within the existing paradigm. The focus shifts to the ways in which insurgent, troublesome, or merely odd or 'different' groups can be contained. But this is not just an instance of resistance to paradigm shift emerging from within a community of scholars. As scholars, we live in a political environment, and the politics of the moment, charged with a continuing hysteria, all point in the direction of huddling together, protecting, excluding and walling off.

In *The Contract of Mutual Indifference*, Normal Geras posits the resonant failure to contest forgetfulness as the violation of a simple moral imperative (an imperative, at least, which is simple to pronounce): '… human beings *need not* remain peaceful, silent, in the presence of atrocity' (1998: 10, italics added). Geras sees this attitude as a symptom of moral failure in the post-Holocaust world. But it also seems to me that indifference, elision or softening of this sort can also lead further to a kind of debilitating amnesia, with real epistemological consequences. True, the anger and pity are lost, but also a certain sharp edge to knowledge.[2] Thus, I want to suggest that the pathways of racial domination in the United States, for example – the real movement of slave trade and plantation slavery, inscribed in blood – have also been shadowed by a regressive movement in understanding, and that this regression is often smoothed by a commitment to a triumphant national story. The premise behind the argument is that losing the compelling urgency of human suffering is not simply a lapse, a forgetting, a vacant aporia, but in fact requires discursive effort. One must try to forget. Of course, the demands of empirical research impose their own limits, and researchers have differed earnestly and sharply on the quality of life experienced by the enslaved. But the patriotic *national project* of 'building a nation' and of incorporating the black population has always been uppermost in framing the central problems. The big thought was to find a place for peoples of African origin in which they could make a sustained contribution to the US economy – through the middle half of the nineteenth century the engine of growth was, in fact, the booming cotton industry in the South – but, at the same time, to find ways to keep black people in their place.

For Americans, then, the black experience became, irresistibly, a story within the national story, intended to recapitulate the stories of other migrant groups. This case can illustrate a more general process in the disciplining of ethnicities. In the first instance, the suppression of hybridity is accomplished on the grounds of a group's encounter with the dominant culture – this is the stuff of the 'distinct historical experiences' to which Clifford refers. But there is also a second disciplining as insurgent cultural groups are read out of history, now understood as a historiographic or theoretical tradition. This last is a discursive move. Yet, ironically, with the celebrated turn to ethnicity and culture, reclaiming the lost history of domination and struggle sometimes becomes more difficult to achieve. If the practical realities of racialization are ignored or suppressed, 'difference' is disembodied and separated from political and economic structure. Then, the historical accumulation of advantage and disadvantage fades, and is replaced by an innocent, gentler celebration of ethnic particularity. Under this lens, hybridity may mark nothing more than a decorative attribute, and no longer that dynamic tension that Du Bois understood for peoples lodged in conflict between two antagonistic worlds.

Indeed, when we turn to the large corpus of writings on slavery in the American South, we find a continuing attempt to avoid or soften the moral impasse imposed by the violent harms done by slavery – for example, in Phillips's (1918) efforts to picture America's big tobacco, cotton and sugar farms as schools for a Christian civilizing mission, or Stanley Elkins's (1959) understanding of the regime as an energetic enterprise that nevertheless stripped away African culture, terminating diasporic connections and substituting the notorious 'Sambo' personality. Given its ambitious psychological claims, Elkins's account is of particular importance. Writing in the shadow of the Holocaust and assuming greater accessibility to this first-hand information than to the disparate and scattered records in Africa and the Americas, Elkins (1959, esp. 129, 129–30n. 101) lays out a provocative analogy between the circumstance of American slaves and prisoners in the camps – a psychic profile of coffle line and dreaded Atlantic passage, seasoning in American ports and sale on the auction block in Charlestown or New Orleans, as compared with the sequence of shocks administered by the Nazis: humiliating capture, lightening-quick; miserable transportation in closed trains; the reaction of Jewish prisoners, especially middle-class men, to their loss of status as heads of families; the identification with Nazi symbols; reactions to collective punishment; and the eventual mass regression by prisoners to an infantile attitude.

Every comparison entails risks, but the problems in this one are enhanced by the very selective dependence on a single account by Bruno Bettelheim (1943), developed from an orthodox Freudian viewpoint. For Bettelheim, being treated as a child led inmates to a catastrophic dumping of the superego, as the old moral sense was violently emptied 'like a bucket', and in a radically changed setting, acquired new contents (compare Elkins 1959: 118). Soiling oneself, nakedness and beatings were the kinds of degrading insults which might very well be understood by the population of aspiring, Middle European Jews who had witnessed the involvement of figures like Mahler and Freud at the margins and even the centre of German-speaking culture; thrown from the comfort of imagining acceptance in gentile society, it led the inmates, in despair – or so Bettelheim claims – to turn against their relatives and fellow-prisoners, at the same time identifying with Gestapo symbols and swagger – the frightening, notorious and repulsive toughness of the SS (Bettelheim 1943: 436–8, 441, 449). It is another striking instance of metonymy, as the author – opaque about his standing as a member of the old Jewish–German bourgeoisie – constructs a vision of infantile regression as a mass-conversion experience in which the camp guards stand in for Freud's biological father, the demanding, rough, but always high-minded disciplinarian featured in the Oedipal configuration (Freud 1961 [1925]). But unlike Freud, Bettelheim insists that circumstances exist where the deep connection between child and parent can be utterly overthrown, thrusting the camp inmate – and, later, for Elkins, the American slave – into a condition of hopeless dependence on those who whip him until he bleeds, humiliate and torment him, and threaten, at every moment, to end his life.

Indeed, it is a nightmare vision equally violent and extreme as that urged by Fanon to describe the colonial subject driven to an absolute and murderous rejection of the occupying power – a species of cold hell – but it foregrounds a figure (unlike Fanon's) who does not fight back but only obeys, and, as such, serves powerfully to consolidate a paradigm of stability. No scope remains for the victim's resistance, even for that feigned and edgy obedience that, even under sexual torture (compare Agger 1989; Kaplan 2002: 187–8), admits the power of the oppressor while refusing to make one complicit with the oppressor's violence through shame and guilt. In Kaplan's discussion of torture in Chile and Argentina in the 1960s and 1970s, for example, the possibility remains open for resistive identifications – a potent connection of the victim with a sense of urgent political mission or moral obligation, or with a community of loved ones who are still psychologically present – connections which limit the psychological harm imposed, even under conditions of utmost physical brutality.

Taken to its conclusion, Elkins's portrayal of American slavery shows how understanding is distorted when contradictions are viewed in a one-sided way. His notion of cultural hegemony does more than dominate: it excludes alternatives. This, of course, is the hallmark of the assimilation perspective at the extreme, which notions of diaspora were meant to contest. And, indeed, it is urged upon us by the author for what he explains as an extreme case, illustrating the dynamic of 'unopposed capitalism' in the US. But this example also reveals what hybridity generally becomes when it lacks a basis in the hard currency of political power. In this chapter, I have urged that the cultural concerns properly foregrounded by the literature on diaspora and ethnicity be matched with close attention to the foundations of cultural strength. Some of these foundational elements have been

def, of culture & its place constantly shifting

noted: the possession of economic resources, including the formation of solidary units such as families or other groups in control of the means of subsistence; political organization; and the securing and defence of cultural rights through the law. If one wishes to understand how dominant identities are successfully challenged, negotiated and renegotiated by diasporic peoples, these foundational elements must be kept in clear sight. I have argued that the assertion of hybridity always contains an irreducible political element, and cannot be understood simply as the discursive addition of an ethnic narrative. As well, although the words and ideas of artists and intellectuals can provide great insight into the experience of personal estrangement and the difficulties of living in two worlds at the same time, these should not be confused with the experience of populations exiled from their homelands by virtue of economic or political force.

Notes

1 This is movingly described in Nasri Hajjaj, 2004.
2 I am indebted to Susan Babbitt for suggesting a key element of this argument. See Babbitt, 1996.

References

Agger, I. (1989) 'Sexual torture of political prisoners, an overview', *Journal of Traumatic Stress* 2(3): 305–25.
Alcoff, L. and Potter, E. (1993) 'Introduction: when feminisms intersect', in L. Alcoff and E. Potter (eds) *Feminist Epistemologies*, New York and London: Routledge, pp. 1–14.
Anthias, F. (2001a) 'New hybridities, old concepts: the limits of "culture"', *Ethnic and Racial Studies* 24(4): 619–41 (July).
——— (2001b) 'The material and the symbolic in theorizing social stratification: issues of gender, ethnicity and class', *British Journal of Sociology* 52(3): 367–90 (September).
Babbitt, S. M. (1996) *Impossible Dreams: Rationality, Integrity, and Moral Imagination*, Boulder: Westview Press.
Ball, H. (2000) *The Bakke Case: Race, Education and Affirmative Action*, Lawrence: University Press of Kansas.
Bassett, J. S. (1968) *The Southern Plantation Overseer As Revealed In His Letters* [1925], New York: Negro Universities Press.
Bettelheim, B. (1943) 'Individual and mass behavior in extreme situations', *Journal of Abnormal and Social Psychology* 38(4): 417–52.
Braidotti, R. (1994) *Nomadic Subjects*, New York: Columbia University Press.
—— (1996) 'Reizende therieën in een multicultureel perspectief', in G. Wekker and R. Braidotti (eds) *Praten in het Donker. Multiculturalisme en anti-racisme in feministisch perspectief*, Kampen: Kok Agora, pp. 15–56.
Brubaker, R. (2001) 'The return of assimilation? Changing perspectives on immigration and its sequels in France, Germany and the United States', *Ethnic and Racial Studies* 24(4): 531–48 (July).
—— (2005) 'The "diaspora" diaspora', *Ethnic and Racial Studies* 28(1): 1–19 (January).
Clifford, J. (1992) 'Traveling cultures', in L. Grossberg, C. Nelson and P. Treichler (eds) *Cultural Studies*, London and New York: Routledge, pp. 96–112.
——— (1994) 'Diasporas', *Cultural Anthropology* 9(3): 302–38.

Cohen, R. (1997) *Global Diasporas: An Introduction*, Seattle: University of Washington Press.

Cornell, S. and Hartmann, D. (1998) *Ethnicity and Race: Making Identities in a Changing World*, Thousand Oaks, California: Pine Forge Press.

Elkins, S. M. (1959) 'Slavery and personality', in Elkins, *Slavery: A Problem in American Institutional and Intellectual Life*, New York: Grosset and Dunlap, pp. 81–139.

Fanon, F. (1967) 'The fact of blackness [1952]', in *Black Skin, White Masks* (Peau noire, masques blancs), trans. C. L. Markmann, New York: Grove Press, pp. 109–49.

Freud, S. (1961) 'Some psychical consequences of the anatomical distinction between the sexes [1925]', in Freud, *Standard Edition of Complete Psychological Works, Vol. 19* (1923–25), London: Hogarth Press, pp. 248–51.

Geras, N. (1998) *The Contract of Mutual Indifference: Political Philosophy after the Holocaust*, London, New York: Verso.

Gilroy, P. (1987) *There Ain't No Black in the Union Jack: The Cultural Politics of Race and Nation*, London: Hutchinson.

—— (1993) *The Black Atlantic: Modernity and Double Consciousness*, Cambridge: Harvard University Press.

Gordon, L. R. (1995) 'Antiblack racism and ontology', in Gordon, *Bad Faith and Antiblack Racism*, Highlands, New Jersey: Humanities Press International, pp. 130–7.

Hajjaj, N. (2004) 'Where does the Palestinian go after his death? Edward Saïd: a case study', *International Conference on 'Out of Place': Text, Memory and Exile*, Institut Supérieur des Sciences Humaines, Université El-Manar, Tunis, Tunisia, December 1–3.

Hall, S. (1992) 'New ethnicities', in J. Donald, and A. Rattansi (eds) *'Race', Culture, Difference*, London: Sage, pp. 252–60.

—— (1996) 'Gramsci's relevance for the study of race and ethnicity [1986]', in D. Morley and K-H. Chen (eds) *Stuart Hall: Critical Dialogues in Cultural Studies*, London: Routledge, pp. 412–40.

Kaplan, T. (2002) 'Reversing the shame and gendering the memory', *Signs* 28(1): 179–99.

Kibria, N. (1998) 'The contested meanings of "Asian American": racial dilemmas in the contemporary United States', *Ethnic and Racial Studies* 21(5): 939–58 (September).

Kuhn, T. S. (1996) *The Structure of Scientific Revolutions*, 3rd edn., Chicago: University of Chicago Press [Orig. 1962].

Macey, D. (2000) *Frantz Fanon, a Life*, London: Granta.

Margold, J. A. (1999) 'From "culture of fear and terror" to the normalization of violence: an ethnographic case', *Critique of Anthropology* 19(1): 63–88 (March).

Neckerman, K. M., Carter, P. and Lee, J. (1999) 'Segmented assimilation and minority cultures of mobility', *Ethnic and Racial Studies* 22(6): 945–65 (November).

Ong, A. (1996) 'Cultural citizenship as subject-making: immigrants negotiate racial and cultural boundaries in the United States', *Current Anthropology* 37(5): 737–62 (December).

—— (1997) '"A momentary glow of fraternity": narratives of Chinese nationalism and capitalism', *Identities — Global Studies in Culture and Power* 3(3): 331–66 (January).

Pels, D. (1999) 'Privileged nomads: on the strangeness of intellectuals and the intellectuality of strangers', *Theory, Culture and Society* 16(1): 63–86.

Phillips, U. B. (1918) *American Negro Slavery: A Survey of the Supply, Employment and Control of Negro Labor as Determined by the Plantation Regime*, New York: D. Appleton.

Pierre, J. (2004) 'Black immigrants in the United States and the "cultural narratives" of ethnicity', *Identities — Global Studies in Culture and Power* 11(2): 141–70.

Reed, A. L., Jr. (1997) 'Du Bois's "double consciousness": race and gender in Progressive Era American thought', in *W. E. B. Du Bois and American Political Thought: Fabianism and the Color Line*, New York: Oxford University Press, pp. 93–125.

Safran, W. (1991) 'Diasporas in modern societies: myths of homeland and return', *Diaspora* 1(1): 83–99.

Said, E. W. (1990) 'Reflections on exile [1984]', in R. Ferguson (ed.) *Out There: Marginalization and Contemporary Culture*, Cambridge, Massachusetts: MIT Press, pp. 357–66.

Shields, R. (1994) 'Fancy footwork: Walter Benjamin's "Notes on Flânerie"', in K. Tester (ed.) *The Flâneur*, London and New York: Routledge, pp. 61–80.

Tadman, M. (1989) *Speculators and Slaves: Masters, Traders and Slaves in the Old South*, Madison: University of Wisconsin Press.

Wright, R. (1935) 'Between the world and me', *Partisan Review* 2: 18–19 (July–August).

5   Islam and consecrated tortures

Ezat Mossallanejad

We live in a 'spiritually orphaned' and alienated epoch – the age of estrangement, anxiety and universal stress. Unlike an older age when uprootedness was a sort of deliberate punishment against undesirable elements by ruling authorities, in our modern time of economic globalization, tyranny, gross human rights violations, warfare and polarization, exile has taken the form of mass exodus of faceless, amorphous and innocent people (80 per cent of whom are women and children). They are uprooted from their native places mostly because of reasons beyond their control. For example, refugees and migrants from Islamic countries are forced to leave the lands of their birth due to their secular views or their progressive interpretation of Islam. Moderate Muslims have been victimized and tortured by fanatical governments who use Islam as a tool for maintaining tyrannical powers.

The choice to escape from one's home is often a choice between life and death. In this chapter, my focus is on the uprooted individuals who have escaped countries where the rule of Shari'a is the order, specifically those who have experienced Shari'a-based torture. At face value, the term Shari'a is defined as 'the sacred law, grounded in the will of God', that comes from the *Koran*ic tradition and a consensus among theologians. But, in real terms, Shari'a is only a specific interpretation of Islam by dominant clergy in the form of a strictly religious jurisprudence (Gragg 1969: 103). Imposition of the anachronistic rule of Shari'a as such has caused havoc and has led to various methods of religiously consecrated tortures. Many uprooted people from Islamic states have actually experienced types of torture that are sanctioned by government and consecrated by religion. In a way, the whole society, in some Islamic countries, looks like a gigantic torture chamber. The implementation of the law of *tazir* – public hanging, flogging and stoning – has had devastating impacts on ordinary citizens and especially on the intellectual strata of society, forcing millions of people – and particularly intellectuals – to leave their countries and seek refuge, predominantly in Western societies such as Canada.

Survivors of religiously consecrated tortures in diaspora try to cope with the after-effects of their torture. Coping, however, is not easy. Everything in the host society can act as a trigger to remind them of their traumatizing past. Their anxious eyes constantly look back to their homeland, longing for the day when there will be no tyranny and they can return. But the prospect for a return to safety and

Misuse of shari'a's part of discouragement to radical Islam

Tyranical Sharia encourages exodns

dignity is not bright. The merciful God of Islam has retreated before the triumphant Allah of Shari'a. This chapter is a modest attempt to analyse religiously conse-crated torture in Islamic countries. Drawing upon the testimonies of survivors of rape and other forms of torture, with whom I work in my capacity as a service provider for the Canadian Centre for Victims of Torture (CCVT), I try to demon-strate the lasting impacts of these crimes on survivors in the diaspora.

Hell: A background to torture

To understand how torture can be executed in certain societies in the name of God, and analyse its impacts on victims, we need to look at its religious roots. The concept of hell, once found in outmoded books of religion, and its revival for public consumption in some Islamic countries – including and, especially, Iran – is a good starting point. This concept is used to constantly brainwash people that their worldly punishments will be supplemented by divine torture in hell. Indoctrinations, as well as the imposition of various religious rules on citizens, have converted the whole of society into a real inferno on earth, and have led to the exodus of hundreds of intellectuals and technocrats.

There are more than 150 verses about hell in the *Koran*. Islam has intensified the techniques of torture illustrated by the Zoroastrian and Christian hells. Some Islamic teachings suggest that all Muslims have to pass through hell: 'There is not one of you who shall not pass through the confines of hell; such is the absolute decree of your Lord' (*Koran* 19: 72). The Islamic hell, *Jahannam*, is located beneath a bridge, *Sarat*, over which all souls must pass. Similar to the Zoroastrian *Jinood* Bridge, the Bridge of *Sarat* is as narrow as a hair, as sharp as the edge of a razor and as hot as a flame. It turns into a wide road for the virtuous, but sin-ners will fall from it into the deep pits of hell (Petroshevsky 1988: 81).

Hell and heaven are interrelated concepts in the *Koran*. While the former is for actual and potential rebels, the latter is for obedient servants of God and his Apostle: 'We have appointed hell a dungeon for the disbelievers' (*Koran* 17: 8). 'And for those who have faith and do good works, we shall admit them to gardens with waters by running streams …' (*Koran* 4: 55–6).

Fire is the main method of torture in *Koran*ic hell. *The Holy Koran* speaks about many different types of fire: 'Fire is your home. Abide therein forever' (6: 128); 'But as for those who disbelieve, for them is fire of hell; it taketh not complete effect upon them so that they can die, nor is its torment lightened for them. Thus shall the thankless be awarded' (*Koran* 35: 36). It seems that hell is also a horribly overcrowded place: 'Allah will separate the wicked from the just. He will heap the wicked one upon another and thus cast them into hell' (*Koran* 8, Anfal: 37); 'And when they are flung into a narrow place thereof, chained together, they pray for destruction there' (*Koran* 25: 13).

Apart from burning in fire, there are other methods of torture occasionally used in Islamic hell. Sinners are frozen to death in the deepest region of hell called *Havieh*. Torture by eating and drinking (ingestion) is carried out through a tree called *Zaqqum*: 'We have made this tree a scourge for the wrongdoers. It grows in the nethermost part of the hell, bearing fruits like devils' heads: on it they shall feed, and with it they shall cram their bellies, together with draughts of scalding water' (*Koran*, Al-Saafat 38: 58); 'They shall burn in the face of hell, a dismal resting place. There let them taste their drink: scalding water, festering blood, and other putrid things' (*Koran*, Sad 38: 39–55).

Unlike earthly tortures, torture in hell is not intended to extract information or confession. The focus here is on human deeds on earth: 'And a voice will say to them: this is the fire which you denied.... Burn in its flames. It is alike whether you are patient or impatient. You shall be rewarded according to your deed' (*Koran* 52, Toor 16). In this context, the target is not only disbelievers, but also believers who may go astray: 'Believers, guard yourself and guard your kindreds against the fire that has fuel of men and stones, whose keepers are fierce and mighty angels who never disobey Allah's command' (*Koran*, Al-Tahrim 66: 6–7).

Islamic hell has seven divisions, or gates (*Koran*, Alhijr 15: 44), 19 fire-keepers and innumerable torturers. As in earthly torture chambers, God has appointed His most loyal and trusted servants (in this case, angels) to enact his punishments. The technique of keeping victims in limbo is used, too and, very similar to today's modern practice, torture is surrounded with utmost secrecy:

> What do you know what the fire of hell is like? It leaves nothing, it spares no one; it burns the skins of men. It is guarded by nineteen keepers. We have appointed none but angels to guard the fire and made their number a subject for dispute among the unbelievers....
>
> (*Koran* 74, The Cloaked One: 19–33)

While Christianity speaks about 'unquenchable fire', Islam goes a step further, and warns that vicious people will suffer in hell forever. There is no forgiveness, and we can easily see a disturbing disproportionality between the crime committed in life and the punishment received after death. Allah seems to be all vengeful: 'The wrongdoer shall suffer an everlasting punishment' (42: 46).

With the spread of Islam to non-Arab countries, the notion of hell was developed to serve the requirements of paternalistic feudal societies. The following are quotes attributed to Mohammad: 'The Prophet said: "I was shown the hellfire and that the majority of its dwellers were women who were ungrateful." It was asked, "Do they disbelieve in Allah?" (Or are they ungrateful to Allah?) He replied, "They are ungrateful to their husbands and are ungrateful for the favours and the good (charitable deeds) done to them"' (Al-Bokhari 1957: 643).

The *Koran*ic account of hell has been exaggerated in the course of time by various theologians and different schools of religion, and has acted as a justification for earthly tortures. What follows is one of these exaggerations:

> The wine of hell is blistering water and the food is *Zaqqum*. Scalding water of hell is nothing but dirt and sore. The smell is so stinking that if one drop of hell's water mixes with the water of all oceans in the world, the foul smell would kill all living creatures of the earth. There is a valley in hell that

accommodates seventy thousand houses. Inside each house there are seventy thousand rooms. Inside each room there are seventy thousand black vipers and inside the belly of each viper, there are seventy thousand pots full of poison.... The sinners in hell have shirts and coats with red hot copper and their legs are tied together with chains of fire. There are shoes on their feet that are made of fire so hot that their brains boil in their skulls.... The door-man of hell is an angel called *Malik*. He never smiles and is always angry.

(Akhundzadeh 1985: 67–68)

powerful psychology

Constant indoctrination about heaven and hell has created both fear and hope, and has persuaded people to obey and behave in a certain way. It has contributed towards the continuation of the spiritual and material domination of the clergy, along with their worldly tortures, as a prelude to divine tortures in hell. It has, therefore, acted as a root cause of Islamic diaspora.

We should not underestimate the psychological dangers of popular belief in hell as a torture chamber of God. Even those opposed to the rule of clergy may carry their trauma into exile. Several of my clients, including survivors of conse-crated tortures, have shared with me their fear of divine punishment in hell. Some blame themselves for the massacre of family members at the hands of tyrannical regimes back home. They consider themselves sinful and deserving of divine punishment in hell.

The notion of hell has penetrated deeply into the fabric of the psychology of people who have escaped Islamic autocracy. I have seen quite a few clients at the CCVT who suffer from recurrent nightmares about being tortured in hell. I have provided them with the holistic services of CCVT – including counselling, art-therapy, and befriending – and have referred them to psychiatrists and psycholo-gists. I have found the process of their rehabilitation very slow and problematic because they suffer from a specific kind of trauma that is mixed with their con-victions. Effective rehabilitation goes beyond clinical healing. There is a need for long-term public and self-education for the emancipation of the human mind from spiritual enslavement. Religion must become a vehicle of universal love and compassion, and be separated from state politics and the day-to-day affairs of people. Physical and psychological punishments, in the forms exercised in some Islamic states, are in fact the creation of hell on earth; torture is the earthly con-struction of God's torture chamber.

In what follows, I will focus on two common forms of torture – stoning and holy rape – that are used specifically in Iran. Both types of torture demonstrate the gender character of these heinous crimes under the Islamic state and are per-formed through manipulation of Shari'a as interpreted by the Muslim clergy. I will also highlight the impacts on survivors in exile.

origin of quotes

Stoning

Punishment by stoning did not originate in Islam. It has its precedence in ancient human history, including the old tradition of some Jewish tribes (*Old Testament*).

The Christian answer to this 'sin' is forgiveness (*New Testament*, John 8: 3–120). *The Holy Koran* contains 16 verses concerning adultery. One famous one says that if adultery is committed, both parties should be given 100 lashes and not allowed to marry another Muslim (*Koran*, Al-noor, verses 2–4). As the most sacred book of Islam, the *Koran* does not prescribe stoning as the punishment for adultery. There is not a single verse to this effect, but it is used by several Islamic states to punish adultery.

However, the majority of Sunni and Shi'a theologians, including the four Sunni Imams (Abu Hanifa, Shafeyi, Malek and Ahmad Hanbel), holds that the order for stoning to death still exists. They argue that Prophet Mohammad himself had stoned to death adulterers and adulteresses.

In some Islamic countries, stoning is consecrated by religion. It is considered a virtuous action done to please God, and is committed against ordinary people, and especially women. The perpetrators are sure that they are doing the right thing, that it is the work of God. Some 'crimes' punishable by stoning in certain countries include homosexuality and adultery; sometimes an accusation, such as being a pornographer or prostitute, is enough grounds for punishment.

Stoning remains a legal punishment in a number of countries regulated by the rules of Shari'a. The following countries are notorious for stoning: Afghanistan (under the Taliban and even today), Bangladesh, Iran, Saudi Arabia, Pakistan, Sudan, Nigeria and Mauritania. Most of the cases remain unreported and undocumented.

The method is simple: a hole is dug and, in the case of a man, the victim is buried in it up to his belly; a woman is buried up to her armpits. Then a group of people throws stones at the victim from all sides. Stoning is usually carried out in public. According to a sacred rule, if the victim manages to escape the hole and get away, he or she will be pardoned. Stoning officials, however, have frequently broken this rule. There are recorded cases in which victims are recaptured by the authorities and shot to death on the spot.

The atrocity of stoning does not end with the perpetration of this gruesome act. In many cases, the enforcement officials force the victim's close relatives, including children, to watch the process. The law even specifies the type of stone to be used: if it is too small, it will not inflict the requisite damage; if it is too big, the person will die too soon. It has to be 'just the right size', so that the victim's suffering can be maximized to its fullest potential. Sometimes it takes three to four hours for the victim to die.

It is important to bear in mind that there is a difference between this and other types of torture, in that stoning is sanctioned by law. Most torture is perpetrated in secret, by professional torturers. However, stoning is carried out in public, involving the whole community – ordinary citizens are converted into torturers. Sometimes the authorities invite 300 people from the community. You must throw a stone if you are invited, or you too will be persecuted; to save yourself, you must throw something, even a small pebble.

As noted earlier, stoning is not a *Koran*ic ordinance, and the Prophet's traditions, even if substantiated, cannot supersede the scripture. The question then remains: how is it that some Muslims justify stoning as a *Koran*ic prescription?

Justification arises out of the concept of *hadd* (boundary) and *hodoud* (plural for *hadd*) in the *Koran*. Although the *Koran* has not prescribed stoning, it should be conceded that it has set certain *hodoud* for Muslims that they cannot and must not trespass. The *Koran* has categorically mentioned that 'those who trespass these boundaries are oppressors' (*Koran*, Baghara, verse 187). If anybody goes beyond these boundaries, he or she has invaded the boundaries preaffixed by God, and must face special penalties called boundary punishments.

Therefore, *hadd* is a *Koran*ic legal term for the offences and punishments specifically determined by Allah and defined in the *Koran*. Muslim theologians argue that boundary crimes are crimes against God and cannot be forgiven by any human being; they come within the domain of God's Rights. Adultery is among the boundary crimes considered as having been committed against God Himself; punishment is set in *The Holy Koran*, and the only task for true believers is the simple implementation of the penalty. This is a correct argument from the point of view of the Islamic jurisprudence. However, the problem comes from the fact that stoning is not a penalty set by the *Koran*. How then can anybody implement it in the name of the Holy Book?

The propagators of stoning support their contention by relying on *Ahadith* (the Arabic plural of *Hadith*), which refer to quotations and traditions attributed to the Prophet and his successors. The Hungarian Jewish scholar of Islam, Ignaz Goldziher (1981), the founder of the Modern Institute of Islamic Studies, has pointed out that most of these quotations and so-called traditions have no basis in truth and are most probably falsifications. It is sad that so many people have been killed on the basis of myth. The Iranian scholar, Haideh Moghissi (1999: 110), suggests that such practices are:

> … part and parcel of a value system, promoted by the fundamentalists, which sees women and their bodies as possessions of men. In this view, purification of the woman's body and soul is a religious and political duty for the individual man, and through him, by extension, for the Islamic state.

The psychological impact of stoning on the public is horrible. It creates panic and intimidation. People feel helpless and impotent *vis-à-vis* the cruelty of a system that legitimizes itself in the name of an omnipotent God. It helps 'holy' barbarous and inhuman institutions entrench themselves. It perpetuates a highly anachronistic tradition that is a prerequisite for the continuation of the most fanatical and backward elements of a society. A terrible psychological punishment is inflicted upon the victim even before the sentence is carried out. In the reading of most verdicts, the condemned are informed that their bodies are to be burned and the ashes thrown away: another humiliation presented as a prelude to eternal punishment in hell. It is also important to note that the implications of the practice go beyond the act of stoning itself. Since strict proofs are necessary to establish that adultery has occurred, and since adultery takes place under utmost secrecy, with the accused not normally confessing, the only way to prove the charge is by using various techniques of severe torture and other coercive methods to extract a confession of guilt.

Victims of torture who come to the CCVT often express pride in having been tortured because of their commitment to a cause. However, in cases of stoning, victims first undergo a psychological assault in the course of interrogation, at which time they are told that they have committed 'the most dirty sin', that they are 'worse than a pig' and that they will 'burn in hell'. The holy inquisitors and their entourages spare no time in making use of selective quotations from the *Koran*, the Prophet and various saints to degrade and humiliate their victims. Following is a narration attributed to a Shi'a saint:

> A river will run towards hell from the genitals of the adulterer and the adul-
> teress. It will continue to flow for 500 years. Hell's inmates get annoyed from
> the stinking filth. A woman who takes a man to her husband's bed makes it
> necessary for God to torture her in her grave and burn her later in his hell.[1]

I have worked with several women and men who come from countries where the rules of Shari'a are in practice. A number of them have escaped to Canada due to their real or alleged involvement in homosexual or extramarital affairs. I have found them to be highly terrified of being returned to their countries of origin, where they may face the real or imaginary prospect of being sentenced to death by stoning. I have felt the panic of death by stoning haunting women from such countries even though they have not been victims of gender-related persecutions. Some of them suffer from hypersensitivity, hyper-vigilance, frequent nightmares and insomnia. I have frequently heard from them that under the patriarchal rule of Shari'a, any influential fanatic can take the whole judicial system in his hands and drag a woman to the stoning ditch. 'These inquisitional courts', a client told me, 'hardly look for any proof'. In fact, there have been cases where women were accused by abusive husbands of adultery and, due to their husbands' influence with the government, found themselves at risk of death by stoning. They were able to escape to Canada with the help of their parents, siblings or friends.

Fortunately, in many cases their claims were considered gender-related perse-cution, and were accepted by Canada's Immigration and Refugee Board (IRB). But there are tragic cases as well. One such case was that of a woman who had been rejected by the IRB because her story was so horrible that the armchaired refugee-determination panel members failed to believe it. She exhausted all legal remedies available to her and was made a subject for removal. It was only with CCVT's help, through mobilizing the community, that her deportation was stayed; however, she continued to remain in immigration limbo for a long time before obtaining her permanent residence status in Canada.

Another painful case was that of an old client of the CCVT who rushed into my office one day unannounced. He was a well-established Iranian social activist who had not visited us for years due to the fortunate fact of his being all right and not needing our services. The moment he saw me he started crying loudly. I found him highly stressed. I tried to comfort him, in vain. Obviously, something had made him irreversibly despondent. Soon I discovered that watching a videotape about stoning had triggered memories of his own torture. He became so dysfunctional that we had to treat him through an array of CCVT programmes, including art therapy, a mutual support group, ongoing counselling and special psychiatric care.

The holy rape

Holy rape is a combination of gender-based, social, ritual and religiously consecrated torture prevalent in many societies. Under certain circumstances, rape is considered a war crime, a component of the crime of genocide, and a crime against humanity. However, like stoning, rape is being used as a method of torture, and is often consecrated in the name of Allah in societies that are based on religious patriarchy.

I have observed that the impacts of rape and stoning are similar. The after-effects of rape, however, are more difficult to overcome for survivors in the diaspora. Victims, in fact, remain dysfunctional years after the infliction of the initial trauma. Although totally unfounded, survivors usually carry the burden of guilt throughout their lives. They almost always direct the blemish towards themselves. Here again we can trace religious sanctioning of this horrendous experience. *The Holy Koran* has unequivocally permitted the taking of women as captives of war and converting them into sex slaves: 'We have made lawful to you the wives to whom you have granted dowries and the slave girls whom Allah has given you as booty' (Section 33, Al-Ahzab: 50). It rules as well that 'you are also forbidden to take in marriage married women except captives whom you own as slaves. Such is the decree of Allah' (*Koran* 4, Al-Nisa: 24).[2]

The above verses have provided justification for holy rapes. During the Iran–Iraq War (1980–8), military and paramilitary forces from both sides raped women in their occupied zones without compunction, easily finding moral and religious justifications for their actions. Among Muslim fanatics, the Iranian Hezbollah has committed holy rape on a widespread and systemic basis. Torturers in Iranian political prisons approach their victims as 'enemies of God and corrupted on earth'. They believe that all political prisoners are at war with Allah, and deserve the most severe 'divine punishments'. They are specifically hostile to women, whom they perceive as agents of satanic seduction and whose bodies are unclean abodes of viciousness. They use rape as a technique of torture against women whom they label war captives, conveniently using the *Koran*'s permission to legitimately convert them into sex slaves.

Rape is normally the last torture a young girl receives in Iran before her execution. It is sad that rape is the ironic outcome of Islamic compassion for virgin girls. According to the Prophet's traditions, if a woman dies a virgin, she will go to paradise. In their sinister determination to lock the gate of heaven to infidel girls, the executioners remove their victims' virginity just before killing them (Chafiq 2002). What follows is the testimony of Dr Reza Ghaffari, a famous Iranian political prisoner:

> The guards and managers of the prison systematically raped women who were sentenced to death. In this way they tried to make them sinful and deprive them from any chance of going to paradise. According to the multitudes of

verdicts by the clerics, a virgin girl should not be executed. As a sign of their adherence to these verdicts, the guards made sure that no girl in jail dies virgin. Without exception, they raped virgin girls before executing them.

(Ghaffari 1998: 273)

The rapist executioners legitimize their actions by forcefully marrying their victims. Following the girl's execution, the 'bridegroom' takes a box of wedding sweets to the family of his victim as a notification of their beloved's simultaneous marriage and execution. In a written confession in January 1990, Sarmast Akhlaq Tabandeh, a senior Guards Corps interrogator, recounted one such case in Shiraz prison:

Flora Owrangi, an acquaintance of one of my friends, was one such victim. The night before her execution, the resident mullah in the prison conducted a lottery among the members of the firing squads and prison officials to determine who would rape her. She was then forcibly injected with anaesthesia ampoules, after which she was raped. The next day, after she was executed, the mullah in charge wrote a marriage certificate and the guard who raped her took that, along with a box of sweets, to her parents.[3]

Although the *Koran* has specifically assigned punishment for adultery, it is silent about the crime of rape. There is hardly any decree by the clergy about punishment of the rapist. In most Islamic countries the blame would go to the victims. This has provided police, military and paramilitary officials with a green light to rape with total impunity. There are reports about rapes of adolescent boys in Iranian prisons at the hands of 'repentants' – prisoners who had been brainwashed in the course of their imprisonment and torture into acting as spies and informers against other prisoners.[4] The following is the testimony of a former political prisoner: 'The repentants were also behind rapes. They raped teenagers who were put under their guardianship to be educated about Islamic values' (Ghaffari 1998: 118). Vida Hadjebi, a woman who languished in the political prisons of the Shah of Iran for years, has also shared her experience of the secrecy surrounding rapes:

Rape was a big taboo of the prison. It was an untold subject that was haunting everyone's mind. Nobody spoke about it…. We had been told about rape secretly, but we preferred not to speak about it. It was perhaps for the sake of people who were raped; it was perhaps because we had no courage to break this taboo in an open and public manner; perhaps we could not do that because of our families and the culture dominated them. (Hadjebi-Tabrizi 2002: 205–6).

Various reasons, including shame, danger of excommunication, and lack of a safe environment to speak, have contributed to the denial and secrecy around rape. In almost all Islamic societies, chastity is regarded as the most valuable asset of each and every woman. *The Holy Koran* has repeatedly ordered believers, especially women, to maintain their chastity.[5] This has deeply influenced the personality of each and every woman – even if she migrates to the West and accepts the rules of modernism. A survivor of rape at the CCVT revealed her tragic experience to me 20 years after the initial trauma and five years after I became her case worker.

Rape is connected to a show of 'masculine' power. I have heard from my CCVT clients in exile who have been victims of rape that their horrible experiences were combined with ghoulish aggression, roughness, gross expression of power, cruel toughness, inhuman rigidity, degradation and humiliation. The psychological scars will remain with survivors for the rest of their lives.

Conclusion

Uprootedness is essentially a discontinuous condition of human existence. Uprooted people seem to be parachuted to life with no land, no roots and no future. It is, therefore, imperative for them to wage an ongoing struggle to overcome this fragmentation and discontinuity. They can alleviate the trauma of uprootedness by making their best attempts, individually and collectively, to establish vital contacts within their new homes.

But uprooted communities in Western countries are so busy with their own domestic problems that they hardly think of the benefits of uniting under a common platform with progressive people in their host countries to struggle for their rights and to combat racism and xenophobia, as well as challenging anachronisms in countries with Islamic, or otherwise fundamentalist, regimes with a modern and secular approach to life. It is useful to revive past humanitarian traditions and promote the use of arts and literature as vehicles of public education. It is necessary to remind the general population in Islamic countries of the global impracticality of outmoded rules and traditions. Formation of a broad solidarity is essential for any positive changes to be made in the lives of uprooted people on the one hand and in their homelands on the other. Uprooted people can never raise their voices unless it becomes the melody of a choir united for democracy, secularism and social justice.

little unity among anti-radicals [handwritten annotation]

Notes

1 Quoted from Mohammad Shafie bin Mohammad Saleh, *Mojmaa al Moaref va Makhzan al-Avaref*, appended to M. B. Majlessi, *Holyat Al-Motaghin*, Tehran: Elmi Bookshop, p. 138.
2 The same ruling is repeated exactly in the *Koran*, 23, Al-Mu'minum: 5–6.
3 For more on this subject see the Foreign Affairs Committee of the National Council of Resistance of Iran's *Women, Islam & Equality* (n.d.), France: Auvers-sur-Oise.
4 To 'repent' means to acknowledge one's sins, but in the context of Iranian jails, repentants became dangerous torturers, and sometimes executioners, while they were serving their terms in prison. This was a unique phenomenon of the Iranian prison system under the new Islamic regime. Repentants lived alongside other prisoners, playing the roles of both victims and victimizers. With the intensification of torture and execution, they became so powerful that even prison guards would obey their orders. Yet, this did not ultimately spare them from the harsh conditions of jail life – several were executed by the regime they supported wholeheartedly.
5 There are at least seven verses in the *Koran* about chastity. See *Koran*: 5:5, 23:5, 24:30–31, 70:29.

References

Akhundzadeh, F. A. (1985) *Makobat* (Maktoeb Dovvom-e Kamal al Douleh), Murd-e Emrouz Publication.

Al-Bokhari, I. M. I. (1957) *al-Hadith*, Vol. 8, Book 82, No. 816.

Chafiq, C. (2002) *Le Nouvel Homme Islamiste: La Prison Politique en Iran* (The New Islamist Man: The Political Prison in Iran), Paris.

Ghaffari, R. (1998) *Khaterat-e Yek Zendani as Zendamhaye Jomhoori Eslami* (Recollections of a Prisoner from the Prisons of the Islamic Republic), trans. A. Saman, Stockholm: Arash Publication.

Goldziher, I. (1981) *Introduction to Islamic Theology and Law*, trans. Andras Hamori and Ruth Hamori, Princeton, N.J.: Princeton University Press.

Gragg, K. (1969) *The House of Islam*, Belmont, California: Dickenson Publishing Company, Inc.

Hadjebi-Tabrizi, V. (2002) *Dad-e-Bidad, Femmes Politiques emprisonnées 1971–1977*, Vol. 1, Köln, Germany.

Koran, various verses taken from *The Qur'an Translation*, translated by Abdullah Yusuf Ali, published by Tahrike Tarsile Qur'an Inc., Elmhurst New York, 1 January 1999.

Moghissi, H. (1999) *Feminism and Islamic Fundamentalism*, London and New York: Zed Press.

Mohammad Shafie bin Mohammad Saleh. *Mojmaa al Moaref va Makhzan al-Avaref*, appended to Majlessi, M. B. *Holyat Al-Motaghin*, Tehran: Elmi Bookshop (no date of publication).

The New Testament, John, Chapter 8, verses 3–120.

The Old Testament, Leviticus 20:10, Deuteronomy 22:22, Deuteronomy 22:23–25, and Deuteronomy 22:20–21.

Petroshevsky, I. P. (1988) *Islam dar Iran* (Islam in Iran). Trans. Karim Keshavarz, Tehran: Payam Publication, seventh edition.

Part II

Home and exile

Gender and politics of memory

6 Divided communities of memory: Diasporas come home

Mary Ann Tétreault

Introduction

Emigrants, exiles, and refugees create diasporic communities, islands of homeland culture in alien spaces. Separation divides travellers from those they leave behind. Each new environment such exiles encounter comes with its own ethos and material world at the precise time that materially anchored experiences of 'home' no longer are available to them. Their connections become ideational and idealized, products of imagining places, structures, and inhabitants. Such simulacra diverge, often sharply, from how those left behind experience the 'reality' of that other place in this other time (e.g. Brannen 2004; Slyomovics 1998).

Intimate connections woven over time between persons sharing social space produce historical memory, a collective sense of the past whose continuous adjustment creates the perception of a seamless journey to the present. Fragmenting this social space generates diverging historical memories as each community 'remembers' from its own contemporary location. In this chapter, I argue that diasporas launch divided communities of memory that continue within 'reunited' populations once diasporas come home. Focusing on the Kuwaiti experience during the Iraqi occupation, I look at some of the mechanisms that create, aggravate and bridge conflicts when divided communities are reunited.

Diasporas

To define 'diaspora' merely as a national or ethnic community living outside its territory of origin is simplistic. Are all the people who share nationality and/or ethnicity but who left a territory of origin at different times and for different reasons part of the same diaspora? Is a diasporic community originating from the same place and now residing in Detroit the same as one departing at the same time but now living in Marseilles? Is diaspora membership an essential quality of personhood (such as the territorial origin of one's ancestors) or is it also, even primarily, a matter of choice: most 'Americans' are technically diasporans yet, speaking for myself, I do not think of myself that way but rather as an American. Are most diasporans the cutting edge of what Aihwa Ong (1998) calls 'flexible citizenship', sources of support for the nation-state left behind as well as integral elements in political communities abroad? Or are they like me, a citizen of one political community with no political or economic ties to a 'mother' country? No wonder Sita Ranchod-Nilsson (2004) cautions: 'Your diaspora might not be my diaspora'. To avoid confusion from the fluidity of the meaning of 'diaspora', I focus here on 'communities of memory', a plural concept that incorporates socialization and choice.

Historical memory

Historical memory is a collection of narratives transmitting what a people 'knows' about its shared past. It is fluid and plural and, like a highway, constantly under construction and repair. Narratives composing historical memory are partial and frequently contradictory. Whether they come from private conversations or mass media, their relentless consumption fills the mind with myriad possible, impossible, and mutually inconsistent stories about past and present. Observers may regard some narratives as 'truer' than others, but individuals hold all the stories they've encountered somewhere in their minds. Modules and particles of narrative remain available for fashioning an identity to suit current circumstances (Kaufman 2004).

Religion and politics provide coherence in historical memory, offering psychic grounding to community members as they generate support for individual power-holders and governing regimes (e.g. Finkelstein and Silberman 2001; Wolf 1999). The heterogeneity of historical narratives offers raw material that regime leaders and their challengers shape into stories presenting themselves as superior custodians of the people's traditions (Habermas 1973: 70–1; Tétreault 2004). In Islam, for example, the heterogeneity of Muslim tradition is reflected in many ways – one in Hadith – each with its chain of transmission guiding the believer's conscious evaluation of its validity (Ahmed 1992; Spellberg 1994). I emphasize 'conscious' here: even though individuals might accord greater or lesser validity to a particular Hadith depending on the chain of transmission, the messages embedded in other Hadith also remain available to be retrieved and deployed. The heterogeneity of sacred texts and oral transmissions explains why Muslim feminists and Muslim anti-feminists both can find support in them for their divergent perspectives (e.g. compare Afkhami 1995 and Mernissi 1987 to Muhawesh 1990; also Spellberg 1994).

With the invention of mechanical printing, rising rates of literacy, and the coalescence of small, relatively homogeneous local units into larger, more diverse nation-states, governments became more involved in producing historical memories to promote national identity and loyalty to rulers (Anderson 1991; Greenfeld 1992). Even so, religion continues to be a primary generator of historical memory and, during periods of religious resurgence such as our own, is an especially strong challenger to the historical memories propagated by states (Juergensmeyer 1994; Tétreault and Denemark ed. 2004).

Narrative transmission

Visual media are especially powerful in creating and validating historical memory. Conveying the impression that the viewer was 'there' when iconic events occurred, they convey a veracity to images that is rare for mere words. They also produce islands of near-homogeneity around the memories of visual representations as compared to memories that come from narrative sources. For example, the first war that was extensively photographed, the US Civil War, resulted in hundreds of widely reproduced pictures of the dead on battlefields. Together, they conveyed searing impressions of the suffering and death of white Northerners and white Southerners (Sandweiss 2004). With help from post-war propagandists, these photos helped to submerge the causes of the war in slavery and secession by fore-grounding in historical memory images of rows and heaps of dead white men. Few photos recorded the valour of black Americans, whose stories rapidly disap-peared from dominant war narratives (Blight 2001). Similar elisions shaped col-lective memories of World War I through the extensive photographic record of the Western front as compared to less abundant and less well circulated materials from the war in the East. This may explain why many find it difficult to contex-tualize the post-war reconstruction of the Middle East within the frame of this conflict (e.g. Fromkin 1989).

The power of pictures is strongly evident in films, but television is most deeply implicated in contemporary constructions of understanding, memory, and iden-tity. Television pictures are more widely viewed than films or still photos. Their repetition transforms the most compelling into 'floating signifiers', images that acquire meaning independent of their original contexts. Television images of bull-dozers smashing Palestinian houses, the human and other debris from the Afghan wedding bombed on 1 July 2002 by US aircraft, and jets crashing into the World Trade Center on 11 September 2001 are floating signifiers whose origins are embedded in the historical narratives of particular groups, yet also convey emo-tions to uninvolved persons who view them as occasions of violence and tragedy.

Television is a powerful generator of historical memory in part because it is a constant background presence. Programmes are discussed informally in the short-hand we use for life experiences rather than as elements of contending ideas. What is seen is usually interpreted as what is, even when viewed behaviour is crit-icized. Deborah Wheeler notes that Kuwaiti families use US sitcoms as bad examples of values and behaviour when they view them with their children (Wheeler 2000: 440–1), but do not evaluate the authenticity of sitcom stories as true reflections of American life. Jürgen Habermas (1991) says that television destroys critical consciousness, not because visuals create lasting and perhaps erroneous mental images, but because they are passively consumed.

The production of historical memory through television programming is espe-cially effective in conveying and sedimenting lasting impressions. With respect to news, long-running or repeated stories quickly become stereotypical as they are shaped to appeal to what the media entrepreneur perceives as the prejudices and expectations of his target market. This creates 'genres' and style conventions that mass media use to make stories intelligible and palatable to commercially valu-able consumers.

Yet by omitting analysis and discrepant viewpoints, the legitimacy of ques-tioning or dissent to what has been presented is undermined. In the context of historical-memory production, these qualities ensure the presentation of black-and-white frameworks within which self-identity and also alienation from and hatreds of various 'others' are generated (Kaufman 2001, 2004).

Historical memory as contested terrain

Divided communities of memory call for reconciliation (Blight 2001), especially when exiles come home. Importing divergent narratives into historical memory offers opportunities to (re)define the entire group and its common history. Perhaps especially when diasporas are triggered by disasters, such as wars or revolutions, that provide a common experience of trauma, diasporic groups may find themselves in strong positions *vis-à-vis* those they left behind. Exiles also endure loss and pain. They feel entitled to recognition for what they suffered, yet their escape also affirms their agency as individuals and families and their authority to define their communities to the outside world. Think of the influence of well-connected members of the Iraqi diaspora on decisions by the Bush administration: to invade Iraq (Drogin 2003; Hersh 2003); to fail to prepare for post-conflict occupation (Fallows 2004); to put so many exiles in the interim government (Cole 2004; Crane and Terrill 2003); to privatize Iraqi state assets and award so many post-war contracts to exiles and their connections (e.g. Dauenhauer and Lobe 2003); and to believe so firmly that insiders were passive and would accept – even welcome – all of the above (Fallows 2004). Iraqi insiders who bore the brunt of Saddam's excesses suffered from the war, but the most terrible penalty inflicted by the exile partners of the Bush administration is the rampant insecurity resulting from a false pre-invasion picture of conditions inside Iraq, one that promoted the views and preferences of prominent exiles rather than one based on intelligence coming directly or indirectly from insiders. The distortion of historical memory required to support this vast disparity is evident in US policymakers as well, most clearly in the pre-war conviction of US leaders that the United States would be greeted as a liberator by Iraqi insiders. Such a view elides the 1991 abandonment of the Shi'as by the United States when they rose against Saddam following the expulsion of his army from Kuwait (Terrill 2003) and the suffering Iraqis endured from US military activities ever since (e.g. Abu Gulal 2002).

   Exile politics also fuels fears that the United States will increase intervention in Iran to promote 'regime change' there. Iranian exile communities are eager consumers of media content focusing on Iranian issues. Most are intended to preserve Persian culture among diasporans, but some programmes with political aims take stands against the Islamist regime through 'shrill and doctrinaire anti-Islamist and pro-royalist' pronouncements (Nafisy 1993). The historical memory they generate is problematic, because the images convey partial truths fashioned from a few strands pulled from the thick and variegated tapestry of life on the ground in both pre- and post-revolutionary Iran. Tara Bahrampour contrasts the historical memory cultivated by private-school students in West Los Angeles to the 'Iranian-ness' of their middle- and working-class counterparts in the Valley.

[T]he [Westlake] boys identify with Iran, an anachronistic Iran that has more to do with their grandparents' generation than with their own. Parshow imagines Tehran in black and white, as it is in his parent's old pictures.... Daniel imagines Iran with 1950s-era cars, and dreams of hunting leopards with his grandfather. Those images of Iranian life are more meaningful to the boys than their encounters with the Iranian kids in the Valley who get tattoos that say 'Allah' and pick fights with Iranian Jews.

(Bahrampour 2003: 60).

Returning diasporic groups struggle with those left behind to define historical memory following reunion. The diaspora I examine here consists of Kuwaitis who fled or were marooned outside Kuwait during the Iraqi invasion and occupation (2 August 1990–25 February 1991). The Kuwaiti diaspora was coherent, virtually monocausal, and short-lived. Although some Kuwaitis resided outside for other reasons prior to 2 August 1990, the vast majority abroad after 2 August had departed or remained as a direct result of the invasion. Some Kuwaitis actually returned during the occupation, and most of the rest came back during the first three years following liberation. Yet despite its analytical compactness, the Kuwaiti diaspora embraced different communities, each illuminating different qualities of diasporic populations and strategies for reintegration into community life.

Communities of memory: Occupied Kuwait

The diaspora

The Kuwaiti diaspora included communities of persons whose decisions to leave, and their conduct while abroad, diverged in significant ways. *Activist* diasporans mobilized against the invasion. Some worked to convince governments and citizens in the countries that had given them sanctuary to help liberate Kuwait; others organized to combat the physical and emotional devastation they expected to find when they returned. Some were members of the political opposition, contending with the regime for democratization ever since July 1986, when the amir had closed the parliament and suspended constitutional provisions protecting civil liberties. They continued their pro-democracy campaign in exile, banking on a near-term return to Kuwait that, thanks to their efforts, would re-establish a more open regime than the *ante bellum* status quo.

The vast majority of exiles were *refugees*. Some escaped during the occupation; others were already outside and simply stayed. Among those fleeing the invading forces were settled *badu* whose exodus was widely interpreted either as a mark of cowardice or a reflection of the distinctive way in which the remnants of tribal nomads, unlike urban populations, are incorporated into modern nation-states. Tribesmen are presumed to focus their loyalties on the persons of their rulers rather than on a particular territory. In contrast, the loyalties of urban populations are thought to attach to ecological communities (Longva 2000).

This ideational and behavioural distinction extends to members of Kuwait's ruling family. The amir and crown prince, along with most other Al Sabah, chose flight as their response to invasion. A few family members stayed behind, and some acquitted themselves admirably in the resistance (Levins 1997; Rajab 1996), but the head of state and the head of government were at the head of the pack of refugees streaming into Saudi Arabia. Other ruling family members and their allies escaped as soon as they could, some assisted by Bedouin guides sent or paid for by the exiled rulers (Levins 1997; interviews in London and Kuwait 1991, 1992).

Most Kuwaitis acknowledge the key role played by the government-in-exile in the campaign to liberate Kuwait.

> The Iraqi plan [before invading] was to continue the talks in Baghdad and then capture the Kuwaiti prime minister and force him to denounce the amir... In this case, the invasion would appear fairly legitimate; it would look like a ruling family quarrel, with the Iraqis being generous to support the good ones in the family.
>
> (Ghanim al-Najjar, personal communication)

The amir-in-exile was able to tap Kuwaiti wealth located abroad and, as the chief symbol of the nation, could inspire and finance heroic efforts to limit the damage the invaders inflicted precisely because he remained outside the clutches of the occupiers. His financial authority allowed the regime to contribute almost US$25 billion to coalition members to support rollback of the invasion (Tétreault 1992: 9), to commit additional billions to re-entry projects, and to sustain thousands of Kuwaiti exiles, many of them students with few personal resources, during exile. The amir's symbolic role rallied the spirits of 'insiders', the people who remained in Kuwait during the occupation, too. Even Kuwaitis who are relatively cynical about their rulers spoke of the amir's escape as having made the restoration of Kuwaiti sovereignty in their lifetimes a plausible rather than a preposterous goal.

Diaspora communities of memory

The community of memory enclosing the small number of Kuwaiti activists bringing people and supplies in and out of Kuwait or preparing for re-entry after rollback seems the least alienated from the insiders' community of memory. Most *re-entry activists* were technocrats who worked on projects. They were in close touch with insiders, especially family members and colleagues, via fax, satellite phone, and visits bringing in supplies and taking out refugees.

> I was outside and came in for two months and then went back outside. I smuggled [myself] through the border ... and stayed until October. During my presence I participated in the cooperative [neighbourhood-owned and -operated shopping complexes] ... I opened a small supermarket... Also, with my friends, I was responsible for the British Airways crew, to hide them, feed them, and take care of them. The main reason for me to leave Kuwait was my

sister, who was late in her pregnancy. The only way to save her life was to [get her out of the country]... Then I went to the army. I trained at Fort Dix. Then I ... deployed to the eighth evacuation hospital.

(al-Muhanna 1992)

Re-entry activists identified with insiders. Nearly all their waking hours were focused on imagining their situations, assisting them during the occupation, and preparing to reclaim the country they shared and rescue their fellow citizens.

We set up a [national oil company] management group, but working as Kuwaitis, not as officials. We had ... seven people... We started planning with Bechtel, from November 15th until we reentered Kuwait. The planning, the material bought and stored in the Emirates, the scenarios – what if we came by sea and there are no port facilities? We planned for temporary port facilities down to the last crane. Bechtel had maybe two days for Christmas but we all worked day and night.

(Buhamrah 1992)

Because of their close identification with insiders, the community of memory of re-entry activists resembled the community of memory of Kuwaiti insiders. Unlike most other exiles, re-entry activists were full of stories about the bravery of insiders in the face of capture, torture and murder, and especially about narrow escapes and the small and large triumphs that, for many, echoed their own efforts abroad (interviews 1991, 1992).

Public relations activists mobilized support for rollback. Like re-entry activists, most were professionals, but in different fields – social sciences and business instead of medicine and engineering. Rather than taking their cues from the news filtering out of occupied Kuwait, these persons identified with and prop-agated the government's packaged image of a helpless Kuwait ground under the heels of Iraqi invaders, and reinforced this image in media presentations. The most memorable media-produced occupation narrative was also the biggest public-relations disaster of the occupation. False testimony about Iraqi atrocities produced by a professional US public relations firm, Hill and Knowlton, was delivered by a member of the ruling family to a US congressional committee. Its exposure impeached reports of real suffering by insiders in the minds of foreigners and Kuwaitis abroad.

Like re-entry activists, PR activists were effective. At their best, they epito-mized the qualities of Ong's (1998) 'flexible citizenship', operating within the codes of their host countries to advocate the rescue of their home country.

The [Free Kuwait Campaign] was ... the focus of action of the European press. We established very good relations with French TV and radio, Scandinavian TV and radio... We had everybody – the Kuwaiti student union is [Muslim] Brotherhood – we would come in jeans and they ... they operate under codes. I don't know the per cent of women involved, but everyone will admit that, throughout, the women have shone. This is a testament that we as Kuwaiti women never had to fight for the right to do the work – we just did it.

(al-Mousa 1991)

Kuwaiti women were prominent PR activists, the result of their intelligence and passion and also their linguistic skills and 'Western' appearance. Unlike student activists who were members of the Ikhwan, cosmopolitan Kuwaiti women in the London-based Free Kuwait Campaign, wearing jeans and speaking their second and third languages with idiomatic fluency, were enormously attractive to media consumers in Europe and the US. They conveyed the impression that occupied Kuwait was more 'like us' than occupier Iraq (Tétreault 1995). Sadly, the women whose lights had shone so brightly during the occupation found themselves targets in post-occupation Kuwait.

Male Kuwaiti professors who had trained or taught in their host countries also were effective PR activists. Political scientists Shafeeq Ghabra and Saif Abbas Abdulla were especially articulate, analytical, and highly persuasive before US television and radio audiences.

Opposition activists used the occupation to exploit opportunities they had been denied in pre-invasion Kuwait. Supported by pressures from friendly governments interested in rolling back the invasion, opposition activists lobbied the Kuwaiti regime to reinvent itself as the democratic alternative to Iraq. With PR activists, they formed grassroots organizations like the British-based Free Kuwait Association and the Washington-based Citizens for a Free Kuwait, both of which demonstrated exile ability to organize effectively. Their growing prominence pushed the government to take over activist organizations, and to make 'a show of national solidarity' by calling huge mass meetings of Kuwaitis in Jiddah in October 1990 and January 1991 (Viorst 1994: 262). While these meetings acknowledged the desire of Kuwaitis to participate directly in their government and their liberation, they did not confer any authority to do so. Even so, activist exiles came home exhilarated and empowered by their effectiveness in helping to restore their country, and returned ready to claim what they saw as their rightful, prominent place in Kuwaiti political life.

Refugee exiles constitute the residuum. Refugees fled or remained outside throughout the occupation because it was the best alternative for them personally. Some continued their education and prepared for careers overseas; others lived off host hospitality and home-government largesse. The five-star lifestyle was not all it appeared to be from inside, however. Kuwaiti refugees were less optimistic about liberation than their activist counterparts, perhaps because their passivity made them feel helpless. Even people who had gone abroad voluntarily for vacation or study prior to the invasion dreaded spending the rest of their lives in exile, not merely because their standard of living was likely to fall if Iraq were to remain in control of Kuwait but also because their exile status had confronted them with shocking evidence of just how 'Kuwaiti' they actually were. 'Didn't you ever notice how men flip [arrange and rearrange] their *kaffiyas*? They do it differently in Kuwait from how they do in the Emirates or Bahrain. You can always tell they are Kuwaitis by how they do this' (interview in Kuwait, March 1994). Marked by their Kuwaiti accents, their discrepant mannerisms, and their alien status, Kuwaiti refugees in the Gulf were humiliated and haunted by the prospect of permanent involuntary separation from Kuwaiti society.

The diaspora comes home

The diaspora returning after liberation was not uniform. Most diasporans felt some degree of guilt for having escaped the hardships and dangers of occupation, especially those who had not been activists (Muqahawe 1992). Refugee exiles faced shame for their self-centredness. Returning to occupied Kuwait had been possible, easy, and sought by Kuwaiti insiders. Many Kuwaitis knew that adults who had stayed away had done so by choice, even though most non-Kuwaitis were oblivious to the ease with which Kuwaitis could come and go – or come and stay – throughout the occupation.

Diaspora men who had witnessed the unexpected and perhaps undesired public successes of diaspora women were unpleasantly surprised to return to a society in which women had played prominent roles in the resistance (al-Mughni 2001). Many devoted themselves to re-establishing masculine dominance in post-liberation Kuwait society.

The rulers also suffered from masculinity crises. Returning meant confronting a domestic society that had suffered hardships when they had fled before the occupiers to languish in luxury hotels. Their knowledge of the occupation came from CNN broadcasts and insiders who travelled to Taif to collect money for resistance activities. Their 'one-down' position was aggravated by having had to make concessions to opposition activists to demonstrate their democratic credentials, and by unfavourable comparisons to re-entry activists who had worked furiously in exile and, unlike the rulers, returned at the first opportunity to a country that was wrecked, bombed, mined and on fire.

The insider community of memory

The masculinity crises experienced by refugees and rulers were amplified by the heroism of insider-activist women and the self-effacing survival strategies of insider-activist men. Insider women were favoured as resistance activists by the masculinist gender ideology Iraqis shared with Kuwaitis. Although they soon learned to mistrust and abuse Kuwaiti women and to torture and kill resistance activists of both sexes, Iraqis were less likely to stop and search women than men (Akbar 1992; Levins 1997; al-Mughni, personal communication). Foreclosed from conventionally masculine activities that would have brought them into direct confrontation with the occupiers, male insider activists took satisfaction from successfully adapting such 'feminine' strategies as ridicule, trickery, and self-sacrifice to keep their communities alive and intact. Any activity tainted with resistance was risky.

I took another occupation. I became the imam in the mosque. It was very
risky, especially for Friday prayers. You have to give a speech and you have
to be careful. I didn't know how but I did it. I had to act brave and it taught
me something. Even in the last days, when people were rounded up in the
streets, I kept going.

(Bu Yabes 1992)

Mubarak al-Nout was the director of the al-Ardiyah Cooperative Society and
a friend of mine ... I was with a friend trying to get the cooperative to help
handicapped people whose homes are near the society. I saw him keep Iraqi
soldiers from entering the society without a permit ... [After he was arrested]
he was brought to the parking lot of the cooperative and was shot in the head
in front of everybody.

(al-Najjar 1999)

The primary identity of insiders, men and women, was defined in terms of
loyalty to Kuwait as a community of memory and belonging.

We did not leave. We didn't want to sit and beg. I would rather die here, in
front of my house, with my family, than go outside and beg... This is our
place and we can't be anywhere else... Kuwaitis have to wake every morning [and face who they are]. No Kuwaiti cooperated with the occupier.

(al-Wazzan 1992)

How can you have a country where people desert?... These types of people,
I can't depend on them. [My family and] I moved back to Kuwait City to stay
with my folks. In our [city] neighbourhood we had 21 houses. Only one
house was empty.

(Bu Yabes 1992)

Yet it would be incorrect to believe that all Kuwaiti insiders were brave and
resourceful. Like their exile brethren, some insiders were passive, frightened
people. Many such were children, terrified by the dangers to themselves and their
families. Insider extended families organized child care along with their other
tasks, but could not protect their children from sensing the pervasive insecurity
surrounding them all (Haya al-Mughni, personal communication).

Yet, despite their fears, Kuwaiti insiders had learned that they could take
care of themselves under terrible circumstances. Foreigners, Kuwaitis and
bidun – stateless Arabs living in Kuwait – relied on one another for food, community services, information and moral support. When Kuwait was liberated,
insiders were eager to roll up their sleeves and build a new Kuwait, one that
would be less materialistic, less reliant on foreign labour and less subservient
to autocratic rulers. While it survived, this ethic served as a reproach and a
threat to many returning exiles, and reinforced their desire to assert themselves
against insiders.

Divided communities of memory

The post-liberation moral economy was quickly appropriated by exiles. The physical devastation of the country, including more than 700 oil-well fires set by retreating Iraqi troops and the refusal of the ruling family to use resistance networks for food distribution, dictated dependence on re-entry exiles and foreign contractors. PR exiles, convinced that their efforts had been integral to the liberation, expected to resume their former prominence on their return. Refugee exiles, spurred by guilt and fear, sought to assert their authority. Their most energetic challengers were opposition exiles expecting to claim what had been promised at the Jiddah meetings. Having piggybacked their occupation demands on those of coalition governments, opposition exiles continued to use external pressure for democratization after liberation while the returning rulers, who controlled the money, cemented their alliances with refugee exiles through transfer payments.

Insiders were challenged by exiles whose memories of the invasion and occupation were so different from theirs. Suddenly the people lauded in a government publication as 'a giant the enemy did not reckon with' (Khalifouh and Abdul-Moa'ti 1994) found their networks ignored or undermined and themselves relegated to secondary status. Insider demoralization was complicated by exhaustion, post-traumatic stress and reactions to the torture, kidnappings and killings they had witnessed and/or experienced. Insiders had a harder time than exiles putting their lives back together, and they were especially unprepared for the methods exiles used to gain the upper hand.

> Before the invasion there was no equality among the Kuwaiti people regarding their loyalty to the country. They were not equal in front of the law. But during the invasion we experienced equality and the true spirit of liberation… When Saddam Hussein came, he treated us equally. He did not kill Shi'a or Sunna: he killed Kuwaitis… After the liberation I was shocked at how Kuwaitis hated other Kuwaiti men.
>
> (al-Hashem 1992)

The most dangerous and, thankfully, short-lived repression of insiders came from vigilante action and martial law (Tétreault 1992: 7). Virtually all Palestinian nationals residing in Kuwait were expelled, including those with unimpeachable resistance credentials, and *bidun* were prohibited from returning. A stated aim of martial law was to disarm insiders suspected of being fifth columnists and potential leaders of insurrection. Insiders were beaten and some were killed. A vigilante group assaulted Hamad al-Jouan, a member of the suspended 1985 parliament, leaving him a paraplegic. How many and who else had been targeted during this time is unclear. The memories of insiders especially are confused (interviews 1992–2003).

Exiles also used rumours against insiders. During the occupation, the government PR machine had ground out story after story of Kuwaiti women being raped by

Iraqi soldiers to mobilize support for rollback. Kuwaiti insiders watched television news that alleged widespread rape in occupied Kuwait. These programmes were frightening even though the insider community remained closely connected by telephone and through regular attendance at mosques, and almost no one I interviewed knew a rape victim personally or even by hearsay (Tétreault 2003). A deeper injury from the allegations of rape came after liberation, when a whispering campaign accused every Kuwaiti insider family of harbouring at least one raped woman, an insult to family honour and one difficult to confront or erase (interviews in Kuwait October 1992).

Other rumours mocked merchant insiders whose cash and goods had supported insiders and provided bribes to Iraqi officers and soldiers to minimize the hardship of occupation on the population (Porter 1991; al-Wazzan 1992). Outsider stories insisted that the ruling family was the source of these financial resources, but only one of many insiders I interviewed told of any funding coming from outside. Post-war disputes over the source of the money launched a cascade of rumours. Merchant insiders and their agents were accused of profiteering or outright stealing. Merchants' insider roles were belittled by tales of how they had stayed behind not to defend their country or their fellow citizens but to protect their assets.

Grand narratives of the occupation produced by former exiles also were used against insiders. Some were state-generated 'atrocity vignettes' (Tétreault 2000: 93). These were short subjects, like commercials, broadcast between programmes on government-owned television stations. They depicted graphic scenes of terror and violence during the occupation, each of which featured images of passive, victimized insiders and reminders that they had been rescued by strong, autonomous outsiders.

The resistance especially was devalued. Everyone commented on how clever the 'kids' had been to paint over street signs so the occupiers wouldn't know where they were. Stories about adult resistance activities were recounted by activist exiles, but I heard none from refugees. A few resistance women were lauded publicly, such as Kuwait Oil Company petroleum engineer Sara Akbar, who managed to save KOC's well-logging data by smuggling the information out of company premises and concealing it beneath a false bottom in a bedroom wardrobe. Sara's participation as a member of the post-liberation Kuwaiti firefighting team is rarely mentioned (Tétreault 1995). For the most part, the resistance figures honoured most widely after liberation were dead. A Martyr's Office was established in the Amiri Diwan but, despite popular demand, it did not publish a list of martyrs. Some Kuwaitis put up street signs honouring particular individuals but martyrs, like POWs, remained a contentious topic.

In March of 1992, the Kuwaiti government gave information to the Red Cross about 850 persons, two-thirds of them Kuwaiti citizens, who had neither been released nor whose remains had been returned during the post-war repatriation programme (ICRC 1993). The Iraqi government insisted that all prisoners and remains had been returned (Iraq 1998), although some of the bodies uncovered in mass graves discovered following Saddam's ouster have proven to belong to POWs. The Kuwaiti government did little on behalf of the POWs (Middle East Watch 1993). Indeed, the information that had been forwarded to the ICRC came from two Kuwaiti voluntary associations. Their members had conducted the background investigations and obtained information from interviews with prisoners in Iraq that provided the estimates of the last date a POW had been seen alive. In spite of such actions, the government refused to license most Kuwaiti human rights organizations. It was unwilling to confer legitimacy on the activities of autonomous groups able to command independent international channels of communication (Hicks and al-Najjar 1995; Middle East Watch 1993; al-Najjar 1999).

Reasserting masculinities

Kuwaitis found reintegration difficult despite the relative coherence and short lifespan of the occupation-induced diaspora. Some of this can be explained by pre-existing social cleavages: most activists, insiders and exiles, had been prominent in pre-war Kuwait. Most refugees had not. Reinforcing the status cleavage was the need of refugee exiles to resolve masculinity crises. These crises were triggered by guilt and shame at having fled or remained outside, and deepened by the prominence accorded to male activist exiles, evidence of masculine cooperative egalitarianism inside, and female autonomy and leadership inside and out. Wresting control of historical memory became part of their project to reunite the Kuwaiti nation on the basis of their preferred historical narratives.

In post-liberation Kuwait, refugees commanded superior resources. Government refugees held the purse strings and quickly re-established the dependency between citizens and the state that underpinned the legitimacy of their rule. Resistance networks were spurned in favour of government-controlled, administered and financed agencies, even though these were so poorly managed initially that Kuwaitis suffered severe hardships, while re-entry supplies, including materials needed by firefighters, were held up by a single gatekeeper doing business over one fax machine (Tétreault 1995: 140–1).

Martial law and vigilantism also bolstered the masculinity of the refugees. Palestinians and *bidun* bore the brunt of beatings, kidnapping and detentions, but Kuwaitis also were targeted. Although insiders remember Kuwaiti loyalty, the government did not rest until it had identified a handful of quislings, marginal individuals more vulnerable to Iraqi pressure than insider activists who had personal resources and strong networks to sustain them. The 'discovery' of internal traitors helped justify the reversal of the moral hierarchy between exiles and insiders.

Scapegoating drove wedges between activists who might have been expected to show solidarity in the face of renewed government oppression. A prominent opposition exile, Ahmad al-Khatib, was falsely accused of having betrayed Kuwait in statements he was reported to have made during a television interview. Ahmad refuted the charges and won election to parliament in 1992, but few of his political allies were so fortunate. His political group faded steadily over the next decade, withered by the incessant production of counter-narratives with Islamist heroes that shaped the historical memories passed on to the rising generation (interviews in Kuwait 2003).

The most vigorous reassertions of masculinity came from the ruling family. Having been pressured from inside and out to call elections and resume constitutional governance, the regime also resumed interfering in elections. In 1992, these efforts were less successful than anticipated – I interviewed a member of the ruling family who complained bitterly at the dishonesty of voters who had not voted for the candidates they had been paid to support. The rulers were more effective at resisting the constitutional cancellation of decrees published during the parliamentary interregnum. Some limited freedom of the press and one established a Potemkin court to try government ministers accused of crimes (Tétreault 1995, 2000).

That masculinity crises drew battle lines in the struggle to legitimate a historical memory of the occupation favourable to refugees is most evident in narratives about Kuwaiti women. Despite the prominence of a few Kuwaiti women in the Western media, most wartime female activism had taken place inside Kuwait. Exile domination of post-liberation reintegration of Kuwaiti historical memory let women's contributions to liberation slide rapidly from view, along with the sacrifices of other groups – 'liberals', Shi'a and Palestinians – deeply involved in resistance activities. In contrast, the roles that Islamists had played during the occupation were parlayed into political power; indeed, Islamism became a floating signifier powerful enough to capture seats in post-liberation parliaments for refugee candidates (Tétreault 2000).

For 13 years, Kuwaiti feminists endured an intense campaign by post-liberation parliaments to restrict women's autonomy and rights. It was spearheaded by tribalists – that is, people who base their political identities on their tribal affiliation – and Sunni movement Islamists. Expectations that women would be recognized for their contributions during the occupation by allowing them to vote and run for parliament were dashed when the amir remained silent on the subject before the 1992 election. Meanwhile, the tribalist-Islamist coalition lowered the retirement age for women and imposed gender segregation at the university. Following the early dismissal of the 1996 parliament in May of 1999, the amir finally acted, issuing a short-lived interim decree conferring full political rights on Kuwaiti women, but it took six more years, reactions to Islamist violence, and a clever parliamentary manoeuvre to get this measure enacted into law in May of 2005 (Tétreault 2005).

Coming home?

The Kuwaiti example illustrates the advantages enjoyed by diasporans in shaping historical memory for insiders and exiles. Kuwaiti exiles projected a story of rape and victimization not only to themselves and the world, but also to Kuwaitis under occupation, challenging contemporary perceptions as well as post-conflict memories and providing a point of leverage enabling returning exiles to undermine insider accounts of heroic behaviour. Their biggest advantage was that the leaders of the regime were exiles, and as interested as refugees in status rehabilitation. Government control of programming on state television, along with its authority to loosen the strings of a purse that while depleted, was far from empty, allowed the rulers to propagate narratives and build alliances that worked to the exiles' advantage. Although exile stories of the occupation were tarnished by the false testimony before the US Congress and its repercussions all over the world, the tarnish stuck as readily to insiders as to exiles, and diminished the credibility of truthful insider accounts of Kuwaiti life under Iraqi occupation.

The Kuwaiti case can be compared to a different diasporic experience, one that some argue is marked by a lack of interest in reunion on any basis with the population of a new nation-state homeland. The Armenian diaspora sits oddly with the images of other diasporic populations. In its unique adaptation to the trauma of genocide and dispersion, the Armenian diaspora is united by its Armenian-ness, and has generated both a rich collective culture and strong attachments to local cultures in host communities. Unlike diasporan Kuwaitis, Iraqis and Iranians, diasporic Armenia's adaptation as a divided community of memory excludes reunification with a contemporary Armenian state so different from the idealized Armenia enshrined in its historical memory (Brannen 2004).

Diasporas by their nature generate divided communities of memory. Separation ensures experiences of trauma and loss necessarily different from and occasion-ally antagonistic towards one another. Reuniting divided communities of memory is a contentious process. Even a diasporan experience as coherent, compact, and short-lived as Kuwait's resulted in a bitter and violent reunification whose effects continue to ramify. The Armenian diaspora suggests a different mode of recon-ciliation, one that creates separate communities with parallel lives. But the Armenian experience is anomalous; it depends on an 'utter loss' of hope for reunification in the homeland. For the majority of exiles, however, the history of diasporas is a history of odysseys: most diasporas do come home.

References

Abu Gulal, S. (2002) 'UN Economic Sanctions and Iraq: A Critical Analysis of a Failed Policy', *Durham Middle East Paper* No. 69, Durham UK: Institute for Middle Eastern and Islamic Studies, April.

Afkhami, M. (ed.) (1995) *Faith and Freedom: Women's Human Rights in the Muslim World*, Syracuse: Syracuse University Press.

Ahmed, L. (1992) *Women and Gender in Islam*, New Haven: Yale University Press.

Akbar, S. (1992) Interviews in Kuwait, October (petroleum engineer, Kuwait Oil Company).

Al-Hashem, S. (1992) Interview in Kuwait, October (attorney and candidate for parliament in the 1992 election).

Al-Mousa, M. (1991) Interview in London, March (public relations employee, Kuwait Petroleum International, London).

Al-Mughni, H. (2001) *Women in Kuwait: The Politics of Gender*, rev. edn, London: Al-Saqi Books.

Al-Muhanna, Dr M. (1992) Interview in Kuwait, October (veterinarian and campaign advisor to Abbas Khodary in the 1992 parliamentary election).

Al-Najjar, G. (1999) Interview in Cambridge, MA, May (Kuwaiti university professor, human rights activist, UN rapporteur for Somalia).

—— (2001) 'Human Rights in a Crisis Situation: The Case of Kuwait after Occupation', *Human Rights Quarterly* 23: 188–209.

Al-Wazzan, A. (1992) Interviews in Kuwait, October (merchant; later Minister of Labour and Commerce).

Anderson, B. (1991) *Imagined Communities: Reflections on the Origins and Spread of Nationalism*, rev. edn, London: Verso.

Bahrampour, Tara. 2003. 'Persia on the Pacific.' *New Yorker.* 10 November: 52–58, 60.

Blight, D. W. (2001) *Race and Reunion: The Civil War in American Memory*, Cambridge, MA: Belknap Press.

Brannen, S. (2004) 'Diasporic Armenian Nationalism and the 1915 Genocide: The Implications of Memory and Metaphorical Space in Nationalist Ideology', paper presented at the annual meeting of the International Studies Association, Montreal, 17–20 March.

Buhamrah, Khaled, then-deputy managing director of the Kuwait National Petroleum Corporation. 1992. Interview in Kuwait.

Bu Yabes, E. (1992) Interview in Kuwait, October (petroleum engineer, Kuwait Oil Company; chief of the Kuwaiti firefighting team).

Cole, Juan R. I. 2004. 'U.S. Mistakes in Iraq.' Testimony before the Senate Committee on Foreign Relations. 20 April. Gulf2000 Archive.

Crane, C. C. and Terrill, W. A. (2003) 'Reconstructing Iraq: Insights, Challenges, and Missions for Military Forces in a Post-Conflict Scenario', Carlisle, PA: U.S. Army War College Strategic Studies Institute, February.

Dauenhauer, K. and Lobe, J. (2003) 'Massive military contractor's media mess', InterPressService, Gulf 2000 Archives (accessed 25 April 2004).

Drogin, B. (2003) 'U.S. Suspects It Received False Iraq Arms Tips', *Los Angeles Times*, 28 August, Gulf 2000 Archives.

Fallows, J. (2004) 'Blind into Baghdad', *Atlantic*, January/February: 52–4, 56–8, 60, 62–6, 68–70, 72–4.

Finkelstein, I. and Silberman, N. A. (2001) *The Bible Unearthed: Archaeology's New Vision of Ancient Israel and the Origin of its Sacred Texts*, New York: Free Press.

Fromkin, D. (1989) *A Peace to End All Peace: The Fall of the Ottoman Empire and the Creation of the Modern Middle East*, New York: Avon Books.

Greenfeld, L. (1992) *Nationalism: Five Roads to Modernity*, Cambridge, MA: Harvard University Press.

Habermas, J. (1973) *Legitimation Crisis*, trans. Thomas McCarthy, Boston: Beacon Press.

—— (1991) *The Structural Transformation of the Public Sphere: An Inquiry into a Category of Bourgeois Society*, trans. Thomas Burger with the assistance of Frederick Lawrence, Cambridge, MA: MIT Press.

Hersh, S. (2003) 'The Stovepipe', *New Yorker*, 27 October: 76–82, 84–7.

Hicks, N. and Al-Najjar, G. (1995) 'The Utility of Tradition: Civil Society in Kuwait', in Augustus Richard Norton (ed.) *Civil Society in the Middle East*, Leiden: E. J. Brill: pp. 186–213.

ICRC (1993) Message of the ICRC to the President of the I.P.O. (27 April). Online. Available HTTP: http://i_p_o.org/kuwaiti_missing_icrc.htm (accessed 9 April 2004).

Iraqi Government (1998) 'Iraq's Position on the Issue of the Kuwaiti Missing in Action'. May. Online. Available HTTP: http://www.meij.or.jp/text/Gulf%20War/KuwaitiPOW 05001998.htm (accessed 9 April 2004).

Juergensmeyer, M. (1994) *The New Cold War? Religious Nationalism Confronts the Secular State*, Berkeley: University of California Press.

Kaufman, S. J. (2001) *Modern Hatreds: The Symbolic Politics of Ethnic War*, Ithaca, NY: Cornell University Press.

—— (2004) 'Historical Memory and Symbolic Politics in the Palestinian-Israeli Dispute', paper presented at the annual meeting of the International Studies Association, Montréal, 17–20 March.

Khalifouh, A. A. and Abdul-Moa'ti, Y. (1994) *Kuwaiti Resistance as Revealed by Iraqi Documents*, Mansouria, Kuwait: Center for Research and Studies on Kuwait.

Levins, J. (1997) *Days of Fear: The Inside Story of the Iraqi Invasion and Occupation of Kuwait*, Dubai: Motivate Publishing.

Longva, A. N. (2000) 'Citizenship in the Gulf States: Conceptualization and Practice', in N. A. Butenschøn, U. Davis and M. Hassassian (eds) *Citizenship and the State in the Middle East: Approaches and Applications*, Syracuse: Syracuse University Press: pp. 179–97.

Mernissi, F. (1987) *The Veil and the Male Elite: A Feminist Interpretation of Women's Rights in Islam*, trans. Mary Jo Lakeland, Reading, MA: Addison-Wesley.

Middle East Watch (1993) 'Kuwait Closes all Human Rights Organizations', September.

Muhawesh, O. A. (1990) *Fatima the Gracious*, Qom: Anssarian Publications.

Muqahawe, Dr B. (1992) Interview in Kuwait, October (clinical psychologist employed at the state psychiatric hospital; human rights activist).

Nafisy, H. (1993) 'From Broadcasting to Narrowcasting: Middle Eastern Diaspora in Los Angeles', *Middle East Report*, January–February: 32.

Ong, A. (1998) *Flexible Citizenship: The Cultural Logics of Transnationality*, Durham, NC: Duke University Press.

Porter, J. (1991) *Under Siege in Kuwait: A Survivor's Story*, Boston: Houghton Mifflin.

Rajab, J. S. (1996) *Invasion Kuwait: An English Woman's Tale*, London: Radcliffe Press.

Ranchod-Nilsson, S. (2004) 'The Global Indian Family: India's Efforts to Connect with her Diaspora', Public lecture at Trinity University, San Antonio, 29 March.

Sandweiss, M. A. (2004) 'Death on the Front Page', *New York Times*, 4 April: WK 13.

Slyomovics, S. (1998) *The Object of Memory: Arab and Jew Narrate the Palestinian Village*, Philadelphia: University of Pennsylvania Press.

Spellberg, D. A. (1994) *Politics, Gender, and the Islamic Past: The Legacy of 'A'isha bint Abi Bakr*, New York: Columbia University Press.

Terrill, W. A. (2003) 'Nationalism, Sectarianism, and the Future of the US Presence in Post-Saddam Iraq', Carlisle PA: U.S. Army War College Strategic Studies Institute, July.

Tétreault, M. A. (1992) 'Kuwait: The Morning After', *Current History* 91, January: 6–10.

—— (1995) *The Kuwait Petroleum Corporation and the Economics of the New World Order*, Westport, CT: Quorum Books.

—— (2000) *Stories of Democracy: Politics and Society in Contemporary Kuwait*, New York: Columbia University Press.

—— (2003) 'In Search of Justice: Wartime Rape and Human Rights', in Mary Ann Tétreault and Robin L. Teske (eds) *Partial Truths and the Politics of Community*, Columbia: University of South Carolina Press: pp. 285–312.

—— (2004) 'Contending Fundamentalisms: Religious Revival and the Modern World', in Mary Ann Tétreault and Robert A. Denemark (eds) *The International Political Economy Yearbook*, Vol. 13, *Guns, Gods, and Globalization: Religious Resurgence and International Political Economy*, Boulder: Lynne Rienner: pp. 1–30.

Tétreault, Mary Ann and Robert A. Denemark, ed. 2004. Gods, Guns, and Globalization: Religious Resurgence and International Political Economy. Boulder: Lynne Rienner.

Tétreault, M. A. (2005) 'New Spaces for Old Politics: Bottom-up Democratization in Kuwait', paper prepared for presentation at the annual meeting of the Middle Eastern Studies Association, Washington DC, November.

Viorst, M. (1994) *Sandcastles: The Arabs in Search of the Modern World*, New York: Knopf.

Wheeler, D. (2000) 'New Media, Globalization and Kuwaiti National Identity', *Middle East Journal* 54(3), Summer: 432–44.

Wolf, E. R. (1999) *Envisioning Power: Ideologies of Dominance and Crisis*, Berkeley: University of California Press.

7 'Our' reflections in 'their' mirror: Cultural politics and the representation of the Iranian diaspora in the Islamic Republic

Hammed Shahidian

In the autumn of 1993, the heart of a much-loved aunt of mine stopped beating. Like many Iranian women, she managed her family and sustained its social status in their community. She was intelligent, skilful and sociable. Those who knew her respected her charismatic presence and enjoyed her company. Even when her husband was alive, she assumed the role of family representative. I last saw her 15 years before her death, shortly before I left Iran. Her memory is forever associated in my mind with all things beautiful, so I remember her jovial presence, her beautiful face, her bright-red lipstick and her sweet fragrance. And so I wrote about her in a eulogy. The eulogy took some family members by surprise, not because of what I wrote, but merely because I have entertained such memories and warm feelings after so many years of living in *qorbat*, a foreign land, and distanced from friends and families.

As I prepared to write these pages, I kept thinking about the reaction to my eulogy. I was, of course, honoured that my relatives bestowed upon me the task of commemorating such an outstanding woman, but I was also perplexed by their reaction. I thought about the ties that linked my family and me, thousands of miles apart. For me, it was – is – a matter of fact that I cherish their memories. For them, it was a surprising discovery that I did. Yet it was also an expected performance, or duty, of mine as a family member and a writer to prepare the eulogy. That expectation and that reaction best demonstrate the contradictory positions that Iranians abroad occupy in the minds of their compatriots still living in Iran. How are we, I thought – those living outside Iran – reflected in the minds of those who live in Iran? What factors influence their understanding, and often judgement, of our lives? To what extent are their memories products of post-revolutionary politico-cultural developments?

The representation of the diaspora

Two major forces constitute the context for the representation of exiles in Iran: the state and the oppositional current. The Islamic state can directly and indirectly define the acceptable frame of representation based on official stands on the diasporas. The manner in which Iranians abroad are presented to the public is influenced by what the statesmen deem essential to control outbound and inbound population movement, the kind of challenge the exiles are perceived to pose for the regime and economic considerations, such as unemployment, the need for capital and skilled labour.

Yet the state's political influence does not end there. The strict cultural policies of the Islamic state both produce the official version of the story and set for others the parameters of acceptable representation. The 'independent' cultural industry produces fluctuating, if not contradictory, impressions of the populace abroad; it has to survive under censorship and governmental watch. (By 'independent' I mean only not affiliated with the state; speaking of being 'independent' under official censorship is rather bizarre.) These literary products reflect dominant values and ideas, such as the East–West dichotomy, nationality and gender relations, but they also contain revisionist scrutiny about past practices and offer new solutions.

Both official and unofficial accounts deny the diaspora a voice. The representation of the diaspora is predominantly a monologue. The diaspora appears as a patient in a coma, as *Sorraya in a Coma*, the title of a popular novel about Iranian expatriates, suggests. The diaspora are talked about and talked to, but they are rarely a party to the conversation.

In 1991, the Iranian authorities confiscated a special issue of the monthly *Adineh*. The issue contained a series of autobiographical accounts by a number of exiled writers and artists describing their achievements during ten years of exile (Momeni 1995: 85). My own review of Tolo'i's *Illusory Paradise* was denied permission for publication in a monthly (Shahidian 1992); the editor informed me that the authorities did not favour my ideas. But Mehrdad Darvishpour, an exiled Iranian activist and author, was not so lucky. He submitted an article about divorce among Iranian immigrants to *Donyâye Sokhan*. His article was never published in its original form and under his name. Fragments of it, however, appeared in a sensationalist account of the topic (*Donyâye Sokhan* 1993). His objection was also denied publication and Darvishpour (1993) finally had to publish the letter in Europe to set the record straight. As I am writing these words, an invitation is circulating by guest editors of *Bâyâ*, a literary monthly, for submissions by and about the Iranian diaspora. The success of this project is to be seen.

Two other commonalities stand out in these renditions of the diaspora. First, they share an overemphasis on alienation in the 'foreign land', as if the diaspora were integrated and felt 'at home' prior to migration. Second, the diversity of the diaspora in terms of nationality, religion (Baha'is and their horrendous persecution are particularly left out), age and sexual orientation[1] are completely overlooked, except for class and gender.

Class distinction is recognized to emphasize the disparity between the haves and have-nots among the diaspora, the alienation of the former from the realities of the majority of Iranians, and the futility of the latter's search for the mirage of exile. Women are made visible for the role they purportedly play in preserving the purity and continuity of 'the Iranian cultural heritage' and the perils of diasporic life with regards to fulfilling such a task. The rest of the Iranian diaspora are treated as if they form a block.

Exile as a legitimation of challenge

Iranians migrate to many countries around the world, but it is mostly those who go to Europe and North America who have been the foci of the migration controversy. For example, the migration of Iranian human resources to Japan is officially considered 'economically beneficial' (Râzi 1991). But immigrants to Western nations numerically constitute a sizeable population compared to others and attract more attention as they challenge the legitimacy of the Islamic regime. First, the majority of the political opponents of the Islamic Republic of Iran (IRI) are among these groups. Moreover, they constitute a subversive group that shatters the desire of at least one tendency within the Iranian Islamic regime that is concerned with portraying an acceptable image in the West. The diaspora is then a seditious group embodying the IRI's failure on cultural, social and economic grounds.

Overall, the literature on the Iranian diaspora has had four explicit objectives:

- discrediting the exiles on social, political or cultural grounds;
- persuading those susceptible to the temptation of migration not to leave;
- convincing some immigrants to repatriate;
- presenting migration as a danger to the integrity of family, women and nation.

These themes have been present in most writings about Iranians abroad, though their ordering has changed through time. Earlier reactions to immigrants and exiles primarily concentrated on discrediting this group as decadent counterrevolutionaries. Published in the 1980s, Esmail Fassih's *Sorraya in a Coma* represents this trend. Though this theme has not been abandoned altogether, other objectives have taken priority in different periods. For example, Mahmoud Tolo'i's *Illusory Paradise*, published in the early 1990s, admits there are different groups among Iranians abroad, but that differentiation is kept blurry to emphasize the futility of migration.

I divide the reflections of the diaspora inside Iranian media and popular culture into three different periods:

- immediately after the revolution until the end of the Iran–Iraq war, when the diasporas were exclusively portrayed as decadent royalists;
- the postwar period, when calls for economic renovations inspired new discussions about post-revolutionary migrations as infantile mistakes;
- the late 1990s, when hopes for reforms in the regime further increased the need for a positive interpretation of the diasporic experience.

Diaspora as decadent

Fassih's *Sorraya in a Coma* was published in the early 1980s and remained a best-seller for several years. In the novel, Jalal Aryan goes to Paris shortly after the outbreak of the Iran–Iraq war to visit his niece Sorraya, who lies in a coma following an accident. We learn little about her in the book. Aryan is informed in

France that his niece has a slim chance for survival. While awaiting a change in Sorraya's condition, he socializes with Iranian acquaintances and a former lover, Leila Azadeh. Aryan's encounter with Iranian expatriates becomes the central theme of the book.

The diaspora of Fassih's book are mainly the royalists and former high officials of the Shah's government. We are also introduced to a number of other characters who lead a shallow and empty life, a poor imitation of Hemingway's 'lost generation' (Nafisi 1984). This group is counterpoised against a devout Hezbollah. Ghassem Yazdani is everything that the exiled opposition is not: spiritual, dedicated, humble, chaste, family-oriented, faithful and righteous (Fassih 1985, especially 170–8).

Reviews of *Sorraya in a Coma* published abroad objected to this classification of refugees (Shayesteh 1988). It is noteworthy, for instance, that the movement of Iranian students in the West against the regime was strong at the time.[2] Activists brought to public attention the atrocities committed against workers, peasants, women, national minorities, students and the intelligentsia. They opposed the Iran–Iraq war and solicited international support for secular, democratic and leftist opponents of the Islamic regime. None of these efforts is reflected in Fassih's book.

Diaspora as the children of Iran

In the postwar years, especially after the early 1990s, the representation of Iranians abroad underwent some changes. Different groupings among the diaspora were recognized. They were presented primarily as people who had left Iran due to the hardships of revolution and war, yet were still burning with patriotism and willing to return to serve their country. The documentary *Sarâb* (The Mirage), which aired on Iranian national television during the autumn of 1990, portrayed Iranians, especially youths, as having left Iran for the West principally for flimsy reasons such as driving fast cars or going on shopping sprees.[3] Smugglers are reported taking advantage of young men and women. Some deceived souls, the producers of *Sarâb* argued, eventually returned home addicted, penniless and corrupt, while some never made it back alive. The intended audiences were middle- and upper-class youths and their parents, and the message was loud and clear: those who leave Iran have a tragic future – do not follow in their footsteps.

Migration was analysed in the context of social shortcomings and mismanagement. In a society where the majority of the population is under 30 (Mirbâqeri 1993), frustrating conditions for youths could not escape attention. According to one commentator, a young population required jobs, entertainment and room for self-expression (Golbâf 1995a: 5). Toosi Tabâtabâ'i (1980) described how her oldest daughter had to leave the country because she was denied entry to a university following a background check. A few years later, the family was informed that officials had made a mistake and their daughter could start her college education.

The monthly *Gozâresh* included a report on Iranian immigrants' contribution to the American economy (Golbâf 1995b). There was also a shift in governmental approach to immigrants that could also be detected in public discourses. The primary targets of the IRI's repatriation efforts were specialists and, more importantly, investors. An editorial in *Gozâresh* used the analogy of a family to further emphasize this mollifying approach:

> Iranians abroad – excluding those guilty of treason or killing their fellow Iranians – should be considered as children who for minor or major reasons have run away from home and are not on speaking terms with their families. The passage of time has, on the one hand, awakened remorse in these run-away children and, on the other, transformed parents' anger into kindness. All we need now is a mediator to return these children who ran away from the kind bosom of the family to its midst.
>
> (Golbâf 1995b: 5)

There is a marked difference between the picture of the diaspora in analyses of the sort presented above and those of the early 1980s. These later analyses favoured silencing political grievances and emphasized potential roles that Iranians abroad could play in the development of Iran. Despite its conciliatory message, the new discourse was extremely paternalistic. Iranian society and government appear as benevolent parents who should protect their runaway children. The use of words like honour (*nâmoos*) and motherland (*mâm-e mihan*) and the analogy of family also implicitly points to the intersection of nationality with femininity and men's protection of feminine integrity. Considering that women's concerns are muted in these calls, one can assume that the invitations are exclusively addressed to the male diaspora, as professionals and investors, who would then bring along 'their wives and children' – like their other belongings.

Diaspora as surplus or contrite

The representation of the diaspora during the late 1990s and early 2000s share the general characteristics of the preceding period. Those closer to the so-called hard-liners dismiss the significance of Iranians abroad, while others opting for some change favour the resources expatriates can provide. The director of the National Testing Centre, for instance, concedes that 'migration is a prevalent inclination among students'. But he dismissively continues to say that if our educated people wish to leave, let them. 'We must not be worried about losing a bunch of our elite population, because we have so many educated people. So many, indeed, that we are not able to absorb them into the labour force' (*Hayâte* No. 1, January 2002: 11).

A university professor, however, warns that after the bloody attack on university dormitories in the summer of 1999, some 30 per cent of professors requested unpaid leave of absence to travel abroad (*Hayâte* No. 1, January 2002: 11). Other observers are also concerned about the financial aspect of Iranians living abroad. The financial daily *Âsiâ* (6 April 2002) quotes the deputy of the High Council for Iranian Expatriates Affairs that some 2.5 million Iranians live outside Iranian boundaries, and estimates their wealth at some $455 billion – 20 times more than Iran's foreign currency income and equal to Iran's entire foreign currency surplus in 2001. These authors suggest that if the Iranian economy taps into this resource, some of its problems will be solved.

The diaspora's political role is also considered. One commentator suggests that since the constitution allots a representative for every 300,000 citizens, Iranians in the Unites States should have the right to elect a Majlis representative (*Payâm-e Âzâdi*, 20 February 2000). The suggestion sounds unconvincing. Yet we must consider the active role of the diaspora in controversies related to political developments in the homeland, as evident in the efforts in support of President Khatami and the reformist movement as well as in the role some expatriate scholars of women's rights have played in theorizing and promoting the reformist trend in the Iranian women's movement, also known as 'Islamic feminism'. (Both endeavours, I must add, are highly contentious among the diaspora, deepening existing splits and distrusts.)[4]

As people's tension increased with IRI suppression, some inside and outside the government envisioned ways to ease the pressure. The diaspora then became an example of how excessive pressure could alienate people from their government and society. Movies such as *Par-e Parvâz* (The Feather for Flying) have portrayed young people's frustration with constant pressure from both family and authorities. In novels such as in *Gandom*, we hear the voices of young, unemployed and depressed individuals who pronounce a scathing judgement on Iranian society. In *My Share*, Parinoush Sani'i (2004) writes of a teenager, the son of an executed political prisoner, who has to take refuge in Germany after his careerist uncle reports him as an anti-government activist, even though his political involvement was nothing beyond the curiosities of a teenager in the tumultuous times of the early 1980s. Confronted with the 'daily' surge of migration (Zabihiân and Mo'tazed 2002: 55–6), authors have acknowledged such issues as undue control of daily life or impositions on personal and political freedom.

Still, migration is defined as *darmândegi*, helplessness, and *âvâregi*, homelessness (Zabihiân and Mo'tazed 2002: 285). They present the diaspora as victims rather than active agents. It is true that earlier diasporic writings presented exile in a similar light (see, for instance, Sa'edi 1994). But speaking of exile as *âvâregi* in the writings of those days was intended more to single out the IRI as the cause of the unfair expulsion of a people from their land, not to portray the diaspora as helpless. Though nostalgia has remained an important motif in diasporic cultural productions (Naficy 1993), later exilic writings have emphasized the opportunities that accompany migration, especially for women and youth (see, for instance, Moghissi 1999b; Shahidian 2000; Ghorashi 2002). The nuances of diasporic lives are not visible in the mirror that is supposed to reflect us. This is a mirror that obfuscates factors leading to diaspora, as well as the changes in the diasporas' conception of 'home', 'hostland' and 'diasporic life'. The Iranian diaspora appear to have lived a life of monotonous absurdity.

Violence, the Islamic state and repatriation

The diaspora's repatriation, in the formal discourse of the regime, involves a passive process whereby a benevolent power absolves a remorseful loser. In the words of Zabihiân:

If in the strangeness (*qorbat*) of the West, everything revolves around materialism, jealousy, ruthlessness, and lack of feelings, in their [the diasporas'] homeland Islamic kindness awaits them with open arms. The springs of its absolution and compassion will cleanse every distressed heart from the dust of pains and disappointments.

(Zabihiân and Mo'tazed 2002: 224)

Many among the Iranian diaspora have a memory of home that is fundamentally different from Zabihiân's. The 'Islamic kindness' that most exiles experienced included daily harassment, purges, persecution, imprisonment, torture and mass executions, memories vividly recorded in diasporic accounts of their lives, and powerfully portrayed in *The Tree that Remembers*, a recent film directed by Masoud Raouf (2002). Though some Iranians abroad have visited home, many refuse to return, and still many more do not entertain any dream of 'home' as a merciful promised land of poetic streams of humanity and care. Women's recollections of home emphasize not only state violence in implementing Islamist gender policies, but also locate unjust, even violent, gender relationships in places that for most men are merely spheres of nostalgia. An exchange among a group of male and female workers in Germany demonstrates this point. A series of poems by male refugees remembered their common hometown, its restaurants, hangouts, regional dishes and various city personalities. Male 'poets' vied for a day when they could return to a home free from the Islamists. After several nostalgic exchanges, a female refugee intervened, reminding the men of the things women had endured in that 'city of ignorance'. She chastised male revolutionaries who did not protest when the Islamic court condemned 12 women to death by stoning. To her, that city is not the nest of euphoric memories of delicious food, friendly shopkeepers and welcoming streets; it is the cause of a nightmare.

Reducing the concerns of the diaspora to the IRI's restrictions on people's daily lives overlooks the broader picture of the Islamic state's violence and suppression. It presents extremism, especially the wrongdoing of some self-righteous individuals (Zabihiân and Mo'tazed 2002: 56), as the problem. In contrast, many among the exiles consider violence integral to the Islamic state, and individual zealots inseparable from the system that has given them power, tolerated their whims and incorporated their moral vigilantism into its apparatus.[5] There is a painstaking effort to minimize the political dimension of the diaspora. Casual references to 'those few political immigrants' (Golbâf 1995b: 5) misrepresent the exiles by not identifying them as such. Political 'immigrants', connoting a voluntary movement, is substituted for exiles, a group of people with legitimate political grievances who escaped the sickle of death.[6]

To appease the Islamic apparatus, these writers deal with state violence by disregarding crucial aspects of reality in order to manufacture a past unrecognizable to those who experienced those horrid days.[7] These accounts change the meaning of such events as the mass executions of the early 1980s and 1988 and years of political imprisonment, and alter historical memory.[8] Concealing violence in the shroud of silence in itself violates the dignity of survivors and victims of Islamist abuses.[9]

Crucial discrepancy about the meaning of 'home' aside, the power relationship suggested in the preceding excerpt from Zabihiân is also problematic for many exiles who do not find any reason in the history of their relationship with the Islamic state to trust that system. To these individuals, returning home depends not on the absolution of the Islamic state, but rather on their decision to deem the time appropriate for repatriation.

The West: 'Us' and 'Them'

Any assessment of Iranians abroad is also a critique of the West. The equation follows a simple logic: those who have left Iran constitute a 'Westoxicated'[10] segment of the Iranian population who primarily took refuge in the West, which accepted them as a propaganda tactic against the Islamic revolution. Yet most authors shied away from an explicit implication of Western countries in actively attracting Iranian compatriots. Zabihiân stands alone in this regard. To him, the refugee phenomenon is an attempt of the colonizing West to ease its economic hardship following the liberation of former colonies. Britain appears to play a leading role in this effort because 'the aging lion of colonialism' opts to compensate for its economic losses world over by attracting refugees to work as cheap labour (Zabihiân & Mo'tazed 2002: 167).

East and West are presented in the polar opposition of *farhang* and *zedd-e farhang*, culture and anti-culture, sacred and profane. According to a national sociology textbook for the tenth grade, Islamic societies are based on homogeneity, cooperation, moral values and close human relationships. The West, on the other hand, is fraught with conflicting groups and classes, specialization and deteriorating family relationships (Naqavi 1994: 8–10).

Similar ideas are reflected in the writings of many independent authors. S. Tooyserkâni (1991), for instance, the editor of the literary monthly *Donyâye Sokhan*, offers a comparably degrading portrait of the West, devoid of morality and consumed by alienation and materialism; the educational problems of 'Western societies' include the diminishing value of religion and morality, freedom of alcohol consumption, drug addiction and gangs (Khabbâz Beheshti 2001: 116–17). Every possible predisposition, from economic destitution to moral deprivation, from homophobia to the fear of losing control over women, from the dissolution of the family to the substitution of children with dogs, are used against migration. And finally, the strongest weapon is brought in: food.

> The French eat all sorts of frogs, turtles, escargots, and rabbits, which do not please our Iranian taste. Iranians who have lived in that country for a short period die for a bowl of qormeh sabzi, qeimeh bâdemjân, fesenjân, âsh-e sholehqalamkâr, or the superb and delicious Iranian âsh-e reshteh.
>
> (Zabihiân and Mo'tazed 2002: 369)

What is astonishing in the above renditions of 'Western societies' is the entitlement these authors feel to judge a nation without even the slightest concern that what they 'learn' through observing the outer layer of a society, whose culture and history they often do not know and with whose people they have no meaningful contact, is a fertile ground for misapprehension and prejudice. Had a Western scholar even hinted at a criticism of Iran's history or culture, he or she would have exposed herself to the harshest criticisms of being Orientalist or irreverent towards Iranian culture. For the Iranian diaspora – both as insiders and as critics of Orientalism – this 'Orientalism-in-reverse'[11] must be alarming, especially in its implications for the subtle and not-so-subtle mechanisms of social and political control, both now and in the future.

Spatial and cultural distances

A sensation was created around Mohammad Mohammad-Ali's interview with the leading Iranian poet Ahmad Shamlu. Shamlu explained why he had stayed in Iran:

> My land is here. I look at the world, but only from this place. Others know better why they have left. I am from here. My lantern burns in this house...
>
> (Shamlu 1987: 25)

Many immigrants and exiles took issue with the allusion, since their departure from Iran meant turning their backs on the homeland. 'I am from here, my lantern burns in this house' became a popular phrase among Iranians inside and outside Iran, yet with opposing interpretations. For insiders, it meant a hierarchical distinction of loyalty: those who are loyal to their land will remain here. For outsiders, the statement testified to a continued commitment: though we are not there, we have remained loyal to that place.

According to accounts about the diaspora, cultural distance is exacerbated by spatial distance. Utilizing such natural imagery as a tree and its roots to describe one's relationship to home, insiders appear rooted and stable while outsiders – the diaspora – become mobile and dislocated anomalies. Such imagery of exile and home, as Liisa Malkki (1992) has argued, naturalizes and essentializes the congruence of geographies and cultures. In this hierarchical notion of insiders and outsiders, the diaspora appear as the inauthentic imitations of the real natives, 'the bastard child of the nation – disavowed, inauthentic, illegitimate, and impoverished imitation of the originary culture'.

Residence in Iran becomes a validation of ideas. It stations the *dâkheli*, the insider, above the *khâreji*, or intellectuals abroad. Insiders are presented as 'experts' on Iran, the diaspora as out of touch with the realities of Iran (see Shahidian 2000: 84–8). Of course, that these authors themselves have not lived as immigrants does not prevent them from authoritatively representing the diaspora. Yet the fact that immigrants are not in the current of daily life in Iran is used to discredit the diaspora if what they point out contradicts the authors' belief. As Edward Soja put it: 'Space can be made to hide consequences from us.... And power and discipline are inscribed into the apparently innocent spatiality of social life' (1989: 6).

Gender and national honour

I mentioned earlier that a common trait of accounts of the Iranian diaspora is denying them a voice. This characteristic is nowhere more vivid than in relation to women. Save for some rare recent introductions of immigrant women in independent feminist magazines and anthologies (Darvishpour 1999, 2000; Moghissi 2000), written by expatriates, most discussions about Iranian immigrant women are authored by men and are derived from a patriarchal perspective. The author of *Immigrant Iranians* claims that a young refugee woman shared her diary with him, but the style, tone and message of the diary are identical with the rest of his book. Travelogues and commentaries on Iranians abroad have been penned, so far, overwhelmingly by men, though several women artists and authors have travelled to the West. There are rare accounts by women about their diasporic lives; we only read men's descriptions of women, a description that emphasizes idiocy, deception and disillusionment in Iranian diasporic women.

The women in *Sorraya in a Coma* are, without exception, airheads, preoccupied solely with appearing appealing. The smart ones realize that their life is empty, but conclude that they deserve whatever happens to them. In a letter to the protagonist Aryan, Leila Azadeh confesses that she is so overwhelmed with 'corruption' (*fesâd*) that she has no right to contemplate life. Indeed, she is so convinced about being worthless that she believes being physically abused by men is her just lot: 'Who am I? I've been so bad that sometimes I want someone to beat me up… Serve[s] me right!' (Fassih 1985: 153) The solution is clear: women need to live under men's shadow to be safe.

Immigrant women are frequently held responsible for the destruction of family life. They are blamed for being deceived by Western ideas and forgetting their native culture. Women are liable for family breakups. Though some critics acknowledge oppressive values and practices in Iranian culture, little – if any – responsibility is assigned to men. The implicit argument is that men might be old-fashioned, but their wives and daughters should understand them. A report on the roots of divorce among immigrant Iranians argues as follows:

> During the early years of migration, when the man as the head of the household asks his wife to maintain her loyalty, purity, and [spiritual] health, as she did in the past, the immigrant woman first keeps quiet. But her silence does not last long. She finally objects and says: 'Past relationships belong to the past! You should now treat me like a human being! You don't understand what freedom and democracy mean! Those old cultural traditions are not valid here'.
>
> (Donyâye Sokhan 1993: 25)

Musing, of course, has not been the only thing Iranian immigrant men have done in this situation. As several observers have pointed out (Darvishpour 1995; Jalali 1982; Shahidian 1999), living in the West has not curbed family violence among immigrant Iranian families. To confront diasporic challenges to gender relations, traditional family structure is revered, and maintaining traditional gender and intergenerational relationships within the family becomes a social and cultural priority. Critics simply do not understand the intricacies of Iranian culture. Reflecting on a report in *Le Monde* about the patriarchal structure of the Iranian family the editor of *Donyâye Sokhan* writes:

> This inexperienced reporter does not know that if a father, as the leader of the family, orders other members of the family, his ordering is the result of his beliefs and character (vizhegihây-e akhlâqi), not due to rigid rules of patriarchy.... In our culture the father is not the same as in Western culture.
>
> (Tooyserkâni 1991: 20)

According to the exposés of the diaspora, women are easily deceived into leaving their nice cosy life at home in pursuit of a baseless dream (Zabihiân & Mo'tazed 2002: 95). Yet, they can as easily deceive intelligent men. In the movie *Shab-e Yaldâ* (The Night of Yaldâ), a woman deceives her caring husband into giving her and their daughter legal permission to leave the country. In time, we find out that her departure is inspired not by what she told her husband – a desire to improve her family's life chances – but by her love for another man living abroad. Similarly, the refugee claimant woman in Immigrant Iranians deceives her husband, then the UNHCR officials in the UK.

Contrary to this negative portrayal of women, immigrant men are presented in flattering terms. They may cheat on their wives, but at least they keep the sacred family together; if they break apart a family, it is another man's family, not their own.

While women ruin their families in order to emigrate, men emigrate in order to defend their families and try to maintain their 'natural' family bonds – a remnant of their lost homeland. In the movie *Ertefâ'-e Past* (Low Height), though the man hijacks the plane to go to a foreign country, he does so to protect his family. The inclusion of his extended family in this unsuccessful escape naturalizes his attempt to uproot himself. If his roots are severed from the homeland, he takes with him the most intimate expression of his ties to that land. In *Yâs-e Vahshi* (Wild Jasmine), several fighting men simultaneously defend their homeland and a woman. The aura of wild jasmine bursting from the prayer mat of the hero – a memento from the homeland – signals the presence of men who never cut the roots that link them to their motherland.

However, a picture of immigrant women is incomplete without a description of Western women. We learn that French women easily divorce their husbands because the law accords them half of their husbands' wealth. 'Unfortunately', we learn, 'French women think about nothing other than sex. French society is filled with corruption. Men and women do not trust each other; for that reason French men prefer to marry foreign women, especially Eastern women. French women often abandon their children, and do not even visit them, because these women only think about themselves and their desires' (Zabihiân & Mo'tazed 2002: 266–9).

The pivotal role of gender in the debate surrounding the diaspora is clearly manifest in the controversy about a refugee case in the Iranian media. In 1993,

Canada granted asylum to an Iranian woman on the basis of her having had an extramarital affair, an offence that could be punishable by stoning to death in Islamic law. The pro-government *Kayhan Hava'i* (13 October 1993) commented thus on the case:

> Persian newspapers abroad are presently writing about the adventures of women deserters [*zanân-e farâri*] who, despite enjoying a relatively comfortable life in Iran, have escaped to foreign countries, and in the chaotic [*bebandobâr*] Western societies, despite having husbands and children, are engaged in corruption and prostitution [*tanforoushi*].

It is noteworthy that the refugee claimant's affair is portrayed as prostitution. *Tanforoushi*, 'selling one's body', connotes that the women in question would compromise everything to attain their goals in foreign countries. The refugee woman is not even credited for having had genuine interest in her boyfriend.

The reformist *Zanân* objected to *Kayhan Hava'i*'s categorical reference to immigrant women as corrupt (Sherkat 1993a). *Kayhan Hava'i*'s editor argued that the passage, translated verbatim above, referred only to one refugee woman, and not to all. Could we, he asked, with 'Iranian-Islamic culture in our blood', consider a 'morally corrupt' (*fâssedulakhlâq*) woman a compatriot (Salimi-Namin 1993: 4)? Much to his chagrin, *Zanân*'s response was affirmative:

> 'Compatriot' refers to all members of the Iranian society, simply because they are Iranian, irrespective of their healthy or corrupt morality. We do not believe that sociopathological people [*âsibdidegân-e ejtemâ'i*] should be thrown into a kiln and burned.... As a matter of fact, we lament any dishonour and, having 'Iranian-Islamic culture in our blood', we can understand and tolerate such a woman because the Prophet and Imam Ali, and even our chivalrous men [*javânmardhâ*] treated the injured and intellectually weak [*mostaz'fân-e fekri*] in the same manner.... Killing the weak is not appropriate for the powerful.
>
> (Sherkat 1993b)

Zanân's main objection – as manifest in the title of Sherkat's first article, 'Women's Condemnation at the Price of National Honour' – is why the news was reported to begin with, considering that it tarnished Iranian national honour. The refugee claimant is regarded as 'sociopathological', 'injured' and 'intellectually weak', one who should be pitied, not punished. The seemingly opposing viewpoints of the two journals share the dangerous assumption that women are a fundamental source of national honour, and both endorse a specific kind of morality and designate other moral choices as pathological. One contends that corrupt people have no place in the Islamic Republic, and the other believes that Muslims should pity such creatures. A few years later, Mohsen Sa'idzâdeh (1997) took a similar approach to the news of another woman who attempted to leave her husband and child and cross the border to the Republic of Azerbaijan in a sack of rice (for details, see Shahidian 2002b: 56).

Conclusion

Depending on the sociopolitical objectives of the state, the Iranian diaspora have been reflected in the mirrors of the Islamic Republic as either decadent counter-revolutionaries or wayward children. Life in the West is presented as a mirage, an illusory paradise, particularly detrimental to family life and 'female virtues'. In recent years, emphasis is placed upon the services that emigrant Iranians could provide for their country. However the diaspora has been presented, one unchanging objective has been to persuade Iranians to stay in Iran.

The diaspora has been a challenge not only for the government, but also for many intellectuals living in Iran. Exiles have proposed, for instance, to regard gender relations and East–West dichotomy in different lights. The diasporic emphases on refashioning socio-political discourses and casting doubts on accepted definitions and assumptions have contradicted some authors' portrayal of Iran as a kind parent awaiting its children's return. Iranian women also recall a home that denied them basic rights and made them vulnerable to various forms of violence that lurked around every corner in their lives.

A great deal of tension and violence has been associated with the departure of many diaspora from Iran. A complicated encounter of two worlds has set the context of our individual and collective diasporic existence. I see the diasporic experience as an opportunity to broaden politico-cultural horizons, not just for the diaspora who experience different cultures, but also for those left behind. This 'opportunity' does not surface on its own; it must be carved out through a dialogue between the diaspora and their fellow citizens. For, just as the initial reaction of the diaspora to their new condition is often tainted with guilt and disbelief, resentment and dismissal overshadow most reflections by those left behind. This condition becomes infinitely more acute when – as in the case of the Iranian diaspora – the exiles pose implications for the political legitimacy of the state and challenge aspects of the home culture. Reflections of the diaspora in the homeland then mesh with observations about their own refuge in order to safeguard the familiar cultural and political relations of the homeland.

Yet, it is exactly under these circumstances that the diaspora can have a critical intervention in the cultural politics of the homeland. The Iranian diaspora have been quite conscientious about portraying the socio-cultural diversity of Iran in their host countries, but we have spent considerably less time and energy claiming our history in the homeland. Our preoccupation has been predominantly Iranian politics, not the politics of exile. This is in part due to censorship, as honest discussions about the diaspora transgress many 'red lines' that even the less abrasive Islamists, the so-called 'reformists', condone and diligently observe. Restrictions notwithstanding, I think we, too, have not been vigilant enough about our task of speaking from our diasporic experience, perhaps because the Islamic state has so lacked legitimacy among us that we have deemed utterly irrelevant what state officials think about us.

However, we must look beyond the official assertions and challenge assumptions that lay people and educated observers cherish about our society, its diaspora, and its 'others'. And it is in this sense that I believe our exile provides an opportunity for cultural self-criticism, a re-envisioning of home in light of both home and diasporic histories. If we opt for a multicultural society, this is an opportunity to redefine centre and margin in our cultural politics to include ethnic, religious, class and political diversity – the denial of which under the IRI has forced a life of exile on many of us. Though the insiders-diaspora distinction is not impermeable, there exist discrepancies that often lead to tension. Instead of shying away from this tension, and far from reducing the diaspora's role to that of support group for those struggling on the home front, I advocate an interventionist role for the 'exilic, extraterritorial, and unhoused' (Said 2004: 11) critics of the cultural politics of the homeland. If multiculturalism is to transcend a collage of translations from other cultures and become an opportunity to deepen self-knowledge through self-reflection, the spatial and cultural borders of diasporic life ought to be envisioned as an opportunity to bring home other cultures, to debunk our ethnocentric, and often racist, views of others. As people living in multiple cultures, this is a task we cannot neglect.

Notes

1 Some of these distinctions are admittedly understudied by the diaspora themselves or by scholars of the Iranian diaspora. The elderly tops the list. Mary Elaine Hegland's project (see her chapter in this collection) is a welcomed addition in this regard.
2 For the example case of the US, see Matin-Asghari, 1991.
3 To my knowledge, this programme is not available in the West. My description is based on conversations with Iranian immigrants and travellers.
4 Iranian diasporic media are replete with discussions about reformist politics and its implications for the women's rights movement. For some examples of debates on reformist politics, see Said Amir Arjomand, 2000, and Ladan Boroumand and Roya Boroumand, 2000. For discussions on reformism and women's rights, see Moghissi, 1999a; Mojab, 1995; Najmabadi, 1995; Shahidian, 2002b; Tohidi, 1997.
5 On the role of violence in the Islamic Republic, see Shahidian, 2002a, pp. 204–12.
6 On distinctions among various forms of migration, see Richmond, 1993 and Van Hear, 1998. Both Richmond and Van Hear, however, seem to underemphasize the role of human agency in the process of population movement. Exile should be envisioned as a dialectical relationship between punishment and refusal. See Shahidian, 2000b, pp. 79–82.
7 On falsification of state terror, see Manz, 1995.
8 On violence and memory, see Pohlandt-McCormick, 2000.
9 Judith Zur, 1999, considers this the making of a 'historical amnesia' and treats it as a form of political and ideological control.
10 'Westoxicated' or *qarbzadegi* is a term used by Jalal Al-e Ahmad, 1982.
11 I am borrowing this term from Sadik Jalal Al-'Azm, 1981.

References

Al-'Azm, S. J. (1981) 'Orientalism and Orientalism in Reverse', *Khamsin* (8): 5–26.
Al-e Ahmad, J. (1982) *Plagued by the West*, trans. P. Sprachman, Delmar, NY: Caravan Books.
Amir Arjomand, S. (2000) 'Civil Society and the Rule of Law in the Constitutional Politics of Iran Under Khatami', *Social Research* 67(2): 283–301.

Boroumand, L. and Boroumand, R. (2000) 'Illusion and Reality of Civil Society in Iran: An Ideological Debate', *Social Research* 67(2): 303–44.

Darvishpour, M. (1993) 'Yek Dastbord va Yek Gozâresh-e Qeyr-e-vâqe'i' (A Theft and an Unreal Report), *Arash*, November, 8–10.

—— (1995) 'Khânevâdeh va Farhang-e Demokrâtik' (Family and Democratic Culture), *Shahrvand* (209): 20, 21, 25.

—— (1999) 'Zanân-e Mohâjer: Châleshgar-e Naqsh-e Mardân' (Iranian Women: Challengers of Men's Role), in N. Ahmady Khorasany (ed.) *Jens-e Dovom*, Tehran: Nashr-e Towse'eh.

—— (2000) 'Pazhouheshi Tajrobi Darbâreh-ye Nabard-e Qodrat dar Khânevâdeh-hây-e Irani dar Sowed' (Experimental Research on Power Struggles within Iranian Families in Sweden), in N. Ahmady Khorasany (ed.) *Jens-e Dovom*, Tehran: Nashr-e Towse'eh.

Donyâye Sokhan (1993) 'Marg-e Taklif' (The Death of Duty), *Donyâye Sokhan*, May–June, 20–7.

Fassih, E. (1984) *Sorraya dar Eqmâ* (Sorraya in a Coma), Tehran: Nashr-e Nou.

—— (1985) *Sorraya in a Coma*, London: Zed Books.

Ghorashi, H. (2002) *Ways to Survive, Battles to Win: Iranian Women in Exiles in the Netherlands and the United States*, New York: Nova Science Publishers, Inc.

Golbâf, A. (1995a) 'Mâ Kojâ, Ânhâ Kojâ?' (Where Are We, Where Are They?), *Gozâresh*, June–July, 4–5.

—— (1995b) 'Moohebat-e 'Afv Kardan râ az Farzandânemân Dariq Nakonim' (Let Us Not Deprive Our Children from the Gift of Forgiving), *Gozâresh*, September–October, 4–5.

—— (1995) '"Bombay, UK, Yuba City": Bhangra Music and the Engendering of Diaspora', *Diaspora* 4(3): 303–22.

Jalali, B. (1982) 'Iranian Families', in J. G. Monica McGoldrick and John K. Pearce (eds) *Ethnicity & Family Therapy*, New York: The Guilford Press.

Khabbâz Beheshti, Z. (2001) *Mohâjerat: Barrasy-e Moshkelat-e Mohâjeran dar Jahân* (Migration: A Review of Immigrants' Problems around the World), Tehran: Âshiâneh-ye ketâb.

Malkki, L. (1992) 'National Geographic: The Rooting of Peoples and the Territorialization of National Identity among Scholars and Refugees', *Cultural Anthropology* 7(11): 22–44.

Manz, B. (1995) 'Fostering Trust in a Climate of Fear', in E. V. Daniel and J. C. Knudsen (eds) *Mistrusting Refugees*, Berkeley: University of California Press.

Matin-Asghari, A. (1991) 'The Iranian Student Movement Abroad: The Confederation of Iranian Students, National Union' in A. Fathi (ed.) *Iranian Refugees and Exiles since Khomeini*, Costa Mesa, CA: Mazda Publishers.

Mirbâqeri (1993) 'Javânân az Mahdoodiyathâ Shekâyat Dârand' (The Youths Complain about Limitations), *Hamshahri*, 24 August, 12.

Moghissi, H. (1999a) 'Émigré Iranian feminism and the construction of Muslim women' in A. Heitlinger (ed.) *Émigré Feminism: Transnational Perspectives*, Toronto: University of Toronto Press.

—— (1999b) 'Away from Home: Iranian Women, Displacement, Cultural Resistance and Change,' *Journal of Comparative Family Studies* 30: 207–17.

—— (2000) 'Zan-e Irani dar Mohâjerat: Jâygozini, Moqâvemat-e Farhangi, va Taqiir' (Away from Home: Iranian Women, Displacement, Cultural Resistance, and Change) in N. Ahmady Khorasany (ed.) *Jens-e Dovom*, Tehran: Nashr-e Towse'eh.

Mojab, S. (1995) 'Islamic Feminism: Alternative or Contradiction?' *Fireweed* (47): 18–25.

Momeni, M. B. (1995) 'Cheh Bayad Mikardam?' (What Could I Do?), *Mehregan: An Iranian Journal of Culture and Politics* 4(2): 79–85.

Naficy, H. (1993) *The Making of Exile Culture: Iranian Television in Los Angeles*, Minneapolis: University of Minnesota Press.

Nafisi, A. (1984) 'Mashq va Sar-e Mashq' (The Copy and the Original). *Naqd-e Âgâh* 4: 67–95.

Najmabadi, A. (1995) 'Sâlhây-e 'Usrat, Sâlhâye Rooyesh' (Years of Destitution; Years of Growth). *Kankash* (12): 171–206.

Naqavi, A. M. (1994) *Jâme'ehshenâsi* (Sociology). Tehran: Ministry of Education.

Pohlandt-McCormick, H. (2000) ' "I Saw a Nightmare...": Violence and the Construction of Memory' (Soweto, June 16, 1976)', *History and Theory* 39: 23–44.

Raouf, M. (2002) *The Tree that Remembers*, ed. M. Raouf, Montreal: National Film Board of Canada.

Râzi, M. (1991) 'Mohâjerat-e Nirooy-e Ensâni beh Kharej az Keshvar, Angizeh-ha, Payâmadha' (The Migration of Human Resources: Causes and Consequences), *Kayhan*.

Richmond, A. H. (1993) 'Reactive Migration: Sociological Perspectives on Refugee Movements', *Journal of Refugee Studies* 6(1): 7–24.

Sa'edi, G. (1994) 'The Metamorphosis and Emancipation of the Avareh', trans. H. Shahidian, *Journal of Refugee Studies* 7(4): 411–17.

Said, E. W. (2004) *Humanism and Democratic Criticism*, New York: Columbia University Press.

Salimi-Namin, A. (1993) 'Pâsokh-e 'Kayhan-e Hava'i' beh Sarmaqâleh-ye "Zanân" ' (Kayhan Hava'i's response to Zanân's Editorial), *Zanân* (15): 3–4.

Sani'i, P. (2004) *Sahm-e Man* (My Share), Tehran: Rouzbehân.

Shahidian, H. (1992) *Qorbat, 'Mâ' va 'Digarân'* (Living Abroad, 'Us', and 'Them'), unpublished manuscript.

—— (1999) 'Gender and Sexuality among Iranian Immigrants in Canada', *Sexualities* 2 (2): 189–223.

—— (2000) 'Sociology and Exile: Banishment and Tensional Loyalty', *Current Sociology* 48(2): 81–106.

—— (2002a) *Women in Iran: Gender Politics in the Islamic Republic*, Westport, CT: Greenwood.

—— (2002b) *Women in Iran: Emerging Voices in the Women's Movement*, Westport, CT: Greenwood.

Shamlu, A. (1987) 'Man Inja'i Hastam, Cheraqam dar In Khanih Mysoozad' (I Am from Here, My Lantern Burns in This House), *Adineh*, July–August, 20–5.

Shayesteh, S. (1988) 'Rowshanfikran-i Kafeh-ye de la Sanction' (The Intellectuals of the Café de la Sanction), *Kankash: A Persian Journal of History and Politics* 1(2–3): 269–81.

Sherkat, S. (1993a) 'Takfir-e Zan beh Bahây-e Âberouy-e Melli' (Women's Condemnation at the Price of National Honor), *Zanân*, October–November, 2.

—— (1993b) 'Âqây-e Modir-e Mas'ul, Âsibdidegân râ Nemitavân dar Kureh Rikht' (Mister Managing Editor, We Cannot Dump Victims in a Kiln), *Zanân*, November–January, 5.

Soja, E. W. (1989) *Postmodern Geographies: The Reassertion of Space in Critical Social Theory*, London: Verso.

Tabâtabâ'i, T. (1980) 'Mohâjer' (The Immigrant), *Donyâye Sokhan*, 52–4.

Tohidi, N. (1997) ' "Feminism-e Islami": Châleshi Demokrâtik yâ Charkheshy Theokrâtik?' ('Islamic Feminism': A Democratic Challenge or a Theocratic Reaction?), *Kankash: A Persian Journal of History, Culture, and Politics* (13): 96–149.

Tooyserkâni, S. (1991) 'Gozâresh-e Safar beh Qarb: Dirouz-e Roushan, Emrouz-e Khâkestari, Fardây-e Tireh' (A Report of the Journey to the West: A Bright Yesterday, A Grim Today, and a Gloomy Tomorrow), *Donyâye Sokhan*, September–October, 20–8.

Van Hear, N. (1998) *New Diasporas: The Mass Exodus, Dispersal and Regrouping of Migrant Communities*, Seattle: University of Washington Press.

Zabihiân, Y. and Mo'tazed, K. (2002) *Iranian dar Mohâjerat: Panâhandeh beh Qarb-e Bitarahhom* (Immigrant Iranians: Refugees in the Merciless West), Tehran: Alborz.

Zur, J. (1999) 'Remembering and Forgetting: Guatemalan War Widows' Forbidden Memories', in K. L. Rogers, S. L. and G. Dawson (eds) *Trauma and Life Stories: International Perspectives*, London: Routledge.

8   Gender, nation and diaspora: Kurdish women in feminist transnational struggles

Shahrzad Mojab

[handwritten annotation: Foreign communities often affected by events at home]

This chapter examines the gender dimension of diaspora/homeland relations in the newly formed Kurdish communities in Europe. Focusing on activism for Kurdish women's rights in both diaspora and homeland (especially Iraqi Kurdistan), the chapter examines the close ties that bind homeland/hostland relations, and reflects on current theoretical claims about 'Islamic society' and related concepts such as 'Islamic diasporas'. It also critically assesses theorizations of 'diaspora' and 'transnationality', which reduce diasporic entities to cultural phenomena. This study is based on fieldwork in Europe and an analysis of the *Charter for the Rights and Freedoms of Women in the Kurdish Regions and Diaspora*, released in June 2004.

The case: Kurdish diasporas

The Kurds are often described as 'the largest nation without a homeland' or 'the largest non-state nation in the world'. They are the fourth-largest ethnic people of the Middle East, outnumbered only by Arabs, Turks and Persians. In the absence of census data, their number is estimated variously between 25 and 30 million (see Table 8.1)[1]. They do have a homeland, Kurdistan, which was divided between the Ottoman Empire and Iran from 1639 to 1918. In the wake of the disintegration of the Ottoman Empire in 1918, the Ottoman part of Kurdistan was redivided among the newly formed states of Iraq, Syria and Turkey. Kurdish populations were also scattered throughout western and central Asia in pre-modern times and, since the 1970s, over other continents, forming a new global diasporic community (Mojab and Hassanpour 2004).

The new Kurdish diasporas emerged in the context of a bloody conflict over Kurdistan. Kurdish nationalism, which emerged in the late nineteenth century, demands the right to self-determination. The nation-states ruling over the Kurds have used violence in dealing with Kurdish nationalism, proponents of which have often taken up arms in order to achieve statehood or autonomy within each unitary state in which they live. The interstate system and, especially, Western powers have been directly involved in the conflict between the Kurds and the four states that rule over them. Kurdish diasporas are, to a large extent, a product of this conflict, and participate in its reproduction and resolution.

Table 8.1 Populations of Kurds (estimated)

Country	Number of Kurds	% of the population
Turkey	13,700,000	24.1
Iran	6,600,000	12.4
Iraq	4,400,000	23.5
Syria	1,300,000	9.2
Europe[a]	700,000	
Former USSR[b]	400,000	
Total	27,100,000	

Sources: [a] and [b] McDowall (2000: 3–4); *Le Monde*, 18 February 1999.

The Kurdish language is a member of the Iranian branch of Indo-European languages with four dialect groups, namely Kurmanji (Northern), Sorani (Central), Zaza/Dimili and Hawrami/Gorani, both of which are found throughout the region, and Southern dialects. The language has been written for about five centuries, predominantly in the Arabic script, but as of the 1930s, also in the Cyrillic and Roman alphabets. The Kurds are predominantly Sunni Muslims (Shafe'is), with a small Shi'a minority in the southern parts of Kurdistan and several religious minority groups such as Alevis, Yezidis, Ahli-Haq and Christians.

Two developments led to major uprooting and resettlement of Kurdish populations, within the region and internationally, in the latter part of the twentieth century. One was ongoing coercive assimilation, which led to increasing Kurdish resistance, including armed conflicts between the Kurds and the governments in Iraq (intermittently from 1961–2003), Iran (1967–8, 1979–present), and Turkey (1984–present). Western powers and regional states were involved in these and other interstate (Iraq–Kuwait, Iran–Iraq) conflicts, which turned the area into an active and enduring 'war zone'.

The second development was the economic boom of Western Europe in the 1960s, which prompted the recruitment of a large number of 'guest workers' to occupy jobs in Germany and, on a much smaller scale, Belgium, The Netherlands, Denmark, France and Sweden. By the late 1990s, Germany hosted Europe's largest Kurdish population, estimated at about half a million (see Table 8.2).

The Kurdish sources have, since the mid-nineteenth century, argued that Kurdish women enjoy more freedom than their Arab, Persian and Turkish sisters. Western travellers and scholars, too, have found Kurdish women notably different from other 'Muslim' or 'Oriental' women. Although travel literature points to the existence of harems and gender segregation in upper-class and ruling families, it also finds rural Kurdish women enjoying more freedom than Arab, Persian and Turkish women. The evidence cited in support of this relative freedom includes, among other data, the absence of veiling, free association with males, including strangers and guests, and a list of female rulers (Mojab 2005).

Table 8.2   The size of Kurdish diasporas

Country	Population	Source
Europe		
Germany	500,000	(Estimate, German parliament, 2000)
France	100–120,000	(IKP estimate 2003)
Netherlands	70–80,000	(IKP estimate 2003)
Switzerland	7,531	(Number of Kurdish speakers, 2000 census)
Belgium	50–60,000	(IKP estimate 2003)
Austria	50–60,000	(IKP estimate 2003)
Sweden	25–30,000	(IKP estimate 2003)
UK	20–25,000	(IKP estimate 2003)
Greece	20–25,000	(IKP estimate 2003)
Denmark	8–10,000	(IKP estimate 2003)
Norway	4–5,000	(IKP estimate 2003)
Italy	3–4,000	(IKP estimate 2003)
Finland	3,916	(Number of Kurdish speakers, 2002 census)
Russia		
Siberia	35,000	(With 30,000 in Vladivostok, IKP 2003)
Krasnodar	30,000	(IKP estimate 2003)
Central Asia		
Kazakhstan	30,000	(KHRP estimate 1996)
Turkmenistan	50,000	(KHRP estimate 1996)
Kirghizia	20,000	(KHRP estimate 1996)
Uzbekistan	10,000	(KHRP estimate 1996)
Tajikistan	3,000	(KHRP estimate 1996)
Caucasia		
Armenia	75,000	(KHRP estimate 1996)
Azerbaijan	12–30,000	(Müller 2000: 70)
Georgia	40,000	(KHRP estimate 1996)
Middle East		
Lebanon	75–100,000	(Meho, 2001: 28)
North America		
Canada	7,140	(Number of Kurdish speakers, 2001 census)
USA	15–20,000	(IKP estimate 2003)
Oceania		
Australia	2,845	(Number of Kurdish speakers, 2001 census)
New Zealand	603	(Number of Kurdish speakers, 2001 census)

Sources: (KHRP 1996); IKP (2005).

Theoretical issues

Transnational feminism and Kurdish diaspora[2]

Recent shifts in feminist discourse and theory do not provide adequate frameworks for theorizing diaspora/homeland relations from the standpoint of Kurdish women. Earlier shifts away from an internationalist framework to a cross-cultural one (Reinharz 1992: 112) have more recently given way to transnationality as the appropriate perspective from which to theorize population movements in a global context. So far, the concept of transnationalism is still vague and ill-defined. The key to its relevance for social-science research is whether it can account for an emerging phenomenon that is not expressed in a previously existing term (Portes *et al.* 1999). The emergence of mechanisms and technologies that allow diaspora communities to follow, and influence, the day-to-day political developments in their homeland is such a phenomenon. The experience of Kurdish women organizing in diaspora is a case in point. In this chapter I will analyse feminist transnationalism and its theoretical ties to diaspora studies by tracing the activism of a Kurdish women's group in the United Kingdom. This group has successfully negotiated a universal charter of rights for women in the Kurdish regions and diaspora. The full title of this historical document, which was officially launched in London on 22 June 2004, is *Charter for the Rights and Freedoms of Women in the Kurdish Regions and Diaspora* (see below for a detailed account of this case). Several studies on the evolution of transnational political structures argue that their form generally takes root in relation to struggles for civil rights in the host-land (Itzigsohn 2000). However, these studies rarely recognize the gendered nature of these political and economic processes. Other literature on transnationalism focuses on the *visible* results of what seem to be *invisible* human relations (see Sassen 1998). It is the apparent invisibility of these relations that has caused some theorists to argue that transnational politics are those that evade national boundaries and state structures, leading to a trend in diaspora studies of envisioning 'transnationality' as a global characteristic related to the withering away of the state's ability to maintain fixed boundaries in relation to its population.

The literature on transnationalism and gender does not speak directly to the literature on transnational politics. The former emerged out of a critique of global feminisms (see Spivak 1997; Mohanty 2003), the latter out of migration studies (see Ong and Nonini 1997). Nor does transnational feminist literature engage in mapping the mechanisms of women's political participation and non-participation. In my literature review of six feminist journals over a span of a decade, I found very little published work on this topic.[3] The main themes in the feminist scholarship of the last decade are issues of women's identity, community creation in the diaspora, gender and development practices, and international links between so-called 'northern' and 'southern' feminists. There is, however, a paucity of research on the explicitly political organizing of women in the diaspora. In these journals, I came across only two articles that were highly relevant to my current research. One is Suzuki's, which deals directly with women organizing in the diaspora, and argues that the organizing of Filipino women, though mainly in charity groups, is an effort to resist the sexist, racist stereotype of them as prostitutes in Japan (Suzuki 2000). The second, more relevant to the issue of political organizing, is the article by Charles, in which he demonstrates how circumstances particular to Haiti led to the development of the Haitian women's movements during the 1990s. The two circumstances that are argued to be central in this process are the particular policy of gender violence by the state under the Duvalier regime and, more specifically, the resistance to these repressive strategies and the simultaneous migration of Haitians since the 1960s to North America, where middle-class and professional Haitian women, in particular, came into contact with feminist discourses, became engaged in political life, and pushed their agendas to the forefront of the political struggle taking place in the diaspora (Charles 1995).

While 'transnationality' is an emerging analytical framework that appears in several areas of literature, ranging from women's studies to political science, the notion of 'diaspora' is emerging as a separate realm of research that encompasses the previous area of migration studies with a new concern for observing the fragmentation and reconstitution of national groups, rather than seeing homogenized 'immigrants'. One problem of particular concern for an analysis of Kurdish women's organizing is that most of the literature depoliticizes both the machinations of capital and organized resistance to it. Another concern is that most of the literature masks the violence of the 'transnationalizing' of capital. One possible first step towards re-theorizing transnationalism in relation to the state would be to clarify the notion of 'diaspora'.

Diaspora and transnational nationalism

Before wading into the often muddy waters of diaspora theory, I must stress that I understand *diaspora* – that is, the dispersal and relocation of populations – to be the result of colonial relations in the historically specific context of capitalist accumulation on a global scale. This is not to deny that the dispersion of populations is of ancient origins and can be traced to multiple 'causes' in pre-capitalist formations. As a concept that has become increasingly popular in the academy over the past decade, 'diaspora' has had a special appeal for academics discussing 'hybridity' and cultural multiplicity in post-colonial, postmodern and cultural studies (Hall 1994). Brah notes that there have been few attempts to theorize the concept, and proposes that we understand diaspora in terms of Foucauldian 'genealogies' – that is, we should 'historicize trajectories of different diasporas [across] fields of social relations' (Brah 1998: 180). Brah also develops criteria based on the circumstances of 'leaving' and 'arriving', including: conquest and colonization; capture and removal; expulsion and persecution; flight from political strife; war resulting in a new state; and the flow of labour (Brah 1996: 182). However, after developing this set of historicizing categories, Brah claims that it is not the histories of different diasporas, but the 'relationality' between them, that matters (Brah 1998: 183).

If diaspora is a notion that blurs history in favour of identity, it also blurs the relation of subordination and dominance in favour of multiplicity. Brah employs the concept of 'multiple modalities' to refer to 'gender, race, class, religion, language, and generation' rather than considering them as categories of oppression (Brah 1998: 184). Using 'multiple modalities' as a way of understanding social stratification makes it very difficult to see how one person occupies several of these categories at once. This depoliticization of categories empties them of their power as analytical tools for understanding ways in which groups experience violence, oppression and exploitation. Although Brah recognizes that certain concepts (such as 'minority') are politically slippery and a dangerous way of describing oppression, she fails to recognize that she may also be falling into similar ideological traps with the concepts she is proposing. The concept of 'diaspora', defined in these terms, tends to neutralize the violence of population displacement.

The ideological underpinnings of diaspora theory are difficult to ascertain on first reading. The theoretical intricacies, complications and incomprehensibilities in Brah's work are consistent with the depoliticized and obscure nature of postmodernist literature on diaspora (Grewal and Kaplan 1994, 2000). Brah does not connect her series of relational concepts to the larger organizing imperatives of the capital or the state, and outside such a framework, 'diaspora' as a theoretical tool may have little to offer anyone concerned with an anti-colonial, anti-racist project. Brah firmly roots her explication of diaspora theory in the postmodernist stream by tracing key concepts of power and identity from Foucault and Derrida. In a way, Brah's writing serves as an artefact that demonstrates the extent to which concepts of 'difference' and 'multiplicity' have replaced concepts like 'racism', 'oppression', 'exploitation' and 'imperialism'. In the relational sea on which Brah is cast adrift, it is difficult to navigate an anti-racist, anti-colonial, feminist opposition to the violence and oppression of the current world order. Oppositional politics are further submerged by the subsumption of the concepts of 'ideology' and 'political struggle' under the concepts of 'culture' and 'ethnicity'. Brah attempts to remedy this political vacuum by adding another category of multiplicity to an already fragmented world view. Rather than developing an analysis of the ways that capitalism structures and restricts the flight of populations around the globe, Brah *adds* the notion of capitalism to her matrix of descriptive categories.

Although Brah notes that the concept of diaspora 'overlaps and resonates with meanings of words such as migrant, immigrant, refugee, expatriate, guest worker or exile...', she is more interested in 'the economic, political and cultural dimensions of these contemporary forms of migrancy' (Brah 1998: 186). However, the former list is much more useful for identifying class relations, immigration policies, patterns of population flow and material conditions. A more useful exercise might be to interrogate the emergence of the concept of diaspora as a way of obscuring and neutralizing the economic and political relations of human dislocation.

Essentializing 'Islamic society', 'Muslim woman', and 'Islamic diaspora'

It is well known that Western Orientalist knowledge has, since the seventeenth and eighteenth centuries, constructed societies practising Islam in terms of their religion. Islam, the dominant though rarely the only religion, is treated as the engine of these societies. Consistent with this theoretical-political outlook, contemporary governments, popular culture and mainstream media in the West also treat these societies and their diasporas as Islamic. The shift, in the last three decades, to culture, discourse and language as determinants or constituents of human life, has contributed to a new essentialization of these societies as 'Islamic'. The totalization of peoples and societies with an Islamic essence has been effectively critiqued (Said 1987, 2002; Zubaida 1995, 1998). Also, the essentialization of women in these societies as 'Muslim women' in search of a 'Muslim woman's identity' has been challenged on theoretical, political and methodological grounds (Moghissi 1999; Mojab 2000a, 2001a).

Western states, and postmodernist and poststructuralist scholars, are certainly not alone in exceptionalizing or essentializing 'Islamic societies'. Many Islamist groups, especially conservative ones, shield their anti-democratic and misogynist policies under the rubrics of the exceptionalism of Islam. The main target of violence of political Islam has been not the West but, rather, women and secular and radical intellectuals and activists who challenge their politics.

using Islam to beat down dissent

The struggle for women's rights in Kurdish diasporas

Women and patriarchy in the Western diaspora

Kurdish diasporas are products of conflicts between the state and the Kurds in their homeland. Not surprisingly, these diasporas enter into complex and changing interactions with the homeland and with each other, and have already transformed the emerging Kurdish nation into a transnational entity. They actively take part in creating conditions for reproducing, in the diaspora, both the nation and the homeland.

In the contemporary world order, these conflicts rarely remain local or national. The 'Kurdish Question' has intermittently occupied an important space in international diplomacy since the overthrow of the Iraqi monarchy in 1958. Since the collapse of the Iraqi Kurdish autonomist movement in 1975, due largely to intervention by the US, Iran and Israel, the question facing the European nations, and in particular Britain, Germany and Sweden, is on the one hand the settlement and integration of tens of thousands of Kurds and, recently, the restricting of immigrants and refugees. On the other hand, and indeed a more pressing question, is how to juggle the 'Kurdish Question' and the competing national interests of the United States and members of the European Union. Two of the most important Kurdish institutions, the Institut kurde de Paris and the Kurdish Human Rights Project in London, for instance, are funded by France and Britain, respectively.

The recent and, thus far, strongest, convergence of interest between the Kurds and the US dates back to the 1991 Gulf War, during which President George Bush, Sr encouraged the Kurds to rise up against Saddam Hussein and, when they did, left them on their own. Fearing another genocide, about two million Kurds escaped into the mountains, fleeing towards Iran and Turkey. The scene became a televised tragedy for two weeks, forcing Britain, France and the Bush administration to intervene; as a result, the refugees returned to their homes in a part of Iraqi Kurdistan designated a 'safe haven', protected by the air forces of the allied powers until the second American war against Iraq in 2003.

The safe haven soon turned into a new experiment in state-building. Elections for a local Kurdish parliament were held in 1992, leading to the formation of the

Kurdistan Regional Government (KRG), which was dominated by two major guerrilla organizations, the Kurdistan Democratic Party (KDP) and the Patriotic Union of Kurdistan (PUK). The four states of Iran, Iraq, Turkey and Syria were concerned that this de facto state might turn into an independent Kurdistan, and did their best to subvert it.[4]

After the defeat of Iraq in the Gulf War of 1991, much of Kurdistan came under the rule of the KDP and the PUK, which created the KRG. Six of the 105 members of the parliament were women (5.7 per cent). However, in the course of parliamentary elections, male and female voters were segregated at the voting centres. Although virtually independent from Baghdad, the KRG, and especially its KDP faction, refused to repeal the Ba'th regime's personal-status codes and other laws that were lenient in the matter of honour killing. In 1994, women marched from Sulaimaniya to Irbil in protest of the civil war between the KDP and the PUK, which lasted, intermittently, until 1996 and led to the formation of two Kurdish governments. The genocide and the 1991 Gulf War disrupted the fabric of Kurdish society and unleashed extensive male violence, including honour killing; suicide through self-immolation, normally a rare phenomenon, occurred regularly. In the wake of continuing protest, the PUK-led government issued resolutions aimed at criminalizing honour killing, although the laws remained on paper. The KDP justified patriarchal violence as part of Islamic and Kurdish traditions (Çingiyanî 1993), but this organization, too, issued similar edicts.

Kurdish patriarchy, with strong ties to feudal ways of life, is reproduced among diasporans of diverse backgrounds, including rural and urban, educated and illiterate, male and female, young and old, rich and poor. Violence against women, even in the form of honour killing, has occurred in a number of countries. Facing extensive media coverage and increasing Kurdish resistance, especially in Scandinavian countries, a few victims of honour killing were taken to Kurdistan to be murdered there (Mojab and Hassanpour 2002; see below).

A small minority of diasporans expect women, much more than men, to be loyal to the traditional patriarchal regime of the homeland, to the extent that they deny their daughters the right to participate in coeducational activities such as swimming or field trips. Europeans of the extreme right and neo-fascists treat honour killing and other violence as evidence of a 'barbaric culture' that must be discarded together with 'the immigrants'. By contrast, some states, such as Sweden, have taken, with good intention, a culturally relativist policy that advocates diversity and respect for difference by denying diasporan women full citizenship rights guaranteed in the civic nation. This policy is, thus, ethnocentric in so far as it does not accept secularism and a century of feminist struggles as genuine components of Kurdish and Middle Eastern cultures. Some Euro-Kurds, fearing violent racist backlash, take a nationalist position by denying that honour killing is part of their patriarchal culture, and treat it as borrowed, imposed, marginal and incidental. In all three cases, nationalism is in conflict with an internationalist feminist politics that treats male violence as universal – both Eastern and Western – and confronts it with a creative blending of both Western and Middle Eastern feminist experience.

Still, diasporic resistance to both state policy and patriarchal violence has been mounting, leading to increasing feminist consciousness and organizing (Mojab and Hassanpour 2002). Women, for instance, have already formed a growing milieu of intelligentsia and professionals, including poets, writers, researchers, journalists, members of parliament (Sweden, European Union), diplomats (USA), physicians, broadcasters and academics.

Organized resistance against indigenous patriarchy

The diaspora has been a centre of Kurdish nationalist activism. In the 1990s, Kurdish nationalist organizations and individuals published four magazines – none of which has survived – dealing with women's-rights struggles (Mojab 2001b: 18). National liberation looms large in these publications, which focus more on women's struggle against national oppression than gender oppression. Homeland Kurdish political parties, which are active in the diaspora, try to control women's activism.

As a founder of the International Kurdish Women's Studies Network (hereafter called the Network), I witnessed, and struggled through, the creation of the first independent network of Kurdish and non-Kurdish women researchers and activists sharing the following platform of action: to provide a forum for exchange of experience and knowledge among those who are interested in Kurdish women's studies; to value the contribution of community-based, institution-based, academic and independent researchers and activists in all parts of Kurdistan and in the diaspora; to assist those engaged in Kurdish women's studies and activism in all regions of Kurdistan and in the diaspora; to enhance and diversify other areas of studies, such as Iranian, Turkish and Arab women's studies through the introduction of Kurdish women's experience and knowledge; and to contribute to theories and practices of nationalism, democracy, citizenship, and women's rights through the case of Kurdish women. This was the first transnational feminist organizing experiment for Kurdish women with total independence from any of the Kurdish political parties.[5]

The life of the Network was short (1997–2000), but had noticeable accomplishments.[6] As it gained more recognition among researchers, activists, women's NGOs and other international NGOs, new allegiances emerged among its members. The peculiar elements in determining the convergence and divergence of political allegiances among women were national and linguistic boundaries and, more significantly, the conceptualization of feminism.[7] I observed a silent competition among the active members of the Network with regards to who had performed more activities and gained more access to funding, or who was given the status of spokesperson for the Kurdish women. It is important to note that the political-positional differences among Kurdish women do not merely replicate the challenges faced by any other 'women's collective', where power dynamics overshadow the feminist collective agenda. Undoubtedly, Kurdish women's activism faces these power challenges and more.

The women's mode of organizing is deeply rooted in the masculine and patriarchal national project. Thus, nationalism, colonialism, and nation-building projects, as presented by Kurdish national parties, preside over any feminist agenda. This overarching political framework comes with lifelong loyalties to particular Kurdish political parties and, often, also enters into a complicated kinship-like relation in which women are crucially implicated. Rupturing the rigid ideological boundaries and loyalties is daring and risky. A Kurdish woman activist recounts her experience at the inaugural meeting of a pan-European Kurdish organization:[8]

> To begin with, the Kurdish political parties active in Europe have to observe some gender equality rules; otherwise, they won't be able to continue their activity. Therefore, they follow the formality of the rule, though some genuinely would like to adhere to the principle of gender equality and, therefore, once in a while we get an invitation to their planning sessions. A group of us decided to accept an invitation to attend the first meeting of creating a pan-European Kurdish organization. In the meeting a male participant proposed that we use a Kurdish flag and an anthem at the beginning of each event. The flag which was proposed clearly identified a Kurdish political party. A Kurdish woman strongly objected to this and suggested that [they] use something related to the struggle of Kurdish women as the symbol of nationalism. Her objection created such an uproar among the male members of the group that we decided, enough is enough: how many times to do we need to listen and take orders from men? And [we] decided to create our own organization.

Kurdish women who, over the last two decades, have tried to create an 'independent' feminist space for themselves have faced many challenges. From being cast out of the community to being denigrated or, at times, even physically threatened, Kurdish women have fully experienced the hostility of patriarchal-nationalism. Let us listen to an excerpt from my interview with a Kurdish woman activist:

> In 1997–98, a group of us decided to establish a Kurdish women's group. We agreed on organizing an event called 'In Solidarity with Kurdish Women'. Based on my years of experience, I knew that this [was] a huge undertaking. Whenever we wanted to do something for Kurdish women, the political parties wanted to make sure that it stayed within their ideological framework. Kurdish elites wanted to limit its membership to professionals and intellectuals, and the community at large would campaign against it by saying that women's organizations are against family ethics, or are anti-men. Even some women shared these sentiments. I would say that behind all this were the Kurdish political parties, who could not perceive an independent feminist entity. Despite all the odds, we managed to establish ourselves, and began a campaign against honour killing. The most successful event which we organized was a seminar where we brought the leaders of the two major Kurdish parties of Iraq to the table and pushed them to discuss their party position on the situation of Kurdish women. The event happened at the time that these two parties were engaged in an internal war. Despite our success, men continued

to interfere with our affairs, and acted as if they were in a leadership position of our organization.

The Kurdish women's organizing efforts in diaspora in the 12-year period of the first Gulf War (1991) to the time of the US occupation of Iraq (2003) is a rich case of transnational feminist organizing. It embodies the complexities of nationalism, colonialism and imperialism. The emergence of women's NGOs in Iraqi Kurdistan, the flourishing of a women's press (see Mojab 2004), and the presence of women in cabinet posts opened new venues for Kurdish women's activism in the region as well as in diaspora. The state-like structure of the Kurdish region of northern Iraq gave legitimacy to the activism of women. In diaspora, too, the rights-based regime of Europe appended some equality clauses to their funding of Kurdish organizations. Some Kurdish women activists, realizing the closer ties binding homeland-hostland politics, made a bold move by creating an *ad hoc* group called The Network on the Kurdish Women's Charter, aimed at drafting a charter of rights for Kurdish women. The group later renamed itself the Kurdish Women's Project. The goal was to create a document that transgressed borders and encompassed all Kurds living within the boundaries of the nation-states in West Asia as well as in the diaspora.

On 22 June 2004 the *Charter for the Rights and Freedoms of Women in the Kurdish Regions and Diaspora* (hereafter called the Charter) was officially launched.[9] The ceremony was chaired by Lord Avebury, and Baroness Helena Kennedy, Q.C. delivered the keynote address. In the Foreword, it states that (Charter: 9):

> The Charter will be presented to the citizens of the Kurdish regions in addition to international, national and non-governmental organizations in the regions and diaspora, including the UN, European Parliament, human rights and women's rights organizations, political parties, cultural organizations and academic institutes.... It is hoped that these relevant bodies, particularly the Kurdish Parliament and Kurdish Regional Government, will support this document for the rights of women in the Kurdish regions and diaspora. These bodies are urged to consider seriously the domestic incorporation of the rights and needs identified in the Charter in both letter and spirit.

The Charter was widely consulted, and the earlier drafts were presented in Stockholm, Sweden (May and July 2001), Sulaimani and Hewler, Iraqi Kurdistan (July 2001), Gothenburg, Sweden (October 2001) and London, UK (December 2001 and March 2002). The Charter is written in English and in the two main dialects of Kurdish language, Kurmanji and Sorani.

There are two significant points about the Charter. One, as was mentioned above, is that this document applies to all Kurds irrespective of their geographical locations. It is truly a 'transnational' project. Second, its content draws on the recognized and widely accepted international body of legal rights as they pertain to women, including the *Convention on the Elimination of All Forms of Discrimination against Women* (CEDAW) and the *Declaration on the Elimination of Violence against Women*. The Charter is rather short, but it is concise. It consists of nine articles: (1) legal equality; (2) the elimination of discrimination in public and political life; (3) the elimination of discrimination in personal law; (4) equal access to employment and job-related services; (5) the elimination of violence against women in its broadest sense; (6) the elimination of sexual exploitation and trafficking of women and girls; (7) equal educational opportunities; (8) equal access to health; and (9) equal economic access and rights to social services and benefits.

The document calls for the separation of state and religion as the 'only ... guarantee for a free and democratic society', and is '[c]*oncerned* that religion is often misused in order to legitimate an infringement of rights guaranteed in a democratic society and fosters discrimination against women' (Charter: 11). Unlike many Middle Eastern states, which have signed or ratified CEDAW with reservations (Mayer 1999), the Charter does not declare any exceptions. In fact, it rejects many discriminations that are enshrined in Shari'a, for example, polygyny, temporary marriage, and control of reproductive rights. It also bans all forms of male violence.

The secularism of the Charter does not owe much to the location of its drafters in secular European countries. As mentioned earlier, Kurdish nationalism has been predominantly secular since the 1940s. In Iraq, where the US is restructuring the Iraqi nation-state along the lines of fusion of state and religion, women in Iraqi Kurdistan have protested the Islamization of gender relations (see, for example, the following report listed on the website of the Kurdish Women Action Against Honour Killing: 'Women in Iraq: Women's Rights Are in Danger': 10/07/2003, Report From Baghdad). The struggle for gender equality began in the early-twentieth century in the Ottoman Empire. Religion was not a constituent of nationhood and womanhood since the Kurds were, like their adversary, the Ottoman state, predominantly Muslim. Nationalists founded the first Kurdish women's organization (Kürd Kadınları Teali Cemiyeti, 'Society for the Advancement of Kurdish Women') in 1919 in Istanbul, where the size of the Kurdish population had been growing due to forced migrations and war (Alakom 1995).

By the mid-twentieth century, intellectuals, ranging from religious to nationalist to communist, denounced the oppression of women in Iraqi Kurdistan. The most prominent modern poet, Abdullah Goran (1904–62), in his work condemned gender and class violence, especially honour killing. The KDP published, clandestinely, the first issue of *Dengî Afret* (Woman's Voice) in 1953. In Turkey, by the time the leaders of the 1980 military coup d'état suppressed oppositional social movements and crushed any trace of civil society, the Kurdish Marxist director Yilmaz Güney raised the question of women's oppression, and strongly condemned, in his movie *Yol* (Road 1982), the patriarchal violence prevalent in rural Kurdish society.

Conclusions

I have tried, so far, to suggest that theories of diaspora and transnationality, which reduce the complex homeland–hostland relations to culture and identity, fail to account for the Kurdish case. I will highlight two issues that are crucial in these theorizations.

First is the metaphysics of constructing an imaginary great divide between the East and the West. In the case of gender relations, while one cannot document a rich history of feminist theoretical work in any of the four countries, the challenges briefly outlined above point to a steady, conscious struggle for women's rights and against male violence in countries where civil society was stifled by the state. The women's press of the Ottoman Empire, for instance, dates back to the latter part of the nineteenth century. In 1911, a member of the newly established Iranian parliament campaigned for women to be granted suffrage rights. In Turkey, these rights were granted in 1932. In Iran, the autonomous government of Azerbaijan, which ruled over the northwestern provinces of the country, granted suffrage rights to women in 1946.

However, several polities do not consider this century-long history of women's movements part of the history of the Kurds and other peoples of the region. Western states, racist and Islamophobic groups and mainstream media treat patriarchy and its violence as *the* sacred, uncontested, essential and inherent constituent of immigrants' gender relations. At the same time, much post-colonial and postmodernist theorizing also considers feminism a 'derivative discourse' coming from the West and infected with Western biases. This claim is shared by Islamists, nationalists and Third World nativists in the non-Western world.

These shared perspectives of polities with conflictual interests call into question the essentialization of some peoples and diasporas as 'Islamic'. At the same time, there is a commonality of interest in the anti-feminism prevalent in both the East and the West. This comprises, for instance, extensive anti-feminism in the popular culture and media of North America (Hammer 2002). Western conservatives do not consider anarchism, feminism, socialism, communism, Marxism or even the UN to be part of the culture or 'canon of Western civilization'. Even the conflict over separation of state and religion is not over. If, in Iraq, Islamists vie for a theocratic regime, in Europe some states demand the adoption of Christianity as the official religion in the forthcoming European constitution.

Second, the Kurdish case calls into question the postmodernist essentialization of the contemporary world into fragmented, decentred and fluid entities in which the nation-state is on the verge of collapsing. While the contemporary dynamics of capitalist globalization demonstrate centrifugal tendencies, especially in the realm of culture and communication, the sovereignty of the state is still treated as sacred. The United States of America, the most powerful state, has refused to ratify CEDAW in order to deny American women the ability to seek justice outside the sphere of the national state. It has also put up stiff resistance to the formation of the International Criminal Court, which aims at bringing to justice the perpetrators of genocide and crimes against humanity.

The charter of Kurdish women's rights will also remain a scrap of paper in the absence of a state that grants such rights. The *de facto* Kurdish state in Iraq may not survive the recurrent structuring of the Iraqi state. No doubt, women and other social movements in Kurdistan and in the diaspora can turn the document into a means of raising awareness about gender equality and justice. However, it is also true that women demand rights, and these rights make a difference only if they are recognized, granted and enacted by the state. Thus, while much feminist theory considers the state and the institution of law patriarchal, it is through these patriarchal institutions that women's rights can materialize. In the absence of a Kurdish state or even regional autonomy, the ability of Kurdish women to enact, amend and implement this charter is seriously limited. The only alternative is for Kurdish women to promote their rights as citizens of individual states rather than as members of the Kurdish nation. This, in turn, demonstrates the power of the four nation-states in the Middle East to shape diasporic life.

Third, the experience of the Kurdish diasporas exposes the limitations of the concept of 'transnationality'. The Kurds are a transnational entity par excellence. Distinct from internationalism and its project of eliminating national borders, transnationalism is fragmented nationalism. It is a national formation fragmented by national borders, albeit the borders of 'other' nations. Already divided among four states since 1918, about half of the Kurdish people now live outside Kurdistan, either within each state or in fragments scattered all over the world. The contradictions are prominent. Diasporas reproduce the Kurdish nation and its nationalist project for self-rule; at the same time, the four states that rule over the Kurds continue to reproduce their borders in the diaspora, and turn the Charter and similar projects into figments of the imagination.

Finally, the Kurdish diasporas are certainly complex in politics, class composition, culture, language and dialect and religion. They cannot be classed as Islamic diasporas in so far as religion plays a marginal role in the nationalist moment, and it cannot account for the complexity of life in (post)modern times. The marginal role of religion in Kurdish life is not difficult to explain. Kurdish nationalism is in conflict with states that are either Islamic (Iran's theocracy), or with those whose dominant religion is Islam (Arabs, Persians and Turks). Sharing the same religious turf, Islam has not turned into a site of conflict between the Kurds and the nation-states that oppress them.

A more useful understanding of 'diaspora' in relation to feminist organizing would be to think of diaspora as a historical rather than cultural phenomenon (Anthias 1998). A historical understanding of diaspora would focus on the events of, and precursors to, war or repression (before a dispersal, if there has been one), or oppression (in the diaspora itself). These are some of the historical events through which a community comes to understand itself as a political entity. The *culturalization* of diaspora is apparent when considering Kurdish feminists organizing in the European context: in the eyes of European policy-makers and the European media, they are overwhelmingly seen as cultural appendages to the male-defined Kurdish community. This is paradoxical, since the women are overwhelmingly *political* refugees. In fact, it has been argued that the trauma related to resettlement in the Kurdish diaspora should be understood as a change in *political* culture (Sheikhmous 2000).

Notes

1 Tables 8.1 and 8.2 first appeared in Mojab and Hassanpour 2004.
2 The theoretical argument for this chapter is based on Rachel Gorman's extensive literature review of transnational feminism and diaspora studies (see Gorman and Mojab forthcoming a and b).
3 I am thankful to Elinor Bray-Collins for her assistance with this project, in which the following journals were reviewed: *Gender and Society*; *Feminist Review*; *Feminist Studies*; *Signs: Journal of Women in Culture and Society*; *Women's Studies International Forum*; and *Women's Studies Quarterly*.
4 For an in-depth study of the political formation and its development of the Kurdish region of northern Iraq, see Stansfield 2003.
5 It is beyond the scope of this chapter to discuss further the influence of Kurdish political parties which, in subtle ways, finally dismantled the Network.
6 For the account of internal power struggle in the Network see Mojab 2001c, 2000b,c, and 1997.
7 The serious debate on feminism and its political and practical implication among Kurdish women is very similar to Alvarez's observation among Latin American women. See Alvarez 2000.
8 To respect the anonymity of the interviewee, all identifiers, such as names of specific political parties, and the location and specificity of the gathering, have been deleted.
9 For the full text of the Charter, check the website of the Kurdish Human Rights Project at http://www.khrp.org.

References

Alakom, R. (1995) *Kurdish Women: A New Force in Kurdistan* (in Kurdish), Spånga, Sweden.
Alvarez, S. (2000) 'Translating the global: Effects of transnational organizing on local feminist discourses and practices in Latin America', *Meridians: Feminism, Race, Transnationalism* 1(1): 29–67.
Anthias, F. (1998) 'Evaluating "diaspora": Beyond ethnicity?' *Sociology* 32(3): 557–80.
Brah, A. (1996) *Cartographies of Diaspora: Contesting Identities*, London and New York: Routledge.
Charles, C. (1995) 'Gender and the politics of contemporary Haiti: The Duvalierist state, transnationalism and the emergence of a new feminism (1980–1990)', *Feminist Studies*, 21(1), Spring: 135–64.
Çingiyanî, C. (1993) 'An interview with four women belonging to the Union of the Women of Kurdistan' (in Kurdish), *Xermane*, Nos. 9–10: 122, 124.
Gorman and Mojab (a) (forthcoming) 'Dispersed nationalism: War, diaspora and Kurdish women's organizing', *Journal of Middle East Women's Studies*.
—— (b) (forthcoming) 'War, diaspora, learning and women's standpoint', in Maroussia Hajdukowski-Ahmed and Nazilla Khanlou (eds) *Not Born a Refugee Woman: Reclaiming Identities: Challenges, Implications and Transformations in Research, Education, Policy and Creativity*, Oxford: Oxford University Press.
Grewal, I. and Kaplan, C. (eds) (1994) 'Introduction: Transnational feminist practices and questions of postmodernity', in *Scattered Hegemonies: Postmodernity and Transnational Feminist Practices*, Minnesota: Minnesota University Press.
—— (2000) 'Postcolonial studies and transnational feminist practices'. Online. Available HTTP: http://socialchass.ncsu.edu/jouvert/v5il/grewal.htm (accessed July 2002).

Hall, S. (1994) 'Cultural identity and diaspora', in P. Williams and L. Chrisman (eds) *Colonial Discourse and Post-Colonial Theory: A Reader*, New York: Harvester Wheatsheaf.

Hammer, R. (2002) *Antifeminism and Family Terrorism: A Critical Feminist Perspective*, Lanham, Maryland: Rowman and Littlefield Publishers.

Institut kurde de Paris (IKP) (2005) The Kurdish diaspora. Online. Available http://www.institutkurde.org/en/kurdorama/ (accessed 16 December 2005).

Itzigsohn, J. (2000) 'Immigration and the boundaries of citizenship: The institutions of immigrants' political transnationalism', *International Migration Review*, 34(4): 1126–54.

Khayati, K. (2000) 'Diasporic consciousness among Kurdish refugees and immigrants', Paper presented at IMER conference, KHRP (Kurdish Human Rights Project) 1996 *Kurds in the Former Soviet Union*, London: KHRP.

McDowall, D. (2000) *A Modern History of the Kurds*, London: I.B. Tauris.

Mayer, A. E. (1999) 'Religious reservations to the Convention on the Elimination of All Forms of Discrimination Against Women: What do they really mean?' in Courtney Howland (ed.) *Religious Fundamentalisms and the Human Rights of Women*, New York, St Martin's Press, pp. 105–16.

Meho, Lokman, (2001) 'The Kurds in Lebanon: An overview', in Meho, Lokman and Maglaughlin, Kelly (eds) *Kurdish Culture and Society: An Annotated Bibliography*, Westport, Connecticut: Greenwood Press, pp. 27–47.

Moghissi, H. (1999) *Feminism and Islamic Fundamentalism: The Limits of Postmodern Analysis*, London: Zed Press.

Mohanty, C. T. (2003) *Feminism Without Borders: Decolonizing Theory, Participatory Solidarity*, Durham & London: Duke University Press.

Mojab, S. (1997) 'Crossing boundaries of nationalism, patriarchy, and Eurocentrism: The struggle for a Kurdish Women Studies Network', *Canadian Woman Studies* 17(2): 68–72.

—— (2000a) 'Doing fieldwork on women in theocratic Islamic states,' *Resources for Feminist Research*, Spring/Summer, 28(1–2): 81–98.

—— (2000b) 'The feminist project in cyberspace and civil society', *Convergence*, 33 (1–2): 106–19.

——(2000c) 'Educational voyaging in a globalizing planet: The conference of the rich, the poor, and the oppressed', *Atlantis: A Women's Studies Journal* 24(2): 123–34.

—— (2001a) 'Theorizing the politics of "Islamic Feminism"', *Feminist Review*, Winter, No. 69: 124–46.

——(2001b) 'Introduction: The solitude of the stateless: Kurdish women at the margins of feminist knowledge', in Mojab, S. (ed.) *Women of a Non-State Nation: The Kurds*, Costa Mesa, California: MAZDA Publishers, pp. 1–21.

—— (2001c) 'The politics of "cyberfeminism" in the Middle East: The case of Kurdish women', *Journal of Race, Gender, and Class* 8(4): 42–61.

—— (2004) 'No "Safe Haven" for women: Violence against women in Iraqi Kurdistan', in W. Giles and J. Hyndman (eds) *Sites of Violence: Gender and Identity in Conflict Zones*, Berkeley: University of California Press, pp. 108–33.

—— (2005) 'Kurdish women and women in Kurdish national politics', in Suad Joseph (ed.) *Encyclopedia of Women and Islamic Cultures*, The Netherlands: Brill Academic Publishers, pp. 358–66.

—— (2005) 'Kurdish women,' in Suad Joseph (ed.), *Encyclopedia of Women and Islamic Cultures*. Volume II, Family, Law and Politics. Brill: Leiden-Boston, pp. 358–366.

Mojab, S. and Hassanpour, A. (2002) 'The politics and culture of "honour" killing: The murder of Fadime Şahindal', *Pakistan Journal of Women's Studies: Alam-e-Niswan*, June, (9)1: 57–77.

Mojab, S. and Hassanpour, A. (2004) 'Kurdish diaspora', in Ian Skoggard (ed.) *Encyclopedia of Diasporas*, Human Relations Area Files, Inc.: New Haven, Connecticut, pp. 214–24.

Müller, D. (2000) 'The Kurds of Soviet Azerbaijan, 1920–91', *Central Asian Survey*, 19(1): 41–77.

Ong, A. and Nonini, D. (1997) 'Toward a cultural politics of diaspora and transnationalism', in A. Ong and D. M. Nonini (eds) *Underground Empires: The Cultural Politics of Modern Chinese Transnationalism*, New York: Routledge.

Portes, A., Guarnizo, L. and Landolt, P. (1999) 'The study of transnationalism: Pitfalls of an emergent research field', *Ethnic and Racial Studies*, 22(2): 217–37.

Reinharz, S. (1992) *Feminist Methods in Social Research*, Oxford University Press.

Said, E. (1978) *Orientalism*, New York: Pantheon Books.

—— (2002) 'Impossible histories: Why the many Islams cannot be simplified', *Harper's Magazine*, July: 69–74.

Sassen, Saskia. (1998). *Globalization and its Discontents: Essays on the New Mobility of People and Money*. New York: The New Press.

Sassen, S. (2001) 'Cracked casings: Notes towards and analytics for studying transnational processes', in Ludger Pries (ed.) *New Transnational Social Spaces: International Migration and Transnational Companies in the Early Twenty-first Centuries*, London and New York: Routledge.

Sheikhmous, O. (2000) *Crystallization of a New Diaspora: Migration and Political Culture Among the Kurds of Europe*, Stockholm: Centre for Research in International Migration and Ethic Relations.

Spivak, G. (1997) 'Diasporas old and new: Women in the transnational world', in A. Kumar (ed.) *Class Issues: Pedagogy, Cultural Studies, and the Public Sphere*, New York and London: New York University Press.

Stansfield, G. R. V. (2003) *Iraqi Kurdistan: Political Development and Emergent Democracy*, London and New York: Routledge Curzon.

Suzuki, N. (2000) 'Between two shores: Transnational projects and Filipino wives in/from Japan', *Women's Studies International Forum* 23(4): 431–44.

Zubaida, S. (1995) 'Is there a Muslim society? Ernest Gellner's sociology of Islam', *Economy and Society*, Vol. 42, No, 2, May.

—— (1998) 'Muslim societies: Unity or diversity', *ISIM Newsletter*, No. 1, October: 1.

9 Discourses of Islam/secularism and identity-building processes among Turkish university youth

Aylin Akpınar

Introduction

Turkey, with a dominant Muslim population, has applied to be a member of the European Union. A recent survey conducted in Turkey by IKV (Economic Development Foundation), together with the European Union General Secretary, showed that 94.5 per cent of the Turkish population was in favour of the country's membership in the European Union, while 4.4 per cent was against it and 1.1 per cent had no opinion (Economy Service 2004). Being a member of the European Union means 'an increase in the standards of democracy and human rights' for 79.9 per cent of the Turkish population. The results of another survey (Çarkoğlu and Toprak 2000) showed that the majority of Turkish people approved of neither the idea of religious involvement in public life nor the interference of state in religious life.

Those in Islamic circles are arguing that the secular regime in Turkey is violating basic human rights through its opposition to the appearance of Islamic symbols in public spaces. On the other hand, some in secular circles insist on the neutrality of public spaces in accordance with the definition of secularism adopted by the Turkish Republic under the influence of French-style republicanism. As a result of adjustments to the Copenhagen criteria of the European Union, several articles in the Turkish Constitution (2004) have been amended, and this has led to more individual liberties. For example, Article 10 'General Principles' states: 'Women and men have equal rights. The state is obligated to put this principle into practice'. The death penalty is forbidden according to Article 38 of 'Individual Rights and Duties'. Moreover, in cases of conflict between national laws and international agreements regarding basic rights and liberties, priority is given to international agreement principles. However, numerous people in Turkey, especially among the highly educated, are cautious and sometimes sceptical of the deeds of the AKP government.

A similar scepticism about Turkish diaspora prevails in the European discourse. This scepticism is shaped by fears which mainly result from political and social conflicts within Turkey (Pratt-Ewing 2003: 405). Whilst some secularists in Turkey fear that the appearance of Islamic values in daily life may eventually threaten the secular regime, some players in the European Union fear that Turkey's entry into Europe may result in the demise of Europe. Within this fear there is a disguised opposition between Turkey with its Islamic-Ottoman heritage and Europe with its Christian heritage.

Islam is known as 'migrant religion' in Europe. Turkish migrant organizations in the diaspora are fragmented in the same manner as the political scene is fragmented in Turkish society. 'Homeland' politics and politics within the Turkish diaspora continuously feed and affect each other. Avcı (2005: 205) states that Milli Görüş (National Vision) is among the leading Turkish migrant organizations in Europe, with an estimated 300,000 followers. The nationalistic-religious vision is reflected in the term 'Milli Görüş', which has been the key concept in the ideology of Islamic parties in Turkey. The National Vision movement in Europe has a critical approach towards the secular system in the country. Having their own schools, Milli Görüş offers Koran courses, religious education to youth and children, mosque services, weddings, funerals, moral support and support for women (ibid.: 207). Today's governing party, AKP (an abbreviation, in Turkish, of justice and development), which took power in November of 2002, is seen as the reformist wing of the movement. Until AKP took power, Milli Görüş had been considered an unacceptable movement by the secular regime in Turkey. That's why the Diyanet, or Directorate of Religious Affairs, was founded in 1971, so that opposition forces would not exploit the religious needs of Turkish migrants and mobilize them against the interests of the Turkish Republic (Landeman 1997: 220). In order to reach this goal, the Diyanet administers mosques and provides them with imams who stress a unitary 'Kemalist-Islamic identity compatible with the Turkish regime' (Ögelman 2003: 169).

The question of new Islamic religiosity in Europe is directly related to debates in Turkey between 'Islam as ethics' and 'Islam as observance'. The key question within the European discourse on Turkish diasporic youth is whether third and fourth generations will retain a Muslim identity and, if so, what kind of Muslim identity that will be. In recent comparative research conducted on Euro-Turks in Germany and France, Turkish researchers Kaya and Kertel (2005: 83) found that more than 40 per cent of Turks construct their identities by relating themselves both to 'homeland' and host society. Islam, in their case, is represented as 'symbolic religiosity', and is constructed as a protest against their discrimination as 'Muslims'. For example, Islamic Force is a German-Turkish rap group performing under this name to protest existing prejudice against Turkish ethnic youth. The same researchers also found another 40 per cent Islamist and secularist groupings among Euro-Turks, besides a 20 per cent assimilated group. Only 8 per cent of Euro-Turks identified themselves fundamentally as Muslims, in parallel to the situation in Turkey (ibid.: 72–3). With reference to the mentioned 8 per cent Islamists, the research results of the German sociologist Nohl (1999: 107) can be considered. Among Turkish university attendants in Germany, he has come into contact with some youngsters who are trying to construct an Islamic identity within the discourse of authenticity. These youngsters are critical of the Turkish cultural impact on 'pure Islamic practice' as in the case of 'arranged marriages'. They see it their mission to teach the essence of Islam to non-Muslims in Europe and to try to construct an Islamic identity as a response to the 'moral degradation' they think exists in the host society.

According to several researchers (Kaya 2000: 58; Narrowe 1998: 203; Neyzi 2001) who have conducted research on Turkish diasporic youth, many youngsters have embraced a hybrid culture where Islam and Turkishness play symbolic roles as signs of a heritage. There are several subgroups within Turkish youth culture whose members constantly facilitate dialogue between and across nations by using modern means of communication (Ostergaard-Nielsen 2000: 23–38). Muslim youth identity is also encapsulated in this process. The question is the same both in the European discourse on Islam and in the debate between secular and Islamist discourses in Turkey: how will it be possible to have Islamic lifestyles without thereby threatening the democratic and secular society?

Today, Muslim populations who claim the right to lead pious, Islamic lifestyles are taking part in all spheres of economic life and consumption to the extent that they can afford. It is possible to observe a Muslim female director of an under-wear firm covering her head with a chic 'turban' and wearing a fashionable Islamic-style suit while taking care of female and male models who are dressed only in underwear. Muslim women who are wearing 'tesettür' (Islamic-style dress) dye their hair and get their faces made up in elegant beauty salons. Islamic pop music, Islamic fashion shows, five-star hotels with swimming pools and dis-cotheques for Muslim youngsters – albeit segregated for males and females – are some examples of consumption patterns among those in the Islamic community. Would it be possible to state, then, that the more the Turkish population becomes part of consumer society, the more secularized they become? El-Guindi (1999: 134) argues that 'privacy, humility, piety and moderation are cornerstones of the Islamic belief system. Luxury and leisure await Muslims in the next world'. In this sense, Islamic values held by at least middle and upper classes in Turkey are going through a transformation. Does this mean that Muslim people are adopting a secular frame of mind? The answer is both yes and no. Yes, because the orga-nization of economic institutions and social relations in the global world necessi-tate the adoption of a rational mindset. No, because it is possible, at the same time, to organize one's life, and especially family and gender relations, according to Islamic beliefs in line with the idea of gender difference/inequality and sepa-ration of the sexes. It has been agreed upon by feminist scholars (Mernissi 1991; Moghissi 1999) that the main area Islamists try to protect from modernization is the domain of women's rights and family.

Generally, two perspectives about identity, Islam and secularism in Turkey can be identified. The argument of the first perspective, as presented, for example, by the anthropologists Tapper and Tapper (1987: 64–5) is that republicanism and Islam could be thought of as aspects of a single ideology. On the other hand, the sociologist Göle (1997b: 86) argues that by participating in public life, Kemalist, or republican, women were freed from religious constraints but that they had to choose between Muslim and European cultural identities. Göle's position, how-ever, could only be understood in relation to categories of gender, generation and class, and might not be applicable to the experiences of Turkish people in general, whereas the Tappers demonstrate an accommodations tactic used by Turkish people at different levels. First, there is the adoption of the kind of Islamic values that are more appropriate for today's society than others. Consider the following statement:

> [The] Prophet forbade alcohol because he found all Arabs to be drunkards and could discover no other remedy for their excesses, but in fact Islam favours moderation in all things, and if one can imbibe sparingly then one has no need to fear one's soul.
>
> (Tapper and Tapper 1987: 65)

Second, Turkish people believe that republican institutions function in exactly the same way as Islamic ones. An example is the case of paying taxes. Taxes paid to the state go to education, health and the salaries of religious teachers, thereby replacing Islamic alms and tithes. Third, Turks may explain religious values by appealing to secular values, such as the rationalization that fasting in Ramadan is good for health, as the idea is to purge the body, etc.

Conceptual framework, method and analysis

This chapter is based on a series of oral interviews I conducted in two stages. The first stage included conversations with different generations[1] and both genders from varying educational backgrounds to understand how different narratives could reflect the dominant assumptions of the informants about religion. I focused on the informants' family backgrounds, religious/secular socialization, gendered socialization, political socialization, visions for the future and the kind of a society in which they would like to live. I interviewed 16 informants living in Ankara, the capital city of Turkey, and Istanbul, the largest metropolis and a microcosm of Turkey.

My analysis showed that the older generation, comprising those over 60 years of age, relegated Islam to the inner conscience of Muslims. They were brought up with the republican ideals of neutral public space, and expressed their thoughts in the saying, 'In Islam prayer is said in secrecy just as sin is committed in secrecy'. This expression implies that republican secularization considers religion a phenomenon related to the next life, and not a worldly affair.

In the second stage of my fieldwork, I interviewed youngsters aged 18 to 35 who were born or socialized during the era of President Turgut Özal. Özal's legacy meant integration of Muslim identity once again into the public realm.[2] Secular youngsters insisted on the neutrality of public space as the main condition of a democracy where individuals had respect for each other's lifestyles. Narratives of youngsters who identified themselves as Muslim indicated that they all went through an individualization process from being more radical to becoming a Muslim subject.[3]

Since my main objective was to understand the kind of meaning Islam, as a world view, had for young university students, I relied on narrative analysis.

I assumed that only if one approaches religion as a lived experience could one see changes in religion as a world view (Houston 1998: 239). My informants, both young men and women, were university graduates or were attending university. I contacted them through secular youth organizations, such as ADD (The Organization for Kemalist Thought) and ÇYDD (The Organization for the Promotion of Contemporary Living) and through religious groups such as Fethullah Gülen's[4] groups, and Milli Gençlik Vakfı, the youth organization of the former Islamist Welfare Party. I also interviewed youngsters who had attended religious schools. In what follows, a short historical context for the Turkish modernization and secularization process will provide the necessary context for the narratives of the young people who participated in this research.

Contesting schools of thought: Westernists, Islamists, Turkists

In reviewing the Turkish modernization process, it is necessary to go back to the years between 1908 and 1918. These years can best be understood as an attempt to find a new cultural construction for the Turkish people. During these years, three schools of thought, namely Westernist, Islamist and Turkist, fought a ten-year battle in order to solve the problems of Turkish transformation.

According to the Westernist standpoint, the basic solution to the problem of transformation was to leave behind old, traditional/religious values in order to develop a new morality based on modern/Western progressive values such as a scientific mind, reason, and individual freedom (Berkes 1998: 337–43). The cause of backwardness, the Islamist standpoint argued, was the separation of the world and religion into distinct compartments by Christianity. The decline of religion followed the progress of science. Doubt was the enemy of faith.

The Turkist standpoint agreed with the role of mind and reason in Western progress, but stressed that the basic reality in Western civilization lay in nationalism in which religion also played a part. The outstanding figure in the Turkish school of thought, Ziya Gökalp, distinguished culture from civilization, and said that Turks were supposed to appropriate the international modern civilization and not the national cultures of the West (ibid.: 383).

The secularizing reforms of the Tanzimat Period (1839–76), achieved by opening the doors to the West, continued in the Meşrutiyet Period (1908–19), the new constitutional era. In 1924, the Sultanate, the Caliphate and the Ministries of Şeriat and Evkaf (pious foundations) were abolished. Madrasas (religious schools), tarikats (religious orders) and their cloisters were banned, and education was unified under the Ministry of Education. A Directorate of Religious Affairs (the Diyanet) was constituted to manage the administrative affairs of religion. Islam as 'diyanet' (piety) was thought to be a factor of enlightenment.

Kemalist secularism and Islamic idiom

The new Turkish Civil Code, adapted from the Swiss civil code, passed in the National Assembly in 1926. Here the Kemalist regime deviated from the Turkist view based on Ziya Gökalp's theory of the dichotomy of culture and civilization. It was stated that there was no fundamental difference in the needs of nations belonging to the modern family of civilization. Classes in religion were dropped in the urban schools in 1930 and in the village schools in 1933. Polygamy was abolished. Full political rights and duties were given to women in 1934. The Turkish Republic was declared a secular state by a constitutional amendment in 1937 (ibid.: 463–85).

As the 'father of Turks', President Atatürk's goal was to free Turks from the collective control exerted on individuals by Islamic 'gemeinschaft'. Mardin (1994: 164) suggests that Kemalist secularism could not compensate for the patterns of Islam that Turkish Muslims followed at the level of everyday life, and thus was doomed to failure. It is possible to illustrate how Muslim culture worked as an idiom in her life in the following narrative by a 30-year-old, covered Muslim woman. She tells us:

> I learned Islam at home.... It was my grandmother who taught me prayer *suras* in the Koran. She used to pray a lot, both day and night. She would always turn to right before she slept, to 'Kıble'.[5] She never watched television. She would not like us to play with dolls. She was against pictures. All these she had learned in the village. My grandmother told me stories about how women in the village resisted learning to read and write in the Latin alphabet. Later on, she learned to read and write all by herself.... Everyone in our family is covered. I went to summer Koran courses. All of my friends were covered when I was at high school. I was a good student who obeyed the rules.... Every 23rd of April was celebrated as a national holiday. On such an occasion, the school administration placed the bust of Atatürk at the entrance to the school. Two of our teachers stood and waited, one on each side of the bust. We students one by one had to go forward and bend our heads in respect in front of the bust of Atatürk. To show respect by bending my head in front of a bust was irritating for me. I was a child who liked Atatürk. However, to bend my head in front of a stone was not spiritual. I perceived this as a repressive sanction.... At that time, some of my feelings for Atatürk were lost.... After graduation, I covered my head.

In this story, we can follow the traces of a deep conflict between spiritual morality, which is an outcome of Muslim ethos, and secular morality, which is being constructed by the school authorities. For the authorities, bending your head in front of Atatürk's bust during a national commemoration was a sign of showing attachment to Kemalist symbols, as integral to national identity. The construction of Muslim identity, on the other hand, gives priority to Islamic faith and everyday living according to an Islamic idiom. Different interpretations and priorities of secular and Islamic standpoints may clash in everyday life due to 'the moving between sacred space and time and ordinary worldly space and time throughout the day every day' (El Guindi 1999: 81). The conflicts between the priorities of secular and Islamic standpoints create a pseudo-polarization at emotional and symbolic levels.

Reappearance of Islamic identity in the urban public space

Turkish state policy towards Islam has been compromising and integrative. Yet, there is a consensus among researchers (Göle 1997a; Narlı 1996; Cizre-Sakallıoğlu 1996; Zubaida 1996) that Islam reappeared in the public space, making a stark contrast between the 60 years of the Republic and the period since 1980. The Turkish-Islamic Synthesis adopted after the military coup of 1980 has worked as a model for state pedagogic and cultural activities (Güvenç *et al.* 1991). In fact, a more complex identity politics was initiated, beginning with the transition to a multiparty system in 1946 through the establishment of the Democratic Party as the main faction against the Republican People's Party (Göle 1997b: 93). The setting up of İmam Hatip Lycées is important because 'Tevhid-i Tedrisat', the Unification of Education Law, was challenged by their curriculum. The secular elite considered these schools necessary for the education of religious functionaries, but they were not foreseen as an alternative to the secular education system. According to recent research (Çakır *et al.* 2004), İmam Hatip graduates consider themselves the best carriers of moralist, nationalist and conservative values. In the 1970s, these schools started accepting girls as well, because conservative parents preferred to send their daughters to schools where genders were not mixed. Ironically, it was found that these girls have adopted modernist values in contradiction to their parents' conservative values. For example, 84.4 per cent of female students were in favour of women's employment outside home, and 57.8 per cent of them thought that women could travel alone, whereas, respectively, 15.9 per cent and 19.3 per cent of male students agreed with the two propositions (Coşkun 1999: 98). It has been argued that several political parties to the right end of the spectrum have supported the establishment of these schools. This was because conservative Muslims considered İmam Hatip Schools a project of civil society (Çakır *et al.* 2004). The schools were controlled by the Ministry of Education, but the religious education provided by them caused suspicion. In 1997, the Turkish state indirectly brought an end to elementary education in these schools by introducing the obligatory eight-year elementary school. This action created irritation among religious families. It is interesting to hear about the education given in these schools from informants who had attended there. A 29-year-old male who is a graduate of İmam Hatip and the Faculty of Divinity says:

> My father decided to send me to İmam Hatip. The youngsters in our *mahalle* who went to these schools influenced him. These were young, pious men who could sometimes lead the *cemaat* [religious community] in the mosque.... My father liked them. My parents' religiosity was built on tradition; however, I learned in the school and taught them about religion. Most families sent their children to İmam Hatip schools so that they would first learn about their religion and then they would attend university to become doctors, lawyers or engineers.... One of my relatives died during the construction of such a school. He was the foreman. People collected money among themselves and donated it to the government for the construction of İmam Hatip schools....

Families saw a social chaos in society. They saw youngsters becoming drug addicts or using alcohol. They saw pornographic publications. We were taught to observe society from the reference point of our religion. What was lacking in society? How was the average Muslim in the street? How much did he have to do with ideal Islam? We thought that nobody knew about ideal religion in our society. Our society needed us. Our teachers always motivated us in this direction.

One can read this story in two ways. It is possible to argue that İmam Hatip Schools were indeed part of civil society, as they were set up due to the demands of people in the community. On the other hand, it is possible to argue that this İmam Hatip School graduate was in fact modelling religious morality because he felt that through his instruction at the school he had been given a responsibility to do so for society. It is thus possible to understand that a moralistic discourse based on an understanding of spreading Islamic knowledge was constructed in these schools as a remedy for degeneration in society. The social chaos which the informant mentions can be defined as the increased anomie[6] in Turkish society, which has been an outcome of rapid urbanization, internal migration and the spread of mindless commercial populism, including the appearance of numerous private channels on television. Conservative families reacted against this morality crisis by holding on to religious symbols. The basic slogan of the Islamist MSP, the Nationalist Salvation Party, was 'Moral Development' in 1970s. Vergin (1992: 74) argues that as a result of internal migration, rural Anatolians who were living in the periphery came to realize the existing social stratification in big cities. Lifestyles in the metropolises were against their tradition. They became alienated and feared that they were going to lose their collective identity. Thus, people started resisting change.

A 28-year-old female graduate whose parents have sent her to İmam Hatip Lycée argues:

My parents did not ask me whether I wanted to attend an İmam Hatip Lycée or not. Why should I be against or for? I did not know that. Today, I think that I have learned more than I have lost by attending the school. When one talks about an Islamic identity, one has to have knowledge of the sources. One has to know what a *tefsir* [*Koran*ic interpretation] is. What has our Prophet really said and what he has not said? These are all components of an Islamic identity. In İmam Hatip I gained such an education, but the pedagogical outlook was very traditional. To give a simple example, I was not allowed to go out to do shopping with a girlfriend. Our teachers taught us about 'sin' instead of 'shame' of the traditional culture. One can fight against shame, but how can a religious person fight against sin? My classmates came from poor, lower-class families. Their parents left them to teachers' authority. I was the only person who was a doctor's daughter.... Yet I learned at the school that I did not have to believe in every *Hadith* [Prophet Mohammad's sayings] because they might not be His own words. I learned at the school that the *Koran* demanded a *tefsir*. Somebody could interpret it differently in the future. I was confronted with radical Muslim girls at the university who did not accept that.... As a graduate of İmam Hatip School, I knew at least the flexibility of religious knowledge.

It is possible to read this story also in two ways. From the standpoint of the informant, one can argue that learning about religion in a religious school is healthier than learning about religion from unreliable sources. On the other hand, it is also possible to argue that education provided at religious schools – despite the parallel, secular curriculum – is directed to construct an Islamic identity. This informant also had a modernist outlook, like many female students mentioned before, in contradiction to the traditional, pedagogical outlook given in the school.

During the 1980s, female students with religious head-covers or men with the 'Islamic beard' appeared on university campuses and other public spaces. Translations of some radical Islamic journals found their way to Turkish society from abroad. It was under Turgut Özal's leadership (1981–93) that Turkish society was opened up to the outside world as a result of neo-liberal economy, while Özal did not hide his strong connections to the Nakşibendi tarikat. He tried to show that being a pious Muslim and a Western-minded person did not necessarily lead to contradiction: quite the contrary, they could be compatible terms.

Research (Atacan 1990; Vergin 1992) shows that tarikats function in Turkey as 'tampon mechanisms' for the integration of the masses to rapidly changing and insecure economic and social relations in big cities. Next in importance to Nakşibendis has been the order of Fethullah Gülen, an important offshoot of the Nurcu movement. This group was very effective in organizing youngsters who had migrated to cities to study at the university. The section of the population who wanted to lead pious, Muslim lifestyles started challenging the secular public space after having formed their elites and their middle classes (Ayata 1996; Saktanber 1997; Özdalga 1990). The Islamist Party's success in the 1995 national elections among rural and urban migrant populations in Turkey's metropolises was explained by its grassroots approach, and the fact that the party focused on social justice and distributed goods, money and services within these 'gecekondu' (slum) communities (Arat 1999; İlyasoğlu 1998; Secor 2001). The Islamist Refah Party was outlawed in 1997. The Islamist movement organized itself under the name of the AK party. Today the AK party argues that they are a conservative democratic party representing the centre-right majority of Turkish citizens.

The construction of Islamic identity within the discourse of authenticity

Kandiyoti (1997: 114) suggests that the Islamist movement in general captured the existing dichotomy between the Western modern and the Muslim authentic identity. The conclusion that I can draw from my interviews is that the identity politics carried out by the Islamist movement motivated some young Turks to start a search for 'conscious Muslim identity'.

In my own research, I sought to illustrate the emerging identity search among young people who find themselves at a point in life, say around the age of 17, where personal experimentation with life begins. For, as Mannheim (1998: 300–1) argues, young people are closer to the 'current' problems; they are dramatically aware of a process of destabilization, and take sides in it.

The 24-year-old woman informant with whom I had a dialogue was brought up in Istanbul in a secular family. Her father's death led her to interrogate the meaning of life, and she turned to religion. She recalls that when she was afraid of death, she turned to the mercy of God; she became receptive to what God dictated. This state of feeling fear was later turned to love of God. After graduation from high school, she chose theology as a major in order to study Islam. She thought that in this way she would find answers to all of her questions about life and death. She also told me that she had been quite relaxed in her manners with the opposite sex and with her clothing. After becoming receptive to the 'demands of God', she became more conscious of her appearance as well as her conduct. The process whereby she became religious is illustrative of the process of identity construction in terms of the 'other'. Our dialogue follows:

> I used to play the guitar when I was at high school. I played the guitar for almost three years. After I became enrolled at the Faculty of Theology, I asked myself: what does a student of theology have to do with the guitar? This was not possible with my mentality then, and I sold my guitar. The love I had for music urged me to play another instrument, and I chose the *ney* [an Islamic instrument]. But if I thought then how I think today, I would have continued playing the guitar.
> *Do you mean that this is a progress?*
> Yes, I was conservative then. I perceived things in a wrong manner. However, being a student at the Faculty of Theology helped me.
> *How?*
> I mean I changed my mind so that I could play the guitar.
> *Were you influenced by what you read? Or was it because of your teachers?*
> Not much because of what I read. My teachers' explanations and some of my own experience.... Why would it be wrong or strange to play a guitar? Once you start questioning, things become less important....
> *For example?*
> This is a search for identity.
> *What kind of a search for identity?*
> You are a Turk. You live in Turkey; you are a Muslim. What kind of a person do you have to be? I had such kinds of thoughts. I thought that there had to be a difference.
> *From what?*
> You are a Turk and a Muslim. That is, you have to be different from the West, from the people in the West.
> *So, you mean it is necessary to be different.*
> Yes, if I say necessary, I mean natural.

Who is the person in the West? What is the West?
When I say the West, I have never been in a Western country. There are some artists, they are the people of the West.
What kind of artists?
Artists whom we see on television.
So, do you mean that the guitar is a Western instrument?
Yes, yes. Since it was from the West, Christian. It was a reaction to that.
Well, how do you interpret the change in your way of thinking later on, in relation to your thoughts about the West
In that period of my life, I started doing exactly the opposite of what I used to do before. Maybe that was what I needed then. When you make a big change in your life, you concentrate on that change. You make a big effort. You have to forget about the rest. Once you start finding your balance, you start thinking more wisely. In time, your thoughts become more mature. You use your mind; you start using your brains and not your feelings. Once you start thinking like that, your thoughts start to change. Better to say your thoughts become more mature.... For example, I am not as conservative today as I was before. Maybe this is what sociability is. I had isolated myself before.... Now, I am both modern and I am covered. I am trying to be as active as I can be. I am trying to attend several courses ... a course about positive thinking, a course about meditation.... Then I went to Aikido.[7]
So, you attended an Aikido course as a covered woman!
Yes, of course.
Why did you go there? What is Aikido?
I love sports. Sports give me happiness, health, strength and self-confidence. I learned about Aikido on a television programme. It was very esthetical. I have an interest in the Far East and in Far Eastern philosophy. Aikido is not only a sport but also a philosophy....

Then she told me what the philosophy of Aikido was, about the similarity of Sufi philosophy in Islam and about the mixed feelings she had over whether or not to continue the course. She told me how she did not want to do anything against Islamic values. Finally, she dropped the course because she was the only female and she was in dialogue with male peers all the time. She could have continued if there had been another female for her to partner with.

First of all, this dialogue illustrates how identity is always constructed relationally, in terms of the 'other'. The 'other', for a Turkish Muslim woman, is 'the West', because she is confronted with the West all the time. The West is on television, at home, almost everywhere. At first she isolates herself in order not to be tempted by her surroundings. Once she is confident of the essence of her identity as a Muslim Turkish woman, she starts being active again. We can understand from her story that she was not against 'the West' *per se*, but she was questioning the West within her: that part of herself which she thought was influenced by the West. The way she dressed, the way she interacted with her male peers, the instrument she used to play and the music she used to listen to were all parts of Western 'taste'.[8] Her dilemma is the dilemma of many Muslim youth who are trying to construct Muslim identities in modern society and in the global world. Once Islam is defined as life itself, then it becomes difficult to decide what is Islamic and what is not. The construction of Islamic identity within the discourse of authenticity is an act of resistance. This is because Islam is defined as the 'other' by the Western world and as inferior to the Western world. In the same manner, what is considered civilized and what is considered uncivilized were classified in the process of Turkish modernization (Göle 1997b). The European way, 'alafranka', was proper and valuable, whereas the Turkish way, 'alaturka', was improper and valueless. It is interesting to note that Turks then started using the word 'alaturka' to describe their own habits.

As we saw in the dialogue with the 24-year-old woman, she later regretted having given up playing the guitar, which she considered a Western instrument. However, after becoming active again, she joined an Aikido course. This example shows us that the contemporary context for social identity formation not only involves particularities of region, religion, social class and rural/urban extraction, but also a network of influences resulting from the globalization of culture via media images and mass consumption (Appadurai 1990: 1–24).

Now, we can try to understand the responses of secular youth. How did they react to the reappearance of Islamic identity in the public space? Young secular people were irritated by the fact that they were being relegated to a position of 'false Muslims' from the standpoint of the Islamists, who defined themselves as 'conscious Muslims'. The religious lessons, which became obligatory after the military coup in 1980, were criticized because youngsters were being forced to learn how to pray and to memorize prayer *suras* in Arabic. A 23-year-old young man tells us about the experience he had in his school:

> I studied at a quite liberal college, but even there our teacher in religion forced us to memorize prayer *suras*, because he gave us low grades if we did not memorize them. He also forced us to learn how to pray. Once, an inspector came to our school, the inspector of the Ministry of Education. He directed a question to us, which was 'How [does] a human become good?' Nobody could reply, but I did. I said, 'We become good humans if we pray to God'. I thought that this was the answer he wanted to hear, and so it was. Then he told us that in his next inspection he was going to ask us questions about how we pray.... I think this is wrong. One should not be forced to learn rituals of worship. One should learn about the meaning of worship and about the goal of religions.

The 23-year-old informant insisted on keeping religion as a private belief. According to him, a person could be Muslim without performing rituals. He also argued that İmam Hatip Schools should not be closed, but the age limit should be raised to 15, because many families force their children to go to İmam Hatip Schools against their wishes. In a real democracy, he felt, a person should be of an age where he or she is capable of deciding what kind of school they want. A

24-year-old young woman was critical of the Islamist movement's use of the rhetoric of 'human rights and democracy'. As she said:

> They don't know what democracy is. They have not learned about democracy. Democracy means respect for human rights, respect even for the rights of minorities. If they have won 35 per cent of the votes in a municipality, what should we say about the rights of the 65 per cent? Let us say they have won 90 per cent of the votes in municipalities, if 10 per cent wants to eat turkey and drink wine on New Year's Eve, they cannot hinder it. A municipality is an administrative unit, which has to give service to all people. A municipality is not an instrument of a party. A municipality is an institution; it does not belong to a party. They have not understood the difference.

Many secular youth did not believe in the sincerity of the Islamist movement, which wanted to formulate its cause around the rhetoric of human rights and democracy. This suspicion is grounded to a high extent in the fact that university campuses were highly politicized in the 1980s and early 1990s, when on some campuses one could see posters that said 'To put on a veil is God's command'.

On the one hand, the fact that Muslim women's demands for rights to education and entry into public spaces while wearing the turban was a progressive movement. As Leila Ahmed (1992: 225) argues, 'Islamic dress can be seen as the uniform, not of reaction, but of transition', or as 'the uniform of arrival, signaling entrance into, and determination to move forward in, modernity'. On the other hand, to the extent that it was seen as a sign of an alternative, hegemonic political project, it aroused intense anxiety among secularist circles. In this anxiety, 'veiling', as a tradition signalling the Islamic-Ottoman past, was ridden with the implication of the imagery of the 'harem' and the seclusion of women (Kandiyoti 1997: 128). Highly educated Muslim women soon realized their own power and the differentiation of their interests, as women, from Muslim men, who held patriarchal attitudes about women's place in Turkish society. However, during this period, due to restrictions on covered women's university attendance, many young women had to give up studying or migrated abroad in order to study at the university level. It seemed that the hegemonic power struggle between secular elites and Islamist movements in Turkey was being carried over to the identities of Turkish women, 'who always have been the subject matter of major social engineering projects from above' (Kadıoğlu 1994: 660).[9] However, major surveys (Çarkoğlu and Toprak 2000; Erdem 2003) showed that women who were covering their heads were not increasing in numbers, as was commonly believed; on the contrary, their numbers were decreasing.

Towards a democratic society: Some challenges

Tolerance and democracy were concepts that appeared all the time in young people's narratives. It seems that Turkish youth are longing for a more democratic society where human rights are respected. At the same time, the results of a representative survey of Turkish people's values showed that the percentage of people who would try to understand others' preferences was as low as 34 per cent (Esmer 1999: 91).[10] The low percentage of tolerance as a value held by its citizens is the biggest obstacle in terms of creating a more democratic and pluralistic society in Turkey. In a recent survey conducted by the European Values Research Group, it was shown that there were some considerable differences between the values held by Turkish and European people (Caldwell 2004).[11] Whilst 62 per cent of Turks believed that 'politicians who do not believe in God are not suitable for performing public service', this value was 18 per cent among Europeans but almost 39 per cent among Eastern Europeans. These results suggest that the majority of Turkish people maintain that only Muslim politicians may serve honestly in public service. According to the same survey, the percentage of Turks who do not want to have a homosexual neighbour is 90 per cent, while this percentage is only 19 among Europeans. This result is also probably related to strong religiosity among Turkish people.[12]

The individualization process whereby Muslim youth are changing from radical Muslims to more moderate Muslims by reflecting upon their identities is at the same time a process whereby lifestyles in the rural periphery become integrated into lifestyles in urban centres. Muslim informants in my study were reflecting upon their identities as Muslims through their engagements in cross-cultural and cross-generational interactions with others, in society in general and with their parents and their families in particular. I would suggest that dialogues between young people and their parents in their families and cultural confrontations amongst youth in Turkish society may affect cultural hybridity, and hopefully lead to a more democratic culture in the future. If the democratization of culture in Turkish society brings about a broader discussion about morality, then the pseudo-polarization between secular and Islamic identities may disappear. However, the question still is: how shall we conceptualize secularism and democracy in Turkey so that negotiation between Islamic and secular identities becomes part of the evolution of a democratic process?

Notes

1 For a discussion on the use of generation in social research, I refer to Mannheim, K. (1998), 'The sociological problem of generations', in P. Kecskemeti (ed.) *Collected Works of Karl Mannheim*, (5), London and New York: Routledge.

2 I refer to Seufert, G. and Weyland, P. (1994) 'National events and the struggle for the fixing of meaning: A comparison of the symbolic dimensions of the funeral services for Atatürk and Özal', in *New Perspectives on Turkey*, Fall, (11), 71–98.

3 The French sociologist Alain Touraine says: 'What I am calling the subject is an individual's ability to reflect upon his or her own identity', in Touraine, A. (1997) *Critique of Modernity*, Oxford: Blackwell, p. 274.

4 Members of the Nurcu movement are the followers of Said Nursi (1873–1960) who maintained a Muslim opposition to secular Kemalist reforms. They came up with a rather sophisticated analysis of Islam. See: Mardin, S. (1989) *Religion and Change in Modern Turkey: The Case of Bediüzzaman Said Nursi*, New York: State University of NewYork Press.

5 *Kıble* means direction of Mecca.
6 Anomie is a condition of society marked by the absence of moral standards.
7 Aikido is a Far-Eastern sport about individual defence. It has a philosophy of peace as it is not offensive.
8 See Bourdieu, P. (1998) *Distinction, A Social Critique of the Judgement of Taste*, London and New York: Routledge, where Bourdieu says (p. 173): 'Taste, the propensity and capacity to appropriate (materially or symbolically) a given class of classified, classifying objects or practices, is the generative formula of lifestyle, a unitary set of distinctive preferences which express the same expressive intention in the specific logic of each of the symbolic sub-spaces, furniture, clothing, language or body hexis.'
9 For a similar argument pertaining to France, see the article written by Moruzzi, N. C. (1994) 'A Problem with Headscarves – Contemporary Complexities of Political and Social Identity', in *Political Theory*, 22(4), 653–72.
10 This result can be compared with international results (USA, 74%; Spain, 71%; Japan, 78%; Australia, 72%; Nigeria, 59%) stated in Esmer, Y. (1999) *Devrim, Evrim, Statüko: Türkiye'de Sosyal, Siyasal, Ekonomik Değerler* (Revolution, Evolution, Statusquo: Social, Political and Economic Values in Turkey), İstanbul: Tesev, p. 91.
11 The mentioned research which is referred to in *The Weekly Standard*, 19–26 July 2004, by the editor Christopher Caldwell, has been published in the newspaper *Frankfurter Allgemeine Zeitung*.
12 A recent project on conservatism among Turks shows that religious values play a role in choosing a party leader by 65 per cent, choosing a friend by 70 per cent and choosing a marriage partner by 85 per cent (Yilmaz 2006).

References

Ahmed, L. (1992) *Women and Gender in Islam, Historical Roots of a Modern Debate*, New Haven and London: Yale University Press.
Appadurai, A. (1990) 'Disjuncture and Difference in the Global Cultural Economy', in *Public Culture*, 2(2), 1–24.
Arat, Y. (1999) *Political Islam in Turkey and Women's Organizations*, İstanbul: Tesev.
Atacan, F. (1990) *Sosyal Değişme ve Tarikat, Cerrahiler* (Social Change and Tarikat, Cerrahis), İstanbul: Hil.
Avcı, G. (2005) 'Religion, Transnationalism and Turks in Europe', in *Turkish Studies*, 6 (2), 201–13.
Ayata, S. (1996) 'Patronage, Party, and State: The Politicization of Islam in Turkey', in *The Middle East Journal*, 50(1) 40–53.
Berkes, N. (1998) *The Development of Secularism in Turkey*, London: Hurst & Company.
Bourdieu, P. (1998) *Distinction, A Social Critique of the Judgement of Taste*, London and New York: Routledge.
Caldwell, C. (2004) 'Gizli değil tutarlı gündem' (Not a secret but a consistent agenda) in *Radikal*, translated from *The Weekly Standard*, July 19–26.
Cizre-Sakallıoğlu, Ü. (1996) 'Parameters and Strategies of Islam-State Interaction in Republican Turkey', in *International Journal of Middle East Studies*, 28, 231–51.
Coşkun, M. K. (1999) 'Comparative Study of Secondary Schools in Turkey, Example of İmam Hatip Schools', unpublished MA thesis, M.E.T.U (Middle East Technical University), Ankara: Department of Sociology.
Çakır, R., Bozan İ., and Talu B. (2004) *İmam-Hatip Liseleri Efsaneler ve Gerçekler* (İmam-Hatip Schools Myths and Realities), İstanbul: Tesev.
Çarkoğlu, A. and Toprak, B. (2000) *Türkiye'de Din, Toplum ve Siyaset* (Religion, Society and Politics in Turkey), İstanbul: Tesev.

Economy Service (2004) 'AB Üyeliğini en çok Güneydoğu İstiyor' (South-East Region of Turkey is most Positive to EU Membership), in *Milliyet*, June 3.

El-Guindi, F. (1999) *Veil, Modesty, Privacy and Resistance*, Oxford and New York: Berg.

Erdem, T. (2003) 'Türban Dosyasi 4' (Turban file 4), in *Milliyet*, May 30.

Esmer, Y. (1999) *Devrim, Evrim, Statüko: Türkiye'de Sosyal, Siyasal, Ekonomik Değerler* (Revolution, Evolution, Statusquo: Social, Political and Economic Values in Turkey), İstanbul: Tesev.

Göle, N. (1997a) 'Secularism and Islamism in Turkey: The Making of Elites and Counter Elites', in *The Middle East Journal*, 51(1), 46–58.

—— (1997b) 'The Quest for the Islamic Self within the Context of Modernity', in S. Bozdoğan and R. Kasaba (eds) *Rethinking Modernity and National Identity in Turkey*, Seattle and London: University of Washington Press, pp. 81–94.

Güvenç, B., Şaylan, G., Tekeli, İ., Turan, Ş. (1991) *Türk-İslam Sentezi* (Turkish-Islamic Synthesis), İstanbul: Sarmal.

Houston, C. (1998) 'Alternative Modernities, Islamism and Secularism on Charles Taylor', in *Critique of Anthropology*, 18(2) 234–40.

İlyasoğlu, A. (1998) *Örtülü Kimlik* (Veiled Identity), İstanbul: Metis.

Kadıoğlu, A. (1994) 'Women's Subordination in Turkey: Is Islam Really the Villain', in *Middle East Journal*, 48(4), 645–60.

Kandiyoti, D. (1997) 'Gendering the Modern, On Missing Dimensions in the Study of Turkish Modernity', in S. Bozdoğan and R. Kasaba (eds) *Rethinking Modernity and National Identity in Turkey*, Seattle and London: University of Washington Press, pp. 113–32.

Kaya, A. (2000) *Berlin'deki Küçük İstanbul, Diyasporada Kimliğin Oluşumu* (Little İstanbul in Berlin, Formation of Identity in the Diaspora), İstanbul: Büke.

—— and Kentel, F. (2005) 'Euro-Türkler: Türkiye ile Avrupa Birliği Arasında Köprü mü Engel mi?' (Euro-Turks: A Bridge or Obstacle Between Turkey and European Union?). Online. http://goc.bilgi.edu.tr/documents/EuroTurk.doc

Landeman, N. (1997) 'The Islamic Broadcasting Foundation in the Netherlands: Platform or Arena?' in S. Vertovec and C. Peach (eds) *Islam in Europe: The Politics of Religion and Community*, London: Macmillan.

Mannheim, K. (1998) 'Essays on the Sociology of Knowledge', in P. Kecskemeti (ed.) *Collected Works of Karl Mannheim*, 5, London and New York: Routledge.

Mardin, Ş. (1989) *Religion and Change in Modern Turkey: The Case of Bediüzzaman Said Nursi*, New York: State University of New York Press.

—— (1994) 'Islam in Mass Society: Harmony Versus Polarization', in M. Heper and A. Evin (eds) *Politics in the Third Turkish Republic*, Westview Press, pp. 161–70.

Mernissi, F. (1991) *The Veil and the Male Elite: A Feminist Interpretation of Women's Rights in Islam*, Reading MA: Addison-Wesley.

Moghissi, H. (1999) *Feminism and Islamic Fundamentalism – The Limits of Postmodern Analysis*, London and New York: Zed Books.

Morizzi, N. C. (1994) 'A Problem with Headscarves – Contemporary Complexities of Political and Social Identity', in *Political Theory*, 22(4), 653–72.

Narlı, N. (1996) 'Women and Islam: Female Participation in the Islamicist Movement in Turkey', in *Turkish Review of Middle East Studies*, 7(9), 97–109.

Narrowe, J. (1998) *Under One Roof: On Becoming a Turk in Sweden*, Doctoral Dissertation, Stockholm Studies in Social Anthropology, Stockholm: Elanders Gotab.

Neyzi, L. (2001) 'Object or Subject? The Paradox of "Youth" in Turkey', in *International Journal of Middle East Studies*, August (33), 411–32.

Nohl, A. M. (1999) 'Breakdans ve Medrese: Göçmen Gençlerin Çok Boyutlu Habitusu' (Breakdance and Medrese: Multidimensional Habits of Immigrant Youth), in *Toplum ve Bilim*, (82), 91–113.

Ögelman, N. (2003) 'Documenting and Explaining the Persistence of Homeland Politics among Germany's Turks', in *The International Migration Review*: New York, Spring, 37(1), 163–193.

Ostergaard-Nielsen, E. (2000) 'Trans-State Loyalties and Politics of Turks and Kurds in Western Europe', in *SAIS Review*, The Johns Hopkins University Press, 20(1), 23–38.

Özdalga, E. (1990) 'Türkiye'de İslami Uyanış ve Radikalleşme Üzerine' (Islamic Revivalism and Radicalism in Turkey), in *İslami Araştırmalar (Journal of Islamic Research)*, 4(1), 57–60.

Pratt-Ewing, K. (2003) 'The Problem of Deceit and the Effects of September 11', in *The South Atlantic Quarterly*, Duke University Press, 102(2/3), 405–31.

Saktanber, A. (1997) 'Formation of a Middle-Class Ethos and its Quotidian: Revitalizing Islam in Urban Turkey', in A. Öncü and P. Weyland (eds) *Space, Culture and Power: New Identities in Globalizing Cities,* London and New Jersey: Zed Books, 140–56.

Secor, A. J. (2001) 'Toward a Feminist Counter-Geopolitics: Gender, Space and Islamist Politics in Istanbul', in *Space and Polity*, 5(3), 191–211.

Seufert, G. and Weyland, P. (1994) 'National Events and the Struggle for the Fixing of Meaning: A Comparison of the Symbolic Dimensions of the Funeral Services for Atatürk and Özal', in *New Perspectives on Turkey*, Fall, (11) 71–98.

Tapper, R. and Tapper, N. (1987) '"Thank God We're Secular!" Aspects of a Fundamentalism in a Turkish Town', in L. Kaplan (ed.) *Studies in Religious Fundamentalism*, London: Macmillan, 51–78.

Touraine, A. (1997) *Critique of Modernity*, Oxford: Blackwell.

Turkish Constitution (2004) Adjustments 2004.

Vergin, N. (1992) 'İslam Kenti Yeniden Muhasara Ederken' (Islamic Siege of the City), in *Türkiye Günlüğü*, (20) Autumn, 72–5.

Yilmaz, H. (2006) 'Türkiye'de Muhafazakarlik Aile, Din, Boti: ilk Sonuçlar Üzerine Genel Degerlendirme' (Conservatism in Turkey Family, Religion, The West: General Evaluation on First Results), Unpublished Project Report. Project supporters: Open Society Institute and Bogaziçi University. Public Opinion Research: Infakto Research Workshop. Supervisors: Dr. Emre Erdogan, Güçlü Atilgan, Research assistants: Bahar Başer, Ömer Ak.

Zubaida, S. (1996) 'Turkish Islam and National Identity', in *Middle East Report*, April–June, 10–15.

Part III

Contested terrains

Islam, gender and struggles for continuity and change

10 The hijab controversies in Western public schools: Contrasting conceptions of ethnicity and of ethnic relations

Marie Mc Andrew

Introduction

In many multicultural societies, the legitimacy of allowing young Muslim girls to wear the traditional hijab within public schools has raised passionate debates. The most obvious case is France, where, since 1989, *les Affaires du foulard* have almost become a national sport.

There, the ongoing struggle (Lorcerie 1996; Gautherin 2000a,b; Stasi 2003) between those who hold a traditional conception of *laïcité* as a strict neutrality of the public space, and partisans of *laïcité renouvelée*, which would allow for the expression of religious diversity by individuals, if not by the state, has recently been won by the former with the adoption of law 2004–228, which came into application in September of 2004 (Ministère de l'éducation nationale, de l'enseignement supérieur et de la recherché 2004). Other societies (Shadid and Van Koningsveld 1996; Renaerts 1999; Centro de estudios para la integracion social y formacion de inmigrantes, 2003) have not been immune, either: Belgium, Germany, Spain, even Canada, at least Quebec, in 1995 (Mc Andrew 2001), have witnessed school personnel, politicians, media and the public engaged in sometimes simplistic, and sometimes surprisingly complex, controversies concerning, among other things, the relationship between gender equality and religious diversity, and the guidelines that would allow a democratic state and its school system to limit the expression of diversity in the context of growing fundamentalism within both majorities and minorities.

The analysis of such controversies (Mc Andrew 1996; Mc Andrew and Pagé 1996; Ciceri 1999) within governmental, academic or community circles has mostly followed three sometimes complementary, but often separate, paths:

- reduction of the entire debate, on the one hand, to Islamophobia and, on the other, to political fundamentalism disguised as piety;
- analysis of the matter as another illustration of the sexist nature of all religion and of the necessity to give priority to gender equity over religious pluralism whenever they come into conflict;
- consideration of the issue as a classical case of liberal versus communitarian dilemma in political philosophy.

Although each of these interpretations holds some truth, to various extents depending on context, they all share one common limit: assuming a particular and often simplistic, albeit inexplicit, conception of ethnicity and of ethnic relations.

The aim of this chapter, thus, will be to revisit national case studies of the hijab controversy from a sociology of ethnic relations perspective.[1] I will first explore the limits of single conceptions of ethnicity, whether essentialist, heterocentrist or individualistic, both from a theoretical point of view and from a practical one, when applied to a specific policy issue, such as the accommodation of religious diversity in public schools and its relation to gender equity. From there, I will argue that only a manifold perspective on the construction of ethnic boundaries and a context-specific analysis can fully reflect the complexity of the dynamics that are at stake within such controversies. Guidelines regarding the principles that should guide public action in this regard will also be proposed.

The limits of single conceptions of ethnicity

Cultural essentialism: The hijab as a non-issue

The paradoxical maintenance of ethnicity throughout the twentieth century, and even in some instances its heightened salience, has been understood from different theoretical perspectives. Within the academic community, only a few analysts have seen it as the justification of an essentialist paradigm, where the maintenance of 'ethnic groups' is explained mainly by their cultural differences. Today, essentialism is almost agonizing, due to the additional impact of the criticisms to which it has been subjected for 30 years from three main sources: social psychology; the sociology of ethnic relations; and political philosophy. In the first case, following numerous experimental studies, it is now widely accepted that ethnic identity is a moving phenomenon, and that its salience for an individual, in relation to his or her other ascriptive (gender, social class) or voluntary (lifestyle, professional) identities, is essentially situational (Tajfel 1982; Oriol 1988, 1991; Taboada-Leonetti 1990; Bourhis and Leyens 1994). The current critical sociological and anthropological perspectives (Barth 1969; Guillaumin 1977; Roosens 1989) also question the rigid and ahistorical nature of an essentialist perspective on ethnicity. They show, among other things, that cultural markers are continuously being transformed within diverse communities, while inter-group boundaries, although sometimes redefined, are pretty resilient overall. Finally, cultural essentialism has also been criticized from a normative perspective stemming from political philosophy, which emphasizes the risk of antidemocratic drifts linked to the non-critical ascription of individuals to their groups of origin (Kymlicka 1995; Touraine 1994, 1997).

Thus, it is not currently popular, at least in academic or government circles, to be considered a cultural essentialist. The dominant perspective is indeed constructivism, which views ethnic identity as a dynamic phenomenon, regardless of whether one takes an analytical or a normative point of view.

Nevertheless, one could argue that for ordinary citizens, cultural essentialism is still, if not the dominant, certainly a very important system of interpretation of ethnicity, as numerous analyses of spontaneous narratives or even more reflective public discourses reveal (Buyck and Fall 1995; Juteau 2000; Helly 1992). Indeed, most people experience their belonging to a specific group and culture as a relatively stable phenomenon and, even if they give it a second thought if exposed to some of the criticisms raised above, in everyday life ethnicity is widely lived as a given, and not questioned.

Moreover, when one turns to schooling debates, cultural essentialism is even more popular, especially among minorities. The control of specific institutions constitutes one of the dominant themes of this current, which is mainly interested in the cultural-reproduction function of schooling (Krukowski *et al.* 1969; Holmes 1981; Glenn and De Jong 1996). Ethnicity, from this perspective, is considered as content to be reproduced as faithfully as possible through education, in opposition to a majority group to which an equally coherent culture, as well as a clear intention to assimilate other groups, is attributed. The transformation of ethnic boundaries, or the creation of a new, hybrid culture, is not on the agenda in this current, and the selection function of schooling and the debate on equality play only minor roles.

In such a perspective, which is exemplified by the reaction of some Toronto Muslims to the 1995 Quebec controversy, the hijab question could be characterized as a non-issue (*Globe and Mail* 1995). People who hold cultural-essentialist perspectives on ethnicity wonder what all that fuss is about. Hijab is considered an integral part of religion and culture, and the role of public schools in that regard is seen as pretty straightforward: respecting the wishes of parents.[2] For the community, nevertheless, tolerance for the wearing of the hijab within public schools is often only a 'second-best' choice; the control – and most of all the funding – of specific institutions whose ethos reflects the full extent of religious values would be preferred (Sarwar 1994; Halstead 1986; Forum Musulman Canadien 1999; Venel 2004).

Cultural essentialism is not only popular among minorities, but is also widespread among majority groups, most of the time in the form of a lenient, multicultural version that leads its proponents to support tolerance for the wearing of the hijab along the same line of argument (Cicéri 1999). But hard-core racists can also be comforted by such a perspective in their belief in the incompatibility of cultures (Taguieff 1987; Potvin 2000) and in some cases they even welcome the claims of minorities for more segregation in education.[3]

Although certainly compelling for the individuals who share such a belief, the limits of cultural essentialism as a system of interpretation of or justification for the wearing of the hijab in public schools are obvious. First, such a perspective totally neglects the potential contradictions, for the Muslim girls at stake, between their gender and their ethnic identities. It also assumes that all individuals belong non-critically to their group of origin, which can dictate their behaviours, and that minors, instead of being actively engaged in a process of building their own personalities and beliefs, should merely be the reflection of their parents' wishes. Finally, it refuses to look at, even if only to later reject its relevance, the legitimacy of longer-term concerns regarding on the one hand the potentially negative impact of religious socialization on women's equality and, on the other, the promotion of rigid religious identities on the democratic character and the quality of intercultural relations in modern societies.

Heterocentrist constructivism: The hijab as symbol of the failure of integration and/or a sexist/fundamentalist plot

Rejecting the conception of ethnicity as a 'given', the constructivist perspective is interested in boundaries between groups, the cultural markers used to legitimize their specificity, and the fluctuation of these two phenomena (Juteau 2000). In this regard, the analysis of material and symbolic inequalities within different social fields, notably in education, and the identification of the competing interests of different groups and sub-groups, such as ethnic elites (Vermeulen and Govers 1966), is considered essential. Notwithstanding this wide consensus, different versions of constructivism as a system of explanation of ethnic relations have developed since its domination of the field some 15 years ago.

A first conception (Bernier and Elbas 1978; Freitag 1981; Zylberberg 1994, 1995) can be characterized as 'ethnicity as the production of the external boundary'. It focuses on the central role played by the dominant group in the maintenance of ethnic boundaries through its perceptions, its discourses and, above all, its socio-political economic domination. According to this school of thought, the persistence of ethnic identity must be analysed, first and foremost, through the lens of inequality. The belief, shared by individuals, of belonging to distinct groups or of being the carriers of cultural differences are often merely reduced to an ideology (in the critical meaning of the concept), which alienates them from their genuine interests.

Although heterocentrist constructivism (which dominates thinking about ethnicity in France and is popular in various other European countries, including Great Britain) has the value of stressing the importance of the social-class variable and of unequal power relationships in the production of ethnicity, it has numerous shortcomings. First, it sometimes falls into 'conspirationism', giving to the state a quasi-monopolistic power in the production of ethnic identities (Fontaine 1993). Moreover, it strongly underestimates the role of internal boundaries, such as historical memory and individual attachment to specific allegiances, in the production of ethnicity. By stressing only one dimension of ethnicity, the Marxist or republican 'egalitarians' thus often adopt a paradoxical and somewhat paternalistic stance: attempting to liberate, against their will, the 'oppressed' for whom they purport to fight.

These characteristics are also reflected in the position heterocentrist constructivists adopt in matters of schooling. The school's primary mission with respect to minority-group students is, first and foremost, defined in terms of equality of opportunity and struggle against inequalities (Bowles and Gintis 1974; Giroux 1981). Because ethnicity is largely looked upon as an illusion, it is not believed, from such a viewpoint, that schooling should contribute to its reproduction. The intensity of the struggle regarding the definition of curriculum, a frequent point of contention between majority and minority groups, is thus usually underestimated.

When the socialization function of schooling is addressed, it is more often to promote an objective of social transformation or producing common identities, rather than maintaining pluralism. A traditional 'civic education', in which ethnocultural diversity is seen as an obstacle to be overcome in the process of constructing an egalitarian and fraternal society, is often promoted (Mc Andrew *et al.* 1997).

When confronted with claims regarding the respect of religious prescriptions in public schools, heterocentrist constructivists can react in two complementary manners,[4] depending on the importance they place on intra- or inter-group inequalities in matters of ethnic relations. In the first instance, the wearing of the hijab by young Muslim women (which is, revealingly, usually termed as the *persistence* of wearing...) is interpreted mainly as a reactive gesture, the symbol of the failure of a genuine integration blueprint. This interpretation, which has almost totally dominated the French debate (Cicéri 1999; Stasi 2003; Lorcerie 2004), whether people support tolerance or banning, is certainly well-grounded in the current sociological reality, both at the national and international level. It would, indeed, be difficult to deny that the racism experienced personally, or current world Islamophobia, might play a role in the decision of some women whether or not to wear the hijab. But it would also be quite paternalistic to assume that the entire cultural and religious motivation of individuals belonging to minority groups is a by-product of their relationships with the dominant group(s). Moreover, such a position gives very little concrete indication regarding the course of action to be followed. The origin of any particular sociological phenomenon does not tell us if it should be welcomed or contested. As every cynic on the planet knows, good things can come from negative realities, and vice versa.

Putting the stress on intra-group power relationships makes positioning easier. Indeed, if the wearing of the hijab is either the reflection of the domination of Muslim men over Muslim women, or of the clerical elites promoting a fundamentalist definition of Islam over the moderates, it becomes extremely difficult to foster tolerance of such a practice. The hijab as a sexist or fundamentalist plot has, thus, an extremely strong appeal in public opinion, both in countries whose official policy supports or bans the expression of religious diversity within public schools and among majorities and minorities (*La Presse* 1994; *Le Monde* 1995; Geadah 1996; Amara 2003).

Here again, however, reductionism and paternalism are obvious. Many cultural practices or beliefs upheld by citizens of various origins are partial products of unequal relationships or of uncritical acceptance of the influence of various institutions, such as churches, clubs, political parties or even the media. Nevertheless, unless physical or other constraints are applied, it is usually considered that individual freedom to make choices deemed unwise by others, however enlightened the others may be, has to be respected (Beiner 1995; Kymlicka 1995). Such a position recognizes that motivation for action is always manifold, and that it cannot be reduced to the inequalities that may have influenced it. Heterocentrist constructivists (Kepel 1989) sometimes advocate that we should apply to ethnic, and especially Islamic claims, a different set of rules than that which is usually accepted in democratic regimes to decide whether a practice is acceptable or not. Unless we accept their contention that ethnicity is only a by-product of internal or external oppression, it would be extremely difficult to follow them on that path.

Individualistic constructivism: The hijab as a choice

A second school of thought adopting a constructivist perspective on ethnic relations can be characterized as 'ethnicity as the production and the prerogative of the individual'. Strongly influenced by social interactionism (Berger and Luckman 1967), its partisans are mostly interested in the interactional processes by which the individual is led to believe that he is different and by which he gradually defines his allegiances. On a normative basis (Bourgeault *et al.* 1995), they insist on the moral autonomy of the person who must construct a cultural formula for himself by weighting various claims and influences linked to individual or social belongings.

The main interest of the 'ethnicity as the production and prerogative of the individual perspective' is to give back an important role to social actors in reaction to social determinism. Nevertheless, this ideology often appears to be limited by a somewhat unsophisticated voluntarism. It is as though individual subjects would construct their identity or their 'narratives' independent of major social relations. To paraphrase Orwell, individualist constructivists often seem to ignore the fact that if all individuals are free to choose their identities, some are freer than others in this regard (Probyn 1987). Furthermore, they sometimes underestimate the autonomy and the permanence of group allegiances embodied in a specific history and in common institutions, as if identities and belongings were mere commodities that could easily be discarded at will.

The cultural production and reproduction function of schooling is central for the proponents of this approach. Indeed, school, a unique space of intensive socialization between peers of different origins, at an age when identities and attitudes are being formed, is considered a laboratory where ethnic boundaries are redefined by every generation (Guttman 1987; Abdallah-Pretceille 1992). Because the liberty and the moral independence of the subjects must be preserved, the final, expected outcome of this contact is not identified a priori. Partisans of such a current neither condone nor condemn pluralism or assimilation. Their only ideological stance concerns the necessity of interactions, which minimally brings them to endorse common school institutions within which intercultural negotiation can happen. The potentially different consequences of such a perspective on the cultural reproduction of dominant and dominated groups are rarely discussed, and, while individual inequalities may be acknowledged if they emerge through interaction within the school system, a critical macro-sociological analysis of the selection function of schooling is clearly lacking.

Individualistic constructivists favour the accommodation of religious practices within public spaces, as long as the claims in this regard reflect *personal choices*. They would nevertheless object to any imposition by the community of a belief not sustained by the individuals within the community, whether in public or ethnospecific institutions. In this line of reasoning, they are consistent with the general rulings of Canadian and American courts and, more generally speaking, with the renewed liberal philosophical perspective, which set as the only legitimate limits to the recognition of diversity the balance of rights and the respect of democratic values (Bourgeault *et al.* 1995; Kymlicka 1995; Bernatchez and Bourgeault 1999). The hijab as an individual choice has been, for obvious reasons, extremely popular among the partisans of its tolerance, whether they belong to majority or minority groups (Ramadan 1994; Commission des droits de la personne du Québec, 1995; Commission ontarienne des droits de la personne, 1996). In the Quebec case, for example (Cicéri 1999), this position was shared by both the leadership of feminist organizations, such as the Fédération des femmes du Québec, and devout Muslim women actively involved in the fight for greater recognition of their religious rights within public institutions. The fact that social interaction is so important for proponents of this current probably also explains why they are inclined to compromise when the very preservation of common institutions might be at stake.

As attractive and globally satisfying as this perspective may seem, it is nevertheless not without shortcomings, especially in education. To start with, the mere concept of what constitutes a *genuine* free personal choice, and the identification of the type of context within which it can be exercised, is a difficult one (Hargreaves 1996). In line with the limits of social interactionism, the complex grid of constraints linked to internal and external power relationships that Muslim women face when they have to decide for themselves whether or not to wear the hijab is often not fully acknowledged. On the one hand, some Muslim pressure groups have used the concept of free choice with such laxity that its status is often reduced to mere rhetoric (Gautherin 2000a,b); on the other, some opponents of the practice (Cicéri 1999) have set the threshold so high that anything one does in society that is influenced by one's cultural heritage and socialization would hardly qualify.

Moreover, the controversy surrounding the wearing of the hijab in public schools does not concern adults entitled to moral independence, but children and teenagers in the process of learning to exercise their rights and still defining their own personal systems of belief. The conflict, in this regard, thus, often opposes two groups of adults – the parents and the school personnel – each invoking its own definition of the 'interest of the child' (Mc Andrew 2003a). Each of these parties has a legitimate role to play. The parents are legally the bearers of the rights of their children until the latter are capable of exerting them (MEQ 1994). But the school's preservation of a climate of free debate and exposure to pluralism is also a prerequisite for the later exercise of personal choice by young women (McLaughlin 1992). The two parties often also disagree about the moment when parents should step aside and leave the decision concerning the hijab to their teenagers.

Examining hijab controversies from a manifold perspective on ethnic relations

Single conceptions of ethnicity either reify it as a given or, if adopting a constructivist perspective, reduce its production/reproduction to the power relationships between dominant and dominated groups or to the action of an autonomous subject. The above analysis clearly illustrates the necessity of transcending the limits of these perspectives, while recognizing that each provides a useful light in the understanding of the dynamics of ethnic relations, the relevance of which varies depending on the specificity of contexts.

The first task in this regard is to reinforce in our analysis what Danielle Juteau (2000) has so aptly named the 'internal boundary' of ethnic identity. Indeed, recognizing that the minority is defined and redefined by its relation with the majority should not cause us to think that the former is a mere creation of the latter, nor that cultural differences or community allegiances are only an epiphenomenon of this relation. We also need, in conjunction with the social interactionists, to reaffirm the Subject's central role and his or her autonomy in this dynamic process. Nevertheless, the individual cannot be considered as the creator of ethnicity in a social vacuum, but rather as a mediator whose influence is maximized at the point of contact between the external and internal boundaries of ethnicity.

This third perspective, which could be characterized as 'ethnicity as the combined production of external and internal boundaries and mediation by the Subject', presents the decisive advantage of best reflecting the complexity of the process we are studying. On a normative plan, it also reflects the dilemma of citizenship in a pluralistic society that tries, at the same time, to recognize the reality of inequality and exclusions and the legitimacy of multiple forms of diversity while preserving the autonomy of individuals in search of their own identities and conceptions of the Good.

In the area of school policy and practices, because it recognizes that ethnicity is influenced by external and internal factors and that cultural differences exist outside power relationships, a manifold perspective can simultaneously justify a respect for pluralism and the development of a critical vision of the socio-historic inequalities that partially caused its emergence, and continue to contribute to its definition. Depending on the specificity of contexts, it can, thus, legitimize the interventions designed to maintain minority languages and cultures as much as it does the opposite: refrain from prioritizing this objective at the expense of equality. By the same token, a manifold perspective on ethnicity allows room for a critical questioning of the inequalities within each group, as well as for a consciousness-raising pedagogy that sometimes challenges various elements of the traditional identity.

Regarding the specific controversies surrounding the wearing of the hijab in public schools, a complex position on the production of ethnicity, because it is, by nature, context-specific, recognizes, first, the many, many meanings of the practice. Indeed, it can be everything we have covered above and even more: a 'natural' gesture that someone carries out spontaneously as part of her culture and religion, without questioning it; a protest against the current state of integration of Muslims in different immigration countries, or their treatment by the international media; a deeply grounded personal choice, in a process of spiritual and social development; or a constraint imposed on young women by patriarchal culture or fundamentalist thinkers using the issue to make a point in their fight against the Western world. Moreover, these are overlapping realities, even within individuals. Symbolically speaking, thus, it is often the case that one wears more than one hijab.

A manifold perspective on ethnicity also stresses that any policy in this regard must seek equilibrium among three important social goals, often complementary but sometimes antagonistic: the maintenance of pluralism; the promotion of equality, including that of women; and the freedom of individuals to define their community attachments. It thus recognizes the necessity for students belonging to minorities that schooling contributes to the development of their culture, language, and religion, while defining – and sometimes limiting – this obligation through a human-rights perspective reflecting the importance of the Subject as a mediator between the internal and external boundaries of ethnicity.

The position in this perspective of the wearing of the hijab in public schools could be summarized as follows:

- A clear obligation for schools to respect the freedom of parents and of students to express their religious beliefs in the public space, whatever meaning one attributes to various practices in this regard, unless legally justifiable exemptions to this rule apply. In this regard, school personnel should be especially cautious not to impose their own definition on *which* hijab is acceptable, or to fall into unrealistic expectations about what constitutes a legitimate threshold of *genuine freedom*, as discussed above.

- The necessity to define potential exemptions to this rule through the lens of a human-rights perspective. In the more general domain of religious accommodation, the following guidelines, whose relevance to each specific context of hijab-wearing should be scrutinized, enjoy a high consensus (Commission des droits de la personne 1995; Commission ontarienne des droits de la personne 1996; US Department of Education 1999; Ministère de l'Éducation Nationale de la France 1989): first, refusing any practice that would have a direct discriminatory impact on the equality of access to education for minority students; second, maintaining a school climate, exempt from proselytism, that guarantees the freedom of choice of parents and students regarding religious practices; and finally, ensuring minimal security rules for both majority and minority students. Until now, the analysis of different national case studies, including court rulings, reveals that it has never been possible to establish a direct link between the wearing of the hijab and unequal access to education, and that there is only a very slight relationship with security (for example, during technology workshops). The issue of proselytism has been highlighted by France, which now uses it as the main argument to justify its new law (Stasi 2003). Nevertheless, this claim is based mainly on personal testimonies expressed during a highly emotional process of consultation, and not on a thorough investigation.

- An equal commitment to protect the right of the individual not to conform to religious practices, even when this contradicts the wishes of the organized community. Schools, above all institutions, must be immune from community ascription or differential treatment of students based on their assumed and essentialized ethnicity. Nevertheless, when conflict in this regard arises between parents and students, while respecting what specific national legislations have to say about the age when children and teenagers enjoy different rights, schools should see their role as that of facilitators of value-conflict resolution, both between parties and within the student torn between two cultural universes (Hohl and Normand 1997). Indulging in emancipatory fantasies, as it is often the case among women teachers (Hohl 1996), would only be falling into the trap of reducing ethnic attachments to power relationships and internal oppression, a position whose limits have been clearly illustrated above.

- The necessity, in a context of growing cultural and cognitive relativism, to fully preserve the school's unique function of exposing all students to critical knowledge and values differing from those of their community of origin, especially while teaching history, citizenship education or cultural perspectives on religions. In this regard, it must be clear that the acceptance of one's expression of religious beliefs does not imply a commitment to foster all the values the bearer of a hijab – or for that matter of a cross or a kippa – thinks it stands for, especially if some appear incompatible with basic democratic principles. Nevertheless, public debates in the classroom on religious practices and their meanings – both spiritual and mundane – must always be carried on in a spirit of respect and with an open mind.

- An increased awareness among decision-makers, educators and also Muslim parents, who do not always condone their teenagers' practices, that what may at first appear as a local educational issue cannot be understood outside the bigger picture of current international Islamophobia. Whether one likes it or not, the external boundary of their ethnic identity is being reinforced day by day among Muslim teenagers. In such a context, the concept of personal free choice, already complex, becomes elusive, and the distinction between a religious and a political hijab more blurred. This is a reality that any class discussion on the issue must take into account. Moreover, one should be especially conscious within school settings, but also in the context of nationwide public debates, not to fall into demagogic or racist traps disguised as democratic concerns. In line with the constructivist literature reviewed above, it is especially important, in this regard, to denounce any essentialist discourse in which 'us' and 'them' are presented as homogeneous and dichotomist realities, most often at the expense of the 'other'. Stereotypical presentation of either the whole Muslim community, explicitly or implicitly, as reduced to its fundamentalist, even terrorist, faction, or of Muslim women as passive victims of external manipulation, is certainly not an asset for the development of a cohesive and equalitarian society, whatever one's particular position regarding religious accommodation in public schools. Hijab controversies should also not be transformed into battles between Good and Evil, nor should they permit to advocate, in the name of the superior interest of the nation – and in some instances of the religious community – practices that democratic values would not condone in other circumstances.

Some of these points may sound like amiable banalities but, unfortunately, various analyses confirm that these basic principles are far from always being respected in recent major national debates concerning the extent to which schools and society should adapt to pluralism.

Notes

1 My analysis is largely based on the theoretical framework developed in Mc Andrew (2003b), synthesized and applied to the specific issue at stake.
2 As stated in the *Globe and Mail* article quoted above: 'My hijab is none of your business …'.
3 The surprising willingness of the French government – and even eagerness, in the case of the National Front representatives – to accept parallel schooling at home for Muslims not wishing to abide by the new law could be, if not totally, certainly partially analyzed through such a lens.
4 Public and individual discourses in this regard often combine both elements. Nevertheless, they differ on the stress they put on each of them.

References

Abdhallah-Pretceille, M. (1992) *Quelle école pour quelle intégration?* Paris: Hachette.

Amara, F. (2003) *Ni putes, ni soumises…*, Paris: La Découverte.

Barth, F. (1969) *Ethnic Groups and Boundaries*, Boston: Little, Brown and Co.

Beiner, R. (1995) *Theorizing Citizenship*, New York: State University of New York Press.

Berger, P. and Luckman, T. (1967) *The Social Construction of Reality*, Harmondsworth: Allen Lane, Pergamon Press.

Bernatchez, S. and Bourgeault, G. (1999) 'La prise en compte de la diversité culturelle et religieuse à l'école publique et "lobligation d'accommodement"', Aperçu des legislations et des jurisprudences au Canada, aux États-Unis, en France et en Grande-Bretagne, *Canadian Ethnic Studies/Études ethniques au Canada*, XXXI(1): 159–71, a special edition edited by Marie Mc Andrew.

Bernier, B. and Elbaz, M. (1978) 'Présentation', *Anthropologie et sociétés*, 2, 1–14.

Bourgeault, G., Gagnon, F., Mc Andrew, M. and Pagé, M. (1995) 'L'espace de la diversité culturelle et religieuse à l'école dans une démocratie de tradition libérale', *Revue européenne des migrations internationales*, 11(3), 79–103.

Bourhis, R. and Leyens, J. J. (eds) (1994) *Stéréotypes, discrimination et relations intergroupes*, Liège: Mardaga.

Bowles, S. and Gintis, H. (1974) *Schooling in Capitalist America: Educational Reform and the Contradictions of Economic Life*, New York: Basic Books.

Buyck, M. and Fall, K. (1995) *L'intégration des immigrants au Québec: Des variations de définition dans un échange oral*, Sillery: Les éditions du Septentrion.

Centro de estudios para la integracion social y formacion de inmigrantes (2003) *Actitudes ante la escolarizacion de menores de origen extranjero en la comunidad valenciana* (directores de centros, profesores y padres), Valencia: Centro de estudios para la integracion social y formacion de inmigrantes.

Ciceri, C. (1999) Le foulard islamique à l'école publique: analyse comparée du débat dans la presse française et québécoise francophone (1994–5). Working Paper, Immigration et métropoles.

Commission des droits de la personne du Québec (1995) *Le pluralisme religieux au Québec: un défi d'éthique sociale*. Document soumis à la réflexion publique, Montréal: Gouvernement du Québec.

Commission ontarienne des droits de la personne (1996) *Politique sur la croyance et les mesures d'adaptation relative aux observances religieuses*. Approuvée par la Commission le 20 octobre.

Fontaine, L. (1993) *Un labyrinthe carré comme un cercle*. Survey on the Minister of Immigration and Cultural Communities and on his real and imagined actors. Montréal: Éditions l'Étincelle.

Forum Musulman Canadien (1999) *Mémoire présenté à la Commission parlementaire de l'éducation, Assemblée nationale du Québec*, Montréal: Forum Musulman Canadien.

Freitag, M. (1981) 'Théorie marxiste et réalité nationale', *Pluriel*, 26, 3–38.

Gautherin, J. (2000a) 'L'universalisme laïque à l'épreuve', in A. Van Zanten (ed.) *L'école, l'état des savoirs*, Paris: La Découverte.

—— (2000b) 'Au nom de la laïcité, Pénélope et Jules Ferry', in J.-L. Derouet (ed.) *L'école dans plusieurs mondes*, Bruxelles: De Boeck.

Geadah, Y. (1996) *Femmes voilées, intégrismes démasqués*, Montréal: VLB Éditeur.

Giroux, H. (1981) 'Hegemony, resistance and the paradox of educational reform', in H. Giroux, A. Penna and W. Pinar (eds) *Curriculum and Instruction: Alternatives in Education*, California: McCutchan Publishing, pp. 400–25.

Glenn, J. U. and De Jong, E. (1996) *Educating Immigrant Children: Schools and Language Minorities in Twelve Nations*, New York: Garland.

Globe and Mail (1995) 'My hijab is an Act of Worship – and None of Your Business', 15 February.

Guillaumin, C. (1977) 'Race et nature: systèmes de marques, idées de groupe naturel et rapports sociaux', *Pluriel*, 11, 39–55.

Guttman, A. (1987) *Democratic Education*, Princeton, NJ: Princeton University Press.

Halstead, J. M. (1986) *The Case for Muslim Voluntary Aided Schools: Some Philosophical Reflections*, London: The Islamic Academy.

Hargreaves, D. H. (1996) 'Diversity and choice in school education: A modified libertarian approach', *Oxford Review of Education*, 22(2).

Helly, D. (1992) *L'immigration pour quoi faire?* Québec: Institut québécois de recherche sur la culture.

Hohl, J. (1996) 'Résistance à la diversité culturelle au sein des institutions scolaires', in M. Pagé, M. Mc Andrew and F. Gagnon (eds) *Pluralisme, citoyenneté et education*, pp. 337–48, Montréal/Paris: L'Harmattan.

—— and Normand, M. (1997) 'Construction et stratégies identitaires des enfants et des adolescents en contexte migratoire: le rôle des intervenants scolaires', *Revue française de pédagogie; L'école et la question de l'immigration*, 117, 39–52.

Holmes, B. (1981) *Comparative Education: A Study of Educational Factors and Traditions*, London: Routledge and Kegan Paul.

Juteau, D. (2000) *L'ethnicité et ses frontières*, Montréal: Presses de l'Université de Montréal.

Kepel, G. (1989) 'L'intégration suppose que soit brisée la logique communautaire', in C. Wihtol de Wenden and A. M. Chartier (eds) *École et intégration des immigrés; Problèmes politiques et sociaux*, No. 693.

Krukowski, T. (1969) 'The other ethnic groups and education', Study of the Royal Commission on Bilingualism and Biculturalism, Ottawa: Imprimerie de la Reine.

Kymlicka, W. (1995) *Multicultural Citizenship*, Oxford: Clarendon Press.

La Presse (1994) 'Des principes fondamentaux sont en jeu dans le débat sur le foulard islamique', J. É. Gaudet, 28 septembre.

Le Monde (1995) 'Le Conseil d'État refuse l'interdiction totale du foulard islamique à l'école', P. Bernard, 12 juillet.

Lorcerie, F. (1996) 'À propos de la crise de la laïcité en France: dissonance normative', in F. Gagnon, M. Mc Andrew and M. Pagé (eds) *Pluralisme, citoyenneté et éducation*, Montréal: L'Harmattan, pp. 121–36.

—— (2004) 'Un point d'orgue dans la crise de la politique française d'intégration: le débat dans son contexte', Journées d'études IREMAM-IEP d'Aix-en-Provence, *La politisation du voile islamique en France en 2003–2004; Acteurs, espaces, enjeux*, sous la direction de Françoise Lorcerie, Aix-en-Provence, 7–8 avril 2004.

Mc Andrew (1996) 'Diversité culturelle et religieuse: divergences des rhétoriques, convergences des pratiques?' in F. Gagnon, M. Mc Andrew and M. Pagé (eds) *Pluralisme, citoyenneté et éducation*, Montréal: L'Harmattan, pp. 287–320.

—— (2001) *Immigration et diversité à l'école. Le débat québécois dans une perspective comparative*, Montréal: Presses de l'Université de Montréal.

—— (2003a) 'L'accommodement raisonnable: atout ou obstacle dans l'accomplissement des mandats de l'école?' *Options CSQ*, 22 (automne), 131–47.

—— (2003b) 'School spaces and the construction of ethnic relations: Conceptual and policy debates', *Canadian ethnic studies/Études ethniques au Canada*, 35(2), 14–29.

Mc Andrew, M. and Pagé, M. (1996) 'Entre démagogie et démocratie: le débat sur le hijab au Québec', *Collectif interculturel*, 2(2), 151–67.

McAndrew, M., Tessier, C. & Bourgeault, G. (1997). 'L'éducation à la citoyenneté en milieu scolaire au Canada, aux États-Unis et en France: des orientations aux réalisations'. *Revue française de pédagogie*, 121, 57–77.

McLaughlin, T. H. (1992) 'Citizenship, diversity, and education, a philosophical perspective', *Journal of Moral Education*, 21(3), 235–50.

Ministère de l'Éducation du Québec. (1994) La prise en compte de la diversité religieuse et culturelle en milieu scolaire: un module de formation à l'intention des gestionnaires, Montréal: Direction des services aux communautés culturelles, 103 pages.

Ministère de l'éducation nationale (France) (1989) Avis du Conseil d'État et déclaration du Ministre concernant le port de signes d'appartenance à une communauté religieuse dans les établissements scolaires. Paris: MEN.

Ministère de l'éducation nationale, de l'enseignement supérieur et de la recherche (France) (2004) Circulaire du 18 mai 2004 relative à la mise en oeuvre de la loi n° 2004–228 du 15 mars 2004 encadrant, en application du principe de laïcité, le port de signes ou de tenues manifestant une appartenance religieuse dans les écoles, collèges et lycées publics. Paris: MENESR.

Oriol, M. (1988) Les variations de l'identité. Étude de l'évolution de l'identité culturelle des enfants d'immigrés portugais en France et au Portugal, two volumes, Université de Nice-IDERIC.

—— (1991) 'Les communautés culturelles et la recherche', in E. Tarrab, G. Plessis-Bélair and Y. Girault (eds) Les communautés culturelles au Québec et la recherche en éducation, Montréal: Publications de la Faculté des sciences de l'éducation.

Potvin, M. (2000) 'Some Racist "Slips" About Quebec in English Canada between 1995 and 1998', *Canadian Ethnic Studies*, vol. XXXII, no. 2, 1–26.

Probyn, E. (1987) 'Bodies and antibodies: feminism and the post-modern', *Cultural Studies*, 1(3), 340–60.

Ramadan, T. (1994) *Les musulmans dans la laïcité. Responsabilités et droits des musulmans dans les sociétés occidentales*, Lyon: Éditions Tawhid.

Renaerts, M. (1999) 'Processes of homogenization in the Muslim educational world in Brussels', *International Journal of Educational Research*, 31, chapter 3, 283–94.

Roosens, E. E. (1989) *Creating Ethnicity. The Process of Ethnogenesis*, Newbury Park: Sage Publications.

Sarwar, G. (1994) *British Muslims and Schools*, London: Muslim Educational Trust.

Shadid, W. and Van Koningsveld, P., dir. (1996) *Muslims in the Margin: Political Responses to the Presence of Islam in Western Europe*, Kampen: Kok Pharos.

Stasi, B. (2003) *Rapport au président de la République*. Rapport de la Commission de réflexion sur l'application du principe de laïcité dans la République, 12 décembre.

Taboada-Leonetti, I. (1990) 'Stratégies identitaires et minorités: le point de vue du sociologue', in C. Camilleri, J. Kasterszteyn, E. M. Lipiansky, H. Malewska-Peyre, I. Taboada-Leonetti and A. Vasquez (eds) *Stratégies identitaires*, Paris: PUF, pp. 43–83.

Taguieff, P.-A. (1987) *La force du préjugé. Essai sur le racisme et ses doubles*, Paris: La Découverte.

Tajfel, H. (1982) *Human Groups and Social Categories*, Cambridge: Cambridge University Press.

Touraine, A. (1994) *Qu'est-ce que la démocratie?* Paris: Fayard.

———— (1997) *Pour vivre ensemble, égaux et différents*, Paris: Fayard.

United States Department of Education (1999) Secretary's Statement on Religious Expression, Farell//A: Online. Available HTTP: http://www.biblecurriculum.org/bibcdocs/ReligionInPublicSchools2.pdf (accessed 14 December 2005).

Venel, N. (2004) *Musulmans et citoyens*, Paris: Presses universitaires de France.

Vermeulen, H. and Govers, C. (1996) 'Introduction', in H. Vermeulen and C. Govers (eds) *The Anthropology of Ethnicity, Beyond Ethnic Groups and Boundaries* Amsterdam: Het Spinhuis Publishers, pp. 1–11.

Zylberberg, J. (1994) 'Le nationalisme québécois. De l'ethnoreligion à la religion étatique', *La pensée et les hommes*, 27, 93–8.

———— (1995) 'Les transactions du sacré', *Sociétés*, 1, 9–12.

11 Islamophobia and women of Pakistani descent in Bradford: The crisis of ascribed and adopted identities

Haleh Afshar, Rob Aitken and Myfanwy Franks

groups forced to choose often go with their friends

Islam as a faith and Muslims as a whole have found themselves under something of a siege in a climate of Islamophobia (Allen and Nielsen 2002). This is particularly difficult for ethnic minority Muslim women who have chosen to identify publicly with the faith and wear the scarf as a badge of honour. Islamophobia creates a wide gap between Muslim women's perceptions of who they are and the ways in which they are viewed by the host society. Groups on both sides of the divide demand of them that they either abandon their faith or conform to particular forms of male interpretations of where *mohajabehs* should be and how they should be living their lives. Groups such as the Hisb ut Tahrir announce that it is no longer possible for youth in the UK to be both British and Muslim, and declare it necessary to 'choose' between faith and nationality (*Sunday*, BBC 4, 24 August 2003). Parties such as the Al Muhajerun paraded their 'choice' in London by calling a conference on 11 September 2003 to glorify the suicide bombers, calling them the 'Magnificent 11'. These aggressive political positions may be described as part of a concerted effort by Islamist revivalists in Britain to create a male, combative Islamic political identity that seeks to unite the Muslim community in opposition to rising Islamophobia in the host society. Their high-profile, propagandist moves are countered by equally abrasive moves such as the decision by the French parliament in April 2004 to ban the hijab from all government-funded schools and banish the *mohajabehs* to Islamic schools, thereby barring the most common avenues towards cohesion and multiculturalism.

Such decisions by the French government, and the continuing carnage in Iraq, resulted in some of the participants in our studies changing their views about Western democracy. One of the sisters who had been at the Hisb ut Tahrir hijab-ban conference held in London in January 2004 told Myfanwy Franks that she did not wish to 'integrate' because of the contradiction between liberal democracy and Islam. Another noted that the West wished to 'impose' democracy on Iraq but did not allow much freedom to her:

> They say here you can do whatever you want, but that's a contradiction, because clearly they do not want you to wear the scarf.
>
> (The sisters' study circle of two generations of women held in Bradford, Sunday, 28 June 2004, Franks, 2004)

situation is growing worse

The fears of the Muslim community that Islamophobia is dictating public policy leads to political backlash on both sides, and can play into the politics of groups such as the British National Party, which capitalizes on fear of the 'other'. At the same time, restrictive policies that specifically target Muslims are fuelled by measures such as the Terrorism Act, which has led to wholesale arrests of rafts of Muslims in Great Britain. Many have been released, but some still remain in prison. These measures locate Muslims as emblems of combative Islam, and place Muslim women at the crossfire between faith and state policies. In a follow-up email conversation, a sister from the Bradford sisters' meeting told Franks:

> I told you about people I met who converted after 9/11. One thing I do find is that many Muslims are also becoming more aware of their belief after 9/11 as we see a major clampdown on Muslims in Europe and [the] US due to the threat of 'terrorism', meaning many are arrested or treated with suspicion without any basis, e.g. arrests of people in Manchester a few months ago, all of whom were later released without charge. This has created two 'camps', which I feel is the plan of the Western governments (e.g. [George W.] Bush's, 'You are either with us, or with the terrorists'), where you have to choose to be either a 'moderate' (liked and integrated) or you are a 'fundamentalist' (an enemy within)... Anyway, this is a challenge for Muslims.

(Franks 2004)

The umma

Hisb ut Tahrir has countered Islamophobia by calling for supranationality. It claims that Muslims belong to the single community of the *umma* which, according to the teachings of the Prophet, recognizes no divisions by race, class or nationality. The power of such calls can be heard from the tape of Mohammad Sidique Khan, who blew himself up at Edgware Road underground station on 7 July 2005. In his recorded message, Khan rejects national identity in favour of the *umma*, the global community of believers, declaring that the violence will continue as long as the government continues to 'perpetuate atrocities' against 'his Muslim brothers and sisters'. He also makes an important theological point often overlooked by Western observers but deeply relevant to activists who might be considering violence; he says that bombs are justified because the *umma* is under attack, that violent resistance is an obligation for all believers, and that 'collateral damage' in the form of the death of innocents is thus acceptable (*The Observer*, 4 September 2005). However, from the very inception of the faith the *umma* has been, and has remained, more an ideal than a reality. It has been a concept that facilitated participation without imposing debilitating practical constraints. The millennial empire of Islam did not demand of its people that they make a choice between nationality and faith; indeed, it accommodated a vast diversity of faiths and nations under its melliat governance that allowed for peaceful coexistence and mutual respect between people of different colours and creeds. The melliat system recognized and respected different faiths and group identities, and accommodated their needs. History denounces subversive statements such as those made by Hisb ut Tahrir that it is not possible for Muslims to be both British and Muslim, and by the Muhajerun that the teaching of Islam condones acts of unprovoked violence. These are specifically male interpretations, made by men and for men in a very specific time and place: namely, the West in the aftermath of 9/11. They are declarations that seek to secure the cohesion of the Islamic brotherhood and its fearless solidarity in the face of adversity. But they represent the views of small minorities on the margin; Qaiser M. Talib, writing in *Q-News*, which describes itself as 'the magazine for the global Muslim', argues that commitments of air and print space to 'this country's extremist groups are in reality an Islamophobic journalist's dream', and that 'those who wish to damage the image of Islam in the West instead choose to interview those who they know will spout hogwash' (Talib 2003: 17). They orchestrate these views and the responses, which include the demonization of Muslims by some politicians and newspapers in Britain and the USA, and spur on the galloping progress of Islamophobia. There is also a fear on the part of Muslims of the spread of a new, violent form of imperialism, illustrated by the occupations of Afghanistan and Iraq as well as by the threats against Iran and Syria.

The calls for fraternity of the *umma* are specifically constructed as a reaction to a crisis. They are primarily addressed to young men, and recall the ideal state where Muslims had a single, overriding political identity, one that extended beyond mere borders, nationalities and political-party allegiances. At the same time, with the emergence of the disastrous scarf affair, the *umma* is seen as requiring the explicit and public support of its women, who are expected to endorse the 'traditional' gender hierarchies that many of them may no longer wish to accept (Buijs 1996; Moghissi 1999). There is a simplistic assumption that Muslim women as a whole, and those who wear the hijab – the *mohajabehs* in particular – do so not only as a matter of faith, but also as a political endorsement of specifically Islamist political views. This is not the case.

It is the contention of this chapter that Muslim women understand the demands of politicized, radical Islam differently. As Muslims, women from ethnic minorities, particularly the *mohajabehs*, may have more in common with their 'white' British sisters than their male, cradle-Muslim brethren. Thus, although there is a shared experience of Islamophobia, for Muslim women the *umma* subsumes, without excluding, their race, ethnicity and nationality. Nor is it impermeable to feminists' demands for active political participation at all levels. For Muslim converts, the decision to wear the hijab in the West is a public assertion of the right to belong to the community of Muslims; it is not a rejection of home and hearth or kinship relations with their non-Muslim families and parents. Within liberal, democratic states and feminist contexts, their decision to wear the hijab is merely a matter of faith, and not a delineation separating them from their communities.

This chapter is based on a series of interviews in a three-generational study (Afshar 1989a, 1989b, 1994) and research conducted by Franks with 'white' converts and cradle-Muslim women who had taken the revivalist path (2001), as well as interviews with Muslim women over 60 in West Yorkshire (Afshar *et al.* 2001) and a series of interviews conducted in 2003 with Muslims of Pakistani origin in West Yorkshire as the British part of a Toronto-based international study of Muslim diaspora. Haleh Afshar has retained informal links with six of the 'migrant' Muslim women in West Yorkshire who in the late 1980s and early 1990s were choosing to don the hijab and identify themselves as 'Muslims' (Afshar 1989a, 1989b, 1994). Since the mid-1990s, younger siblings and friends, as well as 'white' converts, have joined this informal circle.

Nationality, culture and community

Region and country of origin, together with religion, have formed dominant markers in popular and official understandings of multicultural communities. This dominant model tends to equate community, defined in terms of region or country of origin, and sometimes religion, with culture. So, people in Southall, London, act on a model of five communities – White, Black, Asian-Sikh, Asian-Muslim and Asian-Hindu (Baumann 1997) – each with its own culture. However, this model of distinct ethnic communities masks the differences within them and alternative bases of community and identity.

Much of the ethnic identity of migrant groups is shaped by their history of migration and their hopes and aspirations for return to and reconstruction of their communities, often in the remembered images of the past, within the new host society. The situation and circumstances in which women find themselves in host countries have an important impact on identity formation (Ghorashi 2003). The nation is imagined (Makdisi 1990) and referred to as 'something outside' the self (Cohen 2000: 165). But 'for the purposes of personal identity', the nation is reconstructed and mediated through the self (Cohen 2000: 166). It is also constructed through the stories of 'authentic' pasts that help shape the dreams of the future (Subramaniam 2003: 161). For the first generation of migrants, particularly amongst the kin group, there is little need to define what is meant by the nation, since there are clear points of reference: particular places, people and stories that can be repeated (Afshar 1989b). They define themselves in terms of their kin groups, their social position, and the locality in which they grew up. It is only after migration that they become an 'ethnic minority' and acquire a unifying, ascribed group identity (Afshar 1994; Rouse 1995), which may or may not accord with their own notions of self and nationhood. Though different groups have different histories and different memories, their shared 'nationality' in Britain is based on a communality of historical points, often a shared education and language that has enabled groups of similar background to assume a shared understanding. The communality of experience is more intense within the kin group (Afshar 1989a) and groups of the same social and class background, but considerably less so amongst groups with different political views and aspirations. Thus, even first-generation migrants are sharply divided by class, education and politics, and some feel closer to the host society than to their own. This is particularly true of divorced or widowed women, who may have found it advantageous to migrate independently to start a new life. Mrs X., a teacher who left Pakistan for a job in Britain after a difficult divorce, taking her daughters with her, told Afshar that she rejoiced in her new 'anonymity'. She found the non-judgemental attitude of her colleagues liberating. 'It makes my life worth living', she said.

Whereas nationalities may be defined as masculine, there is a tendency to see culture as the domain of women, and an effective means of securing a sense of community and ethnic identity. Women help to shape, develop and recreate the differing cultures and histories in which they find themselves. Culture in this context is understood not as an 'add-on', but as an integral part of human beings and their relationships with others (Bhavnani *et al.* 2003). It is this interactive process that enables 'migrant' Muslim women to participate as active agents who help change and conceptualize the norms, mores, habits and customs that shape their lives. But there are tensions and cleavages between genders and generations in terms of choice and prioritizations. They differ in their preferences in matters such as dress codes and cooking. Younger women may choose to replace the traditional scarf, such as those worn by their mothers, with the stricter hijab, which covers the head and is not loosely hung on shoulders, but often they also discard the traditional *shelvar kamiz* in favour of jeans and loose shirts. For formal family celebrations, however, most women of South Asian origin revert to the beautiful sari.

First-generation migrant women construct their own power base by reconstructing their 'nations' through stories, food and networks that create a functional power base for them within the domestic sphere. Hospitality, good food and care are seen by the older generation as an inalienable part of culture and networking. Talking about and remembering the ceremony with a sense of achievement, a Muslim widow told us:

> I cooked, my daughters and my daughters-in-law cooked a lot of food, and it was very nice food and everybody shared. We had a lovely time ... we really had a lovely time... It was good while everybody [was] there...

But for the younger women, who are often in full-time employment, cooking has become more and more simplified, and 'authentic' food is only to be found in the homes of grandmothers. Thus, of necessity, 'cuisine', which may be recognized as an important cultural signifier (Samad 1998a), becomes diluted and changed, and frequently acquires British characteristics included for convenience and speed.

Whereas culture may be developed and perpetuated by them, it may be argued that nationality is a poor identifier for women; it has long applied differently across the gender divide. The historical construction of nationhood and nationalism is masculine in terms of its character and demands (Adnan 1993; Afshar 2003; Basch 1997). Women, who have been the bearers of nations, have been given the nationalities of their fathers and husbands, and when migrating have lost their birthrights to their homelands, only to acquire that of the male on whom they have been defined as a 'dependant'. They are subject to laws and requirements that are formulated and articulated as if all citizens were male. The construction of nation and citizenship on the basis of 'fictitious ethnicities' (Radcliffe and Westwood 1993) makes women invisible, and does not meet their needs and demands. It is therefore not surprising that the primary identification of many older-generation British Pakistanis is with country or region of origin, rather than religion, although they automatically assumed that this implied that they were Muslims (Modood *et al.* 1997; Samad 1998b: 432–3).

Second-generation migrant women have little reason to revert to a nationality they have not experienced. Often, they have not even seen their homelands; a British-born girl of Pakistani origins told Afshar that 'Pakistan' to her 'brings images of beautiful jungles and wild deer running along rivers'. It was the beauty of the place and the delicious food that delighted B., who had only visited her parental village as a tourist. Other young women who had returned to rural areas have told researchers that they were struck by the general levels of poverty, the lack of facilities and the restrictions placed on them (Jacobson 1998). Young women who returned to cities were struck by the level of freedom and mobility enjoyed by women who had not been raised in the ossified atmosphere of being an ethnic minority in the West (Afshar 1994). They found it hard to reconstruct their national identity on the basis of brief visits and the myths and stories heard from their mothers. They are all too aware that these recreated notions of nation-hood were both idealized and unreal (Afshar 1989b).

However, the younger generation could not easily define themselves as British. In the 1980s many young schoolgirls told Afshar (1989b) that 'British' meant 'white' nationals. In the playground, even those who were born and bred in the UK felt excluded by colour and creed. They, their mothers and their grandmothers were all seen by the host society as 'immigrants'. They could choose a hyphen-ated identity of British-Muslim, but the boundaries created by such a label hide complex intra- and inter-familial tensions as well as the links and friendships made across the boundaries. Østberg expresses this complexity, rejecting hyphen-ated identity as an analytical concept and replacing it with the concept of 'inte-grated plural identity' (2003: 167). Many amongst the younger generation who talked to us saw themselves as British-Pakistani Muslims. When asked 'What country do you define as your home country?' 23 women out of an almost evenly divided sample of 96 males and females defined their country as being Britain or England; two of these were older women over 60 years of age, and 21 participants – these were mostly older women, though two were under 19 and one of these was born in the UK – described themselves as Pakistani. Two women described them-selves as 'both', and one said, 'I'm not sure … Pakistani, I think'. The majority who defined themselves as Pakistani were born in Pakistan, and the majority who defined themselves as English were born in England. The older women who par-ticipated in the Economic and Social Research Council study gave more complex identities. Since they were responding via an interpreter, their replies may well have been influenced by the perceived necessity to explain the complexities to someone who was not of their own background.

Young people of Pakistani origin have developed fluid relations between appar-ently opposing cultural styles (Knott and Khokher 1993; Østberg 2003). Østberg writes of the ease with which Norwegian Pakistani children move between cultures, and quotes Saima, 14, who said, 'I am wearing hijab and listening to techno', without expressing any conflict between these aspects of her identity. Similarly, 'Khalid' (a pseudonym) contacted friends and Norwegian girlfriends by mobile phone. He got to know the cousin in Pakistan whom he was most likely to marry by chatting on the Internet.

Hijab

The return to the hijab and the open and public adoption of the identity 'Muslim woman' is something that many of the older generation of women either had not thought important or had gradually discarded (Afshar 1994). For them, Islam as an identity is both a matter of faith and a matter of cultural norms and practices and 'traditions', old and recreated, which are not necessarily accepted by their children (Afshar 1994; Ali 1992; Jacobson 1997). Young women who had chosen to wear the veil found themselves unwittingly labelled as standard-bearers of 'fundamentalism' (Franks 2000). But there is also a contestation between the understanding these women had of their faith and its demands, and that of many members of the youth movement and also of the older generation and kinship group. The revivalist young men and their religious leaders wish to adopt the veiled presence of Islamist women as an emblem, but they do not always include the 'white' *mohajabehs*.

There are very different understandings of the positionality of women, of marital rights and duties of men, of the lifestyles that the women should lead and of their demands for equality. The return to 'real Islam' created different understandings of possible pathways. There are divisions amongst Muslims' communality of understanding and the aspirations of feminist Muslims (Afshar 1998; Hassan 2001; Govandi 1995; Kandiyoti 1991; Karam 1998; Mir-Hosseini 1996, 1999; Mirza 2000; Sardar Ali 2002). Education and the Islamic principle that places no intermediaries between people and God allow Muslim women to strive for their own definition of the true Islam and to defend their own interpretations against obfuscating scholarship (Afshar 1998; Hassan 2001; Mernissi 1991; Mir-Hosseini 1999; Mirza 2000). The new feminist Islamism is constructed in contestation with that of many male religious leaders and youth revivalists in terms of rights and duties, ranging from those who defend the traditional scholarship and its demands for submission, polygamy and invisibility (Roald 2001) to feminists who contest these views.

Young *mohajabehs* are far stricter, and generally choose to cover completely, some even going so far as to wear a face veil, or *neghab*. Paradoxically, these women, who have been educated in Britain and have chosen to wear the formal hijab, construct a 'new ... British form of Islam' (Vallely and Brown 1995) with a degree of liberalism and individualism. This results in an interpretation stripped of cultural accretions and focused on the teaching of the *Koran*. Often they have moved beyond the scholastic divides that impose limitations according to the different schools and have emerged as 'Muslims' rather than Shiias or Sunnis or

Malekis or Shafeis. They have grasped the unity taught by the 'true' Islam. Many have interpreted the faith in terms of mutual obligations and understandings and have expectations that are similar to those of their 'white' Muslims sisters (Franks 2000), but may be very distinct and different from those of the young Muslim men.

The hijab can also provide a means of escape, of free movement and the possibility for women of going to school (Valayati 2003), and particularly to university. Although the proportion of *mohajabehs* is small, they make a disproportionate impact for being different, and for very obviously choosing to be so. Yet, in France, as in the UK, they had for some considerable time managed to have a presence without being persecuted. The negative outcomes in recent years have little to do with the young women and much to do with government decisions to make hijab a major political issue. The French ban on the scarf followed a relatively uneventful year. In the school year 2003, of the 1,256 young girls wearing the scarf in France, only 20 had been defined by the authorities as 'problematic'. There had been six 'exclusions', of which three were sent off as a result of the disciplinary council's decision, and the other three were withdrawn by their parents to avoid their having to go through the process (*Le Monde*, 17 December 2003). What is of interest is that according to Hanifa Cherifi, France's national educational mediator, the number of problems arising from the wearing of the scarf had fallen from 300 per year in 1994 to 150 in 2003 (*Le Monde*, 10 December 2003). Islamophobia may be a more understandable reason for the French government's decision to ban the scarf.

Young Muslim women have had a wide range of reasons for choosing or accepting the wearing of the hijab, and few, if any, of them have anything to do with what the host community has labelled, and demonized, as 'fundamentalism' (Afshar 1995; Franks 2000, 2001).

> In the Western world, the hijab has come to symbolize either forced silence or radical unconscionable militancy. Actually it's neither. It is simply a woman's assertion that judgement of her physical person is to play no role whatever in her social interactions.
>
> (XURL:http:/so146.essex.ac.uk/users/rafiam/women4.htlm
> 11/1/96 quoted by Franks 2000: 924)

The decision to wear modest garments in general, and the hijab in particular, as a deliberate choice of many Muslim women, had in the first instance been an assertion of faith and an act of solidarity with the *umma*. However, it has been understood and interpreted differently by men and women, and cannot be subsumed as part of a singular identity or ethnicity. Nor can it be seen as a final and permanent position chosen by the women, or as a choice that is not necessarily transmitted across the generations.

Many amongst the *mohajabeh* have liberal interpretations of the faith and may even accept their daughters' choice not to wear the hijab. As a matter of fact, *mohajabehs* themselves do not always stay covered; many of the young girls who were wearing the hijab in the 1980s, when they first talked to Afshar, had discarded their headscarves by the year 2000.

Frequently, the women who chose to wear the veil did not come from families who practised seclusion or insisted on the wearing of the hijab; usually their mothers and grandmothers dressed modestly, and if from the subcontinent, often wore the 'traditional' sari or *shelvar kamiz*, but not the hijab. The head-cover that has been worn by young women, particularly in the West, is very much a late-twentieth-century, Western product. It is a reconstructed emblem that allows the wearer to combine jeans and jackets with a new tradition of the hijab.

Far from an indication of submission or docility, the decision to wear the hijab makes a statement that places the *mohajabeh* in the full light of the public gaze, something parents and kin groups do not necessarily wish to see. It may even be seen as a clear indication of their new radical interpretation of the faith, which they define as liberating rather than constraining.

Different Muslim women at different times and for different reasons have decided to wear or discard the hijab. It is often adopted and worn as a badge of honour by the younger generation of 'white' and 'non-white' as an identifier that delineates a clear difference. It is a symbolic construct that otherizes the *mohajabeh* and creates a communality that celebrates an Islamic identity, and is not bounded by race, class or ethnicity. It creates a new category of believers who can, and often have, their roots or their aspirations in feminism (Franks 2001; MacDonald 2003). By doing so, they often fit uncomfortably within Muslim kinship groups.

For the 'white' veiled converts, this hybridity sits uncomfortably with the norms of the host society. The often open and at times violent objections of individuals in the host society to the veil (Barrett 1996) make the wearing of it a political act. Franks was told by a white Muslim woman who wears the hijab that she was seen as a 'traitor'. An Irish convert said, 'I have been called many things … "white Paki" being the cleanest so far' (Franks 2000: 922). A young, high-powered 'white' executive, who had married a Muslim and had 'Muslim' children, told Afshar that she had had to move house because neither the Muslim community nor the 'white' community in her initial neighbourhood were willing to accept her children. Nevertheless, the decision to choose the hijab has not meant that the women concerned have abandoned their 'British' nationality.

Hybridity

Many of the *mohajabehs* were comfortable with a multiplicity of identity, and defined themselves in terms of faith and nationality as British Muslims. In this there is a unity of understanding and aspiration, and a communality of belonging that is shared by Muslim women across the boundaries of race, ethnicity and place of birth. There is little need to abandon the hyphenated British-Muslim identity for the singularity of political Islam. The hyphenated identity of these *mohajabehs* is part of the complex, self-ascribed identities they share with some Muslim men. For instance, many male and female members of Young Muslims UK (YMUK) who talked to Franks (2001) described themselves as being British *and* Muslim. But then, YMUK and the Islamic Society of Britain have been labelled 'lassi Muslims' (the equivalent of champagne socialists). However, it is precisely within this forward-looking Islamist context that young women of all colours and ethnicities can fit and function. Often women who define themselves as Muslim have a clear appreciation of both the rewards and the duties and obligations that the faith imposes on believers in their everyday lives. These may not be the same as those which the more zealous men assume to be part of the meaning of Islam.

The interactions of history, culture and society, along with the dynamic processes of change, construct identities which are pluralist, fluid, multifaceted and multidimensional (Fischer 1986; Friedman 1994; Giddens 1991). Identities are much more a process of change and continuity than a static attribute (Barth 1994; Bhavnani and Phoenix 1994; Fischer-Rosenthal 1995; Ghorashi 2003). The continuity is sustained by shared memories, stories and cultural practices; change is both a reaction to circumstances and a process of negotiation, which results in a multiplicity of identities that 'may or may not contradict each other' (Ghorashi 2003: 29).

However, multiple identities are not disempowering; they may have a situational aspect. Where individuals have a choice in defining their identities, aspects of identity may be mobilized in different situations: they may present themselves differently in different contexts (Edwards 1998; Ghorashi 2003), adopting a single or a hyphenated identity. Women of all generations may think of themselves as migrants, as wives, as mothers, or as British Muslims. In an interview conducted as part of our older-women study, R., who is 64, responded via an interpreter that she thought of herself as a resident of this country now, as a British Muslim. But because she felt she belonged to Pakistan and still had links to Pakistan, she said that she was Pakistani as well.

Muslim women who talked to us generally accepted cultural, ethnic and national identities that defined them in different ways in different circumstances. Hybridity and hyphenated identities come more easily to women who through their lifecycles move along and between identities. They are not necessarily assimilated, but many share the problems of women as a whole and have communality of experience with 'white', converted Muslim women who also cannot easily 'assimilate' within their own society. In terms of construction of an identity, both the person and the face that they present is distinct and different from that of the older generation of Muslim women; it is also different from the youth-led Islamist revival (Castells 1997) in the West.

However, migrants such as R. often do not have agency and cannot exercise a choice; they live in contexts of unequal powers (Bhabha 1994; Ghorashi 2003) that disregard their understanding of who they are and categorize them as 'migrants', thereby ascribing identities to them in terms of their creed, colour or ethnicity. It may be that young Muslim women, with their shared concept of *umma* and their commitment to being British, may be forging a new way towards social and political cohesion through hybridity. Younger female members of Muslims UK, the Islamic Society of Britain and FOSIS are from Arab, African, South Asian and white British backgrounds. They told Franks that they were interested 'in finding ways of being Muslim and British' (2001). One respondent, the daughter of an

Indian father and a white, English mother, talked about the problems she faced as an English Muslim who could not find a place for herself in either community. Some members of the white community hurled abuse, whilst many Muslims, more influenced by culture than by faith, found it hard to 'locate' an 'English Muslim' (Franks 2001: 137). A high-flying, professional woman, daughter of a Sudanese mother and a British father, told Afshar, 'I can never say that I am British. When I do, people immediately ask, "But where are you from originally?"'

Faith

Muslims in West Yorkshire are divided by their religiously and ethnically defined communities. They recreate their cultures on the basis of mutually independent cleavages of language, regional background and national loyalties. Kinship networks support and enhance these divides (Afshar 1989a; Vertovec 1998). Most marriages and joint commercial activities take place within kinship groups (Ballard 2001; Jacobson 1998). Political alliances are usually made amongst specific biradary[1] groups and endorsed by the community mosque. Many of the older generations are more involved, and interested, in the politics of their homelands, and tend to accept the mosque's lead in voting in the UK. There is reluctance to vote for 'outsiders'. Politics is understood and participation secured through kin and community networks. The moral economy of kin (Afshar 1989a) demands of members of the younger generation that they elect the kin group's candidate, despite the reality that the young often have political positions that do not necessarily accord with those of their parents. The fears engendered by Islamophobia, and the dependence of many Muslims on support within their communities, make it much harder for the young to resist kin pressure in ongoing matters of local politics and at election times. Biradary kin groups are able to deliver local councillors who sometimes do not even speak English, but who have the support of their community.

There is a generational divide, in terms of political and social adherence and activities, which is not easily bridged and is becoming increasingly more pronounced. Amongst the youth, Islam has become a more important identity signifier than it is for their parents (Samad 1998b). Yet, this is not always a sign of increased religiosity. Whereas young women either choose the hijab or adopt their hyphenated identities, young men often have difficulty defining themselves in terms of host or kin community. Some have been described as being perched precariously between the role models of 'Lord Ahmed and Ali G' (Lewis 2001).

> In West Yorkshire some young second and third generation males project a 'hard' image of tough aggressive macho men ... [and claim] membership of Hamas and Hisb-ut-Tahrir ... Yet the same individuals do not know what Hamas or Hisb-ut-Tahrir represent and are unaware [of] who the Shiias are, and how they differ from Sunnis.
>
> (Samad 1998b: 434)

However, for these and other young Muslims, Islam as a religion is a core part of their personal and political identity, although their interpretation of it is different from that of their parents. Given that 'identities are the product of exclusion' and constructed through difference in relation to the 'other' (Hall 1996), it may be that this particular kind of masculine youth identity needs to be considered in the light of the 'compensatory masculinities' constructed by minority youth, which are 'racialized' and 'ethnicified' (Frosh *et al.* 2002; Majors 1990; Sewell 1997) and formed in opposition to the experience of oppression and dominant discourses of masculinity and attainments. Following the 1995 Bradford 'riot', members of the Pakistani Muslim community attributed the manifestation to the expressed frustration of 'disempowered and disenfranchised youth' (Burlet and Reid 1998).

However, there are young Muslims brought up in Britain who have a clear understanding of their faith. They are literate in English and their understanding of Islam is textual, often produced by Islamist groups in English, while that of their parents mainly derives from an oral tradition (Samad 1998b: 434). This generational divide is countered by the greater proximity of views and attitudes amongst some of the younger generation of Muslims. The language divide that separates the communities is bridged by the young, who generally are fluent in English and not in their own mother tongues (Jacobson 1998: 96–8; Samad 1998b: 431–2; Lewis 2001). An interviewee who was a member of Young Muslims UK told Franks how she was introduced to the *Koran* as a child and made to read it at the *madrasa*, but it was only when her brother introduced her to an English translation that she was able to connect with it, and subsequently reorient her life towards Islam (Franks 2001).

However, there is a gender divide, and some of the young women have very different interpretations of the teachings of Islam from their male counterparts. Indeed, in the diaspora interviews we found that in one university the women had started their own Sisters' Islamic association for students. Given the gendered understanding that traditional Hisb ut Tahrir supporters have, it would not have been easy for them to oppose the segregation. This is not to say that there are no joint activities. In specific cases, such as the Women's Seminar: Hijab Ban in France, held on 21 January 2004, a meeting was organized by the Sisters of Hisb ut Tahrir.

But often women meet the challenges differently. In the past couple of years, some sisters have made a shift from 'spiritual' to 'political' Islam. As S. explained to Franks in a telephone interview:

> [The Hisb ut Tahrir-associated sisters] have their own organization, and they mainly concentrate on the political side of Islam. A lot of people would say, 'That's not right, you should concentrate on the spiritual side', but I think those who probably have developed their spiritual side, and who have moved that step further ... then go on to advance into the political side of Islam as well.
>
> (Telephone interview 29 June 2003)

They have also become integrated into women's groups and bridge the generations. The Sisters network includes both Hisb ut Tahrir and other women who meet mainly through university women's Islamic groups. A recent meeting attended by Franks included Muslim and non-Muslim women. Some young mothers brought their children; three young women brought their mothers, and one brought her non-Muslim mother (Franks 2004). Evidently this was normal; mothers and daughters go to conferences together. B. said she likes her mother to know what it is she is involved in.

September 11, July 7 and the subsequent intensification of Islamophobia (Allen and Nielsen 2002) created social contexts that constructed new meanings (Castells 1997) which produced both solidarity and further generational and inter-gender tensions in the Muslim community as well as between the hosts and the Muslim communities. Though, by 1993, 87 per cent of second-generation Muslims aged 16 to 24 were born in the UK (Jones 1993), the young found that they were still ascribed an identity that defined them as 'migrants' and, after September 11, as 'Muslims' who carried attributes of fear, terrorism and discord. The host society and the media were ascribing identities to these people that distanced them from the host community and connected them to a constructed notion of their faith group. The new labels of 'evil', 'the enemy within', and 'terrorist' allowed little room for manoeuvre. Many reacted by defining themselves as Muslims. In a recent set of interviews, conducted as part of a current Toronto-based international study of Muslim diaspora, a majority of the younger participants said that their faith had become stronger in recent years. The faith they embrace does not necessarily comprise the traditional beliefs that their elders wish them to have. Nor is their Islam limited to culture or constrained by the diaspora; their Islam is one that forms part of an imagined, dynamic and unbounded world community: the *umma*. This is a righteous, strong and united Islam that does not prevent its followers from retaining their identities as British, Pakistani or Gujarati, but instead encompasses all those identities within a permeable, unbounded communality of dreams and aspirations. The imagined community that the young refer to is not a homeland; it is not a geographical place, and there is no intention of return. They have a universalistic, Islamist consciousness that is not so much diasporic (Saint-Blancat 2002) as rooted in the global concept of *umma*, the geographically unbounded single community of believers. There is no homeland; the earthly experience is merely a path towards eternity. It is the correct path, or *seratol mostaqim*, that matters, not the earthly political or regional divides. For many women, the first step on that path is through the adoption of a strict dress code and the wearing of the hijab.

Marriage

For Muslims in general, marriage is not so much sacramental as contractual; it is a matter of a contract between consenting partners. The marital requirement stipulates that the husband must make an initial down-payment of *mehre*, before the consummation of the marriage, in order to secure the sexual services of the wife. In addition to payment for the consummation of the marriage, husbands must also pay *nafaqeh*, or maintenance, for the household as well as wages for housework and the suckling of babies. Islamic law recognizes the sexual aspect of the marriage as a service that is bought or rented by the husband, and considers domestic work a form of employment, which is valorized through wages. Thus, men are obliged to pay wages for housework, and women even have the religious right to claim back-pay after their husband's death. The failure of either partner to fulfil his or her contractual obligations provides more or less compelling grounds for divorce. This practical, unromantic approach to marriage has made it an institution vulnerable to instrumental use in firming up kinship connections and securing familial interests. In the Middle East and Southeast Asia, particularly amongst the urban, middle classes, these 'arrangements' have, over the years, become diluted and rather relaxed. But in the ossified culture of Muslim migrants in West Yorkshire, marriage is the cornerstone of the biradary and an important means of linking families across continents.

It is assumed that daughters and sons will accept these arrangements, which would protect them from the 'corruption and immorality' of the host society and, at the same time, benefit the family. Some of the second generation of Muslim women had in earlier years, in theory, accepted the notion that they would marry men chosen by their parents (Afshar 1994). In practice, however, young women raised in the West who, despite the best efforts of their parents, had become familiar with the celebrated ideas of romantic love, found it increasingly difficult to accept the parental choice. At the same time, many parents found themselves locked in arrangements that they did not think they could break. G., a young woman who had been educated in Britain and held a high-powered administrative post, told Afshar about the problems she had faced. G. met her second cousin, M., at the wedding of her sister and fell in love with him. The feelings were mutual. The young man, a professional who had been educated in England, seemed to her to meet all possible parental requirements. But her parents had promised her to a second cousin 'back home', and were horrified at her decision to marry M. The couple went ahead and married anyway, but they were shunned by the kin group for five years. It was only when the first baby was born that G.'s mother decided to go over and see her grandchild. Relations remain fragile, but G. is optimistic that they will improve over time.

It is, however, difficult to generalize, since there are cases of white converts joining the groups and, in one case, marrying a young man within two weeks of meeting him. The young woman in question went home and told her mother that not only had she married, but she had also converted to Islam. In another case, a *mohajabeh*, J., decided to marry a non-British Muslim; once more, the parents were given little notice and little choice in the matter. The marriage was arranged rapidly and the young bride soon left to meet her in-laws.

However, familial negotiations between newlyweds differ considerably; J.'s new husband had already been married and divorced by another British-born, 'white' Muslim, and another professional, 'white' convert, M., told Afshar that she already had two divorces behind her. Both times she had accepted an informally polygamous marriage and both times she had divorced the husbands.

The assertive positions and ideas of the *mohajabehs* have, in practice, made them undesirable brides for the kinship network. They know too much about their rights and have too little respect for the 'traditions'. Often these women are more learned in terms of *Koran*ic teaching than their parents. It has become difficult to marry them off in arranged marriages and even more difficult to argue with them, since their arguments are always presented in terms of 'the true Islam'. An inter-viewee for the Muslim diaspora research, an art student who wears hijab, told Franks, 'The more Islamic I become, the less likely it is I will be pushed into an unwanted marriage'. This is because her parents are unable to criticize her if she is following *Koran*ic teaching. Young women often use their textual understanding of Islam to contest the traditions and restrictions imposed on them by their parents (Samad 1998b: 435; Jacobson 1998: 107–9; Shaw 1988; Ali 1992).

These intelligent and learned young women cannot be subsumed in Hisb ut Tahrir's demand for the acceptance of a singular, male-defined, Islamic identity. The young women who have been talking to the authors of this chapter have grown up with a clear understanding of diversities, and have constructed an Islamic identity that is British but embraces the *umma* and also sometimes accom-modates 'feminisms'. It is not an identity that could be easily hijacked. They have worn the hijab, and by doing so have made themselves the subject of the 'white' gaze. Despite the rising Islamophobia post-September 11, the young women who have defined themselves in solidarity with the *umma* retain a clear understanding of what 'their' Islam implies in terms of rights, duties and obligations. They are not willing to be subsumed in cultural mores that they no longer share. They are independent guardians of the future of Islam and its feminisms.

Conclusions

The Muslim women interviewed are creating a feminist identity that embraces the transnationality of *umma* and does not confine itself to minority Muslim groups; faith supersedes nationality (Schmidt 2002), race and ethnicity. Young revivalist women who are born and bred, or largely raised, in the West often disagree with the cultural interpretations of Islam of their parents. Alliances between Muslim women of different colours and ethnicities, and their radical interpretations of Islam and its teachings, have helped create a new dynamic formulation of British Islamic identity that is bridged by bonds of friendship and scholarship. The new Muslims may be 'lassi' Muslims, but they are also enlightened, cohesive and able to place themselves within both their kin and community groups and within the host society. They may be the ones who reach out and even marry across the eth-nic divides and forge religious alliances. Their lived experiences make it possible for them to have hyphenated identities which are experienced as enrichment rather than as lack. They are the groups who are least likely to respond to the political demands of the zealous on either side of the faith and ethnicity divide. It may be that the realities of lives and choices made by the new *mohajabehs* mark the first steps towards a new, multicultural identity and cohesion.

Notes

1 *Biradari*, literally translated, means brotherhood. It is used colloquially to mean the kin group.

References

Adnan, E. (1993) 'Letters from Beirut', *Mediterraneans*, 5: 107–10.

Afshar, H. (1989a) 'Gender roles and the "moral economy of kin" among Pakistani women in West Yorkshire', *New Community*, 15(2): 211–25.

—— (1989b) 'Education: hopes, expectations and achievements of Muslim women in West Yorkshire', *Gender and Education*, 1(3): 261–82.

—— (1994) 'Growing up with real and imaginary values amidst conflicting views of self and society', in H. Afshar and M. Maynard (eds) *The Dynamics of Race and Gender in Britain*, London: Taylor & Francis.

—— (1995) 'Islam empowering or repressive to women?' in Michael King (ed.) *God's Law Versus State Law: The Construction of an Islamic Identity in Western Europe*, London: Grey Seal Books.

—— (1998) 'Strategies of resistance among the Muslim minority in West Yorkshire: impact on women', in N. Charles and H. Hintjens (eds) *Gender, Ethnicity and Political Ideologies*, London: Routledge.

—— (2003) 'Women and wars: some trajectories towards a feminist peace', *Development in Practice*, 13(2–3): 178–88.

——, Franks, M., Maynard, M. and Wray, S. (2001) 'Empowerment, disempowerment and quality of life for older women', *Generations Review*, 11(4): 1153–61.

Ali, Y. (1992) 'Muslim women and the politics of ethnicity and culture in Northern England', in G. Sahgal and N. Yuval-Davis (eds) *Refusing Holy Orders: Women and Fundamentalism in Britain*, London: Virago.

Allen, C. and Nielsen, J. S. (2002) 'Summary Report on Islamophobia in the EU after 11 September 2001'. Online. Available HTTP: http://eumc.eu.int/eumc/material/pub/anti-islam/Synthesis-report_en.pdf.

Ballard, R. (2001) 'The impact of kinship on the economic dynamics of transnational networks: Differential trajectories of adaptation amongst Mirpuris, Jullunduris and Sylhetis', Supplementary Report, Section 3 of the *Bradford Race Review*. Online. Available HTTP: http://www.bradford2020.com/pride/docs/3.doc.

Barrett, C. (1996) Confrontation at Creil: secularism, multi-culturalism and the 'head-scarves affair' in France. Online. Available HTTP: http://www.york.ac.uk/depts/poli/casestud/fullst.yrk/cs025.htm.

Barth, F. (1994) 'Enduring and emerging issues in the analysis of ethnicity', in H. Vermeulen and C. Govers (eds) *The Anthropology of Ethnicity: Beyond Ethnic Groups and Boundaries*, Amsterdam: Spinhuis.

Basch, L. (1997) 'Introduction: Rethinking nationalism and militarism from a feminist perspective', in C. R. Sutton (ed.) *Feminism, Nationalisms and Militarism*, Arlington VI: American Anthropology Association.

Baumann, G. (1997) 'Dominant and demotic discourses of culture: Their relevance to multi-ethnic alliances', in P. Werbner and T. Modood (eds) *Debating Cultural Hybridity: Multi-cultural Identities and the Politics of Anti-racism*, London: Zed Books.

Bhabha, H. K. (1994) 'Between Identities', interviewed by P. Thompson in *Migration and Identity*, Volume 3 and R. Benmsyor and A. Skotnes (eds) *International Yearbook of Oral History and Life Stories*. New York: Oxford University Press, pp. 183–99.

Bhavnani, K. and Phoenix, A. (eds) (1994) *Shifting Identities, Shifting Racisms: a Feminism and Psychology Reader*, London: Sage.

—— Foran, J. and Kurian, P. (eds) (2003) *Feminist Futures: Re-imagining Women, Culture and Development*, London: Zed.

Buijs, G. (ed.) (1996) *Migrant Women: Crossing Boundaries and Changing Identities*, Oxford: Berg.

Burlet, S. and Reid, H. (1998) 'A gendered uprising: political representation and minority ethnic communities', *Ethnic and Racial Studies*, 21(2): 270–87.

Castells, M. (1997) *The Power of Identity*, Malden, MA: Blackwell.

Cohen, A. (2000) 'Peripheral vision: nationalism, national identity and the objective correlation in Scotland', in A. Cohen (ed.) *Signifying Identities: Anthropological Perspectives on Boundaries and Contested Values*, London: Routledge.

Edwards, J. (1998) 'The need for a bit of history: Past and place in English identity', in N. Lovell (ed.) *Locality and Belonging*, London: Routledge.

Fischer, M. M. J. (1986) 'Ethnicity and post-modern arts of memory', in J. Clifford and G. E. Marcus (eds) *Writing Culture: The Poetics and Politics of Ethnography*, Berkeley, CA: University of California Press.

Fischer-Rosenthal, W. (1995) 'The problem with identity: biography as solution to some (post) modernist dilemmas', *Comenius*, 3: 250–66.

Franks, M. (2000) 'Crossing the border of whiteness? White Muslim women who wear the hijab in Britain today', in *Ethnic and Racial Studies*, Special Issue, Vol. 23, No. 5: 917–29.

—— (2001) *Women and Revivalism in the West: Choosing 'Fundamentalism' in a Liberal Democracy*, Basingstoke: Palgrave.

—— (2004) 'Before and After: The hijab as a focus of religious tolerance and intolerance prior to and post 11th September 2001', European Association for the Study of Religions, 4th Annual Conference, Santander.

Friedman, J. (1994) *Cultural Identity and Global Process*, London: Sage.

Frosh, S., Phoenix, A. and Pattman, R. (2002) *Young Masculinities: Understanding Boys in Contemporary Society*, Basingstoke: Palgrave.

Giddens, A. (1991) *Modernity and Self-identity: Self and Society in the Late Modern Age*, Cambridge: Polity Press.

Ghorashi, H. (2003) *Ways to Survive, Battles to Win: Iranian Women Exiles in the Netherlands and the United States*, New York: Nova.

Govandi, Z. (1995) 'Ejtehadeh zanana' (Women's Ijtehad), *Zaneh Ruz*, 23 December.

Hall, S. (1996) 'Who needs identity', in S. Hall and P. du Gay (eds) *Questions of Cultural Identity*, London: Sage.

Hassan, R. (2001) 'Challenging the stereotypes of fundamentalism: An Islamic feminist perspective', *The Muslim World*, 91(1/2): 55–69.

Jacobson, J. (1997) 'Religion and ethnicity: Dual and alternative sources of identity among young British Pakistanis', *Ethnic and Racial Studies*, 20(2): 238–56.

—— (1998) *Islam in Transition: Religion and Identity Among British Pakistani Youth*, London: Routledge.

Jones, T. (1993) *Britain's Ethnic Minorities: An Analysis of the Labour Force Survey*, London: Policy Studies Institute.

Kandiyoti, D. (ed.) (1991) *Women, Islam and the State*, London: Macmillan.

Karam, A. M. (1998) *Women, Islamisms and the State, Contemporary Feminisms in Egypt*, Basingstoke: Macmillan.

Knott, K. and Khokher, S. (1993) 'Religious and ethnic identity among young Muslim women in Bradford', *New Community*, 19(4): 593–610.

Lewis, P. (2001) 'Between Lord Ahmed and Ali G: Which future for British Muslims?' in W. A. R. Shadid and P. S. van Koningsveld (eds) *Religious Freedom and the Neutrality of the State: The Position of Islam in the European Union*, Leuven: Peeters.

Majors, R. (1990) 'Cool pose: Black masculinity and sports', in M. Messner and D. Sabo (eds) *Sport, Men and the Gender Order*, Illinois, IL: Human Kinetics Books.

Makdisi, J. S. (1990) *Beirut Fragments: A War Memoire*, New York: Persia Books.

Mernissi, F. (1991) *Women and Islam, a Historical Theological Enquiry*, Oxford: Basil Blackwell.

Mir-Hosseini Z. (1996) 'Stretching the limits: feminist reading of the Shari'a in post-Khomeini Iran', in Yamani Mai (ed.) *Feminism and Islam Legal and Literary Perspectives*, Reading, Ithaca Press: pp. 285–320.

—— (1999) *Islam and Gender; the Religious Debate in Contemporary Iran*, Princeton University Press.

Mirza, Q. (2000) 'Islamic feminism and the exemplary past', in J. Ridendown and R. Southland (eds) *Feminist Perspectives on Law and Theory*, London: Cavendish.

MacDonald, L. (2003) 'Islam and feminism', paper presented at the Development Groups seminar, Department of Politics, University of York, May 2003.

Modood, T., Berthoud, R., Lakey, J., Nazroo, J., Smith, P., Virdee, S. and Beishon, S. (1997) *Ethnic Minorities in Britain: Diversity and Disadvantage*, London: Social Policy Studies Institute.

Moghissi, H. (1999) 'The construction of "Muslim Woman" and émigré Iranian feminism', in A. Heitlinger (ed.) *Émigré Feminism*, Toronto: University of Toronto Press.

Østberg, S. (2003) 'Norwegian-Pakistani adolescents: Negotiating religion, gender, ethnicity and social boundaries', *Young Nordic Journal of Youth Research*, 11(2): 161–81.

Radcliffe, S. and Westwood, S. (eds) (1993) *'Viva': Women and Popular Protest in Latin America*, London: Routledge.

Roald, A. S. (2001) *Women in Islam: The Western Experience*, London and New York: Routledge.

Rouse, R. (1995) 'Questions of identity: Personhood and collectivity in transnational migration to the United States', *Critique of Anthropology*, 15(4): 351–80.

Saint-Blancat, C. (2002) 'Islam in diaspora: Between reterritorialization and extraterritoriality', *International Journal of Urban and Regional Research*, 26(1): 138–51.

Samad, Y. (1998a) 'Imagining a British Muslim identity', in S. Vertovec and A. Rogers (eds) *Muslim European Youth: Reproducing Ethnicity, Religion, Culture*, Aldershot: Ashgate.

—— (1998b) 'Media and Muslim Identity: Intersections of Generation and Gender', *Innovation*, 11(4): 425–38.

Sardar Ali, S. (2002) 'Testing the limits of family law reforms in Pakistan: a critical analysis of the Muslim family law ordinance 1961', *International Survey of Family Law*, pp. 317–35.

Schmidt, G. (2002) 'Dialectics of authenticity: Examples of ethnification of Islam amongst young Muslims in Sweden and the United States', *The Muslim World*, 92(1–2): 1–17.

Sewell, T. (1997) *Black Masculinities and Schooling: How Black Boys Survive Modern Schooling*, Stoke on Trent: Trentham Books.

Shaw, A. (1988) *A Pakistani Community in Britain*, Oxford: Basil Blackwell.

Subramaniam, B. (2003) 'Imagining India: religious nationalism in the age of science and development', in K. Bhavnani, J. Foran and P. Kurian (eds) *Feminist Futures: Re-imagining Women, Culture and Development*, London: Zed.

Talib, Q. M. (2003) 'The rise of the morons', in 'Contentions', *Q-News*, October 2003, p. 17.

Valayati, M. (2003) Female rural-urban migration of Azari women in Iran: The case study of Tabriz. Ph.D. thesis, York University.

Vallely, P. and Brown, A. (1995) 'The best place to be a Muslim', *Independent*, 6 December, pp. 2–4.

Vertovec, S. (1998) 'Young Muslims in Keighley, West Yorkshire: Cultural identity, context and "Community"', in S. Vertovec and A. Rogers (eds) *Muslim European Youth: Reproducing Ethnicity, Religion, Culture*, Aldershot: Ashgate.

12 Diasporic narratives on virginity[1]

Fataneh Farahani

I remember we had a fig tree at our home. I don't know how I succeeded in climbing the fig tree, but when I wanted to come down, I got frightened. The height made me terrified. I was around eight or nine years old. I remember my mother and grandmother standing by the tree. My grandmother said, 'If she slips and falls, she will lose her *parde-ye bekarat* [virginity, the hymen or, more literally, the virginity curtain]'. I didn't know what the *bekarat* was. I don't remember how I came down. I don't recall if someone helped me down or I came down by myself. But I remember very well that I scratched my crotch [she shows me where she means]. There was a big veranda in our house. I remember when I came down, my pants also tore. My grandmother seemed very anxious and kept asking my mother to check me. In sum, they laid me down on the veranda, I remember clearly. There were two to three more people there. There were no men. This was so horrible for me that even now when I think about it, I feel repulsion in the pit of my stomach. They pulled down my pants to expose my lower parts, and the area close to my private parts was injured. My grandmother was crying and kept saying, 'For sure, she has lost her virginity'. Then they looked more closely. I was just a little girl. Three people were staring at my bare crotch. Sometimes, I think probably the reason that I still hate to go to the gynaecologist so much probably relates to my feeling of being as exposed as I did that day … I think I went through my first gynaecological examination when I was eight or nine years old. The ridiculous thing is that even in that situation, no one explained to me what *parde-ye bekarat* was, and what would happen if I lost it. Does one die? Does one become physically disabled? Does one become mentally disabled? [She laughs.]

Shirin and I sit in the kitchen in her place in a mid-size city outside Stockholm. It is early spring. We have tried to make plans for this meeting for more than five weeks. I am amazed by her great sense of humour and her exceptional talent for storytelling; I cannot stop thinking it was definitely worth the wait. It seems she reads my mind, and as she looks at me thoughtfully, she says: 'Believe me, prior to this interview, I did a lot of thinking about these issues, because they are very important to me. I tried to think back and remember my childhood and youth…. During these four or five weeks that we've been trying to meet, I have really tried to think a lot about how I have related to my body.'[2] Then she tells me the preceding story. Afterwards, we laugh out loud together. But Shirin expresses irritation, too; she further regards her mother and grandmother's manner as 'ignorance, cruelty and lack of compassion'.

Months later, when I look at my notes, I am preoccupied once again with mixed feelings. This story wakes some memories from my own childhood, which is not drastically different from Shirin's experience or from what other women have shared with me. Shirin and I laughed together, but the story took us back to another time – a time when all these prescribed behaviours promoted numerous questions in our young minds, questions that hardly anyone was willing to answer in any meaningful or logical manner. I try to detach from the pain in order to understand what makes a mother or grandmother who 'normally loves' her offspring put the fear of her lost virginity ahead of concern for her physical safety? What kinds of rationalizations lie behind the behaviour of Shirin's mother and grandmother? What kind of normalized and internalized social values govern their attitudes?

In this chapter, I will engage in critical analyses of these questions. Furthermore, since the demand for female virgin status, as a hegemonic concept, is supported by contemporary legal, social and cultural discourses, I will also examine how this demand affects women's lives in general, and how cultural values and social practices surrounding the maintenance of virginity enter women's personal narratives. By studying how virginity is valued through mechanisms of discipline and regulation, I will also pay attention to the operation of power, which as Michel Foucault advocates, 'is not ensured by right but by technique, not by law but by normalization, not by punishment but by control, methods that are employed on all levels and in forms that go beyond the state and its apparatus' (1990: 89).

The concept of virginity and women's narratives

The concept of virginity is developed within and across the intersections of different discourses such as religion, science, medicine, law, literature and culture (Kathleen Coyne Kelly 2000). By exploring the experiences of ten Iranian-born women who, except for one, spent their childhood and early youth in Iran, I seek to examine how multiple discourses on virginity intersect and interact with each other. While my intention is not to establish a grand narrative of how all Iranian women view virginity, by adapting some of the research participants' narratives of the first instructions and advice they received regarding the preservation of their hymen, I will explore how the concept of virginity is discursively constituted and normalized in Iranian contemporary culture, and how these women now view it at this stage of their lives and following their experience of migration. By examining Iranian-born Swedish women's narratives, I attempt to demonstrate the potential of these life stories to offer an understanding of women's perceptions of their own bodies and sexual experiences that diverges from dominant patriarchal discourses. Taking into account cultural and religious factors, these narratives reflect women's attempts to negotiate complex social relations in which they can claim agency as social actors.

Despite the apparent disparity between discursive analysis, in which the subject is constructed by discourses, and narrative analysis, in which the formation of the subject is witnessed through the (re)creation of the life story, it is necessary to incorporate both analytical methods as a means of both constituting the subject and simultaneously constituting the agency of the subject. Identity-formation processes take place within particular socio-cultural conditions that reveal the values of the culture that are intelligible and accessible through discourse. As George C. Rosenwald notes, '[W]hen people tell life stories, they do so in accordance with models of intelligibility specific to the culture' (1992: 265). As a result, the narrators present cultural specificities and manifest historic diversities relating their past and present lives. They reconstruct their past through the specific intelligible and accessible culture of the present experienced in their everyday lives. On the other hand, while discourses condition our thoughts and our lives, reflection upon individual 'choices' is also significant for understanding the power relations we acknowledge or resist. By focusing on parental and socio-cultural instruction about the importance of maintaining virginity and the anxiety over 'losing virginity',[3] I aim to understand the social codes and gendered boundaries across different discourses (such as religion, culture, law, medicine and literature) that underpin women's sexual behaviours. I am also interested in understanding women's acceptance or rejection of values that, indeed, contribute to the transformation of the discourse of virginity through time and place.

At this juncture, however, it is important to note that engaging topics such as (women's) sexuality within Islamic cultures is by no means an easy task; therefore, this area of inquiry has been very much underdeveloped and unexplored. While the women's movement and gender-based organizations have been a primary focus within the increasing body of scholarly work in Muslim societies, focus on sexuality has been lacking, and it remains poorly examined (Ikkaracan 2000). By voicing the relatively mute female narrative, I hope to generate new understandings on this topic.

Who is a virgin?

A sexually inexperienced person is called a virgin. In view of the fact that a sexual interaction between two women is still unrecognized in many places in the world – culturally as well as legally – sexual experience predominantly implies vaginal, heterosexual intercourse. The lack of recognition of homosexual desire and sexuality, particularly sexual interactions between women, and the suppression of female sexuality by patriarchy, has been the subject of many feminist scholarly studies (Irigaray 1980; Rich 1981; Segal 1994) which have challenged the very notion of virginity as feminine and 'loss of virginity' as a heterosexual occurrence. For instance, by deconstructing the phallocentric patriarchal order, Luce Irigaray suggests that for men:

> In their [men's] system … 'virgin' means one as yet unmarked by them, for them. Not yet a woman in their terms…. Not yet presented or proposed by them…. A virgin is but the future for their exchanges, their commerce, and their transports. A kind of reserve for their explorations, consummations and explorations.
>
> (1980: 74)

Moreover, Kathryn Schwarz, scholar of English literature[4] (2002), defines virginity as the following:

> Virginity is a speech act that masquerades as a bodily state, a male fantasy that locates feminine will at the heart of heterosocial production, a licensed performance that incorporates, co-opts and conspires with the body beneath. In this sense chastity, as an attempt to describe and fix the social useful-ness of virginity, only returns us to the stubborn problem of intent: whether grounded in abstraction or flesh, strategies of female sexual bondage reveal the perverse indispensability of female sexual will.
>
> (2002: 15)

Hence, according to the heterosexual definition of sexuality, one is technically considered to be virgin until she or he has had sexual relations with the opposite sex. However, while the spiritual dimension of the word virgin refers to both men and women, its historical, social and cultural reference is predominantly designed for or applied to women (Holtzman and Kulish 1997). In their psychoanalytic study, *Nevermore: The Hymen and the Loss of Virginity*, Holtzman and Kulish indicate that while the word virgin referred to an unmarried and untouched woman, the impracticality of determining the sexual inexperience of women denotes virginity, above all, as a male invention for constraining women's sexu-ality. Furthermore, they also consider the disagreement among classical scholars as to whether or not ancient Greek and Roman scientists were aware of the anatomical existence of the hymen, which in Greek means membrane, and is taken from Hymen, the God of marriage in Greek mythology (Partridge 1958). For instance, Kathleen Coyne Kelly (2000), in her compelling and provocative study on virginity, *Performing Virginity and Testing Chastity in the Middle Age*, affirms:

> The concept of hymen, the notion that it was a normal feature of female anatomy, did not have the same sort of currency in the medical literature of antiquity and the Middle Ages that it has in today's gynaecology. One way to approach the 'discovery' or 'invention' of the hymen is to ask to what degree it has been recognized as a discrete structure in the female anatomy. This is not to say that the structure was not always 'there', but to suggest that its meaning or import *as* a structure was not always in operation.
>
> (2000: 8)

Additionally, Holtzman and Kulish point out that the Latin root of the word vir-gin, not dissimilar to virile, carried the meaning of strength and skill, and didn't necessarily refer to sexual chastity. The connotation of the abstract notion of chastity, they suggest, came with later Christian translations (1997: 18). Therefore, unsurprisingly, the glorified image of Virgin Mary as the foremost ideal of woman-hood, one whose 'hymen remained intact during and after the birth of Jesus' (Gemzöe 2000: 83), made its way into non-Judeo-Christian societies. Hence, virginity is generally and historically recognized as a feminine characteristic. Therefore, like other gender attributes, and probably more than any other, it is not a natural condition and entails a distinguishing, gendered characteristic for women in different social positions. Moreover, the feminization of virginity has in fact contributed to institutionalizing a discourse of virginity established by a model of sexuality based on heterosexual vaginal intercourse, which typically involves pain and might or might not a leave hymeneal blood sign. While an intact hymen has been considered to be the very symbol of female virginity, a similar biological indicator has been absent for men.

According to the anatomical definition, (Sloan 2002) the hymen is a thin, fragile and elastic membrane around the opening of the vagina that generally breaks after the first penetration and often leaves a bloody sign of its breach. No specific function is recognized for the hymen. A broken hymen will appear as a torn, split and tattered membrane and, among the cultures where a 'virginity examination'[5] is frequently practised, there is a compelling belief that a deflowered virgin can be easily identified by a professional gynaecologist, even though the ability to recognize a virgin from a non-virgin is denied by medical doctors. According to anatomical account (Sloan 2002) no one, including a gynaecologist, can determine whether or not a woman is sexually experienced by looking at her vagina. This is because the hymen can be:

- thin as a spider web, or thick and fleshy;
- quite vascular, with a good blood supply, or relatively avascular;
- extremely variable in how much of the vaginal opening is covered;
- sometimes so pliable and flexible that it never ruptures but only stretches, even after childbirth (Sloan 2002: 35).

Not only are there various forms, sizes, looks and levels of flexibility of hymens, but some women are born without them. So, despite the crucial social linkage between hymen and virginity, they are not physically or even literally identical. A woman who has a torn hymen or lacks a hymen is not necessarily sexually experienced, and vice versa. Even though the existing contemporary medical and scientific observations consider the hymen to be an unreliable sign of virginity (that is, being heterosexually inexperienced) the hymen as a sign of virginity is the subject of considerable social judgements placed upon many women in different parts of the world, and mainly among diverse Middle Eastern cultures and some Middle Eastern diasporic communities in Europe and North America.

Nevertheless, despite the fallibility of the physical indicators of virginity, some people still request a virginity examination before the wedding night (or after the wedding night if the bride failed to bleed) in order to provide an authorized certification of the bride's virginal status. What the gynaecologist can offer at best is an opinion about whether or not the girl will leave a bloody sign on the wedding night. They cannot, however, be certain of the reason that one lacks a hymen or has a broken hymen. In other words, one cannot distinguish between an 'accidentally' broken hymen and a hymen broken by intercourse. Then again, flexible hymens, which can withstand intercourse, can present a virgin status without necessarily indicating sexual inexperience. Despite this unreliability, virginity examinations are widely practised in many parts of the Middle East. The written official documentation, predictably, has helped (and still helps) many young girls who have failed to leave a blood sign on the white bed sheet after the wedding night.

Moreover, along with destabilizing the linkage between the 'existence' or lack of existence of the hymen and female previous sexual experience, two Swedish social-medicine researchers, Monica Christianson and Carola Eriksson (2004), recently published a thought-provoking article on the subject. Referring to their lengthy experience as midwives, they announce that in the course of their work they have never come across a so-called hymen. According to them, what we in common parlance call hymen is not a membrane that separates the vagina from the external part of a woman's genital area; the hymen, they argue, 'consists of a membrane fold that surrounds the opening of vagina. The appearance of the membrane fold does not show whether or not a woman is a "virgin" or "not"' (2004: 322, my translation). Therefore, they claim, the hymen is rather a social and cultural construction shaped by the patriarchal social order. Expressions such as 'maidenhood' in English, or *parde-ye bekarat* (virginity curtain) in Persian, are just a few examples that illustrate how they are embodied even linguistically. The very operation of virginity examination and hymen reconstruction, according to Christianson and Eriksson, are among modern techniques that not only render the control of women's sexuality still possible but also contribute to its maintenance.

Contemporary Egyptian novelist and psychiatrist Nawal El Saadawi is one of the first women to write about female children's socialization to womanhood in Middle Eastern contexts. In her pioneering books she demonstrates how family reputation hangs on the existence of 'the very fine membrane called "honour"' (1977: 25). The weight of the unbroken hymen ensures girls' marriageability while it restrains their lives in general and their sexuality in particular. By providing different examples of her 'patients' – young girls who asked for legitimized anatomical explanations for failing to leave a bloody sign on their wedding nights – El Saadawi explains how women's premarital sexual experience is considered to be a source of shame and a symbol of degradation. Furthermore, Fatima Mernissi, the Moroccan sociologist, has for a long time challenged the existing double standards of moral values in the legal system, religious doctrines and cultural practices of Morocco and some other 'Islamic' contexts. The two central questions she posed in the late 1970s and early 1980s are still indispensable for understanding misogynist discourses that proliferate throughout mainstream discourses in different Islamic cultures and contexts. 'What economic need does [female] virginity serve?' she asked, and 'Of what national plan is [female] virginity a part?' (1996: 38). By examining the aforementioned existing double standards in Morocco, she declares the following:

> Curiously, virginity is a matter between men, in which women merely play the role of silent intermediaries. Like honour, virginity is the manifestation of a purely male preoccupation.... The concepts of honour and virginity locate

the prestige of a man between the legs of a woman. It is not by subjecting nature or by conquering mountains and rivers that a man secures his status, but by controlling the movements of women related to him by blood or by marriage, and by forbidding them any contact with male strangers.

(1996: 34)

By gendering the ways in which the establishment of virginity and gender are related, Mernissi attempts to shed light on the cultural practices that lead to the disempowering of women. In other words, she tries to ascertain not only 'what economic need virginity serves' but 'whose economic need it serves'. In this circumstance, virtue and chastity turn into the core ambition in order to make virginity (that is to say, an intact hymen) socially valuable and desirable, while repressing female will.

But what role does religious doctrine (in this case Islam) play in regulating (female) sexuality in general and the demand for virgin status? In contrast to Christianity, Islam rejects celibacy, and celebrates sexual pleasure as a legitimate right of believers. However, it has copious regulations regarding sexual practices. By advocating early marriage, *mut'a* (temporary marriage in the Shi'a Islamic context), and institutionalizing gender segregation, Islamic regulations codify particular sexual practices and define the boundaries that confine sexual intimacy within marriage (*nekah*) and punish *zena* (illicit sex outside marriage). In *Women in Muslim Unconsciousness*, Fatna Sabbah (1988) distinguishes Islamic erotic discourse from Islamic orthodox discourse. In addition to problematizing whether orthodox discourse and its claims to a spiritual dimension differs essentially from erotic discourse and its embodied dimension, Sabbah explains that orthodoxy and eroticism are polarized into a hierarchical relation, with orthodox discourses being dominant. She also suggests: 'In the Muslim universe there is no purely sexual field, there is only a regulated sexual field, coded and systemized according to the options and priorities of Islam as a culture and a strategy of civilization' (1988: 65).

On the other hand, utilizing a disciplinary sexuality, in the means of civilization, symbolizes the maintenance of an Islamic collective moral, which advocates for a collective rather than individual morality. Therefore, society becomes responsible for governing everybody's conduct to *amre be maroof va nahey-e az monker* (enforce the good and prohibit the evil), a well-known Islamic regulatory code. Thus, to avoid the sexual temptations, collective moral imperatives are enacted to control and contain sexual practices and desire. In this condition, the persistence of the necessity of female chastity and pureness generates a monopoly on women's sexual behaviours across a number of different discourses in order to maintain 'moral hegemony' over women's bodies. Therefore, the intact hymen, as *the* sign of virginity, is historically constructed as the existing point where the body and the society meet and interact in different social, religious, legal and cultural contexts.

So, despite the fact that virginity appears to be a matter of physical technicality, a broken hymen often signifies a sexually active woman and is acknowledged to be an indicator for distinguishing between a non-active virgin (a dignified woman) and a sexually active (non-dignified) woman. Thus, when Tunisian Muslim scholar Abdelwahab Bouhdiba, among others, states that 'Islam, then, is an economy of pleasure' (1998: 86), the appropriate question would be 'whose pleasure?' In doing so, Bouhdiba does not merely fail to locate gender within this pleasure principle, but also diminishes the idea of whose pleasure Islam favours. By focusing on some of the paradoxes and dilemmas, Farzaneh Milani (1992), for instance, aims to give details as to how this disproportionate condition is practised. She explains:

> Ironically, though women are allegedly possessed by an uncontrolled sexual passion, men are offered numerous sanctified ways of indulging their sexual desires. Through polygyny (up to four wives at a time), serial unions (unilateral repudiation rights), and temporary marriages, men have a multiplicity of sexual relations at their disposal. Female sexuality, however, is only recognized, even encouraged, within the sanctified boundary of marriage. Celibacy is not approved of for women. Unlike the birds of Christ, who dedicate their lives to God and remain celibate, or the Buddhist nuns, Muslim women are not encouraged to remain virgins. However much valued and cherished, virginity is not an eternal ideal state for Muslim women. Although it is the most essential prerequisite of the ideal unmarried woman because it establishes her purity before marriage, it should not negate or deny her active sexuality after marriage. Even *houris* [fairies] in paradise are not expected to abstain from sex. Promised in the *Koran* to faithful men, they are blessed with renewable virginity. No wonder there is no counterpart for the Virgin Mary in Islamic heritage.
>
> (1992: 40)

Consequently, in this discourse women's sexuality becomes visible and viable only in the service of men's desire. Furthermore, even in paradise, Muslim men are promised sex, as Milani stated, with *houris*, but a similar promise to women is non-existent. In this condition, the demand for virgin status has established a dichotomy of chaste and honourable women on one hand and disreputable and non-honourable women on the other, and has furnished a lower status for women who challenge this demand and will not or cannot provide proof of their sexual abstinence. Therefore, the significance of the unmarried female virgin body has been a powerful element in disciplining and controlling women's bodies. At this juncture, by examining some of the narratives of women, I aim to understand how cultural and religious values surrounding sex and sexuality and various social practices enter women's personal narratives of their 'first lessons on virginity'.

The first lessons on the preservation of the hymen

In the course of analysing the interview materials, I observed that the importance of virginity was one of the issues raised by almost all of the research participants.

This, however, didn't appear extraordinary, since any sexual intimacy between two people who are not united within a heterosexual marriage is legally considered a crime in post-revolutionary Iran, and it was never culturally or socially accepted before the revolution. The legal, cultural and social prohibition, however, has never been able to stop people completely from engaging in premarital sexual interactions. The meticulous directives from their surroundings regarding the importance of preserving virginity are highly present in the women's narratives. Everyone had a story to tell about how they were advised from an early age to be cautious about their socialization with men and about physical activities that could harm them terminally. In the interview process, the women expressed, in different ways, how they have been instructed to stay away from sexuality. They also point out how the constant written and unwritten instructions regarding safeguards against contact with men have led to self-control and self-censorship up to the present. The following examples are some of the stories women shared with me.

Shiva is 40 years old and comes from the capital, Tehran. She recalls how her mother advised her and her sisters to be careful about their virginity. Shiva's mother also made an illuminating distinction between a 'girl' and a 'woman' for her daughters:

> My mother used to say that the difference between a *dokhtar* [girl] and a *zan* [woman] is that a girl has a *pardeh* [curtain]. I remember that my sister always made fun of it. However, my mother said that we should keep that *pardeh*... She always warned us to be careful even when we played... She said that we should keep the *pardeh* until we marry. So this was the case. And when you hear these things not once, not twice, but thousands of times, you think that is the way it should be.

Another research participant, Simin, in her late forties, comes from the Kurdish part of Iran, and remembers her mother's instruction after she began menstruating:

> Simin: After my first period, my mum told me that from now on, I must be very careful and I shouldn't open my legs too much [laughing], or jump from a stream ... because I could lose my *dokhtari* [girlhood]...
>
> *Did she ever explain what dokhtari was? What did she say?*
>
> Simin: ... I think she said that it was a kind of a *pardeh*, a thin layer of I don't know what, maybe a kind of tissue. She used to say that if a boy comes close to you, this *pardeh* will rip and its sign is that it will bleed. She also said that the *pardeh* should be well kept until the time a girl marries; otherwise she would be considered to be a bad girl, and so on ...

The youngest interviewee, Mana, 24, came to Sweden at the age of nine with her family. She considers herself as having been brought up in a liberal fashion by her parents in Sweden. Despite the fact that Mana left Iran at a very young age, she remembers intriguing stories of her grandmother's instructions when she was a little kid. The following is one of them:

Mana: I think the first time I masturbated I was five or six years old.

And you remember it...?

Mana: Yes, I don't remember the very first time. I remember a time I was six years old. I had started to go to school then. My grandmother caught me when I was masturbating. Then we sat and she explained to me that if I continued doing it, I would never be able to get married and that I will actually end up in hell. She also said that it would be clear to everyone that I was a bad girl and no man would choose me nor want to be with me. And then she told a story about hell that was very terrible.

Did you follow her advice?

Mana: No, no [she laughs]. I think one week later I started doing it again. I just was careful that I only did it when she was not around.

As illustrated in the above examples, in the Persian language *bekarat* (virginity) is manifested and acknowledged even in the ways in which females are addressed. A *dokhtar* (girl) is an unmarried and sexually inexperienced woman, regardless of her age. On the other hand, a *zan* (woman) is a married woman, regardless of her age. Therefore, an unmarried mature woman is still called *dokhtar*, which indicates that she is still a *bakereh* (the word means virgin; its literary origin, from the word *bekr*, means pureness), while a married 15-year-old girl is called *zan*. It is even considered inappropriate to call a *dokhtar* a *zan,* since the word *zan* might indirectly indicate that she is, or has been, engaged in premarital sexual activities. This signals how *dokhtari*, or girlhood, as Simin's mother instructed her, is coupled with a girl's *bekarat* and is synonymous with being a *bakereh*, or virgin. The other meaning associated with the word *zan* in Persian is wife. Thus, this reveals how one, by relinquishing her *dokhtari*, not only becomes a woman, but also, simultaneously, a wife. So, being an unmarried female also implies being sexually inexperienced. A female individual turns into a woman only by becoming a wife. This designation entails the impossibility and impracticality of becoming a woman outside the institution of marriage in contemporary Iranian culture.

Consequently, the identification or lack of identification with morally appropriate standards is reinforced and justified through various metaphoric associations. This production and reproduction of cultural values through language simultaneously shapes the social order and informs the social members of the contained messages they entail. For instance, the very word *parde-ye bekarat* (the hymen or, more literally, the virginity curtain) exhibits how a woman's hymen symbolizes a gateway that allows men's entrance.[6] The word *pardeh* (curtain) also indicates the very possibility of 'taking off' or 'unveiling' a virgin woman. It is worth noting here that the word *pardeh* was originally one of the common names, in Indian and ancient Persian, for the veil. Therefore, the very act of defloration signals the act of unveiling of the female.

Considering the importance of marrying 'on time', particularly for a female, there is also a humiliating appellation that is usually associated with women who do not do so, or who marry 'behind schedule'. *Pir-dokhtar* (old girl, spinster) or *dokhtar-e torshideh* (left-behind girl, pickled girl) implies that a girl who is not married by the appropriate time turns sour and unpleasant. She loses her desirability and consequently will have less chance to marry. Obviously, the age limit and other required qualities are observably socially constructed and differ based on class, urban and rural contexts and other factors that vary dramatically over time and place. *Torshideh* women are undesirable women who are 'behind schedule' for marriage, but there is an inconsistency in the reasons that make one turn into *torshideh*. Such women are generally considered to be physically unattractive or 'defective' in some way; otherwise, the thinking goes, they would be able to marry sooner. While 'unattractiveness' is a common feature for many *torshideh* women, being too attractive may also turn one into *torshideh*. 'Not everyone has the courage to propose to a highly demanded and very beautiful young girl', an Iranian male friend once said to me. The good-looking girls, he explained, may have 'high' requirements and turn down all suitors' proposals and, as a result, pass the appropriate time for marriage.

Torshideh women may have defied various norms and standards, or somehow socially 'misbehaved' (sexually or asexually), and as a result are considered rude, disobedient and undesirable for marriage. A woman of ill reputation is one that 'no' man would like to marry. Another group of young women who turn into *torshideh* are, according to some interviewees, women who sacrifice themselves entirely to their family. Due to low family income or the absence of one or two parents, some women become responsible for supporting the rest of the family. These women sacrifice their own lives in order to take care of their younger sisters and brothers and, as a result, suppress their own desires and requirements. Therefore, they also fail to marry on time and become *torshideh*.

Nonetheless, regardless of the grounds on which one joins that socially undesirable group of women called *torshideh*, after she is positioned there, a woman is expected to appreciate "any offer" by "any man" and with any conditions. Improper reputations, lack of economic and social independence and a feeling of inadequacy when it comes to beauty requirements are a few of the reasons many of these women agree to marry someone whom they not only do not love but also consider an inappropriate partner in terms of age, education, class, or other factors. Noticeably, it is worth mentioning that a similar designation is non-existent for men. The only phrase somewhat similar to *torshideh* used for 'older' men is *marde ja-oftâdeh* (mellow, or mature, men), which not only fails to generate any of the negative associations of *torshideh*, but also indicates some positive characteristics. *Ja-oftâdeh* men are considered mature and experienced. Furthermore, while *torshideh* is only assigned to unmarried, 'older' women, *ja-oftâded* can also be assigned to married men.

The illustrated examples demonstrate some of the ways that gendered social moral values are manifested in the Persian language. The language entails various sexual connotations and moral principles that easily enter into daily conversations and supply gendering of bodies and conduct. In these circumstances, the very act of identifying one as 'female' suggests the existence, or lack of existence, of sexual experience. In these settings, meanings, metaphors and language contribute in shaping a complex value system, and consequently maintain the hegemonic practices of disciplining women. As Shiva expressed eloquently, 'when you hear these things not once, not twice, but thousands of times, you think that is the way it should be'. Shiva's explicit reference to how one is socialized into cultural expectations shows how these social contexts construct one's life. Furthermore, due to the reiteration of institutionalized conventional attitudes, as Shiva pointed out, they become internalized and achieve the status of normalcy through time and place. In this climate, each element and practice strengthens other elements and practices and aims to take charge of sexual expressions and women's movement entirely.

However, despite the fact that social values and restrictions make the conversation and open communication around sexuality complicated, in fact, in everyday conversations sex and sexuality are always indirectly present. For instance, in his early study on theatrical games, which are generally played by and for women in Iran, Kaveh Safa-Isfahani (1980) demonstrates how sexuality is obtainable through the symbolic forms in much religious and secular folklore. In addition, Pâknahâd-e Jabaruti (2002) and Shahidian (1999), among others, have examined in different ways how the Persian language is wrapped up with various sexual connotations, often extremely sexist, which frequently come up in private conversations.

The normal body

Some research participants recalled being advised to keep their hymen intact in order to not become *naghes* (defected). For instance, Mitra, a Tehrani woman in her early forties who frequently emphasizes having coming from a non-religious family, unexpectedly and eagerly exclaimed, 'You know what? My mother kept telling me that I was not supposed to jump up and down. She used to scream at me and say, "*Naghes mishi!* [You'll get defected, or ruined]"'. Considering a female with a broken hymen defected demonstrates how the disciplining of a woman's body not only aims to uphold her virginity but also presents this as 'normal'. A female who is not *bakereh* is defected, immoral, impure and undesirable. Thus, women's representations of their bodies and sexual self-understandings rely on institutionalized social regulations and policies that over time become internalized, and as a result 'naturalized' and ultimately considered *the* normative behaviours. They will also exhibit how different attitudes, gendered moral values, beliefs and manners contain sexual significance and how those attitudes, values and beliefs have an impact on women's sexuality. These personal narratives, as the sociologist Ken Plummer (1995) in his study on sexual stories suggests, do not necessarily make the 'sexual' their centre of attention. Nevertheless, they are always related: for instance, Plummer clarifies, 'the personal narratives of Aids providing stories of illness, politics and grief as much as tales of sex; the stories of abortion providing tales that link to motherhood, reproduction, feminism and politics; and tales of rape being as much about power and violence as sex' (1995: 15). Sexual stories, Plummer emphasizes, 'cannot be sealed off hermetically from allied storytelling' (ibid.). Therefore, utilizing women's accounts contributes to comprehending how the disciplinary power-relation system of the institutions of virginity operate in order to impose limits, restrictions and prohibitions on women's daily lives in general, and sexual behaviours in particular. The following example illustrates how women's narratives cover a broader space.

Nooshin is in her early forties and has a very 'feminine' appearance. While she mentions frequently the importance of exhibiting a 'feminine look', she recalls being very 'boyish' as a young girl. I asked her what she meant by that and how the 'boyish style' affected her. Below is an excerpt of our conversation about her 'boyish style' and how the preservation of her virginity has affected her 'boyish style'.

Nooshin: I was a *pojk-flicka* [tomboy: she uses the Swedish term] when I was young.

What signified that boyish style?

Nooshin: I don't know. Maybe when you are a boy, you can do many things more easily. For instance, I used to hear that I was like a boy, and therefore, I was allowed to bike with the guys. And, for example, if you played with your dolls, guys didn't let you enter into their groups and their games.

So you mean the condition of entering the boys' world was that you leave the 'girls' world'?

Nooshin: Yes, by leaving your 'girly world' you could enter the 'boys' world'. Then when you grow older and are around 15 years old, everything changes. You get your period. Evaluation of your body and beauty starts. Certainly, your path in life shifts because of that period. Then you cannot just climb a tree or wall. There is a risk that you could fall and harm your virginity. Probably, my parents didn't tell these things to me in particular. But I remember my mother emphasized and repeated one sentence frequently: '*Nejabat* [chastity/virtue] is the most significant quality for a girl'. And at that time we didn't understand what *nejabat* was at all. I didn't do anything special. I liked to be happy. I liked to jump. I liked to bike. I didn't know at all what she meant by *nejabat*. Or I remember we were told that '*dokhtar mesle shishe mimune, darz var nadare* [girls are similar to glass; they are not supposed to be cracked]'. I still don't understand it. What does *darz var nadare* [not being cracked] mean? Probably, we are very much cracked now and don't even know it! [We both laugh.] However, there were the things that made you self-conscious about what you were doing all the time. What does this *nejabat* mean? What does it mean to be a *dokhtar* [girl]? And these were the things that distinguished your world from the world of boys. Earlier your games were kind of limitless. You didn't think of these things. But when you grew older, your breasts grew too. When you grew older, the way boys looked at you changed too.

Like Nooshin, another woman, Leila, also talks about how her childhood was divided into 'girlish' and 'boyish' worlds. She recalls that a constant battle was going on between her mother and her brothers. Leila's mother, on the one hand, wanted her to remain a little girl with all the 'glitter and girly jewellery' and Leila's brothers, on the other hand, considered all these things nonsense. Leila's brothers took her mountain climbing[7] against her mother's wishes in a time when very few men let their sisters join them in the mountains, particularly in the small city where they were living. Leila seemed pleased about not living according to her mother's 'girlish' world. In response to my wonder, she says, 'My brothers took me with themselves to another world'. In that 'world', Leila gained self-confidence. In the 'boyish/manly' world, Leila became politically active, where she often raised issues specific to women's situations in Iranian society. In the 'boyish/manly' world, she started to read seriously. She could go out. She learned to think 'better', as she says 'I could not do it if I had remained in my mother's "girlish world"'.

It is worth mentioning here that the importance of the role of brothers was raised by most of the research participants. In Iran, brothers 'usually' support and expand the extent of parents' and society's control over and regulations regarding their sisters. In these circumstances, the masculinity of men is persistently defined by the extent to which they control women in their family and friend circles. Men who consciously or unconsciously fail to control the women related to them have a lower status, since their masculinity is highly questioned. These kinds of men are often openly humiliated for refusing to oppress the women in their circles. However, more liberated and less controlling brothers, from which some of the research participants benefited, were able to exploit their family's confidence in them, and their position of authority, to assist their sisters in exercising more freedom. Some women mentioned that they could meet boyfriends, go to parties or engage in political activities, as Leila did, by having their brothers as escorts when they wanted to do something 'inappropriate'. They received permission to leave home with the condition that they go with their brothers, some of whom were even younger than they were. The brothers let them go 'wherever' they wanted, they said, and then picked them up at a designated time and place. Some Iranian women are grateful for these kinds of brothers, who have assisted them in gaining more 'freedom'.

However, while the existence of these brothers and men dispute the homogenized and Orientalist representation of Middle Eastern men as only oppressive and overprotective, the very dependence of women's autonomy on the wishes of their male relatives (more liberated fathers, brothers or husbands) demonstrates how fragile this freedom can be. The institutionalized inequality within the post-revolutionary (1979) Iranian legal system – discriminatory laws such as compulsory veiling, gender segregation, polygamy, men's unilateral right to divorce, criminalization of extramarital sex, and stoning – places numerous obstacles before each and every woman (though some of those laws existed even before the revolution) that the support of no brother, father or husband can easily remove. Moreover, marrying the 'wrong' man and leaving behind a liberated brother or father can change a woman's life dramatically, as was the case for two of the women whom I interviewed. The existing regulations in regard to sexual relations affect the way women internalize moral values, discipline themselves or empower themselves to assert agency through dominant discourses.

Nonetheless, women continue to employ various tactics to challenge dominant gendered moral values, most notably in the area of literature. An important example is the writing of contemporary female novelist Shahrnush Parsipur, who has taken up questions related to sexuality and male and female relationships in Iranian society. Parsipur has endured prison terms under both the Shah's regime and the Islamic Republic, specifically for her *Zanan bedoone mardan* (Women Without Men, 1998), translated into both English and Swedish, which provoked the Islamic government in Iran to ban the book, forcing Parsipur to leave Iran. She now lives in the United States.

Women Without Men is a collection of several interwoven stories about five female characters, who, in different ways, try to escape the relationships and rules of morality forced upon them. A common thread that joins the stories is how they are mistreated as women. They all end up in a magical garden, symbolic of a breathing space for women in a patriarchal society that consistently denies them their rights and the liberty to choose their own lives. One of the women, 38-year-old Munis, still a virgin, is assaulted and killed by her brother for refusing to obey him. Another character, Zarrinkolah, who was a prostitute, marries the 'good gardener' and is later rewarded by going to paradise. Parsipur frequently and openly discusses issues related to women's sexuality. Recently, in an interview with the journalist Soheila Vahadati, she courageously and candidly discussed her thoughts about virginity when she was a young child, her 'sexual game' that left her with the anxiety that she was not a *dokhtar* (virgin), even trying to avoid marrying because psychologically she 'could not tolerate that a man humiliate' her for not being a virgin (2004). Later on, when Parsipur married and didn't bleed on her wedding night, she was even more convinced that she had lost her virginity when she was a little girl, until she talked to other women around her and found out that not all women necessarily bleed during the first sexual intercourse.

Conclusion

As the illustrated examples demonstrate, the demands for safeguarding virginity do not only lead to the requirement for (female) premarital sexual abstinence. The core ambition, after all, is to have virtuous and chaste women who are socially desirable. Therefore, the insistence on the necessity of the virgin female body not only generates a monopoly on women's sexual behaviours, but also has enormous impact on the women's movement, childhood experiences, playing, and future dreams and plans. In other words, the rules and regulations regarding female virginal status spread out to the ways in which female individuals inhabit, move or even dream and plan for her future. Therefore, while the demands for 'being a virgin' produce enormous anxiety in regards to female sexual life, they also generate enormous control over female life in general, replicating a moral panic predicated upon the preservation of men's honour through women's appearance and conduct.

Within this context, the rationale behind the behaviour of Shirin's mother and grandmother, as outlined at the beginning of this chapter, is the dominant expectation for female virgin status. The safeguarding of Shirin's hymen is more important than her injury and her fear, as her marriageability rests on her pre-marital sexual abstinence, and her remaining a virgin guarantees that future. Shirin's story also demonstrates how the disciplinary power relations surrounding the institutions of virginity govern her mother and grandmothers' behaviour and prompts the imposition of limits, restrictions and prohibitions on women's daily lives from an early age.

Women (and men), however, refuse to be merely victims of the existing order, and they try through different means to gain agency and challenge the hegemonic moral order. In other words, the reality that repressive discourses construct the lives of women (and men) does not mean that their lives are predetermined by these discourses or that they cannot gain agency. Cultural and social discourses shape people's lives, but the subject of these discursive and narrative strategies continually negotiates the social and psychical terrains. Paying attention to specific situations can be beneficial to understanding particular forms of resistance and the struggles that may lead to social and cultural change.

Acknowledgements

I would like to thank all the women who openly and generously shared with me the most private part of their lives. Without their contributions this study would not have been possible; I cannot thank them enough. Janet Bauer, Kata Youn Baghai, Taina Chahal, Jane Cleveland, Lena Gerholm, Haideh Moghissi and Natalie Wisniewski and my colleagues and friends at the Department of Ethnology at Stockholm University have read various versions of this paper and provided me with inspiration as well as valuable suggestions and feedback. I am very grateful to them. This study was possible by generous grants from NorFA, the Nordic research programme, 'Gender and Violence', and further supported within the framework of the Bank of Sweden Tercentenary Foundation, Project ORIS (The Orient in Sweden, Grant No. K2002–0395). I owe thanks to them.

Notes

1 This chapter is a small part of an ongoing research project on Iranian-born Swedish women's sexuality. For this research, I have conducted ten in-depth interviews with urban-dwelling, Iranian-born women living in Sweden in order to explore how the sexuality of these women has been constructed by taking into consideration diverse factors such as past and present social and economic locations, level of education, age and feminist self-awareness.

2 Other research participants have also shared with me how the interview process had preoccupied their minds. One woman called me more than a year and half after the interview and said, 'You know what? The reason I am calling you is that I have just finished reading a book [that] made me think a lot about one of the questions you asked me. I remember I told you then that I didn't have any answer for that question, but now after reading this book I think I know why. I just wanted to tell you that.' And then she told me more about the book and the question. I was pleasantly astonished and deeply touched. I never thought that the participants would carry my interview questions with

them so deeply and for such a long time. Other women I met by chance also asked me how my research was going and told me that they still think of some of my questions. They all think it is quite a pity that I write in English, and not in Persian or Swedish, so they could read it.

3   It is worth mentioning that in Persian, as in English, the term 'loss', *az dast dadan*, is used to denote the 'first-time' sexual experience. This illustrates how, despite the fact that many young people today, particularly in the Western context, regard virginity and lack of sexual experience as a burden and a signifier of immaturity, linguistically, the very first sexual experience, which divides one's life into 'before' and 'after', is coupled with the notion of 'loss' and 'losing' something. While 'losing' one's virginity is a critical sign of maturity, marking the passage to adult sexuality, the 'irreversibility' of restoring virginity (at least before the reconstruction surgery now available both in the Middle East and the West), or the impossibility of regaining the mental virginal stage metaphorically, attaches the very first experience to the notion of loss.

4   In her article 'The Wrong Question, Thinking through Virginity', Kathryn Schwarz examines a range of literary, historical and theoretical texts in order to understand the social conventions that govern gender, sexuality and sexual desire in the early modern period.

5   The 'virginity examination' is performed in many Middle East and African societies and some diasporic Middle Eastern communities in Europe and North America. It is worth noting here that while the general belief is that immigrant groups practise their traditions, such as virginity examinations and female genital mutilation, in Western contexts, up until 1979 virginity examinations were practised on Asian immigrants to the United Kingdom to discern real fiancées of British citizens from those merely faking dependency to enter the countries. This practice was banned in February of 1979. The relevant point is that British authorities assumed a general 'virginal' condition for all the unmarried women from Asia, regardless of their class background, education, age and religious or cultural beliefs. This is just an example of essentialist and Orientalist assumptions of the 'other'. It is also interesting to note here that virginity tests have never been practised by Swedish authorities, but the requirement of Islamic wedding ceremonies and certifications, among others, is an example of how the Western system uses the essentialist assumption of the 'other' to enforce their own political means. In a society like Sweden's, where cohabitation is extensively practised, no one asks for a wedding certificate to prove partnership, while Islamic certification (with all the requested conditions, such as fathers' permissions) is requested from women who want to join their partners in Sweden. A similar request is nonexistent for women from Latin America, for instance, who want to join their partners.

6   According to Old English, the hymen was called the 'maidenhood'. This actually mirrors the Persian meaning of curtain or veil, in a sense, as it refers to a hood that a virgin wears over her head and hair to signify and protect her innocence.

7   Mountain climbing was practised frequently by most of the people involved with different oppositional political organizations in pre- as well as post-revolutionary Iran. The reason the politically active engaged in such activity was that, in addition to granting them an isolated and less accessible geographical spot – and therefore a safer place to meet, discuss and interact – a tough sport like mountain climbing was believed to increase resistance capacity if one was detained by police and had to endure physical and psychological torture. Nowadays, in a more depoliticized milieu, most of the young women and men use the mountain areas, for instance in the northern part of Tehran, as a place to hang out and mingle, away from the watchful eyes of the morality police. A close friend of mine, who lives in Iran and used to go up mountains every weekend, wrote me: 'I climb every weekend, with the hope of just sitting up there and letting my hair wander in the free air and enjoy the sun and wind.'

References

Ayt Sabbah, F. (1988) *Women in Muslim Unconsciousness*, Translated by Mary Jo Lakeland. New York: Pergamon Press.

Boudhiba, A. (1998) *Sexuality in Islam*, London: Saqi Books.

'By Her: Myths and Metaphors of Arab Women's Sexuality.' Online. http://www. theglobalsite.ac.uk/press/303her.htm. Accessed March 8, 2005.

Christianson, M. and Eriksson, C. (2004) *Myter om Mödomshinnan: En genusteoretisk betraktelse av mödomshinnans nature och kultur* (The Myth of Hymen: A Gender Analysis of the Nature and Culture of Hymen), in B. Hovelius and E. E. Johansson (eds) *Kroppen och genus i medicine (Body and Gender in Medicine)*, Lund, Sweden: Studenlitteratur.

Coyne Kelly, K. (2000) *Performing Virginity and Testing Chastity in the Middle Age*, Taylor & Francis Bookstore, introduction page 8/13. Online. http://www.dac.neu.edu/ english/kakelly/forth/perfintr.html date 20 October 2004.

El Saadawi, N. (1980) *The Hidden Face of Eve – Women in the Arab World*, London: Zed Books Ltd.

Foucault, M. (1990) *The History of Sexuality: An Introduction (Vol. 1)*, trans. Robert Hurely, London and New York: Routledge.

Gemzöe, L. (2000) *Feminine Matters: Women's Religious Practices in a Portuguese Town*, Södertälje, Sweden: Almqvist & Wiksell International.

—— (2002) *Feminism*, Stockholm: Bilda Förlag, pp. 156–60.

Holtzman, D. and Kulish, N. (1997) *Nevermore: The Hymen and the Loss of Virginity*, Northvale, New Jersey and London: Jason Aronson Inc.

Ikkaracan, Pinar (ed). 2000. *Women and Sexuality in Muslim Societies*. Istanbul: Women for Women's Human Rights (WWHR).

Irigaray, L. (1980) 'When our Lips Speak Together', *Signs*, Autumn, 1980, Vol. 6.1, 74.

Milani, F. (1992, 1994) *Veils and Words: The Emerging Voices of Iranian Women Writers*, New York: Syracuse University Press.

Mernissi, F. (1996) *Women's Rebellion & Islamic Memory*, London and New Jersey: Zed Books.

—— (2000) 'Virginity and Patriarchy' in Ilkkaracan, Pinar (ed.) *Women and Sexuality in Muslim Societies*, Istanbul, Turkey: Women for Women's Human Rights.

Pâknahâd-e Jabaruti, M. (2002) *Farâdasti va Forudasti dar Zabân* (Domination and Subordination in Language), Tehran: Gâm-e Nou.

Parsipur, S. (1998) *Women Without Men*, Translated by Kamran Talat'tof and Jocelyn Sharlet. Syracuse, New York: Syracuse University Press.

—— (2004) Interview with Soheila Vahdati: 7 April 2004 (19 Farvardin 1383). Online. http://zanan.iran-emrooz.de/more.php?id=3933_0_10_0_M.

Partridge, E. (1958) *Origins: A Short Etymological Dictionary of Modern English*, London: Routledge & Kegan Paul.

Plummer, K. (1995) *Telling Sexual Stories: Power, Change and Social Worlds*, London and New York: Routledge.

Rich, A. (1981) *Compulsory Heterosexuality and Lesbian Existence*, London: Onlywomen Press.

Rosenwald, G. (1992) 'Conclusion: Reflections on Narrative Self-Understanding', in G. C. Rosenwald and R. L. Ochberg (eds) *Storied Lives: The Cultural Politics of Self-Understanding*, Yale University.

Safa-Isfahani, K. (1980) 'Female-Centred World View in Iranian Culture: Symbolic Representations of Sexuality in Dramatic Games', *Signs*, Vol. 6, No. 1.

Schwarz, K. (2002) 'The Wrong Question, Thinking Through Virginity', in *Differences: A Journal of Feminist Cultural Studies*, 13.2 (2002), pp. 1–34.

Segal, L. (1994) *Straight Sex*, London: Virago.

Shahidian, H. (1999) 'Gender and Sexuality among Iranian Immigrants in Canada', *Sexualities* 2 (2):189–223.

Sloan, E. (2002) *Biology of Women*, New York: Delmar.

13 Iranian-American elderly in California's Santa Clara Valley: Crafting selves and composing lives

Mary Elaine Hegland, with Anthropology of Aging (Fall 1997 and Winter 2004) and Middle East Anthropology (Winter 1998) Santa Clara University Sudents

Dedicated to the memory of Aghdas Maleksalehi and to Fakhri Aalami, Babi Hogue, Mahin Roudsari, Zia Saeed and Parvin Shahrivar.

One evening in the summer of 1999, as she was joining a monthly gathering of Iranian senior citizens, 'Mrs Tehrani'[1] put out her hand to brace herself against what she thought was a wall. But it was the open door to the bathroom, which then swung away from her into the room. With her weight shifted towards her unsupported and outstretched hand, she was thrown off balance and then onto the floor. People nearby helped Mrs Tehrani get back up again and pulled up a chair for her. She sat resting while other older Iranian women and men arrived. Once in a while she winced during an evening that included a lecture by an Iranian doctor, music and poetry provided by members and an Iranian dinner. Someone brought a full paper plate to Mrs Tehrani.

At the close of the evening, when Mrs Tehrani struggled to her feet, she cried out and sat down again. Calling out to Mr Zia Saeed, a dear, elderly gentleman who makes himself available for service to others, she asked him to ring 911 and get an ambulance to take her to the emergency room. Others gathered around. Mr Saeed was willing to accompany her to the hospital, but she wanted a woman, too, and asked me, an American anthropologist, to come with her. Mrs Mahin Roudsari, the Iranian senior citizens' association president, also planned to come. The ambulance finally arrived. Attendants lifted Mrs Tehrani onto the wheeled stretcher and then into the back of the ambulance. The others drove their cars to the hospital. Mrs Roudsari insisted on staying until the X-rays came back, at about two in the morning, letting us know that nothing had been broken. After Mrs Tehrani obtained her pain pills, she was released. I followed the ambulance back to her apartment, helped her get bedded down, and lay down on the couch.

In the morning, Mrs Tehrani and I phoned her friends. Soon they arrived with cooked food and comfort. In the following days, Mr Saeed was a frequent visitor. Good friends, her children and members of the Iranian senior citizens' association also called and stopped by.

The day after Mrs Tehrani's fall and 911-facilitated ambulance trip to the hospital ER, another member of the Iranian senior citizens' association, 'Mrs Azizi', attended a local Muslim congregation's Friday-evening religious gathering. When she stood up to leave after the services, she too fell. Again, there was a call to 911, and again an ambulance trip to the hospital ER.

Iranian elderly in diaspora

In these cases, we can see something of the lives of the Iranian elderly living in California's Santa Clara Valley. When Mrs Tehrani and Mrs Azizi fell, their families, children, relatives and neighbours – the typical people who stepped in to assist the elderly in earlier times in Iran – were not present. Instead, two constructed communities, one a secular Iranian senior citizens' association and the other a Shi'a Muslim congregation, became stages for elderly Iranian women living in the Santa Clara Valley to call attention to physical problems and express their need for warmth and reassurance.

Because their children had attended university and then stayed on in the US to work as professionals, Mrs Tehrani and Mrs Azizi moved here too, to be close to them. Both mothers live alone, a situation that is not unusual among the many elderly Iranian parents living in the US. Because of the 1970s oil-boom economy's enabling of education abroad, the 1978–9 Iranian Revolution and the subsequent formation of the Islamic Republic, many Iranians are aging in America. Most are relatively comfortable economically, but they face troubling challenges here. They are adjusting to aging and, at the same time, adjusting to a new society and a transformed world in which their expectations of life in older age are usually not fulfilled.

For most elderly Iranians living in America, earlier expectations about what their lives would be like in their later years have not materialized. Some Santa Clara University students and I have looked into how the Iranian-diasporic elderly address this predicament. In the last ten years, I have directed six joint-class research projects interviewing the Iranian elderly, taught two and a half years of two-hour Sunday English classes for Iranian grandparents, and from its inception cooperated with the Iranian Parents' Club (*Kanun-e Pedaran va Madaran*), a South Bay Iranian senior citizens' association. I have also interviewed more than 30 older Iranian persons and spent hundreds of hours in interaction with Iranian elderly, as have the students. Through this intensive anthropological fieldwork, including participant observation, in-depth, open-ended interviewing and discussion with Iranian aging experts, older persons and younger Iranians, along with applied anthropology service in northern California, my students and I have investigated the living conditions, problems, and social and cultural disruptions faced by elderly Iranians in this area.[2] We have looked into their coping methods and some of the ways they try to deal with their Iranian-American lives. We have also noted how some successful Iranian agers have actually gone through a process of thinking about their changed circumstances and how best to use their personal Iranian resources, as well as new American opportunities, to craft modified selves, construct different modes of relational interaction and compose evolving lives. Some Iranian elders have been redefining aging and being elderly.

Challenges

Dislocation to the modernized 'Silicon Valley', located south of San Francisco and a centre of the computer world, has presented the Iranian-American elderly with difficult challenges. The Iranian students who came to the US for university or graduate education in the 1970s – a huge influx, of which many remained here, or returned – have now grown into middle age. Reportedly, some 200,000 people of Iranian background live in southern California, and perhaps 50,000 in the San Francisco Bay area, including the Santa Clara, or 'Silicon', Valley. Some of the problems of the Iranian-American elderly are related to living in a society different from their own. The elderly, their caretakers, and experts dealing with the elderly talk of isolation, depression, anxiety and loneliness. Usually the elderly cannot speak English. Most often they cannot drive in the US. They usually do not live close to other Iranians. They cannot talk with American neighbours. Not understanding English, they may be worried about using buses or walking for fear of becoming lost or running into situations they cannot handle. Their children are usually busy with demanding jobs and schedules, and must tend to their own children, helping them with school, extracurricular activities and social events with other young people. In addition, these middle-aged children have developed their own pursuits, interests and circle of friends, and need time to devote to them.[3] Very often, then, Iranian-American elderly are rather isolated. Whether they live in homes separate from their children, or with their children, they may be alone much of the time, unable to talk with neighbours and unable to travel by themselves to see family, relatives or other Iranians.

Some older Iranians care for their grandchildren while the parents are at jobs. Although enjoying the companionship of grandchildren and happy to help their children, these elderly may be overworked. Because of their child and house-care responsibilities, they may find it even more difficult than others to get away to visit with other Iranians or attend Iranian gatherings.

The elderly frequently face financial, transportation, medical and social-network problems. Along with loss of culture, gatherings, special days, holidays, and language, elderly men usually have been deprived of power, control, status, resources, property, career, finances and patriarchal, head-of-family position.

Iranian elderly are usually not accustomed to being alone, and miss the intense social life typical in Iran. Compared to their lives in Iran, in the US they feel the lack of kinship networks, strong and numerous family bonds and friendly neighbourhoods. They feel the loss of enmeshed social interaction and social life with spontaneous, continuous verbal communication. They grieve for a sense of community and belonging, a sense of comfort with whom and what they are, and a sense of being fully engaged with their lives and social networks. In their estimation, they do not get enough attention, especially from their busy children who, along with their grandchildren, belong to a different and alien world.

Strong family ties and respect for the elderly: Cultural pride and identity for Iranian-Americans

Recent social-cultural transformation in Iran, too, is resulting in changing conditions for aging and the elderly and evolving relations between older people and their younger relatives.[4] Iranians are becoming conscious of the elderly as a social issue, as are government officials, politicians and charity organizations; in 1999, the United Nations sponsored an international conference on aging in Tehran.[5]

In California, Iranians have formed several senior citizens' associations and instituted several elderly day-activity and care centres. The children and grandchildren of the elderly likewise think about their problems, their inability to adjust to current realities, and potential steps for caring for their aging parents. From individuals, the elderly have turned into a foregrounded, problematized category. In the face of the lack of those conditions that made family care and enmeshment for the elderly possible, both the elderly and their children have been called to focus on definitions and expectations regarding the elderly.

Even more than in Iran, in their new Californian cultural environment, the Iranian-American elderly have been faced with the loss of earlier structures and interaction modes. They have been challenged to rethink definitions of 'aging' and 'elderly' and to formulate modified selves and lives. Even under the best of circumstances, adjusting to new realities and recreating oneself can be excruciatingly difficult. Emigration to North America and the surrounding political and cultural identity issues make the loss of older-generation family authority and modes of deference all the more poignant.

In northern California, whether the elderly live locally or are visiting their children from Iran, they are often alone during the day. Unaccustomed to solitude, they want company. Away from friends, neighbours and relatives and isolated because of distance and, usually, the inability to drive, they yearn for friendships, intimate and frequent social interaction, and most of all for close ties with their children. Some older Iranian parents, people have told me, spend their time waiting to be with their children.

Iranians in the US frequently contrast level of respect and deference for the elderly in Iran with how Iranians living in the US behave towards their older relatives. Supposedly, young and middle-aged Iranian-Americans here have been detrimentally influenced by American culture, and thus are more callous towards the older generation. Most Iranians tend to idealize treatment of and respect for the Iranian elderly, particularly in the past before modernization and Western influence. They frequently use the Iranian family and its positive nature and close bonds as the identity markers between Iranians and non-Iranians. Respect for the elderly, the central position of grandparents in the family circle, and the devotion and obedience of the younger generation to their parents and grandparents become a main dividing line between Iranian culture and Iranians, seen as morally superior, and the decadent, morally corrupt Western culture, and Westerners. Older visitors from Iran and those living in the US commonly bring up family practices and attitudes when condemning Western culture and commenting favourably on Iranian culture. They talk about American premarital sex, 'nakedness' and free sexuality. They talk about American teenagers leaving home, or kicked out to be on their own when they turn 18, divorce and weak family bonds, and Americans' treatment of their elderly parents.

Given the familial contrast which most Iranians see between Iranian and American societies, familial behaviour and attitudes become the main means of affiliation with Iranian identity and culture, as opposed to American. Pure Iranian culture and real Iranians uphold family closeness, values of female purity, and respect for older family members, older Iranians feel. To the degree that girls maintain modesty and virginity and the younger generations defer to the older, family bonds remain strong, and older Iranians living in America see themselves and their families as maintaining Iranian identity and culture and living a good life.

Contact with Westerners and loose Western culture are eroding the pure Iranian culture in the view of such Iranians. *Qarbzadegi*, Al-e Ahmad's term meaning corrupted or struck by the West, is destroying Iranian culture. While many northern-Californian Iranians perceive that less Westernized peoples treat the elderly with more respect, they contradict themselves by viewing their own families – urban, upper- or upper-middle class – as being cultured, and therefore knowing how to treat the older generations. They apparently wish to see and present their own families as good at maintaining Iranian culture and, as a corollary, showing extreme deference and respect for the older generations. The wish to present one's own family in a favourable light may discourage frank communication. A grandmother may even go on and on with horror stories about how other Iranian children treat their parents, and what horrible conditions grandparents may live in, using these anecdotes as backdrops to showcase how marvellously her own relatives and children treat the senior generation.

A grandparent's own status is heavily dependent upon how well she or he is doted on by children. Older people talk to others about all their children do for them and how deeply they care for them, how the children do not rest from efforts to make their parents' lives even more pleasant. The reputations of nation and culture, family and self, then, are seen as closely associated with other people's perceptions of how well the younger generation is fulfilling cultural expectations of loving duty to parents.

The Iranian elderly living in the US have undergone great cultural and social change. They have lived through the upheavals and traumas of revolution and war. Most have suffered financial and social decline and the deaths of dear ones. They have left behind their country, culture, language, neighbourhood, relatives, friends, and way of life. Moreover, present Iranian society is something strange and unacceptable to most older people who live in the US. They do not know if the Iran they knew and loved will ever come back again. In the face of all of this dislocation and trauma, the final blow of inadequate attention and devotion from their children brings pain.

The political relations between Iran and the US, and the attitudes of Americans towards Iran, Iranian culture and Iranians further complicate Iranian views about demonstrated respect for older persons. Most Iranians living in the US do not support the Islamic Republic government and conservative clerics' interpretations of Islam and control over society. They are distraught about political, social and economic conditions in Iran and the way of life forced on people by ruling clerics. Distressing incidents, such as newspaper closings, arrests, demonstrations and violence occur frequently. There is not much about present-day Iranian society that they feel proud of. Given its application by ruling clerics, their religion is not primarily displayed as an identity marker. In any case, even while they were still living in Iran, most Iranian grandparents now living in the US, generally relatively secularized and educated professionals, did not go to a mosque regularly. Their religious practices were limited to irregular gatherings, funerals and death anniversaries, or holy-day rituals. However, even people who are unhappy with the current, politically dominant interpretation of Shi'a Islam and opposed to the government (the great majority in the US) can be proud of Iranian family values.

Because of political relations between the two countries and learned negative attitudes towards Iranian society and Iranians in the US, older Iranians feel all the more marginalized in American society. They exchange stories of discrimination and harassment experienced when trying to obtain visas and entering the country. American television and films portray Iranians as irrational terrorists and rigid, religious fundamentalists. Older Iranians feel devalued and defensive when faced with ordinary Americans and government officials. During times of angry international political exchanges, the release of movies featuring negative portrayals of Iranians, and violent incidents blamed on Iranians, they feel particularly anxious. They try, all the more intently, to reconnect with their Iranian cultural roots.

Two foremost conversational topics of older Iranians are the disgusting actions of the Iranian government and the disgusting American culture, specifically its family values and practices – the dissolution of family bonds. Assertive pronouncements about Iranian dedication to parents, in contrast with American callousness, are often almost knee-jerk reactions to introductions of the topic of the elderly.

The Iranian veneration of the elderly appeals even to those who have turned their backs on the other main Iranian cultural marker: control over women and their sexuality. Less conservative Iranian-American women and even more radical feminists who believe in women's social and sexual self-determination can also be proud of the Iranian esteem for parents.

In the face of grief, anxiety, shame and alienation over Iranian politics, society and religion, cultural practices can be seen as free of religious and political stigma. Values of strong family bonds and devotion to parents can be common ground for Iranians who otherwise differ. From conservative supporters of the Islamic Republic to more liberal Islamists, royalists, leftists, feminists and relatively assimilated Iranian-Americans, all feel comfortable promoting the ideals of attachment to older parents. Even middle-aged Iranian-Americans who were educated in this country and did not live according to their parents' views of correct behaviour compare treatment of the Iranian elderly favourably with American practices. Many even attempt to extract from their own American-raised adult children the same obedience and respect for parental values and wishes that they did not give to their own parents.

As devotion to the elderly demonstrates self-worth and symbolizes the good person, grandparents and their children feel pain when the relationship of older person and adult child cannot live up to the idea.

Coping tactics against diminished deference and family enmeshment

In different ways, my students and I found through our case studies, Iranian senior citizens have attempted to cope with their American lives and loss of status, control, attention and more central position in the family so crucial to their definitions of a satisfactory and fulfilling old age. Many of them used one or a combination of the following: cocooning; manipulation and pressuring; separation from other Iranians; attempts to live up to enculturated expectations of service and self-sacrifice; venturing out; applying Iranian culture to lives in America; combining, picking and choosing; rethinking, reforming, recreating.

Cocooning

In the extreme, some elderly became so fearful and helpless that they stayed inside their houses and counted on their children to mediate between themselves and the outside American, English-speaking world. They isolated themselves from their surroundings. They made cocoons for themselves inside their residences – a protected Iranian environment with trusted family, relatives and friends – and avoided venturing out. They retreated from American society or stayed clear of unwelcome or divergent perspectives. They continued to try to live in an Iranian environment, listening to Iranian radio, watching Iranian television, reading Iranian newspapers, talking with Iranian friends and relatives by phone, having children shop for them or going out to stores only in the company of their children, and staying inside their houses unless their children took them on outings or to visit other Iranians. They clung to or catered to their children. In spite of some, or even good, knowledge of English, at least three elders among our interviewees depended almost entirely on their children or husbands to deal with outsiders.

Manipulation and pressuring

Some Iranian parents tried to maintain power and influence through manipulation. They tried to go on as much as possible as if they were still living in the idealized Iranian past, with its hierarchy, social organization and expectations of social relations. Iranian mothers felt the duty of finding wives for their sons weighing heavily upon them. They found prospective brides and urged their sons, who were generally reluctant, to meet their choices. Some parents attempted to use strategies from the cultural repertoire they had learned in Iran to fight against declining control and extract the desired attention and deference. Such strategies included complaining, anger and shouting, accusations and guilt trips, feigned illnesses, underhanded attempts to oversee and manage children's lives, unnecessary doctors' visits, use of 911 and ambulances and hospital stays, and general dramatizing and going public about less-than-adequate assistance and companionship from children. Some parents did not make any effort to adjust to their children's and grandchildren's American lives. Some even took the step of becoming *qar*, or cutting off relations with children, if their progeny failed to follow their wishes or live according to their standards.

Separation from other Iranians

Some older Iranians isolated themselves from other Iranians and, to some degree or another, abandoned Iranian culture. Often, those who chose this strategy to cope with the differences between their Iranian pasts and their American lives had come to the US long ago, or had American spouses. They lived in American society and avoided Iranians. They did not want to interact with Iranians, did not trust them, and did not, they said, like the gossip or styles of interaction of other Iranians.

Attempts to live up to enculturated expectations of service and self-sacrifice

Some of the Iranian-American elderly, and particularly women, did maintain close ties with their families through their usefulness to their children as housekeepers and babysitters. Some worked very hard, almost like a hired nanny, enabling daughters and daughters-in-law to work outside the home. They attempted to gain self- and others' approval by continuing to carry out enculturated behaviour as females and mothers. They had little time or opportunity to enjoy themselves or engage in the intimate conversations typically so much a part of Iranian women's lives. These women believed their highest duty lay in caring for their children and grandchildren. When I urged one older woman to take a couple of hours' break on Sundays and come to our enjoyable English classes, where she could meet other older Iranians, she responded that she was too busy taking care of her grandson and doing housework. 'And anyway', she added, 'helping my son by taking care of the child has more *savab* [religious credit] than studying English.'

Venturing out

Other elderly Iranians were able to start shopping for themselves, going out for walks and, sometimes, finding new Iranian friends to talk with by telephone or visit. They found ways of going places by bus, taxi or government-supported transportation without the assistance of their children. They got rides to Iranian gatherings or performances and there enjoyed the company of new acquaintances or friends, or went to Iranian movies, concerts, religious organizations and gatherings, clubs, such as poetry, cultural or elderly groups, and Iranian life-cycle gatherings. Some became determined to be relatively self-sufficient in the American environment. They learned English and passed driving tests to get a licence. They took classes offered by associations, high schools or community colleges. They learned logistics and work skills. Some took advantage of opportunities in the American setting to learn line dancing, ballroom dancing, flower arranging or computer skills. Some of the elderly worked or made new friends, even among Americans. One lively woman, after the death of her husband, dated and married an American man. These older people did not depend entirely on children and relatives to fill their lives, but added to family attachments from the new opportunities available in the American setting.

Applying Iranian culture to lives in America

Another commonly used and effective strategy to build satisfying lives on foreign soil entailed the use or modification of elders' learned repertoire from Iranian culture, experiences, social gifts, social relations and lives in Iran. Successful agers practised painting, studying and writing poetry, philanthropy, reaching out to and assisting others, socializing, developing family and kin relations, teaching others their skills in music or dance or sharing religious expertise. Many continued the Iranian practice of *doreh*, or regular gatherings with the same circle of friends. One woman took up drumming, an earlier love she had discontinued upon marriage. She took classes and performed with other musicians for Iranian groups and gatherings. Still another made a career of teaching the Koran, reading, leading and reciting at women's home-based religious rituals and serving at one of the local Shi'a congregations. One man, a police general during the time of Mohammad Reza Shah, found solace and fulfilment by continuing to write poetry, which he recited at Iranian groups and gatherings. Another elderly Iranian woman who did not know any English made a full life for herself by gathering ingredients and then cooking Iranian sweets and preserves, distributing them amongst her friends and relatives. One woman practised her positive outlook, liveliness and delightful, loving interaction in her life in the US, even trying to continue doing so as her memory and strength declined. Mahin Roudsari employed her compassion, along with her skills in teaching, leadership, networking, social relations, administration and cooking, to establish the Iranian Parents Club until it grew to host hundreds at its monthly meetings. Zia Saeed, even after the death of his beloved wife, continued to find meaning through a life of loving service to others. He taught English, took a leading role in one of the local Shi'a congregations, counselled couples about to marry, visited the sick and made himself available to help others in any way possible, such as giving them rides to the doctor. He came to Santa Clara University to speak to Anthropology of Aging students, delighting them with his spirit and kindness, and made himself available to students for interviewing. He warmly greeted people coming to the Iranian Parents Club and added his advice and ideas to its planning board meetings. He rose early to pray and exercise, enjoyed visits and trips with friends, and recited his poetry at gatherings.

Combining, picking and choosing

The Iranian-Americans who were aging most successfully combined aspects from the resources of their Iranian culture and pasts with opportunities in their American environment to compose rich and fulfilling lives for themselves. Such elderly people, often enabled by more exposure to education, alternatives and modernization in Iran, used resources from both cultures, like two palettes of colour, choosing what they wanted from each. These grandparents maintained or even increased their attachment to Iranian music, poetry, religion, holidays, food, family and community. Some volunteered their services to teach skills useful to other Iranians in maintaining cultural knowledge and connections. They also augmented and enriched their lives with American opportunities and interacted with other Americans as well as with Iranian-Americans.

Mrs Babi Hogue presents an outstanding example of this strategic approach. After the death of her husband, with the encouragement of her son she began studying ballroom dancing. Through this activity, she met and married an American man who had lost his wife. Warm and sparkling, Mrs Hogue composed a full and happy life for herself with husband, children, membership and leadership in several Iranian organizations, growing roses and bringing luscious bouquets to meetings and gatherings, and hosting parties. She and her husband gave ballroom-dance performances and began teaching dance to both Iranians and other Americans, even printing up business cards with a photo of themselves in a dramatic dip.

Some elderly Iranians used a number of such coping resources and strategies. Prompted by their new surrounding conditions, they rethought and then reformed themselves, their relationships, their lives and the meaning of 'aging' and 'elderly', as the following section documents.[6]

Crafting selves, composing lives, and redefining 'Aging' and 'Elderly'[7]

Rather than attempting to maintain control and impose their own values, family hierarchy and modes of interaction, some creative Iranian-American grandparents were able to become flexible and modify their lifestyles, activities and modes of interaction. They crafted and created new selves, relational modes and ways of being. They did not depend only on children, relatives and Iranian interaction to fill their lives. Instead of futilely attempting to force children and grandchildren into expected behaviour, causing misery for all involved, they drew upon various sources to craft modified selves and evolved relationships. They composed modified lives and reconstructed the meaning and content of aging, elderly, grandparents, their lives, and themselves as older Iranians.

Several Iranian grandmothers presented papers about recreating themselves in the American environment at the workshop on 'Elders and Immigrants in the Bay Area: Iranian Mothers Create Meaningful Lives and Share Wisdom' at Santa Clara University's 'Women's Day 1998 Program Celebrating Women's Wisdom'.

Babi Hogue's paper (1998), 'How to Fall in Love with Life and Self', which she presented at the workshop, conveyed how she had consciously changed her life and her self. In her view, as she said, 'People can change. At any time someone can make a happy life for themselves. If we are happy, we are positive, and we have more self-esteem, we see everything more beautifully.'[8]

Mahin Roudsari studied English and took courses at the community college. She maintains a large circle of friends and has played an important role in taking care of her granddaughters. Some ten years ago, particularly sensitive to the issue because of her own very elderly mother, she began to note the predicament of the Iranian elderly here. She saw a need created by the older Iranians' diasporic condition and turned it into an opportunity to build a meaningful life for herself through helping others. She formed the Iranian Parents Club (*Kanun-e Pedaran va Madaran*), the first Iranian senior citizens' association in northern California. In the process, she became a comfortable leader and public speaker – even in English – and the president of an association that now hosts several hundred members at its monthly gatherings. In her paper 'Bringing Trees to Blossom: How I Established the Iranian Parents Club', which she presented at the 1998 Santa Clara University women's conference, she described the formation of this Iranian senior citizens' club.[9]

Aghdas Maleksalehi's (1998) paper at the conference, 'How I Found a Way to Make a Close Relationship with My Grandchildren', described how she thoughtfully considered her situation as an Iranian grandmother separated from her grandchildren by a cultural and linguistic divide, and then constructed an alternative mode of grandmothering in the American setting. Even her willingness to present a paper in a university setting shows her ability to try new things and learn different persona. She found the courage to speak – in English – to American students, professors and community women at a conference workshop.

> Good afternoon, ladies. I am happy for the opportunity to talk with American grandmothers. I am a grandmother. I used to have a hard time being close to my grandchildren. There were several problems which prevented us from having a close relationship. One problem was language. My language is Farsi or Persian, and their language is English. It is hard to be close to grandchildren when you don't speak the same language. Another problem was culture. I come from Iran, and they were born in the United States. Because my culture is different from their culture, it was hard to talk with them. I realized that the level of love and devotion which I wanted did not exist in our relationship. The children had become distant from me. When I came to their house, their parents would tell them, 'Say hello to Grandmother'. They would say 'Hello, Grandmother' and then 'Goodbye, Grandmother'. Sometimes they wouldn't even say hello to me. We were like strangers. I was sad.
>
> I want to tell you how I found a way to make a close relationship with my grandchildren. I have found out how to participate in their lives. I started to share their activities – reading, playing, going to the park – so that I could become closer to them. I play *takt-e nar* – backgammon – with them. I paint with them. I play basketball with them. We put puzzles together. I play ping-pong with them. My grandson, who is ten years old, is the California state

ping-pong champion for his age group. I and the whole family encouraged him and practised with him, starting out in the garage. I take part in their school programs; I go along with them. When they play in the children's orchestra or have a dance performance, I go and listen and watch. They are glad that I come. If there is a sports game, I go with them. When they play soccer, I go with them and encourage them and cheer for them. And also, my English language has improved so I can talk with them. The children love having me at their school programs. They are delighted that I take such an interest in them and in their activities. Because I share in their lives like this, they have become close to me. They have become very good friends with me.

... Now, when they see me, they say, 'Grandmother!' They are happy to see me, they respect me, they kiss me, they greet me. It is good for me and good for them. They feel my love for them... That sadness which I had felt before has left... I found a way to join in their lives, in everything that they do. I am very happy to see that, little by little, the close relationship between grandmother and grandchildren, which is so important in Persian culture, is returning.

Mrs Maleksalehi saw that she could not just wait for her Americanized grandchildren to come to her and extend to her the automatic respect and attention owed to grandparents in Iranian culture. Propelled by her strong Iranian desire for a close relationship with her grandchildren, she pondered the problem. She changed her grandmothering style. She moved out towards her grandchildren and their interests, learning new activities and venturing into new environments in order to recreate grandchildren–grandmother relationships and become close to them in new ways.

Concluding remarks

With the Iranian diaspora, many older Iranians have emigrated from their country, often to be closer to their children and to leave political conditions in the Islamic Republic of Iran. Most often, they do not freely choose to leave their country and culture, but have been pressured by circumstances. In northern California, many Iranian grandparents face disturbing new realities. In general, elderly Iranians who expected to be at the centre of their children's and grandchildren's lives, and treated with the great respect and deference which their status as elderly and grandparents should confer on them, are disappointed. They are faced with the fact that this does not happen, and they are left to wonder what they should do about it.

Some Iranians want to continue their pre-migrant lives in Iran in the American setting. If they enjoy the resources and support necessary to do so, they may be relatively satisfied with their lives here. Most, however, do not enjoy such a situation. When those older Iranians who maintain more traditional expectations about their lives, expect total devotion from children and are completely reliant on them for all of needs, do not see their wishes fulfilled, they may become very unhappy. If they have high expectations for obedience, respect, deference and lack of disagreement, and their children and grandchildren are not complying, they may feel they are left with nothing. Unhappy about unfulfilled expectations, and unwilling or unable to try to develop or seek substitutes, new occupations, new relationships, new sources of gratification, or new ways and resources to fulfil needs and wants, they may become sunk in depression, bitterness and despair. They may not be able to understand or tolerate their children and grandchildren's lack of attention, obedience, respect and assistance. They may be distraught at children and grandchildren's failure to fulfil Iranian values and expectations for lifestyles and behaviour. Their dissatisfaction and blame might even ruin their relations with children and grandchildren, and lead to cutting themselves off and diminishing their gratification and need fulfilment all the more.

Many older Iranian-American people, however, are able to adjust to a degree over time, perhaps assisted by the three associations established for them in the Santa Clara Valley. Those who are best off are able to take advantage of the positive attributes of both cultures and modes of social interaction. They are attached to various aspects of Iranian culture and interaction, involved with family, relatives, children and, perhaps, religion, and engaged with Iranian holidays, poetry and food. They also find out about and experience new situations, opportunities and circles. They take advantage of the American social environment and interact with both Iranians and other Americans. They learn new things. They have good relations with children, kin and other Iranians, but are not restricted to them only. They are self-sufficient to some extent in that they also have activities outside the family circle and the Iranian community.

These older people are pleased to own their own homes or rent pleasant apartments, have resources, maintain status to a large degree, have some Iranian neighbours and have an Iranian network accessible. Those elderly who had more preparation to live in a transformed world are often more at ease. Those who worked outside home, were exposed to the outside world and other people, and were already more self-sufficient, were better able to make a life for themselves in this foreign country. People who were already prepared or able to rethink interaction with Americanized children and grandchildren can be loving, interactive and supportive. They are not authoritarian, and do not pressure their offspring to comply with their own values and expectations. These grandparents can have the best of two worlds – individual actualization, self-fulfilment and enjoyment, as well as Iranian-style close ties to family and kin, strong and active social networks, a cultural repertoire from Iran, and values regarding home, cooking, people and friendship. They can have some level of self-sufficiency, but also enjoy connectedness. They are open to some aspects and opportunities in American society, but also comfortable with, appreciative of, and practise some aspects of Iranian culture and social interaction. A number of the older Iranians whom my students and I interviewed brought such competency with them to the US and incorporated new opportunities available here. Some, taking advantage of a new situation to grow, were able to reinvent themselves, their lives, and the meaning of 'aging' and 'elderly'.

Notes

1 Tehrani and Azizi are pseudonyms. Anthropologists normally use pseudonyms for the locality in which they conduct fieldwork and for the individuals whose lives they discuss. I have, however, used the actual names of other individuals. In several cases, the individuals gave papers at a Santa Clara University conference and, with their permission, I cite and quote these papers with the authors' actual names. A number of these individuals are public figures; all of them gave me permission to write about them and to use their actual names. Mrs Aghdas Maleksalehi's daughter granted me permission to use her late mother's name and to publish her conference paper. I appreciate the opportunity to honour these Iranian-Americans by publicly acknowledging their accomplishments and their creative and philanthropic activities.
2 See Hegland 1999b.
3 Goli Taraqqi's (1996) short story, 'A House in the Heavens', portrays a devoted mother who no longer had a place in her children's lives abroad.
4 Iranian elderly living in Iran may also experience such conditions. Iranian elderly are even beginning to be cared for in homes for the elderly in Iran (see Sheykhi 2004). However, the tendency for Iranian elderly to live in loneliness and isolation is all the more extreme in the US setting.
5 'International Conference on Aging', 19–21 October 1999, Tehran, Iran.
6 See Hegland 1999a.
7 During a workshop at the UC Santa Barbara Middle East 2000 conference of 24–25 March 2000, anthropologist Nadine Naber used the word 'crafting' to refer to Arab immigrants in America developing and modifying themselves. Anthropologist Mary Catherine Bateson chose the title *Composing a Life* (2001) for her book about her mother, anthropologist Margaret Mead, and her life.
8 See Hogue 1998.
9 See Roudsari 1998. Other Iranian-American grandmothers presented papers with the following titles: 'Teaching the Sweet Words of the Koran' (Chitsaz 1998) and 'Building an Independent Life in the Shade of My Children' (Jehanian 1998).

References

Bateson, C. (2001) *Composing a Life*, New York: Grove Press.
Chitsaz, M. (1998) 'Teaching the Sweet Words of the Koran', paper presented at the workshop on 'Elders and Immigrants in the Bay Area: Iranian Mothers Create Meaningful Lives and Share Wisdom' at the Santa Clara University Women's Day 1998 Program Celebrating Women's Wisdom.
Friedl, E. (1991) *Women of Deh Koh: Lives in an Iranian Village*, New York: Penguin Books.
Hegland, M. E. (1998) 'Payvand and IFWC: Maintaining Iranian Identity in California's Bay Area', with Ashraf Zahedi. *DANESH Bulletin*, Vol. 3, No. 1, 12–17.
—— (1999a) 'Iranian Women Immigrants Facing Modernity in California's Bay Area: The Courage, Creativity, and Trepidation of Transformation', in Golnaz Amin (ed.) *The Iranian Woman and Modernity, Proceedings of the Ninth International Conference of Iranian Women's Studies Foundation*, Cambridge, MA: The Iranian Women's Studies Foundation, pp. 35–62.
—— (1999b) 'Learning Feminist Pedagogy with Students and Iranian-American Grandparents', *Association for Middle East Women's Studies Bulletin*, Vol. 14, No. 3, September 1999, 1–2.
—— (2004a) 'Iranian Village Grandmothers and the Independent Life', paper presented at the May/June 2004 International Society for Iranian Studies Conference in Bethesda, MD.

—— (2004b) 'Zip In and Zip Out Fieldwork', *Journal of Iranian Studies*, Vol. 37, No. 4, 275–583, December.

Hogue, B. (1998) 'How to Fall in Love with Life and Self', paper presented at the workshop on 'Elders and Immigrants in the Bay Area: Iranian Mothers Create Meaningful Lives and Share Wisdom' at the Santa Clara University Women's Day 1998 Program Celebrating Women's Wisdom.

Jehanian, K. B. (1998) 'Building an Independent Life in the Shade of My Children', paper presented at the workshop on 'Elders and Immigrants in the Bay Area: Iranian Mothers Create Meaningful Lives and Share Wisdom' at the Santa Clara University Women's Day 1998 Program Celebrating Women's Wisdom.

Maleksalehi, A. (1998) 'How I Found a Way to Make a Close Relationship with My Grandchildren', paper presented at the workshop on 'Elders and Immigrants in the Bay Area: Iranian Mothers Create Meaningful Lives and Share Wisdom' at the Santa Clara University Women's Day 1998 Program Celebrating Women's Wisdom.

Roudsari, M. (1998) 'Bringing Trees to Blossom: How I Established the Iranian Parents Club', paper presented at the workshop on 'Elders and Immigrants in the Bay Area: Iranian Mothers Create Meaningful Lives and Share Wisdom' at the Santa Clara University Women's Day 1998 Program Celebrating Women's Wisdom.

Sheykhi, M. T. (2004) 'A Study of the Elderly People Living in Nursing Homes in Iran with a Specific Focus on Tehran', *African & Asian Studies* 3(2): 106–19.

Taraqqi, G. (1996) 'A House in the Heavens', in Franklin Lewis and Farzin Yazdanfar (eds and trans.) *In a Voice of Their Own: A Collection of Stories by Iranian Women Written Since the Revolution of 1979*, Costa Mesa, California: Mazda Press, pp. 3–20.

14 Like Parvin, like Najiba, like Heba, we are all different: Reflections on voices of women in diaspora[1]

Afsaneh Hojabri

Framework

The late 1980s to early 1990s was an era when feminist literature, especially in the field of anthropology, was ripe with attempts to capture women's voices through life history and narrative approaches used as tools to problematize the unity of 'us' and the otherness of 'others' and to reveal differences not only between, but also within, cultures. The works of Marcus and Fischer (1986), Thomas (1991), Behar (1993) and Abu-Lughod (1991) are but a few examples of this trend. The challenge was picked up, particularly by female scholars of Middle-Eastern origin, in order to counter inferiorizing images of Islam and Muslim women.

Already in the early part of the twenty-first century, and faced with the intensified misperceptions about and hostilities towards Muslims in the wake of the events of 11 September 2001, it remains a relevant and timely task to deconstruct stereotypical notions that depict Muslims as homogeneous and alien, thereby targeting women and men of diasporic communities in the West (Moghissi 2002). Indeed, as reported by the Canadian Council for Refugees (2004), the degree to which people of Muslim and Arab origin are feeling the destructive impacts in their daily lives of openly discriminatory policies and distorted media images is unprecedented in Canada. Meanwhile, Islamophobia persists in being the principle Western medium for constructing of the 'other' (Henzell-Thomas 2001).

In this chapter, through the life histories of ten women from Pakistan, Iran, Afghanistan and Palestine, I set out to demonstrate the diversity of women's lives while drawing on the momentous shared ideals and struggles that arguably mark these women as a group bound by the experience of diaspora.

My goal in using women's life histories is not to focus on particularities of women's lives in isolation from the larger context within which they operate. Neither do I embrace the postmodern approach of rejecting all forms of universalism, thereby celebrating the significance of individual acts and local meanings. Rather, my objective in using life histories as a tool is simply to demonstrate the differences that exist within a group of individuals who happen to be of an 'Islamic culture' (coming from Muslim countries and/or families). In doing so, I seek to challenge the image and discourse that ascribes to Muslims a monolithically negative mindset and portrays Muslims in diaspora as alien, strange, and even dangerous and threatening. I will argue that these women are differentiated by a set of factors despite the homogenizing forces – namely the imposition of religious and ethnic identity by the dominant society. I will further argue that they are bound by a set of shared experiences and similar features that make them alike in so far as their dilemmas and struggles are not shared by the larger society.

In using women's life histories, I do not intend to give them voice, but rather to benefit from their own words, which most effectively and profoundly depict the complexity of their lives and bring to light their challenges, struggles, restraints and accomplishments. Furthermore, my focus on *women's* life histories is not by any means intended to underestimate the diversity and significance of men's migratory histories and the difficulties that they, too, face in their search for a better life. However, as an Iranian woman in diaspora, I share these women's concerns and stories in many ways.

In this chapter we will meet ten women in varying degrees of focus: two from Iran; two from Palestinian territories; three from Afghanistan; and three from Pakistan. They come from Muslim countries and/or families, with different socio-economic backgrounds, and they have been in Canada for at least four years. Their ages range between 22 and 53, and they include married, divorced, separated and single women. The structure of this chapter necessitated presenting the life histories in fragments; in so doing, I have nevertheless tried to remain loyal to the context. I have used pseudonyms and changed some demographic data to maintain the participants' anonymity.[2]

Diversity in religious beliefs

At the core of the racist imagery attached to Islam and Muslims is the assumption that the sole identifier of people coming from Muslim countries is their attachment to Islam. Such imagery is guilty of several fallacies at the same time: it ignores the immense size and diversity of the Islamic world; it perceives Islam as a monolithic, evil uniform; and it reduces the life experience of people living in or coming from Islamic countries to matters of religion and religion alone (Moghissi 2002; Henzell-Thomas 2001). The women in this study had different perceptions about, and attachments to, Islam, in particular, and religion in general.

To begin with, being a Muslim constitutes different realities and meanings. These differences were articulated by some women and hinted at by others. In responding to the question as to what their religion was, almost all women were quick to specify that they were Muslims of particular sects and backgrounds. Descriptive phrases such as 'I am a Shi'a Muslim with the Pashtoun background', or 'I am Muslim in the sense that I pray and fast during Ramadan, the way things are done in Pakistan', indicated specific characteristics that distinguished their backgrounds as Muslims.

Others specified their different understandings of Islam in ideological and intellectual senses. A young, single woman of Pakistani origin defined her being a Muslim in the following terms:

I am more spiritual than religious. I do practise [Islam], but on my own.
I don't go to the mosque or religious community gatherings. I don't like the
conservatism there ... I am much more liberal in my thinking. I've spent a lot
of time reading about Islam, and progressive, feminist interpretations of the
Koran. They've really shaped my intellectual identity as a Muslim feminist,
and as a progressive Muslim more generally. My faith is related to my intellectual understanding of Islam in a lot of ways.

Furthermore, the two concepts of religiosity and belief in Islam did not always
come as inseparable bundles. While Islam, *per se*, seemed to be very important to
some women, for others a reference to religious beliefs and practices did not necessarily entail any direct link to Islamic ideology and values. In the latter case, the
'religion' not so much as 'Islam' had a psychological or emotional function, serving women with the means to cope during times of stress and hardship.

Afra, an Afghan woman and a courageous, single mother of four who had
endured violence in the family since her early youth and who was now striving to
make ends meet in Canada, said:

Through religion we learn what is good and bad, and the prayers help us in
our struggle through the adversity. I could not have succeeded in my life if I
had no faith in my religion.

Farah, another woman of Pakistani origin whose life history was centred on the
disappointment and distress she felt due to the rupturing of her family over the
course of time in Canada, said:

They say prayer is supposed to make your heart soft, so I guess holding on
to the rope [of God] helped me cope with my difficulties, which by the way,
did not begin or end with my daughter's disappearing on us.

Religious identity imposed

It is crucial to note that for all these women, whether they considered themselves
Muslims, practising Muslims or not Muslims at all, Islamic identity came into
play particularly, and sometimes solely, in connection and interaction with the
larger society. In other words, the Muslim identity imposed by Canadian society
reinforced, and even shaped, women's belief – or disbelief – in Islam.

For example, Sanaz, an Iranian woman who defined herself primarily in terms
of her social activism and her career as an artist, was almost annoyed at my
including her in a study interested in 'Islamic Diaspora':

[One of the factors] motivating me to become an activist is that the majority
of people living here in the West insist on telling *me*, who happened to have
come from the Middle East, that I am a Muslim. I am not a Muslim!.... I have
come from a Muslim country but I am not a Muslim. I am an atheist, and

I feel strongly about it. People in the West think that out there everybody is Muslim. Well, they are not!

For other women who did have faith and belief in Islam, Canadian society still impacted and shaped their religious identity – in positive or negative ways. For example, while some Afghan women found it more difficult to practise their faith in Canada for lack of time, or because of pressure from society, others from the same region appreciated their liberty to practise Islam in their new surroundings.

Umbreen, a Pakistani woman who comes from a family she describes as 'not strictly religious', was not sure about the degree of her religiosity and belief in Islam: 'In terms of practise, I think many people would say that I don't practise the religion, but in my heart, I think I do. I don't cover anything [wear hijab], but I do pray. I'm religious in that way.' Umbreen's religious/national identity was more clearly defined within the Canadian context:

Here, Pakistan seems exotic to people. They don't know a lot. I'm always struggling to give a good image of Pakistan when I interact with Canadians. For example, when I used to fast in Ramadan and go to work, some people would be very nice, but some would also say things like, 'That's so cruel [that your religion makes you do this] ... how can you do that [fast all day]?' If I got offended at that comment, it wouldn't work. Before, I used to say that it was a matter of faith and religion, very seriously. They would take it as if I was a fundamentalist. But then I tried to say that fasting is a cleansing thing; then they understood. One of my co-workers even said, 'Okay, I'll fast with you.' But she never did, of course. They don't really know much.

The meanings, implications and functions of Islam as a religion varied for these women, despite the fact that the dominant society perceives all Muslims alike and reinforces an Islamic identity. By the same token, women's priorities, their degrees of integration into Canadian society and their visions of homeland vary widely, depending on a set of factors of which ethnic identity is only one. Nevertheless, just as the dominant society reinforces women's religious identity, it also highlights their ethnic identity, mostly in negative terms through discrimination and racism.

Diversity in integration, and sense of attachment

The degree to which these women were integrated into Canadian society, and how active they were within their community and the larger society, varied within the group, depending on the person's length of residence, age, educational background, socio-economic status and role within the family. Consequently, we encountered situations as diverse as the number of participants.

For some recently arrived women trapped in turbulent or abusive marital relationships, with little or no education attained in their country of origin, the immediate challenge was to adjust and, at the same time, to seek avenues to negotiate and transform gender relations at home. Most of the time, within the marriage, it was the woman who took the adult-education or language-training courses; sometimes they 'started from scratch'. Consequently, it was the woman, too, who used her education to develop resources and links, to communicate with the children's schools and to secure different kinds of jobs either to help with the family's income or to fully provide it. Seven or eight years into immigration, many of these women expressed strong feelings of appreciation for what they had accomplished in Canada; at the same time, they continued to regard their country of origin as their 'first country', followed by 'Canada', or 'Montreal'.

Afra had some primary education back in Afghanistan, and upon her arrival in Canada at the age of 20, she first took a seven-month course in French with her husband. When her 32-year-old, illiterate husband said he 'felt too old to study', she carried on alone with adult-education courses and found a part-time, blue-collar job. The school and working environments provided her with a network through which she not only took over child-rearing, but also sought help, a few years later, in divorcing her abusive husband. She affirms with pride, 'Since our arrival in Montreal I have been in charge of the children, educational and otherwise…. Separation from my husband over the past year has not made much difference, as I have been in charge of the family's income for a long time now!'

On the other hand, there were 'old-timers' who had immigrated to Canada some 20 to 30 years ago as young, married women, with or without children, had attained higher education in Canada, and now had professional jobs. Among this group, the degree of social activism seemed to be the highest; yet there were still significant differences in the nature of such activities between those who had come to Canada as refugees (with explicit political backgrounds) and those who had come as professional or investor immigrants. The former were active, depending on their interests and professions, in ethnic-based organizations of various kinds, as well as volunteering in health and other service sectors. The latter were involved in more politically charged forums, such as the minority rights advocacy groups. Generally, for political exiles the sense of belonging to a new home country came with delay and hesitation but was eventually strongly grounded. Sanaz is an example of this case.

Since her teenage years, Sanaz has been a member of political opposition groups and participated in protest rallies, first against the Shah's regime, which led to the Islamic revolution, and later against the Islamic regime. She sought political asylum in Canada some 20 years ago, and is now a vocal social activist.

> For a long period, perhaps for 13 or 14 years, I used to live 'temporarily' in Canada. I used to hope I would return to Iran. I did not want to take any serious steps. I used to think that doing so would somehow prevent me from going back. Even in the process of studying and working here, I still used to think if I wanted to do social activities it had to be within my own community…. Eventually, I got increasingly involved [at various socio-political forums]. All these [activities] helped me get to know so many beautiful souls,

without them having to be Iranians at all! I have lived 20 years of my life in my own country and another 20 here in Canada. So, at least I have equal sense of belonging to both. I still dream of Iran and would love to go there some time.... Immigration [to Canada] has been an extremely positive experience in my life. It has changed me dramatically. I am open to so many issues now, and I am not sure I would have been the same, had I never left Iran.

Finally, the whole realm of displacement, immigration and vision of home country is doubly complicated for Palestinians. As Heba nicely, and bitterly, put it: 'Immigration should be defined differently for Palestinians, because they have no state, no country of their own. We are born immigrants and remain immigrants.... It is most difficult and complicated for us Palestinians to belong anywhere.'

Yet, as much as the sense of 'statelessness' is shared by many Palestinians, this characteristic does not entail any easily recognizable pattern of behaviour among this group. For example, the older Muslim Palestinian women who had come to Canada a decade ago and had smooth marital relationships were more active in the larger society, and more adjusted and at peace in Canada. On the other hand, younger women of the same religious and regional background with a shorter period of stay in Canada felt that heightened tensions within their marriage and the challenges of overcoming those tensions dominated their lives in diaspora. As such, they sometimes longed for their families and memories 'back there', and had difficulty growing attached to the new environment.

Samia, for example, immigrated with her husband and two small children to Montreal four years ago. She was not too happy with her marriage in a Palestinian camp where they had lived, but she burst into tears while describing their 'new problems' and 'new frustrations', and the intensified tension with her husband over the course of their migration to Canada. With a bachelor's degree from back home, she now works in a corner store and provides most of the family's income, while her husband studies on and off at the graduate level and 'refuses to find a job'.

> We fight all the time. We scream and accuse one another. The children witness all of this and they become aggressive and angry. I do not know what to do. I tell him to leave me alone and we stop talking to one another and stop sleeping together, but we make up and it is okay for some time. Then the fighting starts again, especially when bills have to be paid and things have to be bought. I can't go back to the camp and I can't go back to live the way we lived in Lebanon. He keeps threatening me [with] going back by himself as soon as he gets his citizenship, regardless of what I do.

Samia has a few friends of Arabic origin, but she feels very strongly about Canada and thinks she and her children have a better future here. She is determined to take night courses to upgrade her education, land a professional job and stay on, regardless of what her husband does.

Ethnic identity imposed

How priorities are defined and how a sense of belonging develops over time depends on an array of factors, including gender roles and relationships, political background and socio-economic status. Moreover, various dimensions of one's identity fluctuate and take predominance in determining one's sense of belonging, self-worth and degree of integration into Canadian society. Just as religion is not the predetermining dimension of one's identity, neither is ethnic identity as far as women themselves are concerned. Meanwhile, just as the dominant society reinforces women's religious identity, it also prioritizes their ethnicity or ethnic identity over other dimensions.

The following quotes demonstrate how these women are constantly reminded of their ethnic and religious background in their daily encounters, and how such references condition their activities within the society. Interestingly enough, right after their accounts of instances of racism and discrimination, most women choose to talk about their sense of belonging to Canada, despite the negative attitudes they endure.

> *Afra*: We were told that immigrants get the same rights as the native Québecois. In the government area, it is true, but outside it is not. When I was working in [a department store], I faced a lot of discrimination from my supervisor. In the same job and the same position, the girls born in Quebec were treated better than I; I was always the last one to get any work privilege, particularly after 9/11. During many interviews, the employers asked about my origin and my religion before even asking me about my competencies. I lost two out of three jobs because of being an Afghan Muslim. I am still proud to be a Canadian citizen and to go and vote today for the municipal elections, and next week for the federal one. I am informed of the world news regularly, and I have made my decision for whom I will vote.

> *Najiba*: I am very happy to be in Canada. I feel good. I love it here. I don't have too many friends. I am working in the cafeteria for a big company as a cook's help. I have a good relation with my colleagues. In the beginning, after 9/11, they were staying away from me because I was a Muslim. I was sad, but then I found it funny. How could I possibly harm them? I was telling them that Islam is a good faith. It is a religion of peace. Muslims are tolerant and pacifist. Over time, our relation [has improved].

> *Roushan*: We had big hopes before coming to Canada, because Canada was favouring the immigration of professionals. Unfortunately, the education outside is not recognized here…. We decided to try and not think about our studies and our professions anymore, and put more emphasis on our children's education. We realized how we were still very fortunate to be here. Some Afghans have lost houses, families and lives in Afghanistan. But we are resilient. It is harder for my husband to avoid thinking about it, but we have no choice…. Afghanistan remains my home country, but I like it better here.

Today, even after Taliban's regime, we have to wear 'chador', and we cannot walk alone and in peace. The life here in Canada is very good for women.... We faced some discrimination at work, but very little compared to what we could have faced in other countries. People are very kind here. [After 9/11], I had to explain to non-Muslims that Muslims are not terrorists. In all religions, there are bad and good people. I tell them that we should respect each other. And I show them my example.

Sanaz: As to the racism, I know that many individuals show it in their encounters with people who look differently, but I don't extend this to the society as a whole. I think the Canadian society is fighting against [racism]. I do protest when I see it, no doubt.... After September 11, [my son was] stopped by the police several times. They would just stop him to ask where he was going, what he was doing, why he was where he was, et cetera. Once he led them to our house and I came out and told the cops off: 'What do you do, harassing my kid...?'

It is noteworthy that the women in this study testified to the fact that men of Middle Eastern origin were subjected to harsher and more explicit racism and harassment after 9/11. All the same, they felt the destructive impact of these attitudes and treatments, as they echoed the racism experienced by their sons and husbands. For instance, Heba recounted how her son was verbally abused by one of his colleagues with phrases such as 'A good Arab is a dead Arab'. And Umbreen said how uncomfortable and distressed her husband felt when his colleagues would start insulting Muslims at a corporate dinner or at a meeting, expecting him to react somehow.

Unity within diversity

In demonstrating the diversity of lives and experiences of these women, I also revealed their most salient shared experience, that of being perceived and treated by the dominant society as a monolithic entity. I showed that women were differentiated by diverse understandings, interpretations and implications of Islam as a religion. Furthermore, women stood at various intersections of time which, in combination with socio-economic factors and gender roles, determined their priorities and choices in adjusting to the society, as well as integrating into and feeling attached to it. In these processes, ethnicity was not always the most determining factor, and neither was the degree of religiosity. At the same time, women shared experiences of racism based on their religious/ethnic identity, and were constantly reminded of an identity which was ascribed to them by the dominant society. Even to this homogenizing force, women reacted with different degrees of awareness and sensitivity.

Evidently, an imposition of religious and ethnic identity by the dominant society is not a similar trait among the group as much as it is an experience shared by it. Meanwhile, there are indeed some similar qualities among these women which, as I will argue, bound them together further as a group. Some of the similarities already touched on include women's perseverance in adjustment, inspiration for education, striving to secure jobs and decent living, appreciation for living in Canada and being exposed to new world views, and seeing the future with optimism. In the following paragraphs I propose to elaborate on a set of similarities at a deeper and more personal level by focusing on the life histories of four women.

As I was listening to the life histories of these women, I was struck by the resilience and courage that they all showed in overcoming often extreme forms of economic deprivation, war, occupation, revolution, social and political upheavals, domestic violence and cultural transitions in the origin, transit and host countries. I could not help but link their past experiences of hardships to their present strength and determination in fighting against odds, coping with new circumstances and taking control of their lives to the best of their abilities. Their courage enabled them most evidently, but not exclusively, to work towards transforming unequal gender relations, and to end long-lived or emerging abusive relationships.

Najiba never went to school, and worked as a live-in domestic worker alongside her mother from the age of 14 in Afghanistan. Her brother married her off, against her will, when she was 17. Referring to her husband, she says: 'The guy was living in a small village. [After a small ceremony], I was brought to his village. Then my nightmare started!' The initial nightmare consisted of shouldering the responsibility of an extended family of 11 and being beaten up by her husband from day one.

The nightmare persisted during the family's stay in the transit country Pakistan, where she continued to be subjected to her husband's abuse, in addition to resuming her job as a domestic worker, giving birth to a child, facing hostility by the host country and struggling with dire poverty. 'During the end of our stay in Pakistan,' she said, 'we had almost no food on our plates. For eight months we were eating bread and yoghurt. Meanwhile, my sister passed away, and we adopted her two girls, three and seven years old.'

Through the Afghan Sponsorship Program, the couple and their children migrated to Canada seven years ago. With the support of family and friends, they soon settled down in Montreal, and started to learn French as well as 'a new way of living'. Najiba soon secured a job and gave birth to a second, and this time a seriously sick, child who had to be operated on at the age of one. Meanwhile, she said, 'There was physical violence all the time. Even when I was following French classes, my teachers noticed it, and suggested that I speak out. But I never said anything to anybody. I was pretending that I had fallen down. I did not want our sponsor to have any problem because of that'.

Her husband had difficulty keeping jobs, refused to contribute to the family's income when he did have work, and continued to physically abuse not only his wife, but also the adopted children. At some point, recounts Najiba, 'My husband left home, and I did not stop him from leaving. After one month he came back; I refused to let him in. I told him that he was not free to leave home and come back whenever it suited him, [that] my house was not a hotel to come for a bed and food and leave when he got fed up. He was not carrying out a husband's or a father's responsibilities and I was unable to support him anymore.'

Two years into the official divorce, she is now in her early 30s, lives with her four children between the ages of seven and 16, and earns the family's income in the service sector. 'His family,' she says, 'still blames me for not having given him a chance [to return].... My life since then is much better. My daughters are growing and I have spared them a violent environment. All my children are going to school. Today everything is back to normal. I have no problem with the behaviours of my children and they are well under control.'

Like Najiba, Parvin was married off to an older man at a very young age against her will and came to Montreal as a young mother of one child. However, she came with secondary education from an economically well-off family, and thereby had easier access to the means of personal development and social adjustment. Unlike Najiba, Parvin never experienced violence at home; however, since the beginning she had felt trapped in a partnership with a man who would go out 'dining and wining' while she, as a 15-year-old mother of a newborn baby, was all alone in a city unknown to her. She describes her experience upon immigrating to Canada at the age of 18:

> We saw an immigration counsellor to help us settle down. The counsellor wanted to send me to French-language school, and my husband kept insisting I should go to housekeeping and sewing courses instead. Finally, with much argument, I did go to the French school. Not only that, at night I attended college, and later the university, and so many other independent courses ... until I finally finished my higher education and started working in my field ... My husband continued his education and finished his master's studies, but he never worked outside home.

Parallel to developing her profession, Parvin started the process of balancing previously unbalanced gender relations by tirelessly creating her social links, 'taking the control' of her private and public life and demanding more responsibility from her husband, who kept returning to Iran and clinging to his traditional values. More than 30 years into the marriage and immigration, Parvin ended a long-lived, yet undesirable, relationship just a few years ago. She has grown-up, educated children, a prestigious job and a position within her community and the larger society. Parvin's life and divorce story strikes me as one redeemed by personal growth and empowerment, but not one with a 'happy ending', like that of Najiba, for example. Parvin herself summarized her story in heartfelt and nicely tuned words:

> [I keep active] in order to escape loneliness. I do feel lonely after my divorce. And I think my migration to Canada, the path I chose, the personal growth I underwent and generally life, which unfolded the way it did, necessitated my divorce. I can tell you, had I not come to Canada, I [would] still [be] living with my husband, happily perhaps...

Heba's life story is another account of how past hardships seem to strengthen one's ability not only to cope and adopt, but also to take over and craft anew. As an educated woman and active member of the Palestine Liberation Organization, Heba, at the age of 20, married her 'co-militant' husband, despite her parent's wishes, about 27 years ago.

Over the course of the political upheavals and wars in the Palestinian territories and Lebanon, the couple moved with one, two, and then three children – first between Lebanon and Saudi Arabia, and later between France and Canada – several times before they finally immigrated to Montreal seven years ago. The constant displacement, the sense of injustice, and the longing for a lost land and home dominate Heba's life history, even today while she is happy living in Montreal. Moreover, all along and in almost all of these cities and countries, Heba has lived geographically separated from her husband as different vocational and political circumstances have driven him away from home.

In describing her 'duties' as a single parent for most of the time, she says: 'It was very difficult when [the] children were young and we were in France. I wished he were present to help when they were sick or simply needed a father, but I managed, because I had to. The responsibility was a very heavy burden...'. Heba feels she has done a great job bringing up her children, and credits herself for being 'an independent and strong woman'. Nevertheless, she feels helpless observing how forced migrations caused her husband to drift apart from her and their children, changing their roles and relationships.

> We see each other, on average, about six months per year since we have been in Quebec. [He is on contract abroad.] Now, when he is around, he feels like an intruder, and expresses it often. The children and I feel the same about him. I sometimes feel my space being invaded by him, and he realizes the awkwardness between us. When he is around, he drives me and helps with the chores and tries to be a husband, but most of the time I feel better when he leaves and we go back to our routine. He has not seen his sons grow up; he has lost a lot and he does not understand them. He trusted me entirely in their upbringing... They love him very much, but I can see a gap in his relationship with the boys.

Not all past experiences of hardship, and the strengths they seem to yield, were translated into efforts to change unequal gender relations, as not all the women inherited unequal gender relations or wished to change existing marital relationships. There were other women, such as Samia, who endured an overwhelming amount of pain and suffering, such as living as an orphan with 11 siblings in deprived refugee camps, and losing her beloved sister in a bomb explosion. In Canada, she continued to experience alienation at home and in the society at large. There were yet others, like Sanaz, whose past history of political activism seemed to have equipped her with the courage to stand up against perceived injustice in the public arena.

Sanaz, who has already been introduced, married at the age of 19 and accompanied her husband to India before rushing back to Iran at the outbreak of the

Iran–Iraq War. Soon after, she returned to India and gave birth to her first and only child. In India, she continued her fights, for freedom at home far away and against the poverty and distress in her new home. Restricted by financial problems, she left her husband behind in India and, with her few-months-old baby, flew to Canada and sought political asylum at Montreal airport. Sanaz told me, with much amusement and a vivid memory of the incident, and perhaps without realizing how indicative of her courage her reaction was, about her first encounter with the Canadian authorities. She remembered a pleasant, first impression she got from a sympathetic immigration officer in charge of processing her file upon arrival. However, she added:

> ... Then at night, when we were taken to a hotel prison – well, they said a hotel, but it was a hotel room without a door! They took us there with a police car. In the car, we were my child and me, another woman and her child. The four of us sat in the back of the car and two cops in the front. It was winter and we weren't dressed warmly enough, because we did not know... The cops had big warm jackets on, with hoods all tied up. On the way, they rolled their windows down! I was surprised ... I wouldn't understand back then why they were doing that. 'It's cold out there!' I said. 'Roll the windows up!' They ignored me as if they could not hear me or understand me. They kept talking to each other in French, but I knew they could understand that much English. I couldn't believe that! For a second I felt, we are in the middle of nowhere at night and they can, at any instance, decide to leave all of us out in the snow. I was so horrified and thought, alas ... we escaped our own country only to be at the hands of these people. It was such a painful experience... The other woman was scared, and kept telling me, 'Don't say anything; they'll do worse'. I said, 'The hell with them doing worse, what is worse than what they're doing now?' At last, I shouted at them, 'You're trying to kill us', and then they rolled the windows up again... Finally, we got to the 'doorless' hotel rooms [laughing].

Conclusion

In demonstrating diversity, similarities are revealed, and in discussing shared experiences, differences are brought into light. Without having to sharply distinguish between the traces of sameness and difference, I believe the women participants in this study are a religiously, regionally, ideologically and intellectually diverse group of women who are at the same time bound by similar ideals and struggles. Furthermore, it is these very similar ideals and struggles which mark the group as 'different' from the mainstream, precisely because their experiences and dilemmas are not shared by the larger society.

The reality of displacement is perhaps the most pronounced experience shared by these women and not by the society at large. Whether convention refugees, exiles or immigrants, for almost all of the women some element of forced migration played a part in their initial moves. Furthermore, in their journey in search of a better life, they often moved through and temporarily lived in a host of transit countries from Palestinian camps in Beirut to Lebanon, India, Russia, Saudi Arabia, Abu Dhabi, France and the US. Life in transit countries was always much harsher than that in the country of origin, and its memories continue to both disturb and motivate many of these women.

Once in the adopted country, the most salient binding experience among the group but not shared by the larger society is an imposition of ethnic and religious identity. This imposition is most evidently felt through discrimination based on religion and ethnic origin, thanks to post-9/11 events. This is not to say that such discrimination is a three-year-old phenomenon. Even within the narrow scope of this chapter, we saw how unwelcoming the Montreal police were in the late 1970s, and how a lack of recognition of their foreign credentials had a negative impact on the lives of some women. Nonetheless, even the most pacifist and peaceful of these women felt the effects of the intensified misperceptions about Muslims and the overt discrimination against them as a result of the 11 September events.

Finally, changes in gender roles and relationships were significant outcomes or by-products of life in diaspora. When they occurred, these changes were mostly orchestrated by women themselves; they were made possible through positive societal medium, and had positive impacts on women's lives, self-esteem and self-growth. At other times, a transformation in gender roles and relationships was the involuntarily consequence of compelling forces, such as obligatory, prolonged geographical separations forced on couples, and they entailed mixed feelings of satisfaction and loneliness.

Women in this study are not the powerless victims of a patriarchal tradition or religion, as the old discourse of colonialism and the persisting imagery of 'Islamophobia' holds. Nor are they entirely empowered and assertive agents of their own lives, as portrayed by the theories of anti-essentialism and anti-universalism. Rather, these women actively adjust to new, often harsh conditions, and courageously challenge and transform unequal power relations at personal and public levels; meanwhile, their actions and decisions occur within structural constraints and are sometimes formed by the forces beyond their control.

Women in this study are similar in so far as they share the ideals and struggles particular to life in diaspora; meanwhile, like Parvin, like Najiba – like 'Susan' and 'Mary' for that matter – they are unremarkably remarkable women, each different in her history, ideals and outlooks, and each so unfitting of any stereotype.

Notes

1 This chapter is based on my participation at the MCRI research project as the project coordinator for 'Diaspora, Islam and Gender' in Montreal, Canada. The underlying theoretical framework of the chapter is informed by the project's hypotheses. The data used is also part of the data obtained through this research project. See the project's website for details of the study at http://www.atkinson.yorku.ca/~diaspora.

2 These life histories were collected through intensive interviews, lasting an average of two hours, over a six-month period. Eight out of ten of these interviews were initially

conducted by a team of my research assistants, consisting of Uzma Jamil, Sultana Natho-Jina, Fatiha Gatre Guemiri and John Asfour. I acknowledge and warmly appreciate their eager contribution. This chapter and study were not possible without the participation of the ten women who devoted their time and trusted us with their life stories. Their lives and life stories have inspired me in countless ways.

References

Abu-Lughod, L. (1991) *Writing Against Culture*, R. Fox (ed.) *Recapturing Anthropology: Working in the Present*, Santa Fe: School of American Research, 137–62.

Behar, R. (1993) *Translated Woman*, Boston: Beacon Press.

Canadian Council for Refugees (2004) *Feeling the Chill: Discrimination against Muslims and Arabs in Canada*, Montreal: Canadian Council for Refugees.

Henzell-Thomas, J. (2001) *The Language of Islamophobia*. FAIR (Forum against Islamophobia and Racism), London. Online. http://www.themodernreligion.com/assault/language.htm.

Marcus, G and Fischer, M. (1986) *Anthropology as Cultural Critique: An Experimental Moment in the Human Sciences*, Chicago: University of Chicago Press.

Moghissi, H. (2002) *Women, War and Fundamentalism in the Middle East*, Social Sciences Research Council. Online. http://www.ssrc.org/sept11/essays/ moghissi.htm.

Thomas, N. (1991) 'Against Anthropology', *Cultural Anthropology*, 6(3), 305–22.

Index

CPSIA information can be obtained at www.ICGtesting.com
Printed in the USA
LVOW10s2255060314

376402LV00003B/38/P